90 03652

D1758013

WITHDRAWN
FROM
'TH

# RACISM, NATIONALISM AND CITIZENSHIP

# Racism, Nationalism and Citizenship

Ethnic minorities in Britain and Germany

WITHDRAWN
FROM
UNIVERSITY OF PLYMOUTH
LIBRARY SERVICES

NICOLA PIPER

## Ashgate

Aldershot · Brookfield USA · Singapore · Sydney

© Nicola Piper 1998

All rights reserved. No part of this publication may be reproduced, stored in a retrieval system, or transmitted in any form or by any means, electronic, mechanical, photocopying, recording or otherwise without the prior permission of the publisher.

Published by
Ashgate Publishing Ltd
Gower House
Croft Road
Aldershot
Hants GU11 3HR
England

Ashgate Publishing Company
Old Post Road
Brookfield
Vermont 05036
USA

**British Library Cataloguing in Publication Data**
Piper, Nicola
    Racism, nationalism and citizenship : ethnic minorities in
    Britain and Germany. - (Research in ethnic relations)
    1. Racism - Germany 2. Racism - Great Britain 3. Immigrants -
    Germany 4. Immigrants - Great Britain 5. Germany - Race
    relations 6. Great Britain - Race relations
    I. Title
    305.8 ' 00941

**Library of Congress Catalog Card Number:** 98-70151

ISBN 1 84014 537 4

Printed in Great Britain by The Ipswich Book Company, Suffolk

UNIVERSITY OF PLYMOUTH

| | |
|---|---|
| Item No. | 9003652757 |
| Date | 21 SEP 1998 Z |
| Class No. | 305·800942 PIP |
| Contl. No. | 1840145374 |

LIBRARY SERVICES

# Contents

# Acknowledgements

This monograph is a revised version of my D.Phil. thesis at the University of Sheffield, Department of Sociological Studies, completed in May 1996.

There are many people and institutions without whose assistance the outcome of this research would have been less satisfactory, if not impossible. First of all, I owe a special debt to my parents for introducing me to the 'world of books' by encouraging my early interest in the written word and teaching me how to read and write. Their support throughout the long years of my education was invaluable.

I also wish to thank my supervisor Simon Holdaway, without whose interest and guidance I would never have started this research. Crucial to the progress of the project was the involvement of senior members of staff of a number of selected NGOs and semi-governmental organizations, either in form of interviews or the provision of materials. I am very grateful for their time and generosity. I am also indebted to a number of friends and colleagues in the Sociology Department who kindly read through some of the earlier drafts. I have particularly benefited from the encouragement and suggestions put forward by Nick Stevenson, Maurice Roche and Alan France. Many thanks to my friends Barbara and Mel who did a great job helping me with the tedious task of 'tidying up' my English. Paul White and Chris Husbands, who kindly served as examiners of my thesis, provived me with many useful comments, however, I was not able to incoporate all of them into this book.

In preparing for a final manuscript for this book, I greatly benefited from the congenial atmosphere of the School of East Asian Studies at Sheffield, with special encouragement and support from Michael Weiner and Ian Gow. Also many thanks to Catherine Brown who kindly edited the manuscript.

I also want to stress that this work was only made possible thanks to the benevolent financial support by the ESRC and the University of Sheffield. The Department of Sociological Studies, Sheffield, was very helpful in financing my research trip to Germany and trips to London.

Last but not least, I would like to express gratitude, affection and appreciation to my partner Kevin who has shared the ups and downs of the long process of completing this research.

# List of Abbreviations

| | |
|---|---|
| BNA | British Nationality Act |
| BNP | British National Party |
| BSA | British Social Attitudes |
| CDU | Christian Democratic Union |
| EC | European Community |
| ECSC | European Coal and Steel Community |
| EEC | European Economic Community |
| EFTA | European Free Trade Association |
| EP | European Parliament |
| EU | European Union |
| EURATOM | European Atomic Energy Community |
| FDP | Liberal Democratic Party |
| FRG | Federal Republic of Germany |
| GDR | German Democratic Republic |
| IGC | Intergovernmental conference (due in July 1997) |
| IPOS | Institut für praxis-orientierte Sozialforschung |
| OECD | Organization for Economic Cooperation and Development |
| OJ | Official Journal of the European Communities |
| PDS | Democratic Socialist Party |
| SEA | Single European Act |
| SED | United Socialist Party of Germany (informer GDR) |

| | |
|---|---|
| SPD | German Social Democrat Party |
| TREVI | Terrorism, radicalism, extremism and violence (group of EC member-states' interior ministers) |
| UK | United Kingdom |

# 1 Introduction

## 1.1 General introduction

### 1.1.1 Background

Virtually every advanced industrialized country[1] has experienced international labour migration in the form of legally admitted foreign workers, undocumented aliens, political refugees or permanent immigrants. There are an estimated thirty million foreign workers and unauthorized aliens in all parts of the world, with an additional fifteen million political refugees (Castles 1993:18). The movement of people across national borders has undoubtedly become a global issue and will likely become an even more salient one in the future as the economic inequalities and the global knowledge about the existence of these inequalities increase.

Of the world's approximately thirty million foreign workers and undocumented aliens, almost half are to be found in western Europe. These migrants originally came during the post-war period as workers to meet the growing demand for labour. Despite a general tendency in Europe towards restrictive immigration policies in the early 1970s, intensified family reunification as well as 'family formation'[2] (Menski 1994) have resulted in a continuous or even higher proportion of immigrants, and meanwhile the permanent settlement of some fifteen million foreigners in western European countries has become the new reality (Layton-Henry 1990). Among European Community member-states, Germany has the highest number of foreign residents with currently around seven million. The largest group in 1991 was the Turks (1.9 million) (OECD 1995). Germany is followed by France with a foreign population of 3.6 million (Castles 1995:298) and Britain where the number of foreign citizens was two million in 1990 (OECD 1995). In the latter case, however, when British-born persons of Afro-Caribbean and Asian origin are included, the overall population of immigrant origin is estimated at 4.5 million (Castles 1995: 300).

Set against a general trend towards restrictive policies dealing with future immigration in western Europe are various differing socio-political responses of each individual state to the situation of newly settled ethnic minorities (Hammar 1985b). In the German context, the dominant aspect of the government's 'foreigners' policy' (Ausländerpolitik) was a double strategy of integration and 'assistance to return' (Rückkehrförderung). In contrast to the de facto permanence of the immigrants' settlement, the immigration status of former 'guest-workers' is still officially denied as reflected in the absence of a governmental immigration policy and the continuous official claim that Germany is not a country of immigration (Layton-Henry 1990:8; Martin & Miller 1990:9; Schönwälder 1995:423).

1

Britain, as opposed to Germany, solved its manpower shortage partly through recruitment from its former colonies in the Caribbean and the Indian sub-continent (the highest number of labour migrants came in actual fact from Ireland) and granted members of the Commonwealth a privileged status as citizens until the introduction of the first Immigrants Act in 1962. In sharp contrast to Germany, legal equality of the ex-colonial immigrants bound up with paternalistic colonial traditions of British society led, as early as the 1960s, to developments of various ideas about integration (Bahringhorst 1991). However, similar to Germany, a double strategy was implemented, although of different character: On the one hand, harsher immigration legislation, and on the other, measures of inclusion such as the introduction of the 'Race Relation Acts' began to be introduced in the early 1960s (Layton-Henry 1992). The final aim was the same in both countries: to limit primary labour migration. With increased secondary immigration (i.e. family reunification and formation) and fairly unsuccessful 'return policies', immigrant or ethnic minority communities of a considerable size developed as permanent parts of both societies.

### 1.1.2  The topic of this book

Given this very brief portrait of immigration in Germany and Britain, this book examines the question of whether citizenship functions, or could function, as a mechanism for inclusion and participation for settled, post-war labour migrants of non-European origin[3] and their descendants. This means that in the German context, the focus will be on the experience of the Turks, who are by far the largest non-European minority, and on the experiences of the diverse ethnic minorities from the Indian sub-continent and the West Indies in the British context (see Appendix I for figures).

The presence of settled non-European immigrant populations of an unprecedented size[4] and diversity 'constitutes a major challenge to the concept of citizenship in modern industrial democracies' (Layton-Henry 1990:vi). Large communities of foreign residents have been established in western Europe and high proportions of these 'as yet,....show little sign of following the path of previous immigrants by integrating, assimilating and becoming naturalised citizens of their new countries of work and residence' (Layton-Henry 1991:107).

This book is an investigation of the ways in which, and the reasons why, these settled immigrants do not enjoy a fully equal status as citizens, despite their long periods of residence and the emergence of subsequent generations raised and/or born in German or British society. Although these migrants generally enjoy secure rights of abode, their political and social participation in the countries of residence is challenged in many ways, such as by right-wing extremist parties and neo-nazi movements (usually in a crude and open way) as well as by members of mainstream parties, supporting a general climate of restrictive immigration/inclusion policies.

Rights to citizenship are central to the issue of who should be included in the national society as a participating member with full access to civil, political and social rights - the three main elements of citizenship, according to Marshall (1950) - and who should be treated as an outsider with lesser rights. However, exclusion from socio-national membership is also reflected in the mingling of nationality and citizenship laws, whereby the notion of 'descent' impedes the acquisition of citizenship. Furthermore, not only the dimension of rights and laws is central to the issue of inclusion, but also the wider dimension of social participation and recognition within civil society[5]. Hence, in addition to citizenship/nationality as a legal status, the aspects of identifying a national/citizen and recognizing a 'newcomer' as belonging (or not belonging) to a socio-national community are also highly relevant.

## 1.2    Integration into the research context

### 1.2.1  *The particular cases of Germany and Britain - a comparative perspective*

This book is mainly a comparison of the socio-political responses to post-war labour migration in Germany and Britain. The primary purpose of discussing these two 'nation-states' is to show that, despite particular historical circumstances, there have been similar trends with regard to the citizenship status of permanent non-European immigrants and their descendants in both societies. As Britain and Germany are members of the European Community,  an investigation will follow of how this trend is dealt with, or reflected, on the European level, i.e. whether the European Community has made any difference to national policies of immigration and inclusion.

Generally speaking, the benefits of comparison are that such an analysis helps to illustrate, firstly, the complex issues involved in different historical and cultural contexts of immigrant-receiving countries and, secondly, an understanding of the dissimilarities and similarities of immigrant peoples' socio-political status in Britain and Germany. In terms of broad characteristics, the comparative analysis of Germany and Britain involves two less divergent societies rather than highly divergent ones. This can be shown with regard to their 'societal frameworks' (for instance, such features as being highly advanced industrial societies based on democratic political systems within the framework of a nation-state and as being de facto multi-ethnic societies).

Apart from sharing similar societal frameworks, there are differences with regard to their histories of developing national membership (based on national identity) and their histories of immigration. A detailed comparison of Britain and Germany, however, will show that despite these different histories,  different concepts of membership to the nation-state have become more similar when approached from the point of view of immigrants. Although these different histories have resulted in different statuses of *formal* citizenship (i.e. in legal terms) for immigrants in these two countries, there have been similar processes of 'ethnicization' (Bös 1993) or 'racialization' (Small 1994) of the concept of membership. Citizenship and nationality tend to be coterminous.

Existing comparative studies which contextualize citizenship and immigration have not emphasized the latter point strongly enough. Brubaker, for example, presents Germany and Britain in the introduction to his edited book *Immigration and the Politics of Citizenship in Europe and North America* (1989) - a historical account of nation-formation processes - as rather opposing examples by emphasizing the early periods of these processes[6]. Thus, he neglects the post-war developments during which unprecedentedly large-scale immigration of non-Europeans took place resulting, as suggested by Bös (1993), in similar 'ethnicization'[7] processes of the concept of membership in both countries.

Comparative studies of societal responses to immigration, such as by Layton-Henry (1990) and Hammar (1985b), rightly point out the liberal position of Britain with regard to naturalization procedures, dual nationality and the granting of voting rights to its ethnic minorities, as opposed to Germany's illiberalism in this respect. However, these studies, which are in places somewhat descriptive, fail to emphasize the particular British historical circumstances which resulted in a more liberal position vis-à-vis its labour migrants, i.e. the peculiarity of the Empire with regard to Britain's concept of common subjecthood and the colonial link between Britain and most of its post-war immigrants. Moreover, they fail to show post-war tendencies of the British and German position approaching each other (i.e. from liberal to less liberal in the former case and from extremely exclusionary to less exclusionary in the latter case) with similar exclusionary implications for ethnic minorities.

In the post-war period, Germany and Britain have accommodated comparatively large numbers of labour migrants from non-European backgrounds with non-Christian religions. They both stopped immigration of workers during the early 1970s and since then implemented harsher and harsher immigration legislation or other types of control. In both countries the 'ethnic' or 'racial' issues have been major components of daily politics (van Dijk 1993) which have been recently characterized by a certain revival of nationalistic and anti-immigrant tendencies[8]. The restrictive immigration policies are, however, not confined to the right-wing/conservative discourse, but it has been suggested that all of the governments elected to office in Germany and Britain took a strong stand on immigration as well as asylum (Small 1994; Faist 1994a and b; Layton-Henry 1991). This has certain implications for settled immigrants in that they are pictured as undesired or even criminalized in the context of immigration control and repatriation (Castles 1993:24). Nonetheless, it seems to be in particular the New Right's discourse[9] which revived a form of 'racially based theory of nationalism' (Cohen 1994:202) where 'the process of national decline is often presented as 'coinciding with the dilution of one homogeneous stock by alien strains' (Sarup 1991; as quoted by Cohen, ibid.). This sort of discourse also involves the question of 'scapegoating' of immigrant populations in times of socio-economic crises. Statements put forward in both countries which centre upon the 'scrounging of welfare service' or defending a narrow nationalism - for whichever reason - do much harm by rendering respectability to intolerant ideas.

Ethno-centric or racist views as to who should qualify as a full member of the national community are either enshrined in constitutional form, as in the German case, or in immigration legislation, as in the British case. Discourses around 'repatriation' of immigrants have played an important role in both countries (Small 1994; Bahringhorst 1991), although a clear policy, by which immigrants were offered financial support for returning to their countries of origin, existed only in Germany. Thus, despite ideals of freedom, equality and democracy, both countries have systematically excluded a significant portion of their population from the benefits of such ideals.

Another aspect of common ground shared by Germany and Britain with regard to their socio-political structure can be found in their membership of the European Community. It has to be noted, however, that Germany was among the founding countries and Britain did not enter until 1973 - a fact which partly explains the different levels of commitment to the European idea[10] and the differing perceptions of the role of the Community. This is also likely to have an impact on the understanding of European citizenship. Therefore, although with the ratification of the Maastricht Treaty both countries are equally involved in the process of European integration and in the materialization and development of European citizenship, the actual ideas behind these processes might not be the same. The latter is of crucial interest here regarding the issue of granting European citizenship to peoples of non-European background living permanently in EC territory. Moreover, a comparative analysis of Britain and Germany should enable the assessment of the likelihood that the European Community could harmonize the various policies of inclusion (e.g. nationality laws, anti-discrimination legislation) that already exist in the individual member-states.

With regard to academic discourse, in both countries a considerable amount of literature has been produced on historical and ideological aspects of nationhood, citizenship and/or nationality. However, in Britain there has been an emphasis on research into what Banton has called the 'race relations problematic' (Banton 1991; see also Wrench & Solomos 1993:157; Wilpert 1993:67). A comparative analysis of Germany and Britain is useful to explain why there is a lack of such theorizing of racism in contemporary German society and why there is a difference in concepts, as reflected in the terminology of racism versus *Ausländerfeindlichkeit* (hostility towards foreigners).

Furthermore, there seems to be a new trend among 'British' academics towards a greater interest in ethnicity and nationalism rather than 'race relations' (Anthias 1995). Authors such as Barker (1981), Gilroy (1987) and Miles (1993) argue that racist discourse now revolves more around cultural identity and national boundaries rather than biological concepts. This line of argument has, however, so far not been contextualized with the issue of citizenship - neither in Germany nor in Britain.

It will be emphasized throughout this book that, despite historical differences and quite different policies of inclusion, the *effects* of nationalism and racism have had similar results in Germany and Britain viz. racialized 'new' ethnic minorities who are excluded from citizenship and whose social and cultural position is mostly below that of the majority.

There is, among others (which are mainly the subject of the chapter on racism), one terminological issue which needs clarifying when employing a comparative analysis of Britain and Germany. This comparison is that of two nation-states. However, in the British case, the overwhelming concentration of ethnic minorities from former colonies are resident in England and all the sources of the empirical data (groups and organizations interviewed) are located in England (in fact in London). In addition, there is this complex issue of Irish, Scottish, Welsh and English identity incorporated in the whole of the United Kingdom. It seems, therefore, almost more appropriate to refer to England. However, all *legal* provisions (the national as well as the EC legislation) regarding citizenship hold for the entire United Kingdom. Also, contemporary attitudes and conduct towards outsiders seem to have their larger British manifestation. Ireland is viewed in this respect as a special case, as its historical attachment to Great Britain has not been as long as that of Wales and Scotland. More importantly, its attachment to Britain has always been violently contested by certain parts of the Irish people so that it is preferred here to exclude Ireland (in particular from the discussion of racism and its history). Thus, this analysis will be mostly confined to Great Britain (which is referred to here as Britain out of mere convenience), and only in sections dealing with historical developments will a clear differentiation be made between England, Scotland and Wales.

In the case of Germany, only post-war labour migration into the western part will be discussed. The situation of labour migrants in the ex-GDR was different and will be ignored here. However, the country has been reunited since 1990 and the new socio-economic problems - having resulted in rising anti-foreigners sentiments - affect former guest workers' social position in the East *and* West (Räthzel 1995). Therefore, reference will always be made to the whole of Germany, unless stated differently.

## 1.2.2 *The analytical framework*

*Inclusion and exclusion* The perception of long-term residents of non-European background as permanent settlers and an integral part of the resident population requires their *inclusion* into the socio-national community to achieve social justice and to maintain social peace[11]. Thus, only those issues which have an impact on the socio-legal inclusion of immigrant minorities and which test their legitimate membership are considered. The outcome of insufficient inclusion would be exclusion[12] which may be based on legal mechanisms (such as sharp distinctions between the rights of citizens and non-citizens, complicated naturalization procedures) or on informal practices (based on, e.g., racism and nationalism within civil society).

*Citizenship and the effects of nationalism and racism* The main argument established here is that there exists a link between racism and nationalism, both of which are understood as ideologies (or discourses) and practices. The relationship between nationalism and racism - which is regarded as symbiotic whereby neither can be given an absolute priority over the other - is reflected on the state level within the intermingling of nationality and citizenship laws as well as within the perception of civil society. Thus, it is argued that this relationship has exclusionary implications for 'new' ethnic minorities' citizenship status.

As the majority of modern states established a link between citizenship and nationality, 'nationality is considered as a necessary, if not sufficient, condition for the exercise of citizenship' (Leca, in: Mouffe 1992:21). Thus, in the context of inclusion of immigrants, citizenship raises a number of issues, 'in one case concerning national identity and the historical role of nation-states as the pre-eminent modern form of organization of a political community' (Bottomore, in: Marshall & Bottomore 1992:85), and in the other case, concerning rights and 'liberties' (Held 1991) of individuals living in a state. Immigrant peoples' membership of a state might be accorded formal recognition in law, while their presence and participation as full citizens is still questioned within civil society.

Nationalism is here understood as the ideological or discursive articulation of national identity, i.e. as ideologies or 'discourses in which [collective, N.P.] identities and counter-identities are conceived and through which they are sustained' (Bauman 1992:678)[13]. In other words, the construct of the 'nation' tends to depict 'the people' with the notion of descent and blood-relatedness, or - as suggested by Arendt - as "one super-human family that we call 'society' and its political form of organization called 'nation-state'" (1958:29). As a result, clear boundaries (or lines) are drawn between those who belong and those who do not belong to the socio-national community. 'These lines are essentially established within the laws of nationality, but they are not at all restricted to these formal relationships.' (Goulbourne 1991:17). The distinction between belonging and non-belonging is, however, not only one of the main purposes of nationalism, but also of racism. Therefore, it is argued here that national identity and identity as a 'race' are intermingled.

*Identity*  There are many forms of identity but only one is of interest here, collective identity. It is described by Passerin d'Entreves as a 'we' identity which is not given but which must be constantly negotiated. '[T]he creation of a 'we' with which we are able to identify both ourselves and our actions...[is a] process of identity-construction [which] is never given once and for all, and [which] is never unproblematic. Rather, it is a process of constant renegotiation and struggle, a process in which actors articulate and defend competing conceptions of cultural and political identity.' (in: Mouffe 1992:157).

One form of collective identity is nationality (as distinct from nationality as a legal status). As a feeling of cultural togetherness, nationality is suggested by Heater (1990) to be a mental construct which does not necessarily have to correspond with a sense (or the perception) of being a citizen.

National identity should not be confused with other types of identity. The aspect which distinguishes nationality from other types of identity derives from the fact that it is a source of individual identity within a 'people' which is seen as the basis of collective solidarity. The 'people' 'is the mass of a population whose boundaries and nature are defined in various ways, but which is usually perceived as larger than any concrete community (Greenfeld 1992:3). Since the emergence of European nation-states, universalistic and particularistic notions of the 'nation' have tended to co-exist (Räthzel 1995; Bauman 1992) and thus, national identity frequently utilizes ethnic or 'racial' characteristics for self-identification as well as for establishing 'a *natural* division of the world's population into discrete categories' (Miles 1993:62; original emphasis).

The second form of collective identity is citizenship. One of the particular features of an 'identity-as-citizen' is 'the way in which it overlays the other social identities the individual inevitably feels.' (Heater 1990:183). These other social identities based on, for instance, class, ethnic or gender divisions, can create intense antagonisms. Citizenship as a political identity, however, can help to generate an awareness of responsibility for conciliating conflicting interests and thus, help to appease social antagonisms. However, 'as nationality became associated in the ideology of nationalism with the doctrine of popular sovereignty, it became important that cultural nationality and legal citizenship should correspond.' (ibid.:185). Hence, the two sources of collective identity, citizenship and nationality, tend to be enmeshed and thus, counteract the conciliatory function of citizenship by involving exclusionary effects for immigrant minorities. I will argue here, however, that not only the identity as a citizen tends to be equated with national identity, but also that the identity as a 'national' is linked to the identity as a 'race'. Therefore, the drawing of boundaries between insiders and outsiders of a socio-national community also involves processes of racialization. This is reflecting in German and British law as well as within civil society.

To sum up, the following questions will be dealt with in this book: How does the relationship between nationalism and racism affect immigrants' citizenship status? Can citizenship diminish the power of this relationship? To what extent does citizenship function as a mechanism for inclusion? To find answers to these questions, the conceptual link between citizenship and nationality with its racializing effects on ethnic minorities will be shown in the historical and legal contexts of Germany and Britain as well as in the wider perception of civil society in both countries.

## 1.3    Chapter guide

The next chapter contains a discussion of the methods of research employed as well as the nature and sources of the empirical data which derive from pressure or lobby groups working in the 'race relations' field in Germany and Britain and which are about views on racism, national/ European identity, and citizenship.

The chapter following the explanations on methodology and empirical data, Chapter Three, will provide a full account of policies of immigration or inclusion and measures established by the European Community and their possible consequences for the position of non-European immigrants in the European context. It will be shown that, from the perspective of post-war labour migration, the EC has minimal influence on matters of inclusion and is rather preoccupied with immigration issues revolving around border controls and visa requirements. To illustrate this point, the creation of 'Fortress Europe' and its implications on third country nationals' position, both within the single member-states and within the whole Community as a whole, are investigated.

Chapter Four deals with the issue of racism and, first of all, explains the conceptual divergence in Britain and Germany as reflected in the different terminologies employed in both countries (racism versus *Ausländerfeind-lichkeit*). It further outlines existing theories on racism relevant in the context of national identity/nationalism and citizenship. These theories will be combined or elaborated to approach the issue of racism from the perspective of national and supranational (European) citizenship.

Chapter Five briefly presents the relevant theories behind the formation of nation-states and national identity. It will be shown how national identity is closely linked to identity as a 'race', internally (identity as superior 'race') as well as externally (vis-à-vis the Other, i.e. the inferior 'race'). In the context of post-war immigration, the new situation that unprecedentedly large, settled ethnic minority populations pose to the issue of national identity will be investigated with the help of the notion of 'identity crisis'. It will be suggested that racializing and thus exclusionary effects of national identity still exist. The possibility of a new form of identity, i.e. post-national or post-conventional, will be discussed.

Chapter Six outlines the relevant theories on citizenship and describes their shortcomings when approached from the point of view of non-European immigrants and their descendants. The development of a conception of citizenship in this context is attempted. The aspect of citizenship is then looked at in more detail in both British and German contexts. In a further section, citizenship is approached from the post-national, i.e. European Union, level and European citizenship for non-European immigrants will be assessed. A final section on future developments explores the potential of local citizenship as a possible result of the establishment of the Committee of the Regions by the Maastricht Treaty and the principle of subsidiarity.

Chapter Seven includes material on 'mass discourse' in both countries. It looks into the viewpoints held by civil society (i.e. the 'indigenous' population) on the racism/nationalism/citizenship issues central to this book as generated by studies on social attitudes and opinion surveys. The findings will show a high degree of polarization of 'the public's opinion', but will nonetheless enable a broad generalization about the general public's attitudes on the relevant issues.

Chapter Eight covers an elite perspective on the three main issues in form of political discourse. Reports of parliamentary debates topicalizing issues of immigration and issues related to ethnic minorities have been selected to show the language and definitions being used and the connections being made between the relevant elements in this thesis. Both chapters (Seven and Eight) will illustrate the inter-relatedness of public opinion and politicians' discourse and its effects on ethnic minorities' citizenship status.

Chapter Nine deals with the data obtained in the interviews structured in sections on the same main topics as above: racism, national identity and, finally, citizenship. Each section is subdivided into the data obtained from 'British' and 'German' sources and the EU source. Similarities and dissimilarities in the findings will be specially pointed out and references to the arguments developed in the 'theory' chapters will be made.

The final chapter contains the conclusion and future perspectives on a more inclusive concept of citizenship.

# Notes

1      The term 'industrialized' instead of 'capitalist' is used here to acknowledge that the phenomenon of 'migrant labour' also existed in socialist countries (such as the former GDR). However, the focus will be here on western European countries with capitalist economies.

2      Family formation' refers to the situation in which, for instance, a Turkish or Asian person who is a permanent resident in Europe, marries a person from the country of origin who is then allowed - more or less easily depending on the host country's regulations - to join the spouse in Europe (Menski 1994).

3      More precisely, it should be people of 'non-western European origin' as Turkey is usually listed (e.g. in statistics on migration 'flows) under 'Europe'. In other words, the focus will be here on people who come from countries which are not members of the European Union.

4      Today, 2.5% of the European Community's population are legal migrants from non-European countries (Garcia 1992:14).

5      The term'civil society' is meant here to refer to the 'indigenous' majority.

6      This is done by Brubaker in more detail in his book *Citizenship and Nationhood in France and Germany* (1992) in which the British situation is not discussed.

7      Ethnicization' in the context of the acquisition of citizenship refers to the shift from the territorial principle to the principle of blood-relatedness or, in other words, from ius soli to ius sanguinis.

8      For right-wing/conservative British political discourse see Gilroy (1987), Barker (1981), CCCS (1982); for German right-wing/conservative political discourse see Faist (1994a+b).

9      For a brief over-view of New Right's schools of thought see Grant (1993).

10    For more details on the British re-orientation from the Empire/Commonwealth towards Europe see George (1990 and 1991).

11    It might be useful at this point to explain the difference between inclusion and integration as suggested by Soysal (1994). Inclusion means legal and organizational incorporation by state-policies and refers to a macro-level process whereby the migrant becomes part of the host polity. Integration involves the adjustment by the migrant to the host society under the assumption of an individual, micro-level process.

12    Exclusion is not understood here as total exclusion which would mean preventing the entry of all immigrants and the total refusal of naturalization etc.

13    For a brief explanation of the difference between 'ideology' and 'discourse' see Hall (1992b:291-295). The author of this thesis is aware of these differences, but decided not to settle on one of them as in the material cited here either one of these terms is employed depending on the respective author's perspective.

# 2 Methods of research

To understand the relationship between nationalism, racism and citizenship and this relationship's impact on immigrant minorities, I reviewed the relevant academic literature, EU and governmental reports or documents, the constitution of the Federal Republic of Germany as well as leaflets and other publications by the interviewed organizations. Public opinion surveys were consulted to establish broad generalizations on the part of civil society, as well as relevant parliamentary debates to gain insight into an elitist perspective of people who are responsible for policy-making and who have a certain degree of influence on public opinion. I then wanted to probe the findings from the literature and my own thoughts from the viewpoint of ethnic minorities. Interviewing of organizations who are actively engaged in improving 'race relations' was, therefore, chosen as a method to gain insight into: 1. differences and similarities in conceptual thinking in Germany and Britain, 2. their views on exclusionary tendencies (based on the combined influence of racism and nationalism) of citizenship, and 3. their ideas on the possibility for a more inclusive concept of membership in the socio-national community as well as on EU-level.

## 2.1 Attitude surveys and opinion polls

A number of surveys and polls, mainly conducted during the 1990s, were selected to show trends in the majority population's attitudes vis-à-vis ethnic minorities. This was done via secondary analysis of already existing data which is admittedly not a perfect method as I did not design the questions myself, and as the questions were, therefore, not necessarily the sort of questions that I would have asked - neither in terms of wording, nor in terms of the issue raised. In particular in a comparative analysis, the fact that data derived from questions designed by different researchers at different points of time, with possibly different objectives, could be regarded as a serious flaw. In addition, the trustworthiness of some of these surveys and polls has to be queried as polling institutions or survey teams are often 'appointed' by governmental ministries or political parties to serve certain purposes rather than to reflect 'reality'. It is, however, not an easy task to theorize about 'mass discourse', and this method was chosen with the aim of establishing very broad generalizations about, and trends in, the attitudes of the 'indigenous' population to ethnic minorities related issues. A further aim of the analysis of attitude surveys and opinion polls was to illustrate the link between 'public opinion' and 'political discourse'.

## 2.2 Discourse analysis

A selection of key parliamentary debates, held during the 1990s, was investigated for the connections made between racialization, nationalism and citizenship by well-established and recognized politicians who played a crucial role in opinion forming or reflecting. In the British context, these debates revolved around the issue of asylum and immigration as ethnic minority related issues are rarely debated in the British Parliament; in the German context, amendments to the nationality/citizenship law and the Foreigners' Law were the main issues debated. Although the German and British debates did not topicalize exactly the same issues, they were analysed by establishing common rhetorical themes and methods.

Instead of interviewing, the method of discourse analysis was chosen as parliamentary debates are usually more mentally developed and appear in the context of attacking the political opponent by claiming to act on behalf of the people's will or for the people's good. It was the aim to show MPs' involvement in the reproduction of nationalism and racialization by way of subtle or indirect forms of rhetoric. It is exactly this type of discourse which influences the public more than the bluntness of right-wing extremists who are only supported by a minority.

## 2.3 The interviews

After having analyzed the general public's attitudes and the elitist perspective of parliamentarians, the next objective was to gain insight into the viewpoint of ethnic minorities themselves. This was done via interviews with representatives of organizations working in the 'race relations' field.

### 2.3.1 Reasons for choice of method

There are different types of interviewing methods and for this book, the semi-structured type was employed. One of the reasons for choosing this type of interviewing as a method of research is its qualitative nature[1]. This is an important aspect as the social world in general is understood here as an interactive process, i.e. as constructed by individuals who actively contribute meaning to it, "both through their interpretations and through actions based on those interpretations" (Hammersley 1992:44). Construction and interpretation of social phenomena can best be grasped by qualitative methods.

One of the reasons why interviewing was specifically chosen among other qualitative methods is that "interviewing offers researchers access to people's ideas, thoughts, and memories in their own words rather than in the words of the researcher" (Reinharz 1992:19). Interviewing differs from ethnography as it does not involve long periods of researcher participation in the life of the interviewees (which was not the purpose here). It also differs from survey research[2] or structured interviewing by including free interaction between the researcher and interviewee and, thus, offers opportunities for clarification and discussion (Reinharz 1992) - an aspect which is also important in the context of power relations (see section on issues of validity).

As the selected interviewees (see appendix) can be regarded as opinion leaders in the 'race relations field' with a lot of experience with, and knowledge of, different levels of governance (i.e. at grass-root or local, national and EC level), their ideas and thoughts are viewed as vital to gain further understanding of the workings of racism, nationalism and citizenship. Most of the interviewees' previous careers were in politics (local and national), administration (local councils) or education (secondary and tertiary). Thus, they are familiar with the main problems and concerns of immigrant communities and are also in full knowledge of governmental policies and of European Community policies - the latter, however, often to a less detailed extent. In this capacity, their responses give a valuable assessment of the author's theoretical and practical ideas and findings from the literature. Moreover, the responses to similar questions in Germany and Britain are seen as helpful to work out the differences and similarities in conceptual thinking in both countries.

## 2.3.2 Selection of interviewees

Interviews were conducted in Germany and Britain with senior personnel working in lobby groups/organizations or institutions in the so-called 'race relations field' (in Germany, this is called '*Ausländerarbeit*').

In Germany, the following groups/organizations were interviewed:

- Forum Buntes Deutschland - S.O.S Rassismus e.V. in Bonn
- Amt für Multikulturelle Angelegenheiten der Stadt Frankfurt am Main
- Ausländerbeauftragte des Senats zu Berlin (two representatives)
- Türkische Gemeinde, Berlin
- Bündnis türkischer Einwanderer in Berlin-Brandenburg e.V.
- TGB Hamburg e.V. (Bund türkischer Einwanderer)
- WIR - Internationales Zentrum, Hamburg;

In Britain, the following groups/organizations/institutions were interviewed:

- Anti-Racist Alliance, London
- Commission for Racial Equality, London
- Joint Council for the Welfare of Immigrants, London
- Indian Workers Association, London
- The Runnymede Trust, London;

At the EC level, the European Union's Migrants Forum was available as interviewee. For more detailed information on the interviewees' organizations, their functions and objectives, see Appendix II.

The German lobby groups or organizations were chosen because they represent different levels of organizations working at the governmental, semi-governmental and grass-root levels. They, therefore, represent different levels of governance. Further, they are involved in different types of activities all centred upon the improvement of 'immigrant' peoples' socio-economic position. For example, there are the Commissioner for Foreigners' Affairs in Berlin and the Office for Multi-cultural Matters in Frankfurt which are federal state, i.e. *Länder*, governmental institutions. Their work, among others, shows how official policies are implemented, what the official approach is to the settlement of the immigrants and what aims there are for the future at the official level. Moreover, as these institutions are in daily contact with smaller groups which work more at grass-root level, they are aware of both the shortcomings of official policies and the demands for improvement as expressed by specific ethnic minorities' organizations or individual members of ethnic minority communities.

The remaining associations work at grassroot level and can be divided into two groups: the first consisting of those run by Turkish people but not exclusively for the Turkish community. The Turks are the largest post-war labour migrant group and ethno-culturally the most distant (Martin & Miller 1990:10). They were, therefore, selected to express their views on citizenship/nationality and racialization. The second group (Forum Buntes Deutschland e.V. - S.O.S. Rassismus and WIR Internationales Zentrum) represents organizations which were originally established by German (indigenous) people to promote inter-ethnic/inter-'racial' relations. The Forum Buntes Deutschland e.V. is the only *nationally* organized lobby group having as its members various local and regional groups.

The British interviewees were also selected because they represent different levels of governance and are engaged in a range of activities in the field of 'race relations'. The Commission for Racial Equality is the only semi-governmental organization (set up by the Race Relations Act of 1976) mainly dealing with legal cases of racial discrimination. The remaining organizations are pressure groups, such as the Runnymede Trust chosen for its specific interest in two of the three main issues of this study (national identity/nationalism and racism), and the Joint Council for the Welfare of Immigrants chosen for its expertise in citizenship/nationality law and immigration law. The Indian Workers Association represents the largest minority group in Britain, and the Anti-Racist Alliance is, as its name indicates, very much engaged in activities against racial discrimination and violence. The latter two tend to work at grass-root level.

The EU Migrants Forum is the only organization established to represent immigrants from non-European backgrounds or who are of non-

EU nationality but resident within an EU-member-state. It is the only European wide organized lobby group which is concerned with citizenship issues and racial discrimination of non-European immigrants. Within the structure of the Community, there is no official institution which works in the 'race relations field'. Immigration is dealt with by intergovernmental meetings outside the Community; issues of nationality and citizenship are for discussion and decision within each member-state (see also Chapter Three).

Eight interviews with senior personnel of organizations in Germany were conducted as opposed to five in Britain. This appears unequal, but it happened so because the first two interviews (Ausländerbeauftragte in Berlin) were conducted as pilot studies to test whether the interview questions made any sense to the organizations and whether they were able to respond. The value of the data collected in these interviews warranted their inclusion in the main study.

### 2.3.3 *Planning, structure, and content of the interviews*

*Planning* After selecting the organizations with which interviews would be conducted and after designing the interview questions, the interviewees were contacted by letter explaining the research objectives and assuring confidentiality. In most cases, positive responses were forthcoming. The first two pilot interviews had been conducted in December 1993, the remaining interviews during the period from February to April 1994.

*Structure and content* The interviews were undertaken with the heads or other senior members of staff of the selected organizations and they were structured around three main issues: national identity/European identity, racism and citizenship. Despite this formal framework of questions (as can be seen in the Appendix III), the interviews were treated as semi-structured and conducted according to the development of each interview situation. The number of responses for specific questions varied because of variations in respondents' expertise about particular issues. In some cases, the interviewees elaborated on a particular area of knowledge and interest of their organizations. This meant that other issues had to be neglected, but it served the purpose of finding out each organization's priorities and main concerns. In general, however, questions about all three areas - national identity/European identity, racism and citizenship - were responded to.

Furthermore, the questions put to the interviewees in Britain and Germany could not always be identical as certain issues are not discussed with the same conceptual thinking and terminology.

All of the interviews were conducted by myself. They were tape-recorded with the consent of each interviewee (which was in fact given by all of them). Generally speaking, the atmosphere during the interviews was very relaxed - apart from two cases which were conducted under time pressure due to the interviewees' unexpected delay in previous meetings. As a result, the interviewees' schedules of the day were disrupted and, therefore, it was tacitly understood that the interviews had to be kept as short as possible.

The interviews lasted from between forty-five minutes to two and a half hours, with the average length of approximately an hour and a half. Most interviewees had their own offices or were interviewed at their home and thus most interviews were conducted without the presence of other people. Interruptions by telephone calls or colleagues/secretaries were rare and did mostly not have a negative impact on the flow of the interviews.

In almost all cases, it was easy to establish good relationships with the interviewees who appeared more than willing to talk. In part, they seemed pleased to get attention (a feeling the author had in particular in Germany when visiting Turkish organizations) and thus they seemed to be positively inclined to express their views on the above issues.

### 2.3.4 The analysis

I started the process of analysis with some systematic procedures such as transcribing each interview personally and reading the scripts over and over again. The resultant familiarity with the data led to the emergence of the sub-themes in each main area of focus (national/European identity, racism and citizenship). These themes evolved throughout the whole research as a development of my own understanding and experience, academic debate and the interviewed organizations' perspectives. This led to a process of selecting key concepts and key interview excerpts.

The categorization of the interviewees' replies under different headings was of course not always clear-cut as the issues involved appeared complex and interrelated. Replies made to questions on exclusionary aspects of national identity, for example, were repeated as aspects of racism and as aspects encroaching on immigrants' formal/substantive citizenship. This inter-relatedness, however, helped to develop part of the argument of 1. the symbiotic relationship between nationalism and racism; and 2. the link between identity as a 'race', a 'nation' and citizens with exclusionary effects on 'new' ethnic minorities' membership - in legal terms as well as socio-cultural.

### 2.4 'Racial matching' - an obstacle to validity?

One immediate issue arising from this research is that of the practice of cross-'racial' interviewing, i.e. the 'racial matching' of interviewer and informant. More than half the interviews conducted for this research have been with members of an ethnic minority (five out of eight in the German context, two out of five in the British case; the interviewee of the EU Migrants Forum was also a member of an ethnic minority).

According to Rhodes (1994), the argument of the critics of cross-'racial' interviewing maintains that racism is an inherent feature of British (this can also be applied to German) social life and that members of ethnic minorities distrust 'white' people in general. Therefore, this mistrust is extended to the 'white' researcher or interviewer, preventing access or distorting the quality of communication. Critics would also argue that people from ethnic minorities are not simply inhibited in their communications to a 'white' interviewer with the information being passed through a 'white' cultural filter, but that there are dimensions to ethnic minorities' experience invisible to the 'white' interviewer who is said to neither possess the language nor the cultural equipment to understand that experience. "In other words, the lack of an insider perspective precludes the white person from access to the black social world, whereas necessity has taught black people to be competent in both" (Rhodes 1994:549).

However, it is agreed here with Rhodes, who criticizes the above line of arguing, that the relationship of power and the lacking of an insider perspective in an interview situation do not always have to work in this way. The interviews for this study, for example, took place in the interviewees' work environment (i.e. in the offices of the respective institution or organization) or in some cases in the respondents' home (EU Migrants Forum, Anti-Racist Alliance) which means that the interviews were conducted in familiar surroundings. In a similar way as described in Rhodes' own study on prospective black foster parents, it was the case that "[t]he interviewer was 'invited in' on terms largely imposed by the interviewee who decided in which room the interview would take place, where the interviewer and they themselves would sit, whether and how to answer the interviewers' questions, and so on" (op.cit.:549). In a similar way, the interviewees for this study, for instance, decided on the length of the interview themselves (although a minimum amount of time necessary was suggested by the interviewer). In the case of the particular circumstances of two interviews, it was tacitly understood by the researcher that it would have been inappropriate to keep the interviewees for the desired length of time even, although the delay had not been the researcher's fault and in spite of the fact that the researcher had been inconvenienced. Therefore, only the main questions were asked.

Also, as opposed to quantitative questionnaire type of survey research during which the researcher determines the interview questions and language, employing qualitative techniques leaves the content and language more open to negotiation. Thus, "[a] more interactive approach can give interviewees greater power in negotiation of the pace and content of the interview, to direct the flow of conversation, and to ask questions themselves. Where interviews take place in respondents' homes [or offices, N.P.], familiar territory generates confidence, the interviewer is invited in as a 'guest' and the balance of power is more likely to tilt in the interviewee's favour." (op.cit.:555). The aspect of having been invited as a 'guest' was strongly felt in the conduct of the interviews for this study. It was totally up to the interviewees when they were 'ready' for the interviews to start and when to finish. Despite a pre-arranged time and a suggested length, the start of the interviews were often delayed, as they mostly took place in the interviewees' work environment. In this way, the interviews did not interrupt the flow of the interviewees' daily work or the completion of a previous task.

Moreover, as Rhodes rightly remarks, arguments for the exclusion of 'white' researchers with ethnic minorities on the basis that the relationship of power between researcher and researched tends to be unidirectional ignores the fact that the researcher is dependant on respondents' co-operation in the research process and the negotiation which occurs during the course of any exchange.

In addition to that, Rhodes suggests that the significance of skin colour does not have to be the same from start to finish of an interview and more can be gained from considering it as an interactive factor in the dynamic context of each interview than from singling it out as the dominating dimension. Also, skin colour or ethnic background are not the only 'social signifiers' and are not always significant to participants depending on the topics discussed. Dimensions such as gender, class, age, education and professional status can all emerge with different significance during the course of an interview. Moreover, according to Rhodes' experience, it may be the case that the 'white' interviewer has the advantage of a certain 'stranger value' (op.cit.:551). In the interviews conducted for this study, I had the impression that education and professional status played an important role in establishing 'common ground' as the interviewees were mostly leading figures in their organizations. In the case of the interviews conducted in Britain, I felt, similarly to Rhodes, that although being 'white', it was of advantage to be German, i.e. non-British. In the case of interviews conducted in both Germany and Britain, it was certainly of advantage for me to have experienced living abroad, i.e. to be an 'immigrant' myself (albeit not in the context of racialization, but certainly in the context of the issues of citizenship and national identity).

However, there still remains the issue of the interpretation usually being the sole task of the researcher and as such, it seems inevitably to be subject to a 'white' cultural filter. But this is not only an issue in the context of 'racial' matching as the personal background of the researcher (in terms of ethnicity, class, gender etc.) is always reflected in any analysis (Stanley & Wise 1993). As for the actual content of this research, the issues of racism, national identity and citizenship in multi-ethnic/multi-cultural societies were all approached from the perspective of the majority in a critical way. The whole content of this research is meant to improve the awareness of the majority for ethnic minorities' situations and concerns in the areas investigated and this was certainly understood by most of the interviewees. The experience of this study has led to an agreement with

Rhodes that "in certain circumstances and for certain research questions, the 'racial' matching of interviewer and respondent *may be* appropriate" (1994:557; emphasis added), but this should not be viewed as a *general* strategy. Non-racial elements can influence the positive or negative outcome of an interviewing situation. Also, the power relationship between researcher and researched in a 'black-and-white' setting depends very much on the specific research content, the research method, and - in the case of interviewing - the actual interview situation. Thus, the balance of power in an interview situation of 'non-racial matching' does not have to tilt in the 'white' interviewer's favour.

On the whole, the interviews with senior personnel of the selected organizations offered valuable insight into the complex workings of racism, nationalism and citizenship for ethnic minorities in Germany and Britain (as well as the EU as a total) in addition to the governmental or EU reports and academic literature. As 'grass-root' organizations or 'mouthpieces' of grass-root groups, a variety of views were expressed by the interviewees adding a number of conceptual and pragmatic aspects to the debate on citizenship.

## Notes

1    ...as opposed to quantitative methods such as survey or experimental research.

2    Hammersley & Atkinson (1983), for instance, reject the survey method on the grounds that it is incapable of capturing the meaning of everyday human activities.

# 3   The European context

This chapter will put the issue of immigrants' permanent settlement into the wider European context and will investigate the EC's competence regarding third-country nationals.

The creation of the European Community and its organizational developments are of great importance in the context of international labour migration as it is the best known and most tightly integrated of the regional organizations of Europe as far as common economic policies are concerned[1]. Essentially, as the EC was in the first place an economic community, the creation of the EC aimed at closer *economic* integration. In general, this meant the creation of a Common Market, including a series of targets for the establishment of common economic policies. In particular, this involved the free movement of capital, goods, services and people as the gradual aim and thus, labour migration was a central feature of EC policy.

The institutional and policy influence of the European Community on migration (internally as well as from outside) will be considered in the following sections. The main argument is that the EC has not had any major impact on the nationally existing policies to include non-European immigrants. Special emphasis will be given to demonstrating the general tendency towards stricter border controls and immigration regulations and a tendency to deal with these in an intergovernmental structure rather than as EC-policies. The predominance of the national level and the little difference the EU has made concerning settled third-country nationals will become clear.

## 3.1  General Community policies on immigration - Fortress Europe?

In the context of immigration from outside Europe and asylum policies, the key point arising from the creation of a single Europe in the post-1992 period is the concern that it will lead to the virtual closure of the EC to non-EC labour migrants and the creation of what has been labelled a 'fortress' (Nederveen Pieterse 1991; Gordon 1989; The Economist 1991; Cohen 1994: chapter six). This image of a 'fortress' derives from the relaxation of internal border controls within the Community (in order to realize the principle of free movement) on the one hand, with the consequence being (for all member-states alike) the prevention of entry to non-EC nationals, in particular those from the so-called Third World, on the other hand. This will require the harmonization of member-states' immigration policies in relation to nationals of non-EC countries through a common EC policy on immigration.

The creation of a 'Fortress Europe' (i.e. stricter border controls and immigration regulations) seems also to be of concern to settled immigrants. To show the implications for these 'new' ethnic minorities, a brief summary of the policy developments concerning migration within and from without the Community follows.

Since its inception, the EC - being mainly an economic organization - seems to have been originally preoccupied with employers' needs for labour. Under the 1957 Treaty of Rome establishing the European Economic Community, freedom of movement and settlement throughout the community was guaranteed to EC workers and their families to enable labourers to move to vacant jobs. The EEC Treaty specifies this right by stating that the freedom of workers shall be secured within the Community and shall also "entail the abolition of any discrimination based on nationality between workers of the Member States as regards employment, remuneration and other conditions of work and employment" (EEC Treaty, Art. 48[2], as quoted by Niessen 1992:677). In other words, the EEC Treaty defines the right of free movement as the right of a national of one member-state to move freely to another member-state to accept offers of employment and to stay there. Community legislation has extended this right to family members of EC nationals who do not need to have the nationality of one of the member-states (Council Directive of 28 June 1990, No. (90/364/EEC), OJ No. L 180/26). This right of residence has also been extended to students, pensioners and other nonsalaried persons (Council Directive of 28 June 1990, No. (90/365/EEC) and (90/366/EEC), OJ No. L 180/28 and No. L 180/30).

The Single European Act signed in 1986 was the next step towards the completion of a single European market comprising 330 million EC nationals with full free movement and settlement rights as of 1 January 1993. With the signing of this Act, negotiations among EC member-states began with the intention to remove all their internal borders in order to complete the free market of goods, capital, services and labour, which the Treaty of Rome had as its aim but which was halted by a general protectionist response due to the recession of the 1970s. With the completion of the internal market by 1993, it was viewed as necessary to ensure that external borders be strengthened to keep strict control on the admission of non-EC nationals.

Until recently the EC has not been concerned with the immigration of third-country nationals, which has been regarded as a matter for each single member-state to regulate. Common immigration and asylum policies, therefore, developed on an ad hoc basis as a response to the perceived common need to ensure that the opening of Europe's internal borders did not entail the free entry and free movement of non-Community nationals. The need for some co-ordination was first acknowledged in 1976, when the *Trevi* group (acronym for terrorism, radicalism, extremism, and violence) of interior ministers was set up at the instigation of the UK government to co-ordinate issues of terrorism. Later, the agenda was to include all the policing and security aspects of free movement, such as immigration, visas and border controls.

Another group, set up to proceed with the abolition of internal borders, is the Schengen group with its agreement signed in 1985 (originally five members - Germany, France and the Benelux countries, later joined by Italy, Spain, Portugal and Greece). Border controls were to be abolished from 1 January 1990, and working groups were set up to develop co-ordinated measures on policing Schengen's external borders to keep out unwanted people. One year after the Schengen group was established, the Ad Hoc Group for Immigration came into existence in October 1986, again at the suggestion of the UK, to end abuses of the asylum process. The Ad Hoc Group consisted of interior ministers of the EC member-states and proposed, among other methods, sanctions on airlines bringing in undocumented asylum-seekers and those with false documents. In 1990, a convention to prevent asylum-seekers making more than one application in the EC - known as the Dublin convention[2] - was signed (Collinson 1994:125) and a draft convention on harmonization of controls at external borders was introduced during the same year, followed by proposals in 1991 for fingerprinting (Webber, in: Bunyan 1993). The plan to fingerprint all asylum-seekers in the EU was launched in the summer of 1993 and approved by the EU Council of Ministers in November 1995 (Migration News 1996b).

There are a few more *drafted* documents which exemplify the general tendency towards stricter border controls and stricter immigration regulations, such as 'The External Border Convention' (expected to be signed in 1991) and 'The Draft Resolution on Family Reunification' (prepared in 1992)[3]. These measures and draft conventions clearly indicate a certain attitude of western European governments and EC policy-makers towards non-Europeans. Since 1973, there has been a remarkable homogeneity of immigration and deportation measures converging towards increasing stringency in relation to non-EC peoples (Baimbridge & Burkitt & Macey 1994; Mitchell & Russell 1994; Cohen 1991; Hammar 1985b). The basic policy response to the refugee problem, too, has been to erect new barriers around Europe in what can only be seen as a concerted movement towards the creation of a fortress-type of Europe. However, as there is no common EC immigration and asylum policy (apart from a common visa policy, see section on Maastricht Treaty), Mitchell & Russell (1994) suggest that the development of 'Fortress Europe' that has occurred to date is not so much the result of imposed 'top-down' supra-national policy processes, but rather as a growth of co-operation between member-states. The drift towards such a 'fortress' has not been orchestrated from Brussels but is the result of a combination of tougher measures introduced by individual member-states and inter-governmental initiatives directed towards the harmonization of policy and practice (such as Schengen and Trevi). Thus, this co-operation among EC-member-states in the field of immigration seems to be a persistence of restrictive trends on national levels.

To sum up, 'Fortress Europe' concretely refers to the developments around the establishment of the Single Internal Market, to the lowering of internal borders by implementing tighter external border controls, and to the plans for a 'European visa'. The key point about the creation of a single Europe is that it will mean the virtual closure of the EC to non-EC nationals, and, therefore, the impact of 'Fortress Europe' will be most sharply felt by people seeking asylum and refugee status in the countries of the EC.

What are the implications of this development for already settled foreign workers in the EC? There seems to be rising concern that - with the abolition of internal borders - there will be (and already is) an increasing use of *internal* immigration checks such as passport raids by the police (Baimbridge & Burkitt & Macey 1994) and the immigration service as well as checks by individual police officers on black and Asian people's immigration status "in the workplace, social security/welfare offices, at train and bus stations, indeed in all public and private space" (Allen & Macey 1992:382; see also Cohen 1991:13)[4]. Björgo and Witte claim that the restrictive EC policies in this area will also have implications for ethnic minorities already settled in Europe as naturalized citizens as "[a] move from external border controls to internal controls will have a massive influence on daily life for non-white ethnic minorities." (1993:2). This could mean that, although a large number of black and Asian people in the UK have full (formal) citizenship rights and the theoretical right to freedom of movement within the EC, it is likely that they are not recognized by immigration authorities as EC nationals and therefore subject to questioning about their status. Groenendijk (in: Institut für Migrations- und Rassismusforschung 1992:518) suggests that skin colour and cultural difference from the norm (such as clothes or appearance) are going to be the criteria for official internal controls by the police. Moreover, according to the same author, there is the danger that these new European regulations contribute to the legitimization of 'racial' discrimination by civil servants and private persons. such as personnel of air companies[5] (op.cit.). Restricted family reunification policies and the 'primary purpose rule'[6] also have serious implications for long-term settled immigrants. Furthermore, restrictive immigration and asylum policies convey the general message that third-country nationals are perceived as a 'problem' quite often related to drug smuggling and terrorism.

There is also evidence of an escalating hostile climate and upsurge of racially motivated violence throughout the EC (Gordon 1989; Björgo & Witte 1993), aggravating the insecure social position of long-term resident non-EC nationals. Various documents on racism and xenophobia have signified the deteriorating public attitudes and actions towards immigrants throughout the EC (1986 Solemn Declaration Against Racism and

Xenophobia; 1990 Report on the Findings of the Committee of Inquiry into Racism and Xenophobia). The danger of Europe becoming a 'fortress' seems, therefore, to be well founded, as there are indications of a relationship between stricter immigration policies and an intensified hostile climate within the general public against non-European peoples - albeit not only as a problem from outside, but also from inside with serious implications for would-be immigrants and asylum-seekers as well as for settled ethnic minorities.

## 3.2 The Treaty on European Union (Maastricht Treaty)

It has been shown so far that the European Community as such has no clear competence for policy making in the field of immigration/integration and asylum matters which are, for that reason, dealt with in separate agreements such as Schengen and in groups such as Trevi and the Ad Hoc Group. The Maastricht Treaty - the latest amendment to the Treaty of Rome - represents a new development in this respect and deserves special mention.

After much heated argument and delays, the Treaty on European Union was signed in Maastricht in February 1992. The Maastricht Treaty represents a major leap forward towards European integration and abandons the initial main emphasis on the economic sphere. The Treaty contains:

1. amendments and additions to the three existing treaties, namely the European Coal and Steel Community (ECSC), the European Atomic Energy Community (Euratom) and the European Economic Community (EEC);
2. provisions on co-operation in the fields of justice and home affairs;
3. provisions on the common foreign and security policy;
4. special rules on social policy (of which the UK opted out).

Provisions for European citizens (Union citizenship; more details in Chapter Six), the goal of a common currency by 1999 at the latest, and increased powers for the European Parliament are new in the Treaty on European Union. Thus, the Treaty combines for the first time the economic and political dimensions on the supranational level, namely economic and financial policy, military and foreign policy, immigration, and law and order - the so-called three 'pillars' of the EU structure (Bunyan 1993).

The Treaty defines how the policies of these 'three pillars' are dealt with in more detail: the Community's institutions are in charge of economic and financial policy (first pillar); the second block establishes formal co-operation on justice and home affairs including immigration policy (conditions of entry, residence, movement etc.); the third pillar is built around co-operation in the field of foreign and defence policy (Dummett &

Niessen 1993). There is also a protocol concerned with social policy. It is not part of the general Community policy because it was signed by only eleven member-states with the exception of the UK. Article 2, paragraph 3 of this Protocol mentions "conditions of employment for third-country nationals legally residing in Community territory". Callovi (1992) suggests, as the usual sentence has been "living and working conditions", that the expression used by the new Treaty seems to limit the scope of proposals to economic rights and to the working environment. Therefore, according to him, more general topics linked to integration and living conditions, such as housing, education, health, equality of social rights and opportunities, seem hardly to be part of the expression "conditions of employment" and thus, subjects for proposals under this Article.[7]

The most important article with regard to immigration matters is Article K which is made up of Title VI Provisions on Co-operation in the field of Justice and Home Affairs (Dummett & Niessen 1993). This Title does not provide for any amendments to the EC treaty but allows for the establishment of co-operation between the member-states in the field of Justice and Home Affairs. This does not provide a legal framework for the European Union as such. The usual procedure of community legal instruments is that the Council and the Commission issue regulations (directly applicable in every member-state), directives (binding as to the result to be achieved but leave the choice of form and methods for incorporating them into national legislation to the national authorities), and decisions (binding on those to whom they are addressed). The meaning of the 'pillars', however, is that governments agree to work together through new channels and thus, these fields of co-operation are tackled outside the Brussels structure.

The Final Act of the Maastricht Treaty contains declarations of which one is relevant to immigration/integration policies. This is the Declaration on Nationality of a Member State which leaves the "question whether an individual possesses the nationality of a Member State ....solely...to the national law of the Member State concerned" (European Union 1993:644). Nationality law, which is very often linked to citizenship entitlements, is not included in the field of EU competence and the treatment of third country nationals is not harmonized.

Among the various critical comments on the Maastricht Treaty, its democratic deficit seems to be of particular concern (Dummett & Niessen 1993; Bunyan 1993). In this context, Webber (in: Bunyan 1993) views a danger of the Maastricht process in that "once the transitional period of intergovernmental co-operation comes to an end, these extremely illiberal conventions and resolutions, drafted solely from the perspective of *policing* and with no regard to the rights of immigrants and refugees, will be incorporated into EC law..." (page 153; emphasis added). The aspect of 'policing' is a very important theme within the political discourse which tries to justify the necessity of intergovernmental co-operation within the field of home affairs and justice. The allegedly 'urgent need of strict immigration controls' has often been linked to crime so that public opinion has overwhelmingly taken on these views. One European survey comes to the conclusion that the most popular Maastricht measure in all member-states is the closer co-operation in fighting drug traffic and organized crime (91% of respondents agree with it) and the third most liked measure is immigration (76%) (the second was common defence) (European Communities, Eurobarometer, No. 39, June 1993). Asked whether certain policy areas should be decided nationally or as a jointly on the EU level in 1996, the fight against drugs scored highest for European Union policy decision (77%), and still 57% of the respondents see immigration policy as better decided jointly by the EU (against 37% who prefer immigration to be decided nationally) (European Commission, Eurobarometer, No. 44, spring 1996).

A further element of undemocratic procedures within the EU structures is seen in the fact that the Maastricht Treaty has not given more power to the European Parliament. Philip (1994) writes in this context that parliamentarians seem to get more and more anxious about the uncontrolled decision-making processes by which decisions on citizens' rights, asylum and immigration matters are being made. There seems to be indeed a lack of democratic control. As a whole, Maastricht adds little that is new to the EU countries' collective activities in the fields of immigration and integration and does not help to improve the legal and social position of non-European residents.

### 3.3 The European Parliament

The European Parliament has always favoured a gradual increase in the rights of non-Community nationals in the Union. For example, its resolution of 9 May 1985 (OJ No. 141, 1985, p. 462) stressed that the right of workers to be reunited with their families should be recognized in accordance with the provisions of the European Convention on the legal status of migrant workers[8]. In a resolution of 15 March 1989 (OJ No. C 96, 1989, p. 61) on the social dimension of the internal market, the EP expressed its opinion on the social situation of non-Community workers. It called on the Commission and the Council to draw up a common policy based on reciprocity for non-Community workers and their families permanently resident in the Community. On 14 June 1990 (OF No. C 175, 1990, p. 180), the EP reiterated that the lack of a common immigration policy with regard to non-Community migrant workers might lead to pressure on the European labour market. There was, therefore, an urgent need for a Community policy in this area.

In its resolutions of 18 November 1992 (OJ No. C 337, 1992, p. 94) and 15 July 1993 on European policy on immigrants, the EP emphasized the need for non-Community workers legally resident in the

EU to enjoy the same social welfare rights as other migrant workers who were EU nationals and called on the Commission to submit proposals to this effect. Yet again, it stressed the importance of the right to family reunion for spouses and children under 18 years of age. The member-states were urged to ensure that it was made easier for non-Community nationals to become naturalized after a reasonable period of legal residence. The right to vote in local elections should be given to those who had been legally resident in a member-state for more than five years. In a resolution of 25 May 1993, the EP pointed out how unreasonable it was that non-Community citizens legally residing in a Community country should require visas in virtually all the member-states, thus being subjected to time-consuming formalities when travelling from one member-state to another. The EP also considers that a common immigration policy should comply with the rules of parliamentary democracy and wants the Parliament's role to be strengthened to the extent that the immigration issue is made a matter for the Community, which it hopes will soon happen.

Moreover, the EP is concerned about the increase of racism in Europe (mainly directed at non-Community nationals) and set up a committee of inquiry in 1984 to carry out a full investigation of the problem. The committee's work resulted in a report which formed the basis of a resolution adopted by the EP on 16 January 1986. This, in turn, prompted the joint declaration on racism and xenophobia by the EP, the Council and the Commission on 11 June 1986 (OJ No. C 158, 1986). Since then, the EP has dissociated itself from the growing intolerance towards foreigners on several occasions, for instance in its resolution on the resurgence of racism and xenophobia in Europe and the danger of right-wing extremist violence of 21 April 1993 (OJ No. C 150, 1993, p. 127). The latest 'action' in this respect is the designation of 1997 as European Year Against Racism by the EP. It calls therein for the isolation of racist parties (Migration News, vol. 3(6), 1996).

All these resolutions show very well which sort of activities the EP would like to see as part of the EU's responsibilities vis-à-vis third country nationals. They also indicate the limitation of the EP's own power. However, despite being fairly powerless, the EP represents at least a forum where these issues are debated.


### 3.4 EU-provisions for third country nationals - a summarizing commentary

So far, I have illustrated the general tendency throughout the EU towards stricter border controls and stricter immigration regulations on the one hand, and a clear lack of common inclusion policies for non-European residents on the other (despite the European Parliament's different stance in these matters).

Internal policies resulting in the materialization of free movement of EU nationals goes hand in hand with external policies resulting in the creation of 'Fortress Europe'. As for settled third country nationals, there are little if any provisions on the EU level. As far as EU immigration policies are concerned, there is a preoccupation with asylum and border controls. Although the member-states of the EU are going to enhance their co-operation in matters related to migration, the emphasis is very much on visa and admission policies, the control of migratory movements and the crack-down of illegal immigration. Thus, the only common policies deriving from a European consensus are about the need to limit external immigration. Common external border controls seem to be agreed upon without solving the questions of national immigration policies, of the historical ties of each member-state to certain third countries, and of Union power to include third-country nationals among the 'peoples of Europe' as referred to in the Maastricht Treaty. However, Callovi (1992) rightly comments that such controls are not the answer to the need for an active policy on immigration.

According to Dummett & Niessen (1993), immigration policy, at Community and intergovernmental level, is defined not only in terms of future immigration but is also considered to include policies on the inclusion of immigrants who already reside on Union territory. However, inclusion of third-country nationals is not an explicit part of either Community policy or intergovernmental policy. Inclusion, according to the above authors, is now generally viewed as a matter of providing rights for resident migrants and their families and it is meant to promote social policies and educational plans. In this way, the responsibilities of the intergovernmental groups and those of the EU's institutions overlap. The EU, in fact, deals with social policies, and thus it has some competence where third-country nationals are concerned (e.g. the Equal Opportunities directives concerning equality between men and women apply to *all* workers). And yet, the Maastricht Treaty prohibits discrimination on grounds of nationality only with regard to EU nationals. There is, therefore, no explicit competence for EU legislation against discrimination on grounds of 'race', ethnic origin or non-EU nationality. However, as Dummett & Niessen (1993) suggest, it would be possible to include anti-discrimination provisions under the heading of the social and economic policy of the Community, if the *political will* were there. Assumedly the political will is partly lacking at the moment as the result of a generally poor economic climate with the common tendency towards narrow and protectionist nationalism.

The system of free movement combined with the protection of workers' rights, as established by Article 48 and 58 of the Treaty of Rome, by certain provisions of the Single European Act (SEA) which amended that Treaty in 1985, and by the Maastricht Treaty, can only be enjoyed by EU nationals/citizens and their families (the latter may be of any nationality or citizenship though). Thus, approximately eight million

(Niessen 1992:678) legally resident third country nationals with official residence and work permits - as opposed to illegal immigrants - on EU territory are excluded from the right of free movement. The right to cross internal borders is only granted to them as tourists and not for seeking a resident permit or employment (Callovi 1992)[9]. What concerns these people from outside the EU is the fact that each member-state has retained its sovereign right to admit or refuse any third country national. It is for each state to decide upon the legal rights it is prepared to grant non-EU nationals and to define its own nationals for EU purposes.

Inclusion in general is, thus, still a matter dealt with on the national level, and despite a limited degree of convergence of national immigration policies, there remains great divergence. Each EU country's immigration history is distinctive, often resulting in special arrangements for 'privileged' aliens (such as 'ethnic Germans' from Eastern Europe or the Irish and immigrants from ex-colonies in Britain). Thus, the only convergence has been an EU consensus on the need to limit future immigration and asylum applications. A concerted EU policy, however, which reflects the permanent settlement of former labour migrants in the form of legal, social and political equality to EU-nationals does not exist.

### 3.4.1 Future prospects

On the basis of the little improvements the Maastricht Treaty has brought for third-country nationals, the Green Paper on European Social Policy of November 1993 has made recommendations towards a better social position for non-EU legal residents. For instance, the Green Paper calls on the EU to give consideration to allowing access to employment in another member-state to third-country nationals who have acquired a permanent right of residence in one of the member-states with the extension of other rights which are a corollary to free movement in Union terms. The main objective of the Union concerning legally resident migrants should be to enhance their social inclusion through equal opportunities in employment, education, housing, social security and health care. On the national level, the Green Paper recommends improved education and information as this should help to reduce ignorance and lack of understanding of ethnic minorities and may counteract racist attitudes. Each member-state should not only sanction violence (which is largely already the case), but implement comprehensive anti-discrimination legislation to offer an integrated and coherent approach to combating racism and discrimination (which is not yet the case in every EC member-state).

For a future potential agenda, Philip (1994) suggests the improvement of the position and rights of long-term resident migrants in the EU who have not acquired the nationality of a member-state. According to him, this concerns a much broader policy discussion about the evolution of nationality policy in the member-states. The refusal of citizenship to long-term immigrants is perceived as a real barrier to their inclusion and to social cohesion. This aspect will be subject to more details in Chapter Six.

As yet, however, there is no evidence of purposeful harmonization or co-operation in granting nationality (citizenship) to third-country nationals. There is still no truly common Union immigration policy, nor a common citizenship policy in terms of its acquisition. In actual fact, as Philips concludes, "West European societies are open in theory, but not in practice when it comes to immigration from outside and *within* the EU." (1994:188; emphasis added).

The issue of exclusiveness or non-existence of EU policies will re-appear in subsequent chapters, in particular in Chapter Six in connection with citizenship. The following chapter will deal with the question whether and to what extent this exclusiveness is based on racialization and how racialization ties into the debate around national identity and citizenship.

## Notes

1     At least since the Maastricht Treaty, however, common policies are not confined to the area of economics, but have been expanded to include social policies.

2     Its full title is *Convention Determining the State Responsible for Examining Applications for Asylum.*

3     See for more information on these drafted documents in Appendix I which draws heavily on Webber's chapter *European conventions on immigration and asylum* (in: Bunyan 1993).

4     The quoted authors do not give any real evidence of these checks and raids. In the interviews conducted for this thesis, problems such as closer checks when travelling across European borders were mentioned (see Chapter Seven), but the issue of internal checks in Britain or Germany did not come up.

5     In this context, the European Parliament's Report of the Committee of Inquiry into Racism and Xenophobia of 1990 mentions to have received "numerous complaints" about "the police and customs authorities". As a result, the Report includes Recommendation 69 which demands "That Member States renew the instructions given to the various services responsible for carrying out checks to avoid any discriminatory harassment likely to suggest to the persons being checked that external characteristics pertaining to a particular race or category may have predisposed them to the checks concerned." (p. 167).

6     This rule refers to the need to 'prove' that in case of marrying a person from outside Europe, the primary purpose for migration is not economic.

7     It seems appropriate at this point to include a remark on the difference between the EC and the EU which has got terminological implications for the remaining sections and chapters. The European *Union*, as explained

above, comprises the intergovernmental pillars of justice & home affairs and defence, as well as the EC pillar (i.e. the original institutional framework). Thus, 'European Union' will refer from now on to the whole structure as set out by the Maastricht Treaty, whereas 'European Community' will only mean the EC pillar in the pre- and post-Maastricht context.

8    The European Convention on the Legal Status of Migrant Workers (in force since 1983) was sponsored by the Council of Europe - a regional organization comprised of the democratic states of Western Europe and established in 1949. The European Convention currently represents the furthest progression of international human rights law with respect to migrant workers. This is because it concerns itself with the life of migrant workers as a whole and not just with respect to the employment relationship (Lillich 1984).

9    The distinction between 'free circulation' and 'free movement' provisions is important in this context. For third-country nationals, the former provisions refer to those that allow for short visits to other member-states, whereas the latter encompass the wider range of rights associated with 'the free movement of persons' under Article 8a of the SEA (Article 7a, Treaty of European Union), including the right of establishment and access to the labour market (Collinson 1994:146).

# 4 Racism

The purpose of this chapter is to provide the first step towards further elaboration of the argument of a symbiotic relationship between nationalism (as the source of national identity) and racism. This will be done by discussing the conceptual roots of racism and by searching for a definition of racism which links up with the issue of national identity and citizenship.

One of the main arguments for including racism in the debate around citizenship as a concept of socio-national membership is that racism has been an integral part of western Europe's period of modernization and formation of nation-states. There is a long tradition within western European societies of separating 'outsiders' from 'insiders' on the basis of 'racial' differences. The concept to describe similar exclusionary processes as well as the dissimilarities within the German and British socio-historical formation of their collective identity (as 'race', 'nation' and 'citizens') vis-à-vis the 'Other' is suggested here to be the concept of racialization.

## 4.1   History and modernity - general remarks on the roots of racism

Racism is an important contributor to economic, social and political inequality in Britain and Germany today (Mason 1995; Beauftragte der Bundesregierung für die Belange der Ausländer 1993a). The groups that suffer from the cumulative disadvantages of current racisms[1] in both countries are mainly those whose origins are from outside Europe.

Contemporary forms of racism have a long history. They are rooted in centuries of oppression and struggle that formed the foundation of relations not only between 'blacks' and 'whites', but also between whichever groups were defined as 'insiders' and 'outsiders' at a particular point of time. Thus, racism has not only functioned to define others, but also as a means for self-identification.

As for the historical roots of racism, western Europe has been suggested to be the crucial place as "racism is inseparable from modernity" which "developed from *European* origins" (Wieviorka 1994:174; emphasis added). In this way, Wieviorka rightly claims a certain unity of contemporary racisms in Europe by nevertheless viewing racism as a set of ideologies and pseudo-scientific doctrines as well as a set of concrete manifestations. In its link to 'modernity', racism is widely held to be the outcome of the immense changes after the Renaissance, followed by the Enlightenment, the age of the democratic revolution and industrialization with Europe at its centre (Jäggi 1992; Nederveen Pieterse 1994). It developed further in modern times re-emphasized by mass migrations, the extension of trading relationships, the formation of the capitalist economic system, and colonization (Wallerstein 1987; Wieviorka 1994). Thus, there are a number of factors in the history of Europe which rendered Europeans more powerful than others in imposing their social categories on other peoples (Banton 1977).

The emergence of scientific discourse as an important constitutive element in the process of modernity has, according to Brah (1994), bearing on the analysis of the inter-relationship between racism, ethnicity and nationalism. The scientificity of modernity is embedded in the construction of Europe's outsiders. "Its grand narratives of 'development' produced classificatory hierarchies centred on Europe as the norm for plotting the 'achievements' of different peoples of the globe" (ibid.). In this way, a Euro-centric view of the world gradually emerged (Jäggi 1992).

In most western European countries, a specifically crude and (pseudo)-scientific racism was much more widespread before the Second World War than tends to be the case today. Colonial racism postulated the inferiority of colonized people of different 'races', and modern anti-Semitism gave a new and active dimension to former anti-Judaism (Arendt 1951), climaxing in the Holocaust (Bauman 1989). This is the reason why Wieviorka rightly suggests the necessity to "introduce a sense of relativity into our perceptions of contemporary racism" (1994:176). When discussing racism, the different historical manifestations have to be borne in mind with their different types of discourses. However, "this idea means not that there is no continuity in racist doctrines, ideologies, prejudice or more concrete expressions, but that a new era in the history of racism began with the retreat ....of scientific racism, the end of decolonization, and, above all, the 'economic crisis' that has in fact meant the beginning of the decline of industrial societies" (ibid.).[2]

In this context, contemporary sociological literature seems to insist on the idea of changing forms of racism or historically specific racisms (Hall 1988). Furthermore, during the 1980s, some British writers argued that the contemporary expression of racism in Britain could not be adequately explained without considering contemporary nationalism as part of exclusionary practices (Barker 1981; Miles 1987+1982b+1993; Gilroy 1987). According to authors such as Barker (1981), a distinction should be made between a classical, biologically scientific racism and a new racism based on a theory Barker refers to as pseudo-biological culturalism. The main point for many scholars is that the new racism, sometimes also referred to as cultural racism or differentialist racism (Balibar 1991)[3], is the main form in the contemporary world, while the biological scientific one becomes secondary. Wieviorka, however, suggests that this should not be regarded as a general theory of racism as firstly, cultural aspects of racism are not new, and secondly, "a purely cultural definition of the Other, as well as a purely social one, dissolves the idea of race" (ibid.). Whenever there is any reference to 'race' in a cultural sense, it is usually only regarded as 'racist' when culture carries the connotation of nature in the sense of an organistic or genetic (i.e. innate) representation of the Other. If the Other is, however, referred to as socially inferior or marginalized, it is usually not referred to as racist. And yet, as Wieviorka rightly concludes, "in fact, in most experiences of racism, the two logics coexist, and racism appears as a combination of them both" (1994:183) - a statement which is supported by authors such as Goldberg (1993), who acknowledges that it is misleading to treat 'race' as about physical difference and ethnicity about cultural difference since cultural difference can become treated as generic and unchanging. Furthermore, Mason contests the existence of a 'new' racism claiming that "reports of the death of the 'old' one [biological racism, N.P.] have been greatly exaggerated" (1992:23).

As it is agreed here with Wieviorka that 'cultural' and 'biological' racism tend to coexist, it is often not possible to separate biological explanations of differences in human beings from socio-cultural ones. This could also mean that racism is not clearly separable from nationalism - an aspect Bauman seems to have had in mind when claiming that nationalism (and thus, the emphasis on culture) is the racism of the intellectuals and racism   is the nationalism of the masses (1992). This view could also be read as claiming that the way *how* distinctions are being expressed depends on class and educational level.

To regard both types - the biological and the cultural - as racism could be criticized as taking any form of differentiating between human beings as racism, and thus inflating this concept. I argue, however, that the main emphasis should not be on the distinction between cultural or biological forms of racism, but rather on the historical processes (such as modernization and the formation of the nation-state) and purposes involved when constructing groups (i.e. 'races' or 'nations'). In other words, the emphasis should be on the specific material and power relations in which these processes are embedded.

### 4.1.1 Racism in German and British society

It is argued here that changing forms of racism have been an integral part of both German and British society. Both countries - while in the process of economic and political expansion - have made use of conquest and exploitation of labour power of people of foreign origin. In the British case, slavery (Fryer 1984) and colonialism have played pre-eminent roles revolving around the exploitation of peoples of colour which has somehow resulted in a 'race problematic' in the British Isles.

Germany had colonies too, but only for a period of thirty years from 1884 to 1914 - a fact which should not be underestimated in terms of the formation of an attitude of superiority towards third world peoples (Mergner 1992; Melber 1992). Moreover, the 'race' ideologies during German colonialism are suggested by Pinn & Nebelung (1992) as having anticipated essential elements of the national socialist 'racial mania'. However, Germany had not maintained any links to its former colonies after having lost them at the end of the First World War - a fact which is also reflected in post-war immigration to Germany which did not take place from ex-colonies as in the British case. Thus, post-war labour migration had never been of peoples of colour and it did not result in the *language* of 'race' and 'race relations' in *today*'s context. This does not mean, however, that Germany has never employed the terminology of 'race'. Even though Germany's colonial period and the contact to peoples of colour was rather short, its expansionist history - which is more characterized by moves into eastern Europe, the exploitation of eastern European peoples (Herbert 1986), and the Nazi ideology including anti-Semitism and anti-Slavism leading to the use of forced (largely foreign) labour and the Holocaust - was clearly accompanied by the ideology of 'race'. In particular during the Nazi-period, the '*Untermensch*' (inferior human being), although not of colour, but of different blood and different culture, was regarded as a separate and inferior 'race'.

Despite these differences, however, both countries have experienced a general history of inferiorizing and racializing other peoples, along with the development of a feeling of racial superiority which has been shared with all west Europeans in their relations with non-Europeans (Goulbourne 1991).

## 4.2 Historical and theoretical groundings of terminology

As Germany and Britain have quite different histories of immigration and have responded to it differently in terms of policies and legal provisions, it is not surprising that there are also differences in terminology and concepts concerned with racism and racialized groups. In the following section, these terminological differences will be analyzed - not only cross-national, but also with regard to controversies *within* each countries' circle of scholars.

### 4.2.1 'Black', 'race' and Ausländer

In Britain, the term 'race relations' and the fact that victims of racism are referred to as 'blacks' evoke, as suggested by Balibar, a "directly post-colonial situation and imagery" (1991:6). Moreover, blackness tends to be used as a political category encompassing the diversity of ethnic minority groups. There are, however, arguments against subsuming all ethnic minorities - the Asian communities, for example - within the term 'black'[4] (Anthias & Yuval-Davis 1992; Modood 1992).

From a German author's perspective, Bahringhorst (1993) argues that the 'colour problematic' in Britain has created a situation in which the dimension of the so-called 'race' differences is superimposed on the dimension of ethnic differences. In her opinion, the domination of the 'colour difference' in the public perception has entailed an almost exclusive adoption of American models of analysis. She further argues that the relationship between ethnic minorities and the British receiving society is said to be often simplified, equated with the relationship between Afro-Americans and the 'white' majority. American strategies to solve conflicts are transferred to the British situation with little modification.

Noticeable, especially for German observers, is the generally uncritical usage of the term 'race' which might have to do with British history being to a much lesser extent burdened by an extreme ideology of 'race' when compared with recent German history. In contemporary context, the terminology of 'race' is rejected in Germany partly on the basis of the 'race politics' of the National Socialists. I argue, however, that a conceptual understanding of differentiating between peoples has to be seen in the context of *modern history as a whole*. Britain - with its distinctive history of a maritime power, of being the first country to experience the Industrial Revolution and the first signs of capitalism[5], slavery and colonialism - was in contact much earlier and to a much larger extent with peoples of dark skin colour[6] than Germany has ever been. In the latter case, anti-Slavism and anti-Semitism played a much bigger role than 'colour' racism. Senoçak suggests in this context that there is a greater reluctance towards using the terminology of 'race' in Germany today because of the quite thorough 'coming to terms with the past' (Vergangenheitsbewältigung) which has not happened anywhere else in Europe with regard to, for example, colonialism. He goes so far as claiming that Germany's special guilt (Schuld) is used by other European nation-states to divert attention from historical crimes which they themselves have committed (1994:72) - and, therefore, the 'easiness' with the usage of the terminology of 'race' in Britain could be partly explained by the lack of a critical approach to British (or rather English) history of slavery and colonialism.

The direct contact to peoples of colour does not only play a role in the context of the terminology of 'race', but also in the development of a 'black & white' dichotomy of which Neveu provides an interesting interpretation. She links the usage of this terminology to the (at least legally speaking) equal citizenship rights which Commonwealth subjects originally had when entering Britain. Post-war immigration was dominated by the movement of subjects of the Empire, and thus, "[t]he British situation was not one in which the boundary between 'us' (the indigenous) and 'them' (immigrants and/or ethnic minorities) could be drawn along nationality....[Therefore] 'black' and 'white' were ready terms to be used." (1989:8). 'Nationality' in this quote must mean being a 'British subject'. Neveu seems to refer to the fact that there was no clear legal definition of who qualified as a 'British national' during imperial days and the immediate post-imperial period. This lack of a legal definition was not solved until the introduction of the British Nationality Act of 1981.

In Germany, when labour migration first began under a governmentally organized recruitment system in the late 1950s and early 1960s, foreign labourers came as 'guest-workers'. There was no connection between them and former colonies as in the British case. They did not, therefore, come as fully equal citizens before the law and were very clearly distinguishable from German people with regard to their citizenship status and rights[7].

Officially, they were referred to as 'foreign employees and their dependants' (ausländische Arbeitnehmer und ihre Angehörigen), a term that clearly indicates an emphasis on the *economic* character of migration. The migrants used to be popularly known as 'guest-workers' (Gastarbeiter), a term that became problematic as it implied that the 'guests' would leave after a short period when no longer needed. The term 'guest-worker' thus gradually disappeared in the mid-1970s (partly as a result of increased family reunification indicating a changed attitude towards permanent settlement on the part of the Turkish community and the failure of government sponsored 'return policies'). Most Germans now speak of 'foreigners' (Ausländer) which seems to be neutral, but in fact tends to take a pejorative connotation, maybe in a similar way as the word 'immigrant' did in Britain a few decades ago (*Ausländer*, literally taken, means 'outsider', therefore not part of society). Those opposed to discrimination prefer to use the term 'foreign fellow citizens' (ausländische Mitbürger) (Castles 1984), but this is misleading as foreigners are not 'fellow citizens', for they are denied crucial citizenship rights. Other progressively thinking people are beginning to speak of 'immigrants' (Einwanderer) as a conscious way of rejecting the official governmental line that Germany 'is not a country of immigration' (Cohn-Bendit & Schmid 1992; Geissler 1991). However, this term is not acceptable in particular to the third generation born and raised in Germany. The emergence of second and in particular third generations did not result in the official abandonment of the term *Ausländer* (which is reflected in the law called '*Ausländergesetz*' and the official policy referred to as '*Ausländerpolitik*') - a fact which can partly be explained by the non-existing ius soli principle (by which anybody born in Germany would automatically be granted German citizenship). As opposed to the official line, it is now widely agreed in the academic literature and by people working in the equivalent of what is called in Britain the 'race relations field' (Ausländerarbeit) that '*Ausländer*' is not the appropriate term to reflect the reality of the migrants' lives in terms of their long periods of residence and contributions to the 'host' society and in particular of their children born and/or raised in Germany (Funcke 1991; Leggewie & Senoçak 1993). There is, therefore, increasing pressure on the government to change its policies and attitude with regard to inclusion policies, such as e.g. procedures of acquiring citizenship (see also Castles 1984:98; Kulluk 1996).

But what is the alternative? Apart from 'immigrants' for the first generation, the best way out of this dilemma is suggested by some authors to be the term '*Nicht-Deutsche*' (non-Germans) or Turkish-Germans (Leggewie & Senoçak 1993). The former term seems to be preferable to '*Ausländer*' as it does not carry the meaning of people from 'outside'. It indicates that immigrants and their children are part of German society (as permanent residents) but still do not have German citizenship. The latter hides the fact that these people (apart from those who naturalized) do not have full citizenship status. I argue that the best solution is not of a terminological nature, but of a politico-legal nature, requiring a change in nationality (or citizenship) and immigration laws. At present, however, the legal terminology (revolving around *Ausländer*) forms part of the process of racialization.

Resulting from the above, the main point is that the conceptual and terminological differences in Britain and Germany reflect differences in individual histories and patterns of labour migration. Although the different terms function in both countries as devices to distinguish between the indigenous population and the immigrant minorities, 'black' and 'race' in the British case indicate legal equality of majority and minority despite any social exclusion, whereas '*Ausländer*' clearly refers to a status as non-citizens in legal *as well as* social terms[8].

### 4.2.2 Racism, racialization and 'Ausländerfeindlichkeit'

As shown in the previous sections, there have been different forms of racism throughout history as well as those in the different societies of Germany and Britain as reflected in their different terminologies, albeit with the same result of excluding ethnic or immigrant minorities. It is argued here that the best way of grasping these differences conceptually is offered by the theory of 'racialization', first evolved by Miles (1982a, 1989) in relation to post-war labour migration in Britain, and advanced further by Small (1994).

### 4.2.3 Racialization and the British context

Miles developed the theory of racialization from his critique of what he has described as the 'race relations problematic' in which he argues that 'race' should not be given analytical status, but that racism should be the object of study (1982a, 1989). One of the main purposes of this critique seems to be to detach the issue of racism from the sole context of 'ex-colonial' immigrants who were distinct by their colour as previously done in studies by, for example, Rex (1983). In much of his work, therefore, Miles gives evidence to processes of racialization occurring in a 'non-black-and-white' context[9]. Summarizing the usage of the term 'racialization' in the literature, Miles concludes that "there is minimal agreement that the concept be used to refer to a representational process whereby social significance is attached to certain biological (usually phenotypical) human features, on the basis of which those people possessing those characteristics are designated as a distinct collectivity." (1989:74). Miles himself employs the concept of racialization to refer "to the historical emergence of the idea of 'race' and to its subsequent reproduction and application" (op.cit.:76). Rather than accept the idea of 'race' as a biological given, this perspective requires the examination of the conditions under which specific processes of 'racialization' have taken place. If 'race' has not got anything to do with biology, Small concludes that the relative implications of multiple factors such as economics, politics, demography, culture, ideology and myth should be unravelled in patterns of 'racialized relations' (1994:33).

Small suggests progression to an analysis of 'racisms', 'racialized relations' and 'white' people. Such a focus "questions the existence of 'races', looks at how groups not previously defined as 'races' have come to be defined in this way and assesses the various factors involved in such processes" (1994:30). In Small's opinion, the problem with a sole focus on 'black' people is that it depicts the 'black' population as a cause of racialized antagonism, rather than it being a consequence of 'white' attitudes and actions. Thus, "the problem is not 'race' but 'racisms', not relations between 'races' but relations which have been racialized, not the physical attributes of blacks or their presumed inferiority, but the motivations of non-blacks, and the obstacles they impose" (ibid.). The concern with racisms, racialized relations and 'whites' transfers the attention from the notion that 'black' people are a 'race' to the historical process whereby Europeans racialized other peoples, as for instance in the case of Africans (Banton 1977) and the Irish (Miles 1982a). Small concludes that when examining the process of 'racialization', common beliefs about 'races' and 'race relations' will result in the acknowledgement that they have more to do with the attitudes, actions, motivations and interests of powerful groups in society, and less with the characteristics, attitudes and actions of those who are defined as belonging to inferior 'races'. Therefore, Small abandons the term 'race' by replacing it with 'racialized group'.

Both, Miles and Small argue for a 'racialization problematic' which assumes that 'races' are constructs which are socially and politically generated. This allows an analysis of the changing forms and meanings of racism. In this connection, the idea of 'the new racism' is more correctly conceived as rearticulated 'racialized discourse'.

However, in his latest book (1994) Small presents the reader with rather fixed categories of 'black' and 'white' which are regarded here as being as much constructed as 'race'. The most important aspect for the comparative nature of this thesis (that racialization can and has transformed a variety of different attributes - not only colour, but also religion, country of origin, language - into categories deemed 'racial') has to be emphasized. In this way, the conception of racialization can be applied to the German context.

## 4.2.4  The German context: Racism  or Ausländerfeindlichkeit?

Labour migration to Germany differs quite a lot from the British pattern. During the Kaiserreich and the Weimar Republic, labourers were recruited from Poland and Russia to work in the agricultural sector in the eastern regions which suffered chronic labour shortages. In terms of official terminology, the phrase *ausländische Wanderarbeiter* (foreign itinerant workers; the part *'Wander '* implies a short stay without settlement) was adopted and was changed later during the Nazi-period to *Fremdarbeiter* (alien workers) who subsequently became during the Second World War *Zwangsarbeiter* (forced labourers). None of these forms of migration for labour were meant to result in permanent settlement - a fact which has enjoyed certain continuity throughout the post-war era up until the present as there still is no official *immigration* policy.

The year 1945 constitutes a distinct break with the labour migratory pattern which had existed until then. With the separation of West and East Germany and the expansion of the Soviet sphere of influence all over eastern Europe, immigration to West Germany came from expellees (Vertriebene) and Germans from the GDR (Übersiedler) until the erection of the Wall in 1961 which brought the influx of the much needed workforce to an abrupt end. Slavonic peoples, too, were not available anymore as they were cut off by the Iron Curtain. A new source of labour was found in the southern regions of Europe and in Turkey, organized in the form of official labour recruitment - the guest-worker system - which was abolished in 1973 as a result of the recession triggered by the 'oil crisis'. As mentioned above, from 1973 onwards a terminological and conceptual shift has taken place from 'guest-workers' to *Ausländer*.

This, then, is the background to the theoretical debate revolving around the issue of whether *Ausländerfeindlichkeit* (hostility towards foreigners) or racism is the appropriate term and concept when referring to the post-war German situation. Since 1945, the term 'racism' has been widely treated as a taboo, on the part of politicians and commentators as well as academics[10] (Wilpert 1993; academics have, however, provided research on post-1945 anti-Semitism as e.g. Bergmann & Erb 1991). In general, the only groups of people for whom the usage of the term 'racism' has seemed acceptable have been right-wing extremists and so-called 'neo-nazis' (Jäger 1993:242). During the last few years, however, this post-war taboo is loosening, and the term racism is increasingly used. However, particularly when compared with Britain, there is still a lack of research into post-war forms of racism as deplored by Jäger (1993:12). The discussion in Germany has so far been centred upon *Ausländerfeindlichkeit* (see also Wilpert 1993). Even though the *Ausländer-Problematik* was publicly addressed and possible negative reactions of the population were pointed out by commentators, politicians and academics, racism has remained a delicate topic. Bielefeld refers to this situation as 'an

insufficient political, intellectual and theoretical analysis and discussion'
(1991:11).

The reasons for this non-acknowledgement have to be related to
Germany's recent past and its disastrous experience of the most extreme
version of racism: the systematic extermination of racialized groups[11]. In
this context, Wilpert notes that today "[r]acism is identified with genocide"
(1993:67). However, even though there has been a break from the political
and ideological system of Nazi-Germany, this break has not been
altogether complete and a certain continuity has to be admitted. Therefore,
the taboo of the term 'racism' indicates partly the attempt to get free from
the 'guilt complex' concerning the shameful events during the Third Reich.
The non-usage of the term 'racism', according to Ruf, has to do with the
specific political culture of the Federal Republic which tries to detach itself
from Hitler's 'politics of race' (in: Antrata, Kaschuba, Leiprecht & Wolf
1989). In my opinion, the non-usage of the term 'racism' can also be
interpreted as the attempt to play down the seriousness of contemporary
events (such as e.g. arson attacks on asylum-seekers' hostels and homes of
Turkish people). Thus, the taboo of the term 'racism' constitutes a form of
repression.

Apart from the context of anti-Semitism and the Third Reich, the
only other context in which racism seems to be viewed as appropriate is
colonialism and the discrimination of Afro-black people. The underlying
message is that Germany did not have a significant colonial past, neither
has Germany experienced large-scale immigration of coloured people,
therefore, this problem does not exist in the German context.

Furthermore, the opposition to a language of racism also indicates
a lack of understanding of both racialization processes and the existence of
historically different racisms. The term used instead of 'racism' -
*Ausländerfeindlichkeit* - is now subject to more and more criticism (mainly
by academics and journalists) for its inappropriateness: the first part,
*Ausländer*, supposes that *all* foreigners are objects of hostility (Kalpaka &
Räthzel 1990) - which is not the case as, for instance, EU-nationals and
white US Americans are not usually regarded as 'foreigners' (see also
Forsythe 1989), whilst the second part, *Feindlichkeit*, seems to imply that it
is a reaction on a personal, individual basis which is understood as 'natural,
understandable and rational' (Bhavnani 1993).

What is at stake here, however, is a *social* problem and not an
individual one, and therefore, the term 'racism' is considered the better
concept to describe a *general climate* as well as institutional forms of
'racial' discrimination. This general climate is suggested as having come
about via 'a racist learning process outlasting generations' (ein
Generationen über-dauernder rassistischer Lernprozess; Jäggi 1992:24).

Similarly, Kalpaka & Räthzel note, with regard to the peculiar
problem Germany seems to have with this type of terminology, that the
concept of 'racism' is not meant to equate today's form of racism with
German fascism, but it is about choosing a concept which makes the issue

of *historical* connection feasible (Frage nach historischer Verbindung; 1990:18) and therefore, the term 'hostility towards foreigners' is not acceptable.

Hoffmann (1991) writes in this context that *Ausländerfeindlichkeit* contains a false legitimation of hostility by calling its objects 'foreigners'. Discrimination, however, is not caused by lack of citizenship (i.e. by being classified as 'foreigners'), but by non-German ethnicity.

Jäggi (1992) approaches this problem from an analytical point of view and criticizes *Ausländerfeindlichkeit* for characterizing an attitude which is not grounded in theoretical explanatory devices.

As a result, I argue that the changing ideological/discursive and practical forms of racism as well as its changing target groups throughout German history, in addition to the fact that Germany has never experienced a 'colour problem' as in the case of Britain, constitute strong arguments in favour of the above mentioned concept of 'racisms' (multiple forms of racism) and 'racialization'. *Ausländerfeindlichkeit* is not a theoretical concept which can explain the changing patterns and target groups of this hostile and discriminatory climate rooted in a long history, nor does it help to explain mechanisms of social exclusion as reflected for example in immigration and nationality laws - which are not elements of individual hostile instances but clearly institutionalized general practices. In a comparative analysis, the concept of racialization is also of great use to explain why not only *Ausländer* ('outsiders', people with foreign citizenship) are victims of 'racial' discrimination but also *Inländer* ('insiders', people who hold the 'host countries' citizenship) of different ethnic backgrounds as in the case of Afro-Caribbeans and people from the Indian sub-continent living in Britain.

Therefore, the concept of racialization provides explanations for the different citizenship statuses of certain immigrants in Germany and Britain in a more useful way than concepts centring upon *Ausländerfeindlichkeit* or the 'race relations problematic'. In a comparative analysis of countries with different migratory patterns, histories and terminologies, racialization is the most appropriate concept to grasp the reflection of these differences in immigrant peoples' citizenship statuses.

## 4.3 Europe, the European Union and Racism

Europe is widely regarded as having a long tradition of latent and/or overt forms of racism whereby some authors would explain the common existence of racism in Europe as a result of modernity (Wieviorka 1994) and others would lay the emphasis more on the historical development of capitalism within Europe (Miles 1994). However, the unity of contemporary forms of racism in Europe should not hide the fact that each country has its own social, political and nation-state forming history with its own international past (Wieviorka 1994).

In the context of the European Community, and in particular since further European integration was launched in 1992, there has been concern about the treatment of third country nationals residing within the EU member-states and a new, daunting European racism in the form of an institutional phenomenon which is accelerated by the 'building-up' of Europe (as 'Fortress Europe') and nurtured by an ideal picture of Europe (Balibar, in: Institut für Migrations- und Rassismusforschung 1992). This image of Europe is described by Solomos & Back as "pan-European Whiteness" (1994:154).

Whether the 'European society', which is still in the process of construction, results in a 'European racism' is a question also posed by Balibar. According to him, the 'European culture' consists historically of two ideological models which are specifically racist: the colonial model and the anti-Semitic model. Both have never been collectively come to terms with and have formed, until today, an integral part of 'European identity'. Balibar further views the originally differing *national* forms of racism in Europe as influencing each other and recently as even converging to form a new phenomenon which could be referred to as 'European racism'. It is an institutional phenomenon which functions in a 'racially' discriminatory way as it defines for each member-state in an equal way at least two categories of migrants with different sets of rights allocated to them, namely EU-nationals and non-EU-nationals (third country nationals) (Balibar, in: Institut für Migrations- und Rassismusforschung 1992; and 1991:6). This new European racism seems to be essentially supported by the intensive efforts made to harmonize immigration and asylum policies as it happened with agreements such as Schengen and organizations such as the Trevi group. These combined efforts are characterized by one crucial result: the criminalization of so-called 'illegal' immigrants or 'illegal' asylum-seekers (Jäggi 1992) which also has certain implications on legally residing immigrants (see Chapter Three).

Another author puts the emphasis slightly differently with regard to the causes of racism in western European societies. Castles views 'two sets of causes' as decisive: the first of which concerns the history of ideologies and practices in connection with the construction of nation-states and colonialism, whilst the second set derives, according to him, from "current processes of social, economic and political changes" (such as the "rapid pace of change in living and working conditions" and the "dissolution of the cultural forms and organisational structures of the working class") (1993:25).

In this context, Sivanandan is quoted by Small as suggesting a pan-European racism generated by the European Community. This Marxist view holds that "[w]e are moving from an ethnocentric racism to a Euro-centric racism, from the different racisms of the different member states to a common, market racism." (1994:93). Primary motivation for this form of racism is, according to Sivanandan, the new competitive pressure felt by European capitalists vis-à-vis "American and Japanese capitalists in an international economic order dominated by multinational companies, new methods of production, distribution and consumption, new technologies and the movement of capital to labour" (ibid.). The interest of European capitalists is said to be the maximization of economic benefits of 'Third World' labour by minimizing the political and social costs, and it is met by the creation of a 'Fortress Europe' "with conditions of entry that suit the economic need of capital, while totally disregarding the personal, social and economic needs of workers" (ibid.). One result of this new Europe is the presence of migrants, guest-workers and undocumented aliens without proper citizenship rights.   Miles objects to the idea of a European racism as put forward by Sivanandan and Balibar. Although he acknowledges criteria of similarities, such as immigration control, as well as processes characteristic for all of western Europe such as the general crisis of the nation-state and structural mass unemployment, Miles emphasizes that these criteria and processes are "neither unilinear, nor identical in their extent or effect, within and between the different nation states of Europe" (1994a:552). Moreover, he stresses the different histories of migration which western European societies have experienced as well as different histories of laws on nationality and citizenship, of different racisms targeted at different groups of people and under different historical circumstances (such as colonialism), and of their place within the emergence of the capitalist world economy. In his view, the notion of 'European racism' is employed to homogenize and totalize a wide range of ideologies and practices, and therefore he suggests "to talk of a racist construct of the idea of Europe" instead (1994b:203).

And yet, I argue that, with this view, Miles ignores racializing or discriminatory effects of policies created by the European Union as a *unity* despite the different histories of immigration in each member-state. These might only be reproductions of similar policies on the national level, but they gain a different dimension in their capacity as European-wide practices and they indicate the exclusiveness of the Union to non-European immigrants. In a different piece of writing, however, Miles clearly makes this distinction by referring to the context of the changing features of racism whereby he draws again on Balibar's work: "[W]hat we might call the dominant official racism that underlies the creation of an EU immigration policy is a racism of *oppression* (cf. Balibar 1991:39) and *spatial exclusion* which has the primary effect of redefining the ideological concept of Europe, and of who has the right to a European identity and to reside in Europe, rather than a racism of *extermination*." (1994a:557, original emphasis). The idea of racism as the result of EU-policies is, however, only seen here in the context of immigration and not in the context of exclusionary effects of European citizenship for settled third-country nationals.

In terms of cultural identity, statements by distinguished politicians  referring to the European Union have been described as defining a "Christian club" (Senoçak, 1994) whereby Muslims and Jews are not necessarily spatially excluded but probably more so culturally - in particular in the case of long-term resident third-country-nationals. This seems to confirm Miles' 'racist construct' of Europe. A shared racialized identity is also clearly expressed in the often quoted 'Bruges speech' of 1988 by the then Prime Minister of Britain, Mrs. Thatcher:

> Too often the history of Europe is described as a series of interminable wars and quarrels. Yet from our perspective today surely what strikes us most is our common experience. For instance, the story of how Europeans explored and colonised and - yes without apology - civilised much of the world is an extraordinary tale of talent, skill and courage.
> (quoted by Solomos & Back 1994:154).

These arguments lead to the conclusion that a clear distinction has to be made between racisms existing in each individual EU member-state and the racializing effects as the outcome of the creation of the European Union as a whole (in form of legislation and ideology/discourse) - i.e. a distinction between *racism in Europe* (as a common phenomenon) and *European racism* (as the outcome of EU policies). These two separate levels, however, have to be treated as related as it cannot be denied that despite particular histories of each member-state, the Union is based on a long history of racialization processes as a universal phenomenon. There are common racializing tendencies in each EU member-state, such as phases of rising right-wing extremist parties and racist violence (see edited book by Björgo & Witte 1993). This common history might be the reason for racialization or racial discrimination as the outcome of common EU policies or non-policies - an assumption which suggests that national practices are perpetuated on the European level. The aspect of common racializing tendencies and the issue of whether the EU has made any difference to national practices are looked into in more details as follows.

### 4.3.1 European racism and racism in Europe

On the supra-national level, the basic document with which the EC was set up in 1957, the Treaty of Rome (which contains the constitution of the EC), does not explicitly mention racism. The Treaty does not guarantee any protection to those who do not receive equal treatment on the basis of 'race', colour, religion, or ethnic origin. The Treaty does, however, forbid discrimination on the grounds of nationality, but only if that discrimination occurs against Community nationals and their families. On an individual level, very few nation-states in Europe have legislation which allows concrete forms of racism to be declared illegal (Bhavnani 1993).

Although the Treaty of Rome does not contain any explicit mention of racial discrimination, there has been growing concern over this issue, in particular on the part of the European Parliament - which has a special stance (albeit with little political power) within the institutional structure of the EU on matters of immigration/integration (as pointed out in the previous chapter). The Report of the European Parliament's Committee of Inquiry into Racism and Xenophobia (1990) and Ford's book *Fascist Europe: The Rise of Racism and Xenophobia* (1992) - an adaptation of the report drawn up on behalf of the Committee of Inquiry into Racism and Xenophobia - focus on common racist features in EU member-states such as right-wing extremist political parties and organizations which have spread all over western Europe as well as right-wing and 'racially' motivated violence and attacks[12]. The report is based on more or less official documents and declarations as well as hearings of ministers and civil servants responsible for combating racism and forming legislation in that field (Ford 1992:5). It mentions opinion-surveys and, in particular in the British case, forms of institutional racism (such as recruitment into the police and the army), however, in the 'country by country analysis' it focuses on right-wing extremist political parties and organizations as well as racially motivated violence. Thus, it tends to neglect the more subtle, less overt, forms of racism among elites in the field of politics, economics, the media and education as identified by Van Dijk (1991 and 1993).

In the section on the 'country by country' analysis, the report tends to focus on the political situation in Europe at the end of the 1980s which was characterized by the presence of extremist right-wing parties that are commonly considered (except by themselves) as being racist. These parties formulate blatantly derogatory opinions about minorities and immigrants and attribute most of the socio-economic problems to minorities or immigrants as the illusionary solution voters may be attracted to. It might be debatable how influential these parties are, in terms of actual seats in national governments and the European Parliament they do not seem to be very powerful. The problem of their presence, however, does have serious implications in that they affect the political positions of other parties. Because of competition for voters or for other political reasons, there seems to be a tendency, among the more conservative parties in particular, to adopt some of the anti-minority attitudes of the extreme right, as has been the case most notably for the conservative parties in Great Britain (see Messina 1990), France and Germany. Quite often the extreme right-wing parties and sections of the traditional conservative parties also promote anti-European sentiments and narrow nationalism. This rather more subtle type of anti-foreigners/minority attitudes is, however, neglected by the above report.

In this context, Wrench & Solomos write that "European politicians and policy-makers are more willing to condemn racism if it is seen as the activity of loony extremists, but are less willing to undertake action which would imply that racism in both its ideological and practical manifestations forms part of the structure of European societies" (1993:157-58).

In its more general section on Community action since 1986, the above mentioned report deplores that no significant changes in national anti-racism legislation have been made nor has there been any action at the Community level "to confront and tackle the root causes of racism and xenophobia" (p. 99). The 1986 Joint Declaration against Racism and Xenophobia is confirmed in this report as a non-binding declaration without any recommendations to the various member-states (p. 100) and as "sheets of paper, with no means of checking whether or not the recommendations are put into practice" (p. 101). In its section on the 'cultural field', the report mentions the mass media's role in presenting ethnic minorities in an often 'poor' and 'biased' way (p. 137). However, apart from the media and their role of providing information about, to and by ethnic minorities, the report does not include any other forms of cultural racism and thus, it only touches upon the many forms of everyday racism as identified by Essed (1991). She partly relates problems of racism to the "domain of conflict between the dominant and the dominated group" (1991:185) with regard to norms and values as well as to another cultural source of conflict concerning the "definitions of social reality" (ibid.).

Reports such as the Inquiry into Racism and Xenophobia only investigate forms of racial discrimination on the national level of each EU-member-state. It does not consider at all the racializing effects the European Union as a whole has on ethnic minority groups residing in its member-states. Nonetheless, I argue that there exists a distinction between 'racism in Europe' and 'European racism' as the outcome of EU policies. A supranational level of racialization cannot be denied. The rather abstract idea of a European identity in the form of 'white and Christian', based on a long history of domination of other peoples, as well as the more concrete provisions of European citizenship as established by the Maastricht Treaty (for more details see chapter on citizenship) certainly result in a new category of racial discrimination by privileging EU-nationals over non-EU-nationals despite their long periods of residence. Also - as was discussed in the previous chapter - the commonly restrictive EU policies in the field of immigration and asylum have negative, if not racializing, effects on the established ethnic minorities. It seems, however, that this *European racism* is a result of *racism in Europe*. The history of racialization had begun long before the establishment of the European Union and it seems, therefore, that this phenomenon which originally manifested itself at the national level is now perpetuated at the European level.

## 4.4  State, national identity  and citizenship - a brief contextualization

The main aim of the remaining chapters is to provide evidence for the assumption of a symbiotic relationship between racism (or racialization) and nationalism (as the source of national identity) and to assess the effects of this relationship on immigrants' citizenship status.

As mentioned previously, the two sets of ideologies/discourses on racism and nationalism show certain similarities in that they are both sources of human collective identity and both categorize human populations into discrete groups, each of which is presumed to have unique characters. Both seek to naturalize the difference they construct, and both invoke narratives of origin referencing defined territory as the natural home of a specific racialized group with its defined cultural traits. Authors such as Banton have pointed out that modern ideas about class, nation *and* 'race' - arising "from the same European milieu" (1977:3) - share points of similarities and that it is unwise to study them in isolation.

There is an important sense in which the ideology/discourse of the 'nation' emerged as an embodiment of changing notions of sovereignty so that a notion of political representation within territorially bounded new political units or states is central to it. Thus, as the latest works by Jackson & Penrose (1993), Miles (1993) and Anthias & Yuval-Davis (1992) seem to have in common, an ideology/discourse of 'nation' underpins the formation and organization of the nation-state. This ideology (or discourse) developed historically as part of a political project aimed at challenging the hegemony of the monarchy and aristocracy.

However, shifts in meaning associated with the idea of 'race' also played a central role in mediating the tremendous upheavals, disruptions and transformations in social relations during the emergence of the nation-states. "When the old usage of the term 'race' in the sense primarily of a 'lineage' lost its purchase because the future destinations of members of the newly emerging classes could no longer be totally fixed by their birth or social origin, the concept of 'race' came to refer to an innate, physical quality. It came to signify an imaginary biological principle asserting the moral, physical and intellectual superiority of the dominant classes over the social orders at home and the 'subject races' abroad" (Brah 1994:809). The similar socio-historical changes the ideology/discourse of 'race' and 'nation' have undergone will be subject to the following chapter. It will be shown - with special reference to Germany and Britain - how identity as a racialized group is very closely linked to the identity as a 'nation'.

Furthermore, as the identity as a racialized group and as a 'nation' is reflected in the intermingling of nationality and citizenship laws, concrete forms of racialization are perpetuated by the granting or non-granting of full citizenship whereby long-term third country nationals tend to be at a disadvantage socially, politically and economically.

As suggested by Jackson and Penrose, the nation-state is "a crucial locus for the articulation of racist ideologies because of the extent to which it embodies the idea of 'race' and legitimizes it through the granting or withholding of citizenship." (1993:9). When governments regulate the movement of people across political boundaries and decide upon whom to grant what type of socio-political membership, they work with a concept of what their nation is and/or should be. Immigration/integration policies, nationality law, citizenship rights and the historical formation of national identity, therefore, have to be seen in a context. The exclusionary effects of these policies and laws "have served the project of nation-building by protecting the integrity of a national character which is thought of as founded on tradition and grounded in experience" (Smith, in: Jackson & Penrose 1993:53). It should not be forgotten, however, that ideas about 'national identity' and identity as a racialized group are not only reflected in citizenship/nationality laws or other legislation (i.e. on the state level), but also within civil society which means that exclusionary and racializing ideology/discourses and practices find their larger manifestation within all levels of society.

As a result of this chapter, the concept of racialization is regarded here as the most convincing concept to investigate the notion of socio-legal exclusion from citizenship through the notion of nationality and national identity. The following chapter will show the racializing processes involved in the socio-historical formation of both German and British national identities which have implications for the ways in which those two societies have responded to post-war labour migration and their willingness to vest these people of different ethno-cultural backgrounds with full citizenship rights.

## Notes

1.   Stuart Hall put this view forward that "[t]here have been many significantly different **racisms** - each historically specific and articulated in a different way with the societies in which they appear. Racism is always historically specific in this way..." (1978:26; original emphasis).

2.   Mason, however, would argue in this context that biologically determinist formulations have never disappeared and that biological reasoning of various kinds is still widespread in popular beliefs about 'race' (1992).

3.   Balibar borrows this term from Taguieff. Differentialist racism is"a racism whose dominant theme is not biological heredity but the insurmountability of cultural differences, a racism which, at first sight, does not postulate the superiority of certain groups or peoples in relation to others but 'only' the harmfulness of abolishing frontiers, the incompatibility of life-styles and traditions" (1991:21).

4.   See for a detailed account of this debate also Brah (1992).

5.   This is of importance as Fryer showed that "it was the drive for profit that led English merchant capitalists to traffic in Africans. There was big money in it. The theory [of racism, N.P.] came later. Once the English slave trade, English sugar-producing plantation slavery, and English manufacturing industry had begun to operate...,the economic basis had been laid for all those ancient scraps of myth and prejudice to be woven into a more or less coherent racist ideology: a mythology of race" (1984:134).

6.   See Fryer's whole chapter seven on "The rise of English racism" for more details (1984:133-190).

7    Rudolph has found that a 'new gastarbeiter system' is being operated in Germany, partly as a result of its mounting post-reunification employment crisis. In terms of migration systems, the tradition of 'temporary labour migration' as opposed to 'permanent settlement migration' is being maintained with this system of contract labour in which hardly any rights are being granted.

8    On the European level, the language of 'black and white' can clearly not be employed as the  history and origin of immigrants on the continent tend to be very different and, thus, have resulted in the acceptance and use of different terminologies. In this book, I decided - although this might not be a perfect solution - to use the term 'ethnic minorities' or to make precise reference to the origin of former immigrants (such as Afro-Caribbeans, Indians, Pakistanis, Turks etc.; see also Modood et al. 1994). The expression'ethnic minorities' (for a detailed definition see Castles 1993:28, footnote no. 3) seems to recognize best that immigrants and foreigners whose roots lay in post-war labour migration have become permanent members of society. In the German context, however, this hides the fact that large parts of the long-term immigrants do not have full citizenship rights. Therefore, when referring to the particular German case, the term 'immigrant' or 'immigrant minorities' will be employed.

9    See, for instance, his chapter on Irish labour migrants (1982a).

10   Jäger, for example, describes his unsuccessful attempt to find funding for his project on 'racism in everyday life' in his publication of 1993 (page 12, footnote 7): "racism does not exist" was part of the explanation why major funding bodies refused to support Jäger's project.

11   Burleigh and Wippermann have shown that not only the Jews were victims of the Nazi killing machinery, but also other groups: gypsies and 'a-socials' such as homosexuals, mentally and physically handicapped people, criminals (1991).

12   As Björgo & Witte remark, this report as well as other studies of the same phenomenon "tend to discuss racism, right-wing extremism and Fascism in general without specifically analysing racist violence as such" (1993:13) - a shortcoming the above authors hope to overcome in their edited book.

# 5 National identity and exclusion

The main aim of this chapter is to argue that there is a close relationship between national identity and the identity as a 'race' in the German and British context.

The formation of Germany and Britain as nation-states will be discussed briefly to show that their formation has origins in the long process of modernization which resulted in a gradual shift from 'subjecthood' to 'citizenship'. However, when the development towards national large groups began to be of a particularistic nature (i.e. ethno-culturally defined), this development entailed the distinction between 'insiders' and 'outsiders' based on ethnic or racial differences. In this way, the conceptual link between 'nationality' (in the sense of ethnic descent) and 'citizenship' was established. '

The racializing effects of this link (and thus, the symbiotic relationship between nationalism and racism) will be discussed below with regard to German and British internal formation of national identity as well as vis-à-vis 'the outsider'. The same effects will then be examined in the post-1945 context with the help of the notion of 'crisis of identity'. The problem of the traditional concept of national identity in the context of post-1945 multi-ethnic/multi-cultural societies might be solvable by developments towards a post-national identity (in the European Union context) and by Habermas' alternative conception of a 'post-conventional identity'.

## 5.1 Some theoretical remarks on the formation of nation-states and national identity

There is a body of literature which contextualizes the emergence of nations and nationalism with the process of modernization. Liah Greenfeld's *Nationalism: Five Roads to Modernity* (1992), Mann's contribution in the edited book titled *Transition to Modernity* (1992) and Joseph R. Llobera's *The God of Modernity - the development of nationalism in western europe* (1994) all make this link with modernity - which reminds one of a similar link which was suggested by Banton (1977) in his discussion of racism.

Elias has explained this development with reference to the concept of the 'civilization process' (1992a&b), running from the late medieval to the early modern period[1]. All three authors (Elias, Greenfeld, Llobera), however, agree that the word 'nation', originally referring to the 'elite', became to be applied to the whole population of the respective country and was thus made synonymous with 'the people'.

The equation of the two concepts, nation and people, implied the elevation of the general populace. The people were thus denoting a positive entity by acquiring the meaning of the bearer of sovereignty and by forming the basis of political solidarity. National identity in its distinctively modern sense is an identity which derives from membership in a 'people' which is characterized by its definition as a 'nation'. As opposed to pre-modern times, a national population, although stratified, is perceived as essentially homogeneous being only superficially divided by the lines of status and class.

Both Greenfeld and Elias make clear that there is a link between 'nation'-formation and state-formation. This relationship is viewed by both authors as the transition from people being subjects to people being citizens - a process starting during the second half of the 18th century. Thus, the nation-state formation process is connected to the gradual democratization and political incorporation of all social strata. This development is seen in the context of modernization (Greenfeld) or of civilization (Elias). In this way, *nation-states* are linked to the phenomenon of nationalism[2] which is the source of national identity as a mass belief.

Greenfeld, along with other authors such as Smith (1994), places England (not Great Britain!) as the first nation in the modern world. Individualistic, civic nationalism (which regards nationality, at least in principle, as open and voluntaristic) then developed. Particularistic nationalism (which views nationality as being inherent) in general is suggested by Greenfeld as not having emerged until the 18th century. Germany is given as one prime example. The same author further claims that the dominance of England in the 18th century, followed by the dominance of the 'West' in the world, "made nationality the canon" (1994:15). In this way, the phenomenon of *national* identity developed as an international process.

At the same time, however, every single nationalism was very much an indigenous phenomenon. Greenfeld assumes that there must have been groups in whose interest it was to import and promote national identity. Prior to that, there must have been dissatisfaction with the identity these groups had. "A change of identity presupposed a *crisis* of identity" (op.cit.:14; emphasis added). This process of importing the foreign idea of the nation and focusing thereby on the source of importation and reacting to it is labelled by Greenfeld as 'resentment' - a term borrowed from Nietzsche (op.cit.:15)[3]. The reason why this identity is *national* is explained by the availability of a certain type of concept. Thus, national identity is understood as a matter of historical contingency rather than necessity. This understanding is similarly expressed by Elias in his study on the civilization process, in which he develops a theory of nation-formation processes which is void of teleology.

With regard to the historical emergence of nation-states, the modernist conception is adopted here. It takes the nation as the result of 'modern phenomena' such as the creation of political and territorial monopolies with the gradual shift from subjecthood to citizenship. The elements which constitute 'modernity' (and also the actual meaning of 'modern period') are, however, contested[4]. And yet, wherever the emphasis is placed, most of the 'modernist' theorists seem to suggest the pertinence of one common element, and that is the depiction of nations as belief rather than a more material phenomenon. Gellner (1983) and Anderson (1983), for example, place an emphasis on the nation as a *construct*, by which they mean the creation of *myths* being part of the make-believe evolving around the origin of a people (such as the claim of common ancestry, common customs and vernaculars, common territory and a common native history as suggested by Smith 1988). The constructionalist view of nations has been criticized by authors such as Heckmann (1992), who holds that nations also have become reality as constructs. According to Nicklas (1994), the idea of the nation as a product of elitist or intellectual discourse needed to be internalized by the whole population which was attempted through, for example, the education system, symbols, and compulsory military service. In this way, a certain level of standardization, which is also referred to as homogenization (O'Brien 1992), was gradually achieved. National identity is acquired and sustained not only through the educational system, but, for example, also through political and social rituals, cultural institutions, and the media. Thus, individuals become conscious of themselves as having a national identity (Poole 1992). These standardizing processes were the prerequisite for the transition from a feudal, agrarian society to a modern society based on capitalistic economy (Bade 1992). Räthzel (in: Jäger & Januschek 1992) describes these processes as horizontal standardization (*Vereinheitlichung* - of various ethnic groups within a unified territory) with vertical standardization happening at the same time (of the various strata, of ruling elites and the ruled), which reminds one very much of Elias' civilization model.

Miles (1991 & 1994) similarly explains the decisive character of a modern nation by the fact that the 'dominating class' and the 'dominated classes' come to regard each other as belonging to the same *national* group. Until the 19th century, the aristocracy, the working class and the peasants were perceived as different 'races' - a fact which Balibar refers to as 'racisme de classe'.[5] The process of nation-state formation, however, resulted in the creation of *Grossgruppen* (national large groups as an extensive cross-class community) (Hoffmann 1992) and thus, also in a changing pattern of racism: It shifted from being a device for *internal* classification to being used *externally*. On similar lines, Bauman refers to nationalism as a specimen of the big family of 'we-talks' which are set apart by their exclusivity promoting "ego-centred binary divisions" dividing "the world into friends and enemies" (1992:678).

It is argued here, therefore, that the early meaning of 'nation' (in terms of the elite) went hand in hand with *racisme de classe* and both notions, nation and 'race', developed from there into external classificatory devices. Thus, in general, there seems to have been a strong connection between the concepts of racism and nationalism throughout their existence, supporting the claim of their symbiotic relationship.

## 5.2 Identity as 'nation' and as 'race': the individual cases of Britain and Germany

### 5.2.1 *Formation of English collective identity*

Historically, *England* is regarded as the first nation that came into existence (Kohn 1940, as quoted by Llobera 1994:39). "By 1600, the existence in England of a national consciousness and identity, and as a result, of a new geo-political entity, a nation, was a fact" (Greenfeld 1994:31)[6] The English nation is seen by Greenfeld as having been originally based on Humanist ideas or ideals as a community of free and equal individuals taking part in the collective and political decision making process. However, the correspondence between the concept of the nation constituted of free, rational individuals and reality was not perfect. "Not all people of England were actually included in the nation in this first century of its existence - and many would, for a long time, remain outside it." (ibid.). Nonetheless, the commitment to the idea of the nation of the political ruling parts of the English population meant, as claimed by Greenfeld, an important change in political culture having an impact on future developments.

English nationalism of the 16th century centred on the figure of the monarch as the important symbol of England's distinctiveness. The other factor that helped the emergence of English national consciousness was Protestantism in the form of the Book rendering the English conscious of being Christian. This, however, led to the exclusion of English Catholics from membership in the nation at this stage. English nationality and religion were one, united in the person of Elizabeth I. Reason and 'rationality' were given a central place in the notion of an English national character, and science was considered the sign of superiority. Its pursuit was a matter of national prestige and was used as a yardstick in the cultural competition with the other continental nations. These developments lead Greenfeld to the conclusion that "English nationalism at this time certainly was *not* defined in ethnic terms. It was defined in terms of religious and political values." (1994:65; emphasis added).

### 5.2.2 *Formation of German collective identity*

The development of German nationalism seems to have differed considerably from the English in that German national consciousness emerged significantly later (Elias 1992c). It was triggered by the Wars of Liberation from Napoleonic, i.e. French, domination in the early 19th century. German national consciousness developed very rapidly and grew from "birth to maturity" between 1806 and 1815 (Greenfeld 1994:277).

The source of nationalistic ideas was not, as in the English case, the aristocracy and the ruling elite, but a peculiar class of educated commoners or professional intellectuals, the so-called *Bildungsbürgertum*.. Their status was higher than that of the middle class but much lower than that of the higher classes, and thus, they found themselves in a marginalized social position (Greenfeld 1994; Elias 1992c). Compared to England, the sense of German nationality failed to take root in the 16th century partly because of its lacking a central authority. Germany at that time, in the form of the Holy Roman Empire of the German Nation, meant a number of territories loosely united. Religion, too, had more of an opposing effect when compared with England as the religious struggles (Catholics versus Protestants) of the first half of the 16th century resulted in the transformation of the Empire into small kingdoms and principalities (Llobera 1994). Thus, the confessional differences and the absence of a national dynasty were the realities of the post-Reformation period and the legacy for internal dissension.

Elias (1992c) allocates the delay of Germany's national integration partly to its geographical location in the centre of Europe. As such, it was the main territory where many European wars were fought resulting in ongoing shifts of territorial borders. Further, as Elias and Greenfeld both hold, Germany's social order remained unchanged for a much longer time than in England. The nobility in particular enjoyed long periods of uninterrupted and, by comparison, unusual stability. The ancient divisions between different strata remained sharp, and the conditions of a static society made it virtually impossible for the middle-class intellectuals to be upwardly mobile. The *Bildungsbürger* found national identity attractive because it elevated members of the national collectivity giving them almost equal status with the nobility.

The indigenous traditions which formed the basis of the character of German national consciousness were Pietism and Romanticism. The latter was a movement of thought responding to the fears and frustrations of the *Bildungsbürger,* generated by the Enlightenment. "[I]t was rationalism that Romantics revolted against" (Greenfeld 1994:330). The peculiarity of the German people became language and land. 'Nation' was synonymous with *Volk*, representing "the inner unity and spirit of the people" (op.cit.:364). As 'nation' was a foreign import, the concept of *Volk* was preferred, but both concepts meant very much the same. The unique character of the nation came to be its language as an object of worship. 'Turnvater' Jahn (creator of the idea of the value of exercising) advised in his work *Das deutsche Volkstum* ('German peoplehood') from 1810 that "the state should develop the teaching of the mother tongue and suggested that the knowledge of German be used as a qualification of citizenship" (op.cit.:368) - an element still vital in today's evaluation of applications for naturalization.

Deriving from this ideological background, nationality was ultimately based on blood-relatedness. German language was regarded as the *Ursprache* (pure, unmixed language), Germans were the *Urvolk* (pure people). Thus, Greenfeld concludes that "German national consciousness was unmistakably and distinctly *racist* from the moment it existed, and the national identity of the Germans was essentially an identity of *race*" (op.cit.:369; emphasis added). She refers to German nationalism as "the most activist, violent, and xenophobic species of the phenomenon" (p. 360). The finishing touch to this type of nationalism, according to the same author, is to be seen in *resentment* - the envy of the successful neighbour France and the feeling of shame over the defeat of Prussia in the course of the French revolutionary wars. Both, Greenfeld and Elias, hold in a similar way that the particular historical circumstances of Germany's nation-state formation have resulted in a proneness to ethnic nationalism - which can certainly be read as suggesting a symbiotic relationship between nationalism and racism[7]. This, then, suggests an explanation of why and how the combination of nationalism and racism under National Socialism was to reach extremes in Hitler's Germany.

### 5.2.3 *Comparative problems*

There are a number of problems with the comparison of the internal formation of national identity and its original components in Britain and Germany as outlined above. Greenfeld provides the reader with an incomplete picture by her comparison of *England* as the very first nation, with its date of emergence being around 1600, and by emphasizing its 'religious and political nature' with that of Germany's 'racial' sense of national identity. There is no doubt at all with regard to her depiction of Germany[8], but her analysis of England is flawed by the fact that she does not take into account the formation of *British* national identity which is certainly not only based on positive political (i.e. democratic) and religious values. By incorporating the Welsh, Scottish and Irish nations, there must have been clashes at least with the 'religious identity' (Protestantism versus Catholicism) having as a possible result the adding of an 'ethnic' component.

Furthermore, as convincingly argued by Colley, after 1707 (the year of the Act of Union joining Scotland to England and Wales), the British "came to define themselves as a single people not because of any political or cultural consensus at home, but rather in reaction to the Other beyond their shores." (1992:6) - whereby Colley does not suggest that the Welsh, Scottish and English lost their distinct cultural traits. Her argument continues that the sense of a common identity did not develop as the result of integration and homogenization of disparate cultures, but rather that "Britishness was superimposed over an array of internal differences in response to contact with the Other, and above all in response to conflict with the Other." (ibid.). The 'Other' is here understood as the hostile party in the various wars during the period of 1707 and 1837 on which Colley focuses.

To show that an 'ethnic' (and thus racializing) component was involved in the process of the formation of both *British* and German national identities, this issue will be approached from the point of view of the outsider or 'the Other'. However, the 'Other' will not be literally understood as the 'outsider' as described by Colley, but the focus will be rather on ethnic minorities on German or British (imperial) territory. The purpose of this is to give a historical basis to the exclusionary construction of the 'Other' which is considered here as having implications for the perception of post-war immigrants.

### 5.2.4 National identity vis-à-vis 'the Other'

Despite the existence of a more complex debate as identified by Cohen, the notion of 'Otherness' is used here in a much more simple way (as suggested by the same author), namely in the sense that "one only knows who one is by who one is not" (1994:198). The Self-Other relationship - as a process of exclusion and inclusion - is partly constitutive of national identity (as one of the outcomes of the nation-state is the boundary drawing between 'us' and 'them'). This relationship is subject to continuous defining and redefining processes.

*The British case*  As already mentioned in the introduction, the case of Britain is very special as it actually incorporates four nations[9]. It has been suggested that England has dominated the other three, and I have argued that this domination was and is based on a sense of 'racial' superiority.

There are a number of authors who have stressed the four different national identities existing within Britain rendering Britishness rather ambiguous (see chapter 7, 8, 9 in MacDonald 1993; Samuel 1989; for a more historical account see Teich & Porter 1993). Nairn (1977) claims that nationalism in these parts of Britain derive from contradictory effects of uneven development which resulted in a defensive type of nationalism of peripheral countries against the core. The terminology of 'periphery' and 'core' is strongly suggestive of a colonial context which is in fact adopted by Hechter's study of the United Kingdom titled *Internal Colonialism* (1975) in which he seems to follow Nairn by emphasizing the unequal development of industrialism within states. He shows how industrialization aggravated already existing conditions of economic dependency and inequality of the Celtic fringe (Ireland, Scotland and Wales) to England and how this situation manifested itself in differential political behaviour and eventually in ethno-national movements. Furthermore - which is of greater interest here - he also underpins the idea that it is difficult to speak of a 'national culture'. What exists is better depicted as a core culture dominating the others by establishing ethnic boundaries. Hechter describes the earliest stages of British nation-building as 'overland expansion of patrimonial states' and therefore prefers the term 'empire-building' (1975:65). This imperial nature of British nation-building leads to his suggestion that "[f]rom the 17th century on, English military and political control in the peripheral regions was buttressed by a *racist* ideology which held that Norman Anglo-Saxon culture was inherently superior to Celtic culture", with the clearest signs of England's domination being in Ireland (op.cit.:342; emphasis added)[10]. English cultural superiority entailed gross denigration of Irish culture by treating it with clear disdain "as the work of barbarians" (op.cit.: 77). This was reflected in the never ceasing attempt to suppress the speaking of the Gaelic language and the practising of Roman Catholicism, as well as in "a steady procession of Penal Laws" (op.cit.:76). These laws began to be introduced from the early seventeenth century onwards, peaking in 1727 when Catholics were prohibited, for example, from being members of Parliament, bearing arms, education abroad, keeping a public school in Ireland, practising law, and acquiring land owned by a Protestant. Finally, the right to vote was taken away from Catholics. These legal measures were operated throughout the period from 1727 to 1829 - the year of Catholic Emancipation.

Similarly, but in a different context, i.e. in a later period and not in a colonial context, but in an immigration setting, Miles (1982a) suggests that the Irish were the object of the articulation of a racist ideology. This happened during the 19th century when Irish labour migration to England and Scotland started to increase (the largest proportion of labour migrants to England have, in fact, come from Ireland). One part of the Irish found employment in the agricultural sector which suffered from labour shortage as a result of indigenous labour migrating to industrial towns. Another part was involved in the improvement of the infrastructure (road, railways). They tended to live in the cheapest and poorest accommodation and did mostly semi- and unskilled type of work. According to Miles, the Irish exclusion was justified by reference to the idea of 'race' and religious adherence - the latter having been a strong element of English national identity as explained above. In certain decades of the 19th century, there was massive opposition to Irish migration on the part of the English as reflected in various incidents of physical violence and riots. Miles supports his claim for this anti-Irish sentiment being a form of racism with evidence found in writings of that time in which the Irish are clearly conceived of as a 'race' in the sense of the 19th century scientific racism - namely as a separate physical type of people with a range of negative social and cultural characteristics (1982a:139-40). Increasing publicity was given to works on scientific racism, and the mid-19th century is said to have been not only the high-spot of scientific racism, but also of Irish immigration. The two strands of anti-Irish sentiment and/or discrimination of the Irish and Anti-Catholicism suggest a combined existence of racism and nationalism, whereby the boundaries between identity as a 'nation' and identity as a 'race' seem to be rather blurred at times.

Another minority group which was declared a separate and 'alien' part of British or English society - and in whose case the link between nationalism and racism becomes quite clear too - were the Jews. According to Holmes (1979), during the period of 1870 to 1930, the idea of a different 'race' became a central element in the construction of the Jews as distinctive to the majority population, although without resulting in "a system of official controls similar to the 1935 Nuremberg Laws" (1991:108) as in the German case.

In addition, Lebzelter (in: Kennedy & Nicholls 1981) suggests with regard to the same period and place (i.e. Britain) that elements of modern Jew-hatred are composed of *racial*, religious, historical and socio-economic arguments corresponding to traditional hostility. The novelty about modern anti-Jewish sentiments as opposed to traditional hostile reactions was that "it was no longer assumed that the Jews should and could be assimilated or absorbed" (op.cit.:88). Lebzelter, therefore, concludes that racism was "the backbone of modern anti-Semitism" (op.cit.:90) thrusting sole economic, cultural or religious arguments into the background. Furthermore, she identifies a clear link between racist anti-Semitism and nationalism as the "anti-Semitic campaign contained the argument of an alleged Jewish world-conspiracy directed against British interests." (op.cit.:92).

The selection of those two examples, the Irish and the Jews, should allow the assumption that British national identity did have an ethnic component and functioned as an identity of (a superior) 'race' vis-à-vis other (inferior) 'races'. Thus, excluding and even racializing implications for those minority groups were involved in the formation of a collective identity.

Another way of testing British national identity vis-à-vis 'the Other' would be to look into ideology/discourse around 'external' colonialism (as opposed to Hechter's notion of 'internal colonialism') and the inferiorization of colonial subjects. Mann writes in the context of the American colonization that "the colonies had institutionalized *racism*" (1993b:139; emphasis added). Fryer devotes a section in his book *Staying Power* to the nature and origins of racism in the context of early colonialism in the West Indies (1984:133-184). Cohen (1994), for example, suggests that during colonial/imperial times, the term 'English' carried connotations of class, linguistic and cultural superiority - an area which can only be touched upon here because of shortage of space, but it is assumed that a detailed look into the period of expanding imperialism would reveal more evidence of racializing effects of British self-perception vis-à-vis other peoples.

As a whole, there seems to be strong evidence in British history for a symbiotic relationship between nationalism and racism, i.e. the formation of national identity as an identity of a 'race'.

*The German case*  In the German context, there is a parallel example to Irish immigrants to Britain, namely that of the Poles. Since the existence of a unified Germany in 1871, the largest group of non-German (labour) immigrants were Polish people[11]. The political discourse during the period 1880 up to the First World War revolved mainly around the admission and re-admission of Polish seasonal agricultural workers and to a much lesser extent around 'German' Poles, the reason for this laying in those two different 'categories' of Poles. The eastern part of Prussia included at that time territory annexed from Poland. The Polish population living there actually belonged to the German Reich and thus enjoyed Prussian citizenship which allowed them, for example, to move on to the western parts of the Reich to find employment in the coal-mines of the *Ruhrgebiet* (Bade 1992). They had been subject to quite successful attempts of Germanization (Germanisierungsbestrebungen) in the form of anti-Polish 'Prussian protection policies' containing, amongst others, the prohibition of the usage of the Polish language. As a result, those Poles were less regarded as 'dangerous for nationalistic politics'[12].

Those Poles, however, who entered the Reich as agricultural workers were mainly from the Russian part of Poland and the Polish territory annexed by Austria-Hungary and had, therefore, not been subject to the same Germanization policies. They were referred to as *Auslandspolen* (foreign or alien Poles). However, both 'types' of Poles had one element in common, this being that their culture was regarded as being inferior to German culture (Herbert 1986) - similar to the English superior attitude towards Irish culture. They suffered from very bad working conditions with sixteen to eighteen hours of work per day. Even Polish women and children were used as a source of labour, as for example in brickworks, which was against the law in the case of German indigenous women and children (Bade 1992:319). It is suggested, therefore, that Polish workers were in a similar social situation to the Irish in England: they formed a 'sub-proletarian foreign second-class working stratum' (op.cit.:320).

There is evidence that the inferiorization of Poles was based on racialization. Bade quotes a statement by a quasi-governmental source in Breslau of 1911, in which Polish workers are referred to as 'unskilled and less intelligent'  by nature (1992:320). Associations, such as the *Ostmarkenverein* and the *Alldeutscher Verband,* were founded to promote anti-Polish propaganda which "carried in a way racist features" (Herbert 1986:46). In a speech, the chairman of the *Ostmarkenverein* mentioned the behaviour of the Poles as giving the impression of a "less educated race" (op.cit.:74). This anti-Polish propaganda was reflected in practical policies. In Westfalen (western part of Germany where the *Ruhrpolen* settled), for instance, Polish schools and the teaching *of* as well as *in*  the Polish language were forbidden, and the request for a Polish priest from the Polish community was turned down (op.cit.:75).  All of these policies show similarities to the anti-Irish Penal Laws mentioned above.

Another similarity to the English case, which has been described above, is the notion of 'internal colonialism'. As indicated with regard to the *Auslandspolen*, the territory of Poland was partitioned until 1918 - the date of the re-establishment of the Polish state by the Treaty of Versailles. As a consequence, national ideologists' claims to the superiority of the Germanic peoples was not only used vis-à-vis the French (as mentioned earlier), but was also used to legitimize German rule over former West Slavs and Polish territories. Ethnic stereotypes, such as the notorious reference to 'uncleanliness of the Slavs' entailed a general perception of Germans having brought civilization to Slavic peoples in general and to Polish peoples in particular (Burleigh & Wippermann 1991:26). "This cultural-political form of *imperialism* was given an historical-messianic quality through the claim that the Germans had a 'mission' to resettle territories once inhabited by ancient Germanic tribes." (ibid.; emphasis added).

The racialization of eastern Europeans resulted further in their being 'used' as forced labourers (Fremdarbeiter) during the period of National Socialism (in particular the years of war 1939-1945). Bade refers to this as the "largest case of forced mass-usage of foreign labour in history since the abolition of slavery during the nineteenth century" (1992:354; free translation). Workers mainly from Poland and Russia suffered from the worst treatment and the worst working conditions when compared with POWs and forced labourers from western Europe[13]. Thus, they occupied the lowest level of the 'racial' hierarchy (Bade 1992; Herbert 1986:153).

A further example which illustrates the co-existence of national identity and identity as a 'race' is that of the Jews. The Jewish population in Germany experienced rising anti-Semitism from the time of unification in 1871[14], partly as the result of Jewish migration to Germany from eastern Europe between 1880 and 1929. The terms 'east' and 'Jews' carried negative connotations "in the language of German nationalistic circles" (Bade 1992:326)[15]. During 1918 and 1923, anti-Semitic activities increased further culminating in the crudest biological-scientific racism of the Third Reich. Hitler was very much influenced by the earlier racial-anthropological, racial-hygienic, and racial anti-Semitic theories. In *Mein Kampf* he "turned them into a comprehensive, self-contained, if totally insane, racial-political programme" (Burleigh & Wippermann 1991:38). The consequences of this ideology and its high degree of political instrumentalization, namely the extermination of six million Jews, is a well-known fact.

## 5.3  The context of the post-war period

The post-1945 period has given a new dimension to the issue of nationalism and national identity in various respects. As a result of a phase of extreme nationalism and national identity based on racial purity during the Third Reich, Germany experienced defeat and total collapse. Britain, on the other hand, emerged from the war as one of the Allies. However, it could not indulge for very long in its victorious position, but had to turn back to its problems of continuous economic decline and the gradual break-up of the Empire. It seems, therefore, as if the post-war period represents the beginning of a new era in the history of nationalism in the wake of the retreat of its extreme racist version, the end of decolonization, and the beginning of a new 'economic crisis'.

Another aspect which began to give the issue of nationalism and national identity a fresh impetus is large-scale post-war immigration of non-Europeans. The presence of a permanent 'foreign' population of a considerable size has resulted, in western Europe, in a common problem of national identity despite historically very different approaches to the role of immigration in each single western European country. This common problem of national identity will be approached by the notion of 'crisis'.

## 5.3.1 Identity crisis

Usually, the issue of 'identity crisis' seems to be related to an individual, personal level. However, as Macdonald (1993:8) suggests, not only individuals suffer from identity crises, but societies can suffer from it too if they have lost hold of their history and roots. Even majority identities need not necessarily be secure and unambiguous - a fact discussed by Forsythe in the context of German identity (1989). Any question of identity is clearly dependent on the social and political environment of a particular period in time and on the categories available for the drawing of boundaries. These elements - environment and boundaries - are subject to changes and can, therefore, result in crises at the moment of redefinition.

The era of integration - to borrow a term from Wieviorka (1994) - during which western European nation-states started their formation processes seemed to have been quite successful in integrating three basic components of their collective life: an industrial society, an egalitarian state and a national identity - a process which was ongoing until the 1960s and 1970s as suggested by Wieviorka (op.cit.). Since then, however, all western European countries have found themselves undergoing a huge transformation which has implications for these three components. The decline of industrial societies, the fading of the working-class movement and the downward mobility of the middle classes, just to mention a few of the outcomes of the present economic situation, seem to be (at least partly) responsible for increasing national populism and a generally rising feeling of insecurity. This is very likely to be attributed to immigrants, thus involving strong anti-migrant attitudes (op.cit.).

In this context, in most western European countries, political debates about nation, nationality and citizenship are activated (see, for example, the 'New Right' debate), and nationalism tends to become again narrower, i.e. loaded with xenophobia and racism. Such a development entails further exclusion of those 'outside' the national society - mostly the ethnic minority groups - leading to stronger identification with their religious and ethnic roots. Thus, the era of integration is suggested by Wieviorka (1994) to have changed into an 'era of destructuration'. This post-1945 social and political environment is, therefore, the frame of historically different problems of national identity.

*The British case* . The symptoms of a crisis of national identity acute to Britain are many-fold. As a country which was once imperialistic, Britain's role in the world has been substantially diminished. Significant economic decline and crisis in the welfare state has had implications for its self-image. Schnapper, therefore, suggests - albeit put in a rather simplistic way - that "[d]ivisions of class, gender, region and 'race' - which are no longer transcended by a grand imperialist project, or by confidence and pride in a political system... seem to threaten the unity of the country" (1994:131).

In Britain, the boundaries of national identity have been for a long time very imprecisely drawn and understood. Historically, the concept of 'belonging' was expressed in terms of being the monarch's subject, i.e. the vertical relationship between monarch and individual (Dummett & Nicol 1990). Since the French and the American revolutions, it has become general practice to define nationality in legal codes and/or constitutions, which is, however, not the case in Britain. The introduction of the first Nationality Act in 1948 is usually quoted as the end of this shortcoming and as having destroyed the notion of 'subjecthood' (Brubaker 1989; Dummett & Nicol 1990). However, according to Cohen (1994), many residues of this status remain.

> It may be argued that these are mere historical residues and denote only token power by the Crown. But if we are talking about mere residues, why is it so difficult to provide a simple, up-to-date, definitive statement of the limits to constitutional monarchy, the nature of parliamentary power, the rights and responsibilities that attach to British citizenship, and above all, the parameters of a national identity? (1994:6).

Prior to the British Nationality Act of 1948, there was the common assumption that all who came under the Crown's power were British subjects with an emphasis on duties and loyalties to the monarch rather than on rights. When large-scale post-war immigration into the core took place, a need was seen to clearly identify British nationality - a fact which was not only triggered by immigration but also by former dependent territories which began to implement their own nationality and citizenship laws, the first of which was Canada in 1947. Whereas the imperial notion of British nationality seems to have been concerned with who was included, the British Nationality Act of 1948 started a process of defining who should be excluded from being British. The only brief period when people from the Indian sub-continent and the West Indies could come to the core, testing the common status and freedom of movement, was between 1949 and 1962 (Goulbourne 1991:95-96). With the large-scale influx of these Commonwealth citizens, "it became increasingly difficult to uphold the idea that a British identity was exclusively a white identity" (Cohen 1994:18). Consequently, post-war British immigration law successively restricted access to the UK leading to a redefinition as a nation-state (as opposed to a multi-'racial' empire). The four main legislative interventions were:

- the British Nationality Act of 1948 (invention of 'Citizens of the UK and colonies' as distinct from 'British subject' and 'British subject without citizenship'),
- the 1962 Commonwealth Immigrants Act,
- the concept of 'patriality' as introduced by the 1971 Immigrants Act (allowing immigration only from people with a British parent or grandparent),
- and finally the British Nationality Act of 1981 which abolished the long-standing reliance on sole ius soli (rule of birthplace) and thus, the automatic acquisition of British citizenship by birth (Cohen 1994; Schnapper 1994).

In particular the concept of 'patriality' and the introduction of the 'ius sanguinis' principle into the Nationality Act of 1981 have been criticized for having racializing implications (Gilroy 1987).

Another factor adding to the identity problems resulting from a radical change from empire to nation-state lay in Britain's joining of the European Community (George 1990 & 1991). There is now the pressure of moving towards a European identity despite the long historical "ties of kinship, economic interdependence and preferential trade arrangements" (Cohen 1994:17) with the Commonwealth.

All these identity problems can be summarized by Cohen's notion of 'fuzzy frontiers'. He identifies six fuzzy frontiers which render British national identity complex: 1. the Celtic fringe, 2. the heritage of the Dominions, 3. the Empire and the non-white Commonwealth, 4. the continuing Atlantic and anglophone connection, 5. the relationship to an emergent European identity, and 6. the British notion of and relationship to 'aliens' (1994:7). As a result, Cohen concludes that British identity is characterized by a general pattern of fragmentation.

> Multiple axes of identification have meant that Irish, Scots, Welsh and English people, those from the white, black or brown Commonwealth, Americans, English-speakers, Europeans and even 'aliens' have had their lives intersect one with another in overlapping and complex circles of identity-construction and rejection. (op.cit.:35).

The various forms of British identity have shifted throughout history as well as space and excluded different types of people. The racializing effects of national identity in the post-war period are mainly directed towards black and Asian immigrants.

*The German case* In Germany, it was the situation of complete destruction in 1945 which caused a radical change in its people's self-perception. The experiences and revelation of the full scale of atrocities during the Third Reich with its aftermath of the expulsion from and loss of eastern territories as well as national division into two separate states resulted in a general inferiority complex combined with a feeling of shame or guilt (Weidenfeld & Korte 1991; Buruma 1994). Since then, as Forsythe (1989) suggests, German identity has been fragile and of ambiguous quality. People's feelings about being German has often been referred to as being bound up with their feelings about the recent past (Habermas 1989; Maier 1988) and is, therefore, a rather touchy and painful topic. Germanness as a positive identity is "*historisch belastet*" (emotionally burdened as a result of the Nazi past; Forsythe, 1989:151) which results, according to Forsythe, in two main attitudes towards being German: either complete and total rejection of anything 'national' (i.e. symbols, terminology) or a more positive view which advocates a 'normal' handling of national identity - which is claimed by representatives of the former attitude as dangerous since any 'normal' handling of national identity is likely to slide back into the pre-war type of nationalism[16]. During the immediate post-war period, the former attitude seems to have prevailed. The memory of the years from 1870 to 1945 tended to make people avoid the use of the word 'national', as it seemed uncomfortably reminiscent of 'nationalistic' and 'National Socialist' (Schwarz, in: Baring 1994). The creation of a positive national identity at that time had to fail because of the "shadows cast upon German self-understanding and historical consciousness" (Bade 1992:432; free translation). In the wake of the 'economic miracle', any feeling of pride in being German was dominated by so-called 'economic patriotism' (Wirtschaftpatriotismus) (Weidenfeld & Korte 1991). Integration into the Western Alliance (Nato) and the European idea helped to ease the 'historical burden'. However, not before reunification in 1990, did Germans actually have to face the issue of national identity (op.cit.).

Meanwhile - between the 'national identity crisis' of the immediate post-war years and the second wave of crisis following reunification - the recruitment of 'guest-workers', in particular of Turkish workers, had largely resulted in their permanent settlement, and thus to the establishment of 'new' ethnic minorities. Until reunification, German policy towards immigrants consisted of maintaining a legal and political distinction between nationals and foreigners. Even today, German policy has hardly changed, treating second and third generations as much as *Ausländer* as the first immigrants (Cohn-Bendit & Schmid 1992). The traditionally ethno-cultural conception of the German nation is still retained in nationality laws (in particular article 116 of the Basic Law which offers immediate citizenship to all ethnic 'Germans' in eastern Europe) and naturalization procedures (Heckmann 1992). The term *Ausländer* and non-recognition as a country of immigration indicate this as well as the right to nationality being still based on pure ius sanguinis (right of descent). Schnapper, therefore, suggests that "[p]olicy of integrating immigrants through their participation in economic and social life alone without giving them citizenship is in a sense the logical outcome of the German national project" (1994:137).

Reunification entailed a new crisis of national identity in various aspects. It is a crisis for West Germany as it has regained full political sovereignty (by the final signing of a peace treaty and the gradual withdrawal of the allied forces) and thus, has to reinterpret its role in European and world politics (Estel 1991; see also Baring 1994). Thereby the terminology of the 'nation' with a *'völkisch'* (ethnic) identity seems to be more emphasized than ever since 1945, being fundamentally contradictory to the notion of a republic - an issue raised by a prominent political scientist (Oberndörfer 1993). It is a crisis for East Germany as it has to come to terms with economic, social and ideological changes created by a new political union of two national identities whose historical paths had been diverging for two generations. For both, east and west, there is the further task of handling the Nazi-past in the light of rising (contemporary) nationalism. The East needs to come to terms with its involvement in the Hitler Era which had been disguised by the anti-fascist propaganda of communism (Bielefeld 1991). At the same time, East Germany has to cope with the revelations of the communist regime and the intrigues of the STASI. Therefore, the official self-understanding of the GDR as a 'socialist country' as well as the propagated version of a sole *Verfassungspatriotismus* (constitutional patriotism; Kluxen-Pyta 1990; Sternberger 1990; Gebhardt 1993) in the West are coming to an end, and there is real concern that narrow nationalism might replace these and, thus, form a 'wrong' new identity (Estel 1991; Oberndörfer 1993).

For the ethnic minority communities, too, reunification seems to have resulted in more awareness of their position in Germany, and for the first time this has triggered a stronger, openly expressed claim for 'an expansion of the concept of Germanhood' to reflect the real composition of German society (Leggewie & Senoçak 1993:11)[17]. The first generation of immigrants in particular has to come to terms with the fact that they have become permanent residents and, thus, part of German society. This was never an issue for those generations born and brought up in Germany. And yet, they too experience identity problems: they actually identify with Germany, but as a result of the exclusiveness of German national identity, the difficulty in obtaining full citizenship rights and raising nationalism/racism, they tend to look back to their ethnic origin as their source of identification (Leggewie & Senoçak 1993). During the rapid process of socio-economic and political reunification - with its enforced distributive struggle over scarce resources resulting in tendencies towards narrow nationalism, i.e. clearer boundary drawing along ethnic lines - the status of ethnic minority communities (in particular the Turkish) had been ignored. Despite the fact that they had come to think of themselves as legitimate members of the nation-state, they were not giving clear political signs (such as full citizenship rights) to confirm their belief in being an established part of German society. In other words, the immediate incorporation of East Germans did not run parallel to a similar incorporation of former guest-workers and their descendants. German society as a whole, therefore, still needs to redefine its identity as multi-ethnic or multi-cultural. One step towards that would be the legal redefinition of nationality which is still based on the ethnic or 'racial' concept of *Volk* (Heckmann, in: Bielefeld 1991; Hoffmann 1991).

The above shows that Cohen's concept of 'fuzzy frontiers' can also be applied to the German situation. Problems of national identity occur in the context of: 1. the (ex-) GDR-citizens, 2. ethnic Germans from eastern Europe, 3. long-term resident *Ausländer*, 4. heritage of the nazi-past, and 5. relationship to other 'aliens' such as asylum seekers.

German national identity shows as much a general pattern of fragmentation as the British. Both countries need to acknowledge the complex composition of their post-war societies. Even today, there are still residues from pre-war periods as reflected in the concept of subjecthood and *Volk* which make the search for a national identity so difficult. Ideas of common descent, common tradition/culture and common history are very backward looking and fail to incorporate large sections of ethnic minorities. Ethno-centristic attitudes and the dominating tendency of majority cultures not only disregard the long history of sub-national traditions in Germany and Britain - which have always existed despite the myth of one national identity - they also have exclusionary and racializing effects on ethnic minorities. Part of the solution in the search for a collective, all-encompassing identity, might be a new concept of post-national identity.

## 5.4 Post-national and post-conventional identity

### 5.4.1 Post-national

The tendencies in the advanced industrialized world towards further internationalization suggest a move into a post-national epoch - a concrete sign of which is the creation of the European Community. Some authors have emphasized the limitations of nation-states in a world which is becoming more and more inter-dependent be it economically, culturally, ecologically or in any other way (Roche 1992, Robertson 1992, Albrow & King 1990). In the context of the European Community, the idea has been expressed that the era of the domination of the nation-state in western

Europe is coming to an end (Nicklas 1993). This is certainly true for common European interests identified so far as mainly economic. Mann adds to this common EC defence interests, but other than that he holds that "[i]t [the EC] is not yet a state, nor is it replacing states" (1993a:128). Thus "European nation-states are neither dying nor retiring; they have merely shifted functions, and they may continue to do so in the future" (op.cit.:133). Nicklas continues to argue that the supranational framework provided by the EU does not change the fact that in everyday life smaller entities, such as the region, are much more crucial for the formation of identity. The results of a European survey seem to confirm this claim by showing that, roughly, the nearer to home the issue, the more people prefer their national government handling it (or even local governments), and only issues which have to do with external affairs get big support for EU action (European Commission, Eurobarometer No. 41, 1994). Thus, despite global ecological, economic and cultural interdependencies, the nation-state seems to remain the dominating *political* form of organization with strong sub-national traditions as in the German case (federal state system!). Castles, too, argues that the nation-state is beginning to lose its position as the centre of political identity and power, and thus some of its functions, but it is not going to dissolve completely (in: Bielefeld 1991).

However, in the context of the European Union, supra-nationality does not only mean taking power away from national governments to supranational institutions, but it also means the regeneration at sub-national levels (urban, regional etc.). The emergence of the EC and its transformation into the European Union has created a new situation "with new possibilities for European regions and sub-nationalities, 'subsidiarity principle', and in particular the development of a Committee of the Regions [which] are elements in the creation of a new political space and potential for the exercise and development of sub-national forms of citizenship and identity." (Roche 1994b)[18].

It is still too early to assume a post-national identity as actually existing. However, there seems to be evidence of shifting politics of identity away from the national to the supranational (i.e. EU) as well as to the local or regional level which might have empowering consequences - with particular regard to a potentially new emphasis on local communities (see also Chapter Six).

*5.4.2 Post-conventional*

In his attempt to define an alternative concept of national identity, Habermas pleads for constitutional patriotism and a post-conventional type of identity. The notion of 'constitutional patriotism' was originally developed by Sternberger as a solution to rid post-war Germany of any national patriotism (1990). Instead of feeling pride for the nation, the object of pride and loyalty should be the constitution (symbolizing the 'state' and not the 'nation') as the sole provision of citizens' rights and liberties.

According to Sternberger, democracy is only possible in the form of the state, and the state is democratic through its constitution. As such, the modern constitutional state (Verfassungsstaat) can produce identity.

This approach towards identity is claimed by Habermas to be too rational. Identity, according to him, has to invoke some sense of community bond that goes beyond rational adherence to normative propositions. Post-nationalistic identity requires recognition of interdependence and community. Habermas tries to overcome the initial incompatibility between a commitment to transnational, liberal values and the collective identity generated by traditional communities.

> If national symbols have lost their influence with the young, if naive identification with one's heritage has yielded to a more tentative relationship to history, if discontinuities are felt more strongly and continuities not celebrated at any price, if national pride and collective self-esteem are filtered through universalist value orientations - to the extent to which all this is really the case, indications of the development of a postconventional identity are increasing. (1989:227).

With this concept, identity derives no longer predominantly from common ethnic and cultural properties, but rather from the *practice* of citizenship. The decisive element for the formation of collective identity and 'community bond' is, therefore, participation and belonging on the basis of being a *citizen*. In this way, the republican strand of 'citizenship' is detached from the idea of belonging to a pre-political community integrated on the basis of descent and a shared tradition/history, and thus it reflects the multiplicity and complex composition of western European societies during the post-war period.

In the British context, the concept of post-conventional identity could help to overcome the present 'identity crisis' with regard to the monarchy, and the last residues of subjecthood could develop into full citizenship. Overall, post-conventional and post-national (i.e. regional and supranational) elements could create a type of collective identity which is inclusive and pluralistic. It must be conceived of as a tradition which is open to development and change (and thus might even lead to a critical approach to the concept of 'tradition'). In this way, the ethnic origin of people would not have any negative effect on their legitimate state-membership, and full participation could be based on residence criteria instead.

This concept of post-conventional identity might be difficult to achieve. Habermas' idea of identity as a 'sense of community bond' and as a 'recognition of interdependence and community', however, lead here to the argument for *local identity* based on *local citizenship* and participation as a useful concept to include all long-term residents - an issue which will be subject to more details in Chapter Six.

## 5.5 Concluding remarks

This chapter has outlined arguments supporting the idea that there is a strong connection between the identity as a 'race' and as a 'nation', i.e. between nationalism and racialization. In other words, the above sections underpin the argument that these two phenomena - nationalism and racialization - tend to be characterized by a symbiotic relationship[19]. By creating national, large groups and by drawing the boundary between these 'insider' groups and 'outsiders', nationalism seems to be easily accompanied by racializing effects. However, nationalism has not only and still does not only work against 'outside' groups, but has also the tendency to racialize minorities from 'inside' who have been part of the nation from its very inception (such as the Jewish population in Germany, and the Scottish and Irish in Britain).

For clarification of the above, the beginning of this chapter included relevant theories examining common features of the genesis of nation-states and nationalism resulting in a sense of national identity. Modernization or civilization processes have been constitutive of the constructed reality of the nation-state and the abolition of a *'racisme de classe'* . Thus, nation-states have developed from interior into exterior classificatory devices. However, national identity came to co-exist with an identity as a (superior) 'race' as the illustration of the British and German cases showed. Therefore, the newly achieved superficial stratification by classes (as opposed to pre-modern times) and standardization of large national groups (a 'people') have had a negative effect on ethnic or religious minorities who did not fit into, or were regarded as a threat to, the prevailing idea of national identity and the dominating majority culture.

The sections on the individual cases of Germany and Britain have shown the different histories and elements of their individual national identities, though with the same result of racialization and ethnic exclusionism. The depiction of England as the first ever nation based on political and universalistic ideas (i.e. territorial or 'civic' basis of membership) has been challenged by looking beyond this early historical period (around 1600) and by approaching the issue of 'nation-state' from the *British* perspective. Internally (in the context of the Scottish, Welsh and Irish nations as well as the Jewish minority) and externally (in the context of overseas colonies) Britain has been described as an 'empire', i.e. as multi-national or multi-'racial'. There is evidence for particularistic tendencies due to the domination of the English culture which had exclusionary effects on, e.g., the Irish, the Jews and the various colonial peoples. Germany's history as a nation-state began in 1871, and the ideological formation of its national identity also involved ethnically exclusionary and racializing elements vis-à-vis its Polish and Jewish residents.

Developments after the post-war period in both countries resulted in 'identity crises' with regard to their historical legacies and with regard to large-scale immigration of people with rather distant cultural backgrounds. These 'new' ethnic minorities tend to be excluded from a general understanding of national identity.

Based on the above, the following conclusions have been arrived at. The traditional concept of the nation, i.e. the myth of common descent, common territory, common customs/culture and common history, has been a problematic issue throughout the history of both Britain and Germany. Neither country has ever been a 'nation' in the ideal sense (i.e. constituted of one ethnic people) and most likely never will be, which indicates the irrationality of this concept with exclusionary consequences for ethnic minorities.

In the contemporary context, internationalization and globalization processes - of which international migration is one crucial feature - reinforce the uselessness of the original concept of the nation. In western Europe, developments revolving around the establishment of the European Community and its further integration into the European Union seem to involve the gradual evolution of a post-national identity and the prospects for a post-conventional identity detached from the prerequisite of common ethnic origin and culture with the emphasis on transnational and subnational values. Collective identity would, thus, be based on a sense of community materialized by the practice of citizenship and not by descent. In this way, it would be inclusive for the whole variety of residents within the state community.

As a whole, it has been shown that the socio-historical formation of British and German national identity with its close link to identity as a 'race' has resulted in an exclusionary response to immigration and the settlement of ethno-cultural minorities. How this response is reflected in the citizenship status of non-European immigrants will be more thoroughly examined in the following chapter.

## Notes

1       Elias identifies some key mechanisms in the nation-state formation process. The first is referred to by him as the monopoly mechanism, meaning the formation of territorial and political monopolies. The second is the institutionalization of power by which he means the tendency of the state to specialize its functions and to develop impersonal bureaucracies. By exploring this process of long term state formation he focuses on certain behavioural patterns (etiquette, ritual) developed by the aristocracy during the late Middle Ages. The so-called 'civilizing process' thus means the gradual imposition of strict rules of behaviour.

2       It is not of importance here to settle on the issue whether nation-states are products of nationalism or the other way round. Both are seen here as inter-connected and somehow as re-inforcing each other.  Also, it should be noted here that there are a variety of theories of nationalism in other

    contexts (Smith 1971; Seton-Watson 1977; Hall 1993), but of interest here is only the German and British context.

3    Mann (1993a) refers to the same phenomenon as 'geopolitical rivalry'.

4    Wallerstein (1987), for instance, places his theory of nationalism within the capitalist world-system. Gellner (1983) provides a theory which hinges upon the requirement of a growth oriented industrial society, and Anderson defines the nation as an 'imagined political community' deriving from the extensive use of 'print capitalism' (meaning that books were the first commodity produced in a massive way generating great profits). Llobera (1994) suggests that modernization as a whole triggered the development of nationalism.

5    A phenomenon which becomes also clear in Eugen Weber's famous study on France where he describes that the notion of 'race' was used to refer to peasants (1976:7) until almost the end of the 19th century.

6    England happened to become the first nation as the result of certain circumstances, the most important of which were, according to Greenfeld (1994), the transformation of the social hierarchy and the unprecedented increase in social mobility throughout the 16th century, the accession of the Tudors to power, and the Protestant Reformtion. The social structure became much more open than had ever been before.

7    It should be mentioned here that 'ethnicity' is mostly regarded as a cultural marker or a container of shared origin and characteristics (Rex 1986). However, it is agreed here with Rattansi who remarks that 'culture' and notions of 'shared origin' "smuggle in ideas of shared *biology*" (1994:53, original emphasis) and are, thus, highly suggestive of 'race' and racism.

8    She does, however, acknowledge that the period she describes is "long before the word 'race' acquired its specific meaning and long before racism, bolstered by the authority of science, became an articulate and presumably objective view" (1994:368-69). This is also discussed by Brah who questions that nations can be connoted as "a 'racial group' at this stage when the word 'race' was not yet part of the vocabulary...." (1994:809). And yet, Greenfeld is very correct in her understanding of the strong ethnic nature of German national identity.

9    According to Llobera, who draws on Smith's typology, the necessary criteria for identifying a nation are: a collective proper name, a specific myth of common ancestry or descent, elements of culture which are shared, and the association with a specific homeland or history (1994:39-40). England, Scotland, Wales and Ireland are claimed to fulfill the conditions required.

10    Again, here are the same reservations to a terminology of 'race' and racism during this period as explained in footnote no. 8 on page 66.

11    The peak during this period was reached in 1914 with 1.2 million immigrant workers (Bade 1992:312).

12    As unification of Germany had only come about in 1871, the presence of a fairly large Polish minority was seen as a threat to the still very fragile

nation-state. This was expressed as a fear of *'Polnisierung'* - Polishization - of the east of the Kaiserreich.

13    There were 2,758,312 Soviets and 1,688,080 Polish forced labourers from a total of 7,615,970 'civilian labourers' and POWs in 1944 (Herbert 1986:145).

14    *Anti-Jewish sentiments* existed, of course, much earlier and were a crucial element in ideologizing a German national identity (see Greenfeld 1992). The German Jews had gained their emancipation comparatively speaking late in 1869/71, and already around 1881 a movement was founded which had as its goal the withdrawal of Jewish equality (Bade 1992). *Antisemitism* was a creation of the scientific form of racial anthropology during the second half of the 19th century (Pinn & Nebelung 1992).

15    Lebzelter writes in this context of a similar attitude towards eastern European Jews migrated to Britain/England. She quotes one observer who wrote in 1908 that "[t]he East-European Jews are treated like dirt." (in: Kennedy & Nicholls 1981:90).

16    For a more detailed account of these positions see the publication of the complete 'historians' controversy' (Historikerstreit) by Piper-Verlag (1987) - a debate between Habermas and a number of distinguished German historians on the consequences of the Third Reich for contemporary German national identity.

17    This is also reflected in a series of newspaper articles published on this topic following the arson attacks in Mölln and Solingen in 1992.

18    For further details, in particular on the subsidiarity principle and the Committee of the Regions, see Chapter Six.

19    Balibar remarks in this context that although "racism is not at all functional from the point of view of nationalism", "there is virtually no historical example of nationalism *without* a racist supplement" (1991:12; original emphasis). Therefore, he thinks that "racism is an elaboration and forward rush of the contradictions of nationalism." (ibid.).

# 6   Citizenship

It is the purpose of this chapter to assess: 1. the effects of nationalism and racism on immigrant minorities' citizenship status and 2. the way in which citizenship functions or could function to minimize these effects and thus, work as a mechanism for inclusion. This assessment will not only be made with regard to nationality/citizenship laws and legal rights but also with regard to immigrant minorities' recognition as full members by civil society. To do so, it is more useful to analyze citizenship along a subdivision of formal (in connection with access) and substantive rights. I regard the link between citizenship and nationality thereby as a major obstacle to equal membership on the formal basis as well as within civil society at large. A concept of citizenship which is disconnected from ethnic descent and based on residential criteria will, therefore, be argued for to resist the power of nationalism and racialization.

The European dimension to citizenship, i.e. its supranational (Union citizenship) and subnational developments (principle of subsidiarity and the Committee of the Regions) and their specific implications for ethnic minorities will be added to this analysis: a) to show the shortcomings of European Union citizenship for the inclusion of non-European long-term residents as it stands at present; and b) to seek a new conception of post-national citizenship.

## 6.1 Nationality and citizenship - brief definitional remarks

Both concepts, nationality and citizenship, are a reflection of state membership. Whereas 'nationality' implies the passive acquisition of membership by birth, 'citizenship' refers to the active carrying out of rights and duties. Nationality actually relates to qualification of state membership by blood-relatedness or shared culture. However, in academic literature and other pieces of writing, nationality is often regarded as a formal personal relationship between the state and the individual. As such, it can be purely nominal or it can create or imply a legal status entailing rights and duties which is sometimes referred to as citizenship (O'Leary 1992). In this view, 'nationality' and 'citizenship' are intermingled which is also reflected in law, as for example in the case of the British Nationality Act (which defines British citizenship).

In the context of immigration, however, I argue that the mingling of 'nationality' and 'citizenship' is not very useful, as post-war immigrants, and in particular in the case of the first generation, tend to be of non-European nationality, but in the wake of permanent settlement and the birth of subsequent generations, immigrants seek full citizenship rights. This issue will reappear in more detail throughout this chapter.

## 6.2 Relevant theories on citizenship

### 6.2.1 T.H. Marshall

As a starting point of almost all contemporary debate in British political scientific and sociological literature on citizenship, T.H. Marshall's essay *Citizenship & Social Class* (1950) is taken in which he argues that the modern concept of citizenship is made up of three combined elements - civil, political and social. Civil rights are considered by him as rights for individual freedom, rights to property, personal liberty and justice. Political rights encompass the right to participate in the exercise of political power, whether by holding office or by voting. The third, social rights, are rights of economic and social security within a modern welfare state. According to Marshall, these rights were extended over the last 300 years in a way often described as 'evolutionary' (Giddens, 1985)[1] by coinciding with the rise of capitalism and its evolving class structure.

Marshall views modern citizenship as a process of expanding rights to all residents in a capitalist nation-state in order to dismantle class inequalities. Therefore, modern citizenship began as a system of rights which developed out of market relations and became a system of rights which were to reconcile formal equality with the continuity of social class division. Marshall's answer to the problem of capitalism versus democracy was the welfare state. With the establishment of the welfare state, he saw the conflict between capitalism's tendency to generate social inequalities and class division on one hand and the democratic developments on the other hand, solved by the creation of citizenship and by its egalitarian and integrative effects. His argument is that social citizenship has tended to reduce certain social inequalities whereby he thinks in particular of class inequality. Social citizenship is viewed by him as the final stage of this development and thus, the evolution finishes here having resulted in a virtual guarantee of citizenship.

Marshall's *Citizenship & Social Class* explains the nature of citizenship in post-World War II Britain, that is, in the context of social reconstruction since the rise of the welfare state. It also provides an account of the emergence of citizenship in the modern nation-state in terms of the historical development of capitalist society. In Marshall's general understanding, citizenship is defined as a status attached to full membership of a community. Those who possess this status are equal with respect to the rights and duties associated with it (1950:28-29). Perhaps the most important aspect of Marshall's theory of citizenship is that it addressed explicitly the question of the relationship between citizenship and social class. In particular social citizenship (i.e. welfare citizenship) has tended to reduce certain social inequalities and has imposed modifications on class, but has not been able to abolish class altogether.

Summing up, it may be said that Marshall's 'citizenship' describes an ideal standard having developed into an 'institution' or 'national status'.

His principal emphasis, despite having to admit that citizenship as a 'system of equality' implies an inevitable conflict with capitalism as a system of 'stratification', is clearly on membership of, and loyalty to, a common (national-societal) civic community. The "extension of the area of common experience and common culture" (Young 1967:9) is seen by Marshall as one aspect of social change towards the reduction of class divisions as the result of the gradual development of a universal status of citizenship. Young suggests that Marshall's idea of a growing common *national* culture can be read as implying a corresponding growth of a *national* consciousness.

> This consciousness - loyalty to a 'common heritage' and to a 'civilization which is a common possession' - is the *integrative* complement to citizenship (1967:9; emphasis added).

Thus, Marshall's' concept of citizenship is essentially a concept of integration (and inclusion) into a national-societal community.

### 6.2.2 Critics

Many of Marshall's critics take as a point of departure the specific period during which Marshall was writing his essay, namely when the welfare state had just been established. The welfare state was identified by Marshall as a key element in his notion of citizenship because of the new opportunities resulting from its provision of social rights to minimum levels of well-being for the sick, unemployed and retired (Twine 1994). More importantly, by taking immediate post-war Britain as the background, Marshall is criticized for taking the socio-political unity of Great Britain for granted. Some authors, such as Turner (1986), however, have suggested that the question of citizenship within Britain cannot be discussed without reference to the Celtic fringe or the incorporation of the working class (Barbalet 1988; Young 1967). More importantly for this study, any debate around citizenship can not ignore the presence of ethnic minorities of non-European background involving the issue of belongingness challenged on the state level as well as within civil society by nationalism and racism. The above criticisms by Barbalet and Young, thus, rightly object to what Turner (1986) considers 'a too homogeneous picture of Britain' as provided by Marshall[2].

Two main features of Marshall's argument seem to reappear in the general critical literature: One concerns the character of the relationship between citizenship and class and the other concerns the socially integrative character of citizenship. The first aspect has been taken up by Turner (1986) who argues that citizenship is not simply about class and capitalism. There are now new social movements for social membership and full participation. Moreover, inequalities are diverse and not only based on class, as some might be less importantly connected with the capitalist-industrial economic order. These two points suggest that racialization might play a role in the claim for full participation and that racialization might be one feature on which inequality is based.

The aspect that inequalities are not only based on class has been similarly taken up, for instance, by Fraser and Gordon who claim that Marshall's periodization with its integrative effects of the three stages of citizenship "fits the experience of white working men only, a minority of the population" (in: van Steenbergen 1994:93). Vogel adds a 'race' dimension to this view by arguing that differences of colour, ethnicity and sex might have long been removed from the formal, legal qualifications of citizen status, but they still have some purchase in the informal mechanisms of today's political culture. She refers to the specific disadvantages suffered by these groups as 'problems of latecomers' to the political arena as they often lack resources that are necessary to make full use of the equal entitlements and opportunities postulated in the idea of democratic citizenship (in: van Steenbergen 1994)[3].

To re-evaluate Marshall's early theory of citizenship at the end of the 20th century, various changes in western European societies should be taken into account when discussing the meaning of citizenship. One of those changes is the settlement of post-war labour migrants and the emergence of 'new' ethnic minorities. In this context, Marshall's concept is flawed as it takes *formal* citizenship for granted. The question of membership in a nation-state, however, can be quite problematic and the intermingling of the concepts of nationality and citizenship has the tendency to render the acquisition of formal citizenship difficult. Thus, Marshall assumed the nation-state as *the* framework and theorized citizenship as a *national* phenomenon. This poses problems not only in the context of immigrant minorities, but also in the context of supra-national and sub-national developments (aspects which will be returned to at a later point). Moreover, Marshall's rather integrative concept of citizenship, as a device to promote social inclusiveness among 'insiders', completely ignores the ways in which racialization functions to obstruct access to full citizenship (Anthias & Yuval-Davis 1992). Large-scale post-war immigration in fact has resulted in the tendency to restrict access to citizenship in countries such as Britain. In other countries (such as Germany), traditionally harsh regulations have hardly been eased. Thus, in this context, citizenship is not a unified, homogeneous set of social arrangements.

### 6.2.3 *The context of immigration and cross-national analysis*

This still leaves the question of a conception of citizenship applicable to the situation of permanent settlement and the emergence of 'new' ethnic minorities. Such a conception should allow the analysis of the effects of nationalism and racism on ethnic minorities' citizenship and the extent to which these effects allow citizenship to function as a mechanism for inclusion. In legal terms, nationality/citizenship laws are to reflect a society's identity as a nation. Therefore, Turner rightly remarks that "any further development of the theory of citizenship will have to deal more fundamentally with societies in which the struggle over citizenship necessarily involves problems of *national identity* and state formation in a context of multiculturalism and ethnic pluralism." (1990:212; emphasis added). The presence of a considerable size of settled post-war labour migrants and their descendants challenges the intermingled concepts of citizenship and nationality and, thus, the fragmentation of identities demands a conceptual redefinition of collective membership to render the exercise of citizenship a more equal basis.

So far, citizenship has been mainly identified with a socio-political status conferring a set of rights upon individuals in a nation-state. However, citizenship is not only comprised of rights, but also revolves around a cultural dimension, i.e. is based upon a sense of belonging to and identification with a socio-political entity. This sense of belonging (or identity) seems to be required in national polities in which large numbers of persons are distant and largely anonymous to each other. It may help to reduce social distance and might function as a basis of solidarity. Therefore, a conception of citizenship is needed which can grasp the legal status' dimension as well as the dimension of national identity (i.e. consciousness of collective membership). In this context, acquisition (access to rights) and social inclusion of immigrants into citizenship (recognition of belonging) have to be elements of such a conception.

These two dimensions can be distinguished with the help of two categories of rights:

- formal rights (i.e. legal access to citizenship in form of methods of acquisition and codification of nationality provisions; civil and political rights; this dimension is connected to the state level) and
- substantive rights (social membership and participation in society as a whole; this dimension involves civil society) (Held 1991; Hammar 1990; Meehan 1991).

In the case of the latter, however, it is somewhat deceptive to refer to this form of citizenship as 'rights' in the same sense as in the case of formal citizenship. Substantive citizenship is not about concrete legal (statutory) rights but their wider practical realization within society and thus, should probably rather be referred to as 'liberties' (as suggested by Held 1991:22).

Ethnic minority groups in fact largely enjoy formal citizenship rights, with the most likely exception being political rights. Most civil rights, for example, such as personal liberty and access to justice through courts, are treated as human rights and thus, apply to every person regardless of nationality and citizenship (Bottomore, in: Marshall & Bottomore 1992). However, when including nationality laws revolving around the acquisition of formal citizenship based largely on the principle of ius sanguinis, racializing elements tend to be involved. Furthermore, there is a difference between having formal (i.e. legal) citizenship rights in theory and how these rights are 'translated' into practical terms (which is expressed here in terms of substantive citizenship). In particular, in the British case where membership of peoples from former colonies is accorded formal recognition, "this recognition is constructed in such a manner that their legitimate presence and participation in Britain are nearly always questioned" (Goulbourne 1991:2).

Equally important, therefore, is the substantive aspect of citizenship as a potential source of exclusionary practices, in particular if understood as 'social citizenship' in a broad sense as suggested by Roche (1992:3) including work, education, health, quality of life. Some of these practices in areas such as housing, work, and education have been taken up by British anti-discrimination legislation. I argue, therefore, that a definition of citizenship in the context of immigrants' settlement has to include the legal and political status of formal membership as well as the notion of participation in public life and recognition by civil society (substantive membership) in order to analyze the combined effects of nationalism and racism.

Husbands' (1992) dimensions of 'welcome' are another way of indicating the level of inclusion or exclusion of immigrant peoples with regard to their formal and substantive citizenship status. These dimensions are extracted from a mixture of legal, institutional and social spheres including the content of immigration (and integration) policies, employment policies, naturalization policies, social rights (i.e. access to social-welfare provisions and to collective-consumption goods such as social housing & public sector education), civil/industrial rights, political rights, equal-opportunity provisions and the general quality of reception given by the receiving country. The latter covers, for instance, the extent to which immigrants are targets of racist hostility and their depiction in the media. These elements help to operationalize the assessment of citizenship within the framework of nation-states which have become multi-cultural or multi-ethnic in composition and which are challenged by supra-national as well as sub-national developments.

## 6.3 Citizenship as a legal device - a historical perspective

Modern citizenship (as opposed to classical forms of citizenship in ancient Greece and Rome) is widely considered to have originated during the French Revolution of 1789 and is tied to the political and administrative framework of the *nation-state* (Turner 1986; Heater 1990; Hammar 1991; Roche 1992; Brubaker 1989; Dummett & Nicol 1990; van Steenbergen 1994). The historical process of territorial integration into states and the emergence of the nation-state resulted in the separation of peoples and the creation of categories for legitimate membership of national societies. Originally, citizenship developed from 'subjecthood' (*Untertanentum*) and was, thus, tied to residence (territorial or residential principle). As a result of territorial and political integration into nation-states and a corresponding shift to particularistic ideas about national identity, however, citizenship began to be more strongly linked to blood-relatedness (principle of ethnic descent). Thus, the process of boundary drawing vis-à-vis 'outside' and homogenizing or standardizing processes 'inside' led to the introduction of the principle of ethnic descent (*Abstammungsprinzip*). This continental European development was triggered by 'national awakening' (*nationales Erwachen*) and as a consequence, the cultural particularity of a people began to gain more importance (Bös 1993; Franz, in: Institut für Migrations- und Rassismusforschung 1992). Common features such as language, tradition, history and in particular the imagination of common descent provided the "kit for a 'we-consciousness' "(Franz, op.cit.:239). Today, in most western European countries, the principle of ius soli (territorial) and ius sanguinis (ethnic descent) exist side by side. The purest form of ius sanguinis exists in Germany, where the notion of Germanhood (Deutschtum) is still a strong element in the citizenship law.

I argue on similar lines to Bös (1993) that, despite any philosophical republican ideas of citizenship about parting company "from the idea of belonging to a pre-political community integrated on the basis of descent" (Habermas 1994:23), the definition of citizenship within the legal systems of Germany and Britain, if not even throughout the rest of western Europe, has adjusted during the last 200 years to the criterion of ethnic belonging (in the sense of being tied to nationality). This can be partly explained as a response to outgoing and incoming migratory movements. Thus, this development is prone to entail racializing effects.

### 6.3.1 *The English/British case*

Originally, the English/British citizenship law, which is considered as having the longest continuous history of codification (Bös 1993), was based on 'allegiance to the Crown'[4]. Every person who owed it became a 'British subject' and had the right of entry and settlement. Since before the Norman Invasion in 1066, a codified ius soli (born 'within His Majesty's dominions') was already established (Dummett & Nicol 1990). Since 1351 the ius sanguinis principle was enforced for the English successor to the throne so that members of the Royal family who were born abroad could become king or queen. The statute *De natis ultra mare* named a list of individuals "'which were born beyond the sea, out of the ligeance of England' and provided that they could inherit on the same terms as those born within the ligeance" (op.cit.:35-36). This statute was intended to provide for a very limited group of persons. Otherwise, the so-called *Calvin's Case* of 1608 became the most important point of reference for English/British law as it represents, within the context of the monarchy, a clear formulation of the 'ius soli' principle[5]. The rule and protection of the king obliged the individual to allegiance and to the position of the 'subject' (Bös 1993:629). The Glorious Revolution of 1688 did not replace this structure as the Parliament was declared the highest sovereign and not the people (Dummett & Nicol 1990:59-70). In 1870, an important change was introduced by the Naturalization Act. Until then, 'perpetual allegiance' was only terminated in the case of the individual's death. From 1870 on, however, subjects living abroad could renounce their citizenship, and naturalization within the dominions was made possible for the very first time.

During the period 1700 to the early 1800s, the Jews constituted one minority for whom the acquisition of citizenship was made difficult, if not impossible. The Jewish population who had been expelled in 1290 and only re-admitted in 1664 soon had legal restrictions placed upon them because of their different faith (Holmes 1979). One major limitation those Jews who were foreign-born had to encounter centred upon naturalization restrictions. "It was generally possible for foreigners to obtain naturalization through Parliament but this was not open to Jews since such petitioning was available only to those professing the Christian religion" and "it was not until 1825 that the sacramental test for naturalization was abolished." (op.cit.:8)[6].

After the Second World War, the British Nationality Act of 1948 was implemented as the result of the vagueness of the traditional law and as a response to growing nationalism in various Commonwealth countries initiating the transition from imperial to national Britain (Goulbourne 1991). With this Act, the principle of ius soli (birth on the territory of the United Kingdom-and-Colonies) was established alongside the principle of ius sanguinis (birth outside the territory to a father there born or there naturalized) (Dummett & Nicol 1990:135). Different categories of 'British subjects' were created:

- 'Citizens of the United Kingdom-and-Colonies',
- 'Citizens of independent Commonwealth countries' with special treatment of 'British Subjects without Citizenship',
- 'British Protected Persons', and
- the Irish (Bös 1993:629).

Thus, the general custom of acquisition by birth was now accompanied by acquisition by descent. The first generation living abroad obtained citizenship via the father's origin whilst following generations could become registered. Goulbourne stresses that the introduction of the BNA of 1948, which did not stop people from Commonwealth countries entering Britain by retaining the imperial definition of 'British'[7], was more a response to nationalism in the dominions and colonies and that it shows a sense for past responsibilities in the light of present realities on the part of politicians and governments.

From 1962, however, continuous immigration from the Commonwealth was brought under control by several changes towards implicit ius sanguinis. The restriction was that only those people whose parents or grandparents were born in Britain could enter freely. Thus, the tendency towards ius sanguinis starting slowly in 1351 and reinforced during the 1960s reached firm consolidation with the British Nationality Act of 1981 which is in principle a *ius sanguinis a patre et a matre* (Bös 1993:630). This historical development - i.e. the 1962 Commonwealth Immigrants Act, the 1971 Immigrants Act and the 1981 Nationality Act - clearly demonstrates the tendency towards linking citizenship with nationality and hence, towards involving an ethnic definition of Britishness by preventing the entry of people from non-white Commonwealth countries.

### 6.3.2 The German case

In the countries which were later to become the German Reich, the ius soli principle was common practice. Citizens were those born on German territory, however, citizenship could also be acquired through permission by the police or after a certain period of residence (e.g. after ten years in Prussia according to a ruling of 1818; Franz, in: Institut für Migrations- und Rassismusforschung 1992:238). Most of the southern German states had taken over this principle from the Code Napoléon. In 1842, Prussia amended its law by introducing the principle of ius sanguinis[8]. Article 13 of this law states "residence within Our State alone shall in future no longer determine qualification as a Prussian" (cited by Bös 1993:627; free translation).

The predecessor of today's still valid citizenship law of 1913 (*Reichs- und Staatsbürgerschaftsgesetz*) dates back to the 'law on acquisition and loss of federal and state citizenship' of 1870 which was in force in the then existing *Norddeutsche Bund* (north-German federation). With unification in 1871, this law was superseded by a modified version called the *Reichs- und Staatsbürgerschaftsgesetz*. On grounds of the Reich's federal structure, national (Reich) citizenship was acquired via federal state citizenship (Bös 1993:627). Thus, until 1934, only federal state citizenship in each of the states of the German Reich existed, but not a general German citizenship. Passports specified the holder as, for instance, 'Prussian' or 'Bavarian'. Even in 1931, the Prussian government still expelled 'undesirable aliens' to the neighbouring state of Hamburg (Engelmann 1991:23)[9].

The National Socialists were the first to institutionalize legally a central German citizenship (Räthzel 1995). Under their regime, the ius sanguinis adopted its most narrow definition by which in particular the Jewish population came to be excluded. Until Hitler's *Machtergreifung* (coming into power) it had been general practice to include Jewish citizens in the common principle of descent. However, as in Hitler's propagated ideology a real German had to be of Aryan descent, the people (*Volksgemeinschaft*) had to be 'cleansed' of such (Jewish) 'elements'. The first step was the removal of Jews from public, i.e. governmental and administrative, positions - a process which was started off with the Law for the Restoration of the Professional Civil Service of 7 April 1933 (Burleigh & Wippermann 1991). In 1933, the law on 'revocation of naturalization and deprivation of citizenship' was implemented which allowed the cancellation of citizenship of 'undesirable persons' (mostly Jews). After the abolition of particular citizenships in the federal states and the introduction of a single German citizenship, the next wave of anti-Semitic legislation was introduced to "achieve legal discrimination, segregation, and precision in the question of who was a Jew" (op.cit.:45). From 1935 onwards, legal claim to naturalization was abolished. These and other measures culminated in the Nuremberg Laws (Nürnberger Reichsgesetze) of 1935 in which a citizen (Reichsbürger) was defined as 'of German and kindred blood, who proves by conduct to be willing and qualified to serve the German people and the Reich' (Engelmann 1991:242). Under the Reich Citizenship Law, Jews were redefined as 'subjects' and distinguished from the definition of 'citizens to the Reich' and thus, deprived of their political and civil rights which were restricted to 'citizens' (Burleigh & Wippermann 1991).

For the Federal Republic, Engelmann (1991) and Räthzel (1995) both suggest that, although the Nuremberg 'Race' Laws are annulled, the idea that citizenship is linked to German nationality (by ethnic descent) has still remained in the 'Basic Law' (German constitution). This is reflected in the immediate granting of full citizenship to ethnic German immigrants (Aussiedler) and refugees from the former GDR (Übersiedler). The existence of article 116 of the 'Basic Law' in which ethnic Germans are defined as citizens of the FRG, if residing in the territory of the German Reich as of 1937, is, however, not only explained in terms of blood-relatedness, but also as a matter of moral and historical duty towards ethnic Germans in eastern Europe suffering from alleged or forced collaboration with the Nazis[10] (Wolf-Almanasreh 1992)[11]. Klusmeyer writes in this context that the 'framers' of the constitution saw themselves as "act[ing] on behalf of those Germans to whom participation [in establishing the constitutional order] was denied" (1993:84). Therefore, they wanted to ensure "that Germans outside the Western occupation zones would not, through the creation of this order, lose their claim to full rights of citizenship" (ibid.). To this end, the Article 116 was established guaranteeing the right of repatriation to any person who had been "admitted to the territory of the German Reich within the frontiers of 31 December 1937 as refugee or expellee of German stock (*Volkszugehörigkeit)* or as the spouse or descendant of such person" (ibid.)[12]. Moreover, any amendments in the citizenship law during the immediate post-war period would have had to acknowledge the separation of Germany and thus, would have destroyed the deliberate provisional character of the (pre-unification)

Federal Republic (Bös 1993). The 'framers' envisaged this provisional state to last until the "entire German people could achieve in free self-determination the unity and freedom of Germany" (Klusmeyer 1993:85). Therefore, it was impossible at this stage to create an individual's citizenship irrespective of ethnic nationality. Thus, there are convincing historical and political reasons for not abandoning the ethnic component by altering the citizenship law in favour of ius soli, in particular during the immediate post-war period. However, it is less understandable, and most of the above mentioned authors agree, that ius soli was not introduced into the new constitution as a *supplement* (see also John 1990). Even less justifiable is the fact that reunification has not resulted in the abandonment of the *sole* principle of ius sanguinis. Today, the same claims to citizenship cannot be denied to 'foreigners' who have been residing in Germany for long periods or who were even born there.

The above showed the development towards a clear link between the legal notions of citizenship and nationality in both Britain and Germany. Although this link has a longer history in the case of Germany, it has to be remarked again that in the British case, *any* clear legal definition did not exist until 1948 or even 1981.

During the immediate post-war period, both countries had to come to terms with their reduced territorial sizes and with past responsibilities as reflected in preferential treatment of *Aussiedler/Übersiedler* in Germany and Commonwealth citizens in Britain (in form of immediate granting of citizenship/nationality). In the latter case, post-war developments went further to eventually exclude non-white members of former British territories from British citizenship. Thus, it does not seem to be too far fetched to claim that there is a parallel of ethnic Germans and mainly white Commonwealth citizens and the way in which these two groups are given preferential treatment in terms of access to German or British citizenship.

The following section will look into the effects of the above described shift towards an ethnic definition of formal citizenship for post-war labour migrants.

## 6.4 Formal citizenship in the context of post-war labour migration

### 6.4.1 The British case

The acceptance of labour migrants followed very different patterns in Germany and Britain. In the latter case, *foreign* workers have formed a very small proportion of its migrant workers. When labour recruitment started in 1956, it was from the West Indies and thereafter from the Indian sub-continent, although the highest proportion of migrant labour came in actual fact from Ireland (Miles 1982a; Layton-Henry 1990). The Ireland Act from 1949 vested the Irish with the same rights as those of every other UK citizen. Caribbean and Asian migrants to Britain were British subjects, either directly as members of British colonies or as citizens of British Commonwealth countries. Thus, they benefited from the residues of the imperial notion of subjecthood which viewed citizenship as allegiance to the Crown resulting in an idea of a common citizenship with freedom of migration throughout the former Empire. In this capacity, the Irish and Commonwealth immigrants had exactly the same political, civil and social (narrow sense) rights as indigenous citizens (Brubaker 1989; Dummett & Nicol 1990; Layton-Henry 1990). Until 1948, all persons within the dominions of the monarch were British subjects. There was no specific citizenship status for colonies, for Britain itself or even for independent Commonwealth countries.

The new situation of the dismantling of the Empire, of ex-colonial subjects of geographical and cultural distance entering Britain, and of the notion of common allegiance to the Crown giving way to the notion of rights (Dummett & Nicol 1990) resulted in the 'need' to slow down immigration and to define legally who was British. This 'need' was met in form of consecutive immigration acts culminating in the British Nationality Act of 1981.

Although citizenship has traditionally been easy to acquire or to reclaim and has been detached from the traditional nation-state, the introduction of immigration legislation and nationality laws were to make the acquisition of citizenship more difficult and to tie access to citizenship rights more closely to nationality. The automatic right to British citizenship by Commonwealth countries' nationals has officially come to an end since the Nationality Act of 1981, and the trend has been to treat Commonwealth and non-Commonwealth citizens on the same basis as far as immigration and citizenship rights are concerned. However, the 'patriality clause' - introduced by the 1971 Immigrants Act - allows privileged access to UK citizenship for people with a close connection with the UK through descent from a British parent or grandparent (and they tend to be 'white') and thus, it is another indication of a stronger link to nationality. Moreover, until the Nationality Act of 1981, all persons born in any British territory in any part of the world could claim British citizenship whether or not their parents were British citizens or legally settled. Thus, the UK traditionally used to be the prime example of a country where the principle of ius soli has applied. After the Second World War, although countries belonging to the British Commonwealth had begun enacting their own citizenship legislation, their citizens continued to be British subjects until the 1981 Act. Now, only those born in the territory of the UK become British citizens provided that one parent has been born or settled in the UK - a fact which does not have serious implications for the ethnic minorities under view here as most of them settled in the UK some time before this Act existed. However, the whole 'package' of legislation dealing with immigration (in particular the 'patriality clause') and nationality/citizenship is suggested by some authors as racializing (Gilroy 1987).

As a whole, for first generation immigrants and their descendants from ex-colonies, the legacy of the imperial notion of 'Civis Brittanicus sum' has had beneficial implications and resulted in their enjoyment of full political, civil and social (narrow sense) rights. However, the idea of a common citizenship and the freedom to migrate seems to be purely theoretical, as Rex & Tomlinson have pointed out (1979), especially in the absence of a Bill of Rights, and was only acceptable to the indigenous people as long as they were not exercised. In this sense, it does not seem too far fetched to argue that common citizenship during the days of the Empire, when encompassing an enormous range of ethnically and culturally different peoples, was not more than an 'imagined' citizenship meaning that as soon as immigration actually took place, restrictive laws started to be introduced. Nonetheless, these specific historical circumstances, even if lasting in practice only for a short time, resulted in a formal citizenship status for first generation immigrants and their descendants which is - at least in theory - totally equal to indigenous people which is fairly exceptional throughout western Europe.

### 6.4.2 The German case

In the case of Germany, the close link between the notions of nationality and citizenship has appeared from much earlier and has been clearer in both citizenship laws and the (written) constitution. Thus, with regard to the automatic right to citizenship, a German citizen is in general at the same time a German national as the citizenship/nationality law is solely governed by the principle of ius sanguinis.

When labour migrants were recruited during the 1960s predominantly from southern Europe[13] and Turkey, they did not only enter Germany as foreigners, but also originally as guest-workers. In this capacity, these workers were not expected to become settled, long-term residents with claims to citizenship rights - an expectation which proved false after the recruitment halt of 1973 when large-scale family reunification began. Therefore, although they enjoy in theory all social rights (narrow sense), political rights - locally as well as nationally[14] - are denied to them. Civil rights are restricted as the law still allows German administration to forbid foreign residents taking part in political activities when important national interests are (allegedly) endangered. Freedom of opinion can be restricted as well in order to protect public order and security (Layton-Henry 1990). The 'Kurdish problem' is a recent example of civil rights being limited for long-term immigrants for fear of disruption of public order (source: newspaper articles[15]). The only right is that of the residential permit which entails the permission to work.

In the absence of ius soli, second and all successive generations remain legally speaking 'foreigners', governed by the so-called 'Foreigners' Law' (Ausländergesetz). Without German citizenship, they have no political rights and only restricted civil rights in the same way as their parents or grandparents. As opposed to Britain, where dual citizenship is common practice, German law does not allow the holding of two passports, although there are exceptional circumstances under which this is possible. Nevertheless, it is officially considered as highly undesirable and there has always been reluctance to approve of dual citizenship. Naturalization, it might be assumed, is under these circumstances relatively speaking easy, but this is not the case. In Britain, by comparison, a person born there who is not entitled to British citizenship at birth, is entitled to be registered as a British citizen after the age of ten years, providing he/she has not been absent from the UK for more than ninety days in any of his/her first ten years. Otherwise, citizenship can be acquired by registration or naturalization. The latter is subject to a condition of residence of between three and five years (de Rham, in: Layton-Henry 1990). The knowledge of English, Scottish or Welsh is required as well as a 'clean criminal record' and a 'good character' (Bös 1993). Germany, on the other hand, has never officially been regarded as a country of immigration. As a result, there is more of a 'protectionist' approach towards the naturalization of foreigners, and the procedures are regarded as among the toughest in western Europe (Cohn-Bendit & Schmid 1992:333). Naturalization is referred to as a matter of discretion (Ermessen) and should only be effected if in the interest of the German Republic (no matter whether it is in the interest of the immigrant) (Bös 1993:628). Among the minimum prerequisites for naturalization are a ten-year period of residence, a clean criminal record, accommodation in Germany, a regular income, good command of the German language, and renunciation of the original citizenship is necessary[16] (Cohn-Bendit & Schmid 1992:331-32). Moreover, it is desirable for a whole family to have a uniform citizenship which means all members should naturalize at the same time (however, this is not obligatory).

Until 1990 - the year when the 'New Foreigners' Law' (Neues Ausländergesetz) was passed - it was not possible to acquire citizenship as of right. Since then, naturalization still remains a very 'complicated procedure' (Forudastan, in: taz, 25.04.90) and has only marginally improved. Juvenile 'foreigners' between the age of sixteen and twenty-three who have been living in Germany for eight years and who went to school for six years can legally claim German citizenship (but again, they would have to renounce their parents' citizenship). Moreover, the fees are reduced to DM 100 (about £ 40). The other 'category' of 'foreigners' who have the same right to citizenship as juveniles are those who have been living in Germany for fifteen years and who have, in the case of unemployment, not caused the loss of their job themselves - subject to the same condition of having to renounce their original citizenship. Apart from the introduction of a legal right to citizenship, the New Foreigners' Law is generally regarded as having had no major positive impact on the 'foreigners' status, in some respects it has even worsened their situation when compared with the old law (e.g. deportation is facilitated, 'data protection' is completely removed) (Forudastan, in: taz, 25.04.90).

Newspaper articles carry information of a recent amendment to the citizenship/nationality law (Hannoversche Allgemeine Zeitung, 18.11.94; taz, 14.11.94; taz, 15.11.94). The latest development in the question of formal citizenship has arisen from new coalition talks between CDU/CSU and FDP after the last general election in October 1994. Pressurized by the FDP, the CDU/CSU was prepared to compromise with the following new rule: Third generation 'foreigners' shall be granted automatic formal citizenship provided that one of their parents had been born in Germany. When reaching the age of eighteen, they have to decide which citizenship they are willing to renounce. Thus, dual citizenship is still not allowed. This new rule has been ironically referred to as '*Schnupperstaatsangehörigkeit*' ('sniffle or sniff citizenship') as it implies a 'tit-bit' acquisition of citizenship (taz, 21.11.94). Moreover, it does not give any protection from deportation nor any help in case of personal conflicts with regard to ethnic origin (Frankfurter Rundschau, 14.11.94). This new development does not result in any profound changes towards generally granting long-term 'foreign' residents formal citizenship, but offers only another slow step in a piecemeal process.

In terms of formal citizenship, the above shows that post-war labour migrants in Britain, although on the basis of particular historical circumstances, have the most preferable formal citizenship status within western Europe. They enjoy full civil and political rights, whereas labour migrants in Germany are denied formal citizenship to a large extent as they are not vested with any voting rights and the safeguarding of civil rights is, in particular for non-EC nationals, infringed because of their insecure residential status. Generally, 'foreigners' in Germany have a much more insecure formal status. In addition, the acquisition of citizenship via naturalization is among the hardest procedures in western Europe.

The comparison shows that the link between nationality and citizenship as a *legal device* affects 'immigrants' more in Germany than in Britain. Although the latter has acquired with the 1981 BNA a nationality law which is based on ius sanguinis, most of the ex-colonial immigrants and their descendants are not effected by it. In the German case, the link between nationality and citizenship would be defensible (especially by having in mind the historical circumstances as explained in an earlier section) if naturalization was an open and straight-forward process for all permanent residents, but this is not the case. Furthermore, recent amendments have not had a major impact on improving this situation. Therefore, the link between citizenship and nationality (and thus the combined effects of nationalism and racism) has remained a major obstacle for labour migrants' acquisition of formal citizens' rights. However, this link does not only affect formal citizenship, but also the substantive side which is subject to the following section.

## 6.5  Substantive citizenship in the context of post-war labour migration

Substantive citizenship tends to be less easily identifiable as formal citizenship, as it refers to what in Marshall's view is described as not only encompassing rights to a "modicum of economic security" (i.e. social rights in a narrow sense), but also entailing a more far-reaching right "to share in the full social heritage and to live the life of a civilized being according to the standards prevailing in the society" (1950:11).  Thus, substantive 'rights' refer to 'social citizenship' which is "concerned with the welfare of people as citizens, taking 'welfare' in a broad sense to include such things as work, education, health and quality of life" (Roche 1992:3). To recall Husbands' 'dimensions of welcome', substantive citizenship includes all aspects of a 'general quality of reception given by the receiving country' which covers the extent of racism (and nationalism) immigrants are exposed to.

Substantive citizenship seems, therefore, to be operationable, for instance, within the scope of studies into elite racist discourse by Van Dijk (1993b) and Jäger (1992) in which the subtle racism of elitist groups such as politicians, academics, and industrial elites are scrutinized. Essed's *Everyday Racism* (1991) and Jäger's *BrandSätze - Rassismus im Alltag* (1993) add to this a non-elitist dimension by showing how racist attitudes and discourse are part of ethnic minorities' daily experience[17]. Other studies which explore the role of the media in connection with ethnic minorities and/or racism, such as Gordon & Rosenberg's *Daily Racism - The press and black people in Britain* (1989), the Council of Europe's Colloquy *Migrants and the Media - from 'guest-workers' to linguistic and cultural minorities* (1987), and Van Dijk's *Racism and the Press* (1991) show the strong tendency in the media to depict these minorities as 'problem makers' and a burden of the welfare state, and thus to the general public. Similarly, the publication *"Ausländerkriminalität" oder "kriminelle Ausländer" - Anmerkungen zu einem sensiblen Thema* (1993b; in English: Foreigners' Crime or criminal foreigners - remarks on a sensitive subject) by the Federal Commissioner for Foreigners' Affairs reveals how police statistics tend to portray 'foreigners' as generally more prone to criminal offences than indigenous Germans. Geissler & Marissen's study *Kriminalität und  Kriminalisierung junger Ausländer - Die tickende Zeitbombe - ein Artefact der Kriminalstatistik* (1990; English title "crime and criminalization of juvenile foreigners - the ticking time bomb - an artefact of criminal statistics") confirms the findings of the Commissioner. On the 'British' side, Gordon's *Black people and the criminal law* illustrates how "the law is not colour-blind, but a means by which black people have been subject to a process of criminalization" (1992:190) whereby he offers concrete examples, such as 'riot trials', juries, and sentencing. In chapter three of *There Ain't No Black in the Union Jack* (1987) in which the law and black criminality is topicalized, Gilroy concludes that "[t]he idea that blacks are a high crime group and the related notion that their criminality is an expression of their distinctive culture have become integral to British racism in the period since the 'rivers of blood' speech[18]." (p. 109).

The Report of the Committee of Inquiry into Racism and Xenophobia by the European Parliament (1990) confirms racist tendencies not only within British and German society, but also suggests a European-wide rise of anti-black and anti-immigrant movements, in particular in form of organized right-wing extremism. Unorganized, more individual hostile attitudes are described in Friedrich & Schubarth's study on *Ausländerfeindliche und rechtsextreme Orientierungen bei ostdeutschen Jugendlichen* (1991; English title: hostile and right-wing orientations with East-German youths) and in Schönwälder's study *Zu viele Ausländer in Deutschland? Zur Entwicklung ausländerfeindlicher Einstellungen in der Bundesrepublik* (1991; English title: Too many foreigners in Germany? About the development of hostile attitudes in the Federal Republic). The former authors base the increasing hostile and (individual) right-wing attitudes on the 'nationalistic-authoritarian syndrome' characterized by elements such as feelings of superiority and intolerance towards the 'foreigner'. The latter author mentions, too, that hostility towards foreigners is based on 'handed down potentials for nationalism and racism' (tradierte Potentiale von Nationalismus und Rassismus).

Another issue is racially motivated violence. Baimbridge, Burkitt & Macey quote official statistics by the UK Home Office stating that racially motivated attacks rose from 4,383 in 1988 to 8,779 in 1993, although the majority of such incidents are said to go unrecorded (1994:427). The information brochure by the Campaign Against Racism & Fascism (carf) continuously reports on racially motivated attacks and deaths (see edition No. 18, 1994:4-8). The edited book by Björgo & Witte titled *Racist Violence in Europe* (1993) provides an analytical approach to the issue of racially motivated violence (see also Gordon, 1990, on the same issue). In addition, there seems to be evidence of discriminatory and racist attitudes within state institutions, such as the police-force (taz 19.04.94; Korell 1994; Gordon 1993; Holdaway 1996).

Furthermore, there are other studies which highlight the housing, working, educational and health conditions of members of ethnic minority communities by giving concrete evidence of their living standards as compared to the general standards prevailing in German and British societies (see, e.g., Skellington & Morris 1992).

This list could be endless. The general message in all these studies and publications seems to be that, whatever the formal citizenship status, the fact of being of different ethnic origin seems to have a negative impact on the ethnic minorities' substantive citizenship status within civil society as reflected by studies on the media, right-wing extremist groups, racist motivated violence, and 'everyday racism'. Most of these studies implicitly or explicitly indicate the symbiotic existence of nationalism and racism[19] as expressed in Euro/Whitecentrism and feelings of superiority by biologically and culturally denigrating ethnic minorities (see for examples Essed's table of 'Frequencies of the Forms of Everyday Racism', 1991:180). In rough outlines, but by acknowledging more complex processes, Friedrich & Schubarth view uncertain economic, political and social conditions as responsible for rising nationalism *and* racism whereby their study focuses on East Germany after reunification with the West. Here, the theme of 'crisis' is strongly indicated, and in this context, the mere presence of peoples of non-European ethnic background tends to be abused for political purposes (e.g. during election campaigns) by a tendency to put the blame for general problems on immigrants as the easy option. In such an environment, the existence of anti-discrimination legislation could be regarded as one concrete means of improving ethnic minorities' substantive citizenship status.

### 6.5.1  Situation of the first immigrants

*The British context*  The socio-economic situation arising from first immigration into Britain is characterized by Rex & Tomlinson as a rather antagonistic relationship of formal and substantive citizenship with regard to ex-colonial immigrants and is therefore, when compared with most of continental Europe, outstanding in two ways. On the one hand, black and Asian communities share fully equal formal citizenship with their indigenous British counterparts, whilst on the other hand, immigration of West Indians in particular has a colour dimension with a specific history that no other immigrant peoples in Europe have, viz. the combination of slavery and colonialism. This has a very distinct impact on the presence of blacks in the UK, and in Rex and Tomlinson's words, West Indians have to be recognized as people "who were taken into captivity" (1979:292) and that captivity meant not only slavery but also cultural suppression. However, Asians too suffer from the legacy of colonial society, but maybe even more so, they also experience discrimination on grounds of their religion (Modood 1992b)[20].

In general, when immigration from ex-colonies began on the basis of freedom to migrate, indigenous British people, confronted with culturally distant immigrants entering in unprecedented numbers, tended to react in terms of the roles which the immigrants played in British colonial history (Rex & Tomlinson 1979). Integration into British society of ex-colonial immigrants is, thus, described by Rex & Tomlinson as a 'traumatic experience' for lower middle- and working class people, because they tended to feel degraded themselves through having to accept these people as equals, as fellow workers and neighbours. To live with black and Asian people was perceived as a threat to one's own status. Rex & Tomlinson, therefore, suggest that the deterioration which indigenous residents in Handsworth (the main focus of their study) came to anticipate was not an accelerated physical deterioration due to the misuses of buildings by black immigrants, but simply a deterioration of the area due to the fact that they were thought of as inferior because of colonial people living there. The above authors believe that this is a more important factor than that of the cultural differences which did exist, but they argue it is more a matter of the place viewed as appropriate for colonial people to occupy in an imperial structure. The immigrants, thus, found themselves in the place allocated to them: The range of jobs occupied by West Indians and Asians was concentrated at the lower levels of the occupational system, they were under-protected by their unions in times of trouble, they worked longer hours for the money they earned and did more shift work. Their houses, apart from the council-built houses, were the worst houses in the city and ones which had not yet been demolished even though eligible for it. Their children went to schools which were largely segregated or were immigrant majority schools. In these schools, they were held back by linguistic and cultural difficulties to which teachers tended to react according to racial stereotypes. Asians suffered in particular form the lack of fluency in the English language, while the West Indians found themselves in a paradoxical situation as they actually shared British culture more than non-English speaking Asians (and herein lay the problem, as argued by Rex & Tomlinson: They had always been taught things which were not necessarily connected to their cultural background, and they had always been called upon to appreciate a culture in which they were systematically downgraded)[21]. The above authors claim that Asian children had less trouble in school, once they had overcome language problems, because they were aided by two factors: They had a degree of security in that their culture had not been destroyed and secondly, the instrumental attitude their parents had towards education helped them to be quite successful. Their problems tended to arise at higher levels. Even though they achieved a good education, they could often not get the corresponding jobs (see also Brown 1984). It is suggested by Rex & Tomlinson that second and subsequent generations who were born and raised in Britain, are likely to be more frustrated by the experience of discrimination as they have higher expectations or different expectations not shared by their parents.

The above is similarly expressed by Layton-Henry when noting that the "feeling and behaviour of native white British people...towards Afro-Caribbean and Asian migrant workers, and their images of them, were influenced by the knowledge that these migrants had been subject peoples of the British empire" (1993:9).

Further studies, such as the early work by Rose et al. (1969) and by Brown (1984) underpin the, comparatively speaking, worse housing and working conditions of immigrants. It seems, therefore, as if the specific historical link of post-war labour migrants with Britain has not only had a positive outcome in terms of equal formal citizenship, but is also partly responsible for a disadvantaged socio-economic position in British society.

*The German context* In the German case, the above explanations of the formal citizenship status of immigrants in the Federal Republic seem to render the discussion about substantive citizenship almost superfluous, as the majority of immigrants do not enjoy a full formal citizenship status which is the first and necessary step towards substantive citizenship. However, in the case of the Turks, there is a slowly increasing number of naturalizations, in particular since the introduction of the New Foreigner's Law (Beauftragte der Bundesregierung für die Belange der Ausländer 1993a:167). Therefore, it is worth mentioning a few of the aspects which indicate similar socio-political problems of immigrants in Germany as in the British example. Moreover, despite largely lacking formal citizenship, and thus legal inclusion, increasing integration on the part of the Turkish minority has been taking place (Sen, in: Leggewie & Senoçak 1993).

The first generation of immigrants into Germany experienced equally bad, if not worse, housing and working conditions as in the British case, as they were recruited as 'guest-workers' and thus, were expected to return after a few years. This fact might have justified the pushing of these workers into the least appealing jobs as well as the exploitative treatment recognized by some Germans as indicated in the 'undercover' operation of Wallraff described in his book *Ganz unten* (1985; English title "The Lowest of the Low"). The life experiences of first generation immigrants have been described by Schiffauer (1991) and Akçam (1993) highlighting the bad socio-economic conditions under which the first guest-workers lived and worked. Many immigrants first lived in hostels provided by the companies they worked for. Others went onto the housing market in search for accommodation, which did not necessarily improve their living situation. An article in the *Handelsblatt* - a major economist newspaper - from February 1967 (as quoted by Herbert, 1986:202-203), for example, describes the most appalling living conditions of Greek and Turkish guest-workers. Crammed into dirty, only very basically furnished rooms of small size (one example mentions 20 square meters for six men), treated in a very inhumane and patronizing way by their landlords/ladies, these workers are quoted as having had to pay a extortionate amount of rent. Since 1973 - the phase of family reunification - most immigrants looked for accommodation on the general housing market. A concentration in certain areas took place where housing was cheap, but also comparatively worse, which led to the creation of 'ghettos' (such as Berlin-Kreuzberg, e.g.). This happened mainly for two reasons: 1. the 'myth of return' was still held onto and cheap housing was required to keep savings as high as possible; 2. a general attitude of rejection on the part of landlords/ladies in better residential areas (Sen, in: Leggewie & Senoçak 1993).

Apart from a generally bad housing situation, immigrants were also concentrated in unskilled or low skilled jobs in rather dirty and dangerous environments (Castles & Kosack 1973). They tended to do the kind of jobs indigenous people began to reject. All these aspects indicate that there was hardly any 'dimension of welcome' - to use Husbands' term - which has partly to do with the fact that these labour migrants came originally as 'guests' (although this term is hypocritical as guests are usually treated preferably) as well as with the fact that Germany has never officially been considered as a country of immigration, and thus, has never had concrete immigration policies (Martin & Miller 1990). This also explains the almost complete lack of inclusionary measures, such as education policies for immigrants' children. Only after 1973 (the year of the recruitment halt) did such policies slowly began to be considered (Castles 1995).

To sum up, the substantive citizenship of first generations in particular was affected by the social position of these immigrants and their perception by civil society - in Britain as 'colonial subjects' and in Germany as 'guest-workers' who would return to their countries of origin after a short period of time. In the latter case, therefore, it seems to be understandable that the guest-worker system did not involve governmentally sponsored immigration and inclusion policies. This situation should, however, have gradually been reversed after 1973 with the arrival or birth of family members.

### 6.5.2 Subsequent generations

*The British case* It is difficult to assess to what extent the situation has improved for the generations of ethnic minorities born and brought up in German or British society. It depends very much on the criteria chosen to make this assessment. In terms of general acceptance, it is assumed here that in the British case, colonial attitudes have faded away with the emergence of majority generations born after the dismantling of the Empire. Multi-ethnicity of British society seems to have found general acceptance - as reflected in a shift from assimilationist to pluralist policies (Castles 1995:301) - and upward social mobility of ethnic minorities, to a certain extent, can certainly not be denied (in the context of the Indian minority see Modood 1992b). Anti-discrimination legislation, too, seems to have had some positive outcomes.

However, since the time of first immigration, the economic situation has dramatically changed, and the long-term recession has resulted in high unemployment which is suggested by many authors as having had a worse effect on ethnic minorities than on the majority. What this situation has certainly brought about is a re-emerging protective, narrow nationalism (Goulbourne 1991) represented not only by certain successes of the BNP, but also in statements by politicians such as Powell, Churchill Junior, Thatcher, Tebitt and Portillo who "openly seek to delineate 'the Other'" (Cohen 1994:209).

Ethnic minority youths are still faced with many problems that their 'white' counterparts do not experience in a similar way. Research done by Wrench & Solomos into the "processes of discrimination which exclude young migrant-descended school-leavers from training and employment opportunities" shows the still existing and often "subtle and indirect way that institutional procedures perpetuate racial discrimination" (1993:157).

Collinson notes that the integration of 'second' and 'third' generations[22] has attracted special attention "since it has become increasingly apparent that the marginal position of immigrants in housing, employment and public life has tended to be perpetuated in the case of their children and their children's offspring" (1994:109). Levels of unemployment among descendants of immigrants are often higher than among the immigrants themselves (ibid.). In this context, the notion of 'inherited disadvantage' seems to be highly suggestive - 'inherited' not as a biological fact, but in a socio-political sense. It is, therefore, probably safe to say that the exclusionary effects of racialization which cut across class and gender (as suggested by Anthias & Yuval-Davis 1992 and Essed 1991) have still got a major impact on the daily lives of ethnic minorities in Britain.

Recent studies - in particular those on ethnic minorities' labour market position (such as by Owen & Green 1992) - have pointed out that the experience of the various ethnic minority groups cannot be seen anymore as a monolithic block and that any attempt to generalize about 'ethnic minorities' is fraught with difficulty (Mason 1995). Jones' re-analysis of the Labour Force Survey, for instance, reveals that the position of ethnic groups is becoming more complex as the experience of members of different groups begins to diverge (Jones 1996). Male members of some minority groups are beginning to experience employment patterns increasingly similar to those of white men (i.e. African Asian, Chinese, and Indian men). Among those of Afro-Caribbean, Bangladeshi, and Pakistani origin, however, there is much less evidence that suggests any progress. Some groups display remarkable polarization: Both Indian and Chinese men are represented in large numbers in the highest as well as in the lowest job categories. "This may suggest that men from these two groups enter a relatively narrow range of occupations, either at the top or at the bottom end of the job market." (Jones 1996:72).

Successive studies (Brown 1984; Jones 1996) have shown that persons of ethnic minority groups are more likely to be unemployed than 'white' people. Even among Indians who are usually identified as *the* group experiencing progress (Modood 1992b), the unemployment rate was about 25% higher than the rate among 'white' men and twice as high among women (Owen 1993b:6). Young people are in particular affected by unemployment: The rates for 16 to 24-year-olds are higher than those for the economically active as a whole (Jones 1996:127; Owen 1993b:8). Studies on earnings have revealed that patterns resulted from earlier studies (Brown 1984) have remained the same during the 1980s and 1990s (Mason 1995): Ethnic minority employees earn between ten and thirty percent less than their 'white' counterparts (Jones 1996:81). The growth of minority enterprises in recent years has also attracted much interest. Self-employment is generally more common among ethnic minority groups than among the 'white' population, and more among those classified as 'Asian' than among others. Ram estimates that more than one-fifth of Asians in employment are either self-employed or employers (1992: 601). However,

Bangladeshis are much less likely to be self-employed than other South Asians (Owen 1993b:4-6). Ram has revealed in this study (1992) the specific problems most of these enterprises encounter, partly because they are run as 'family businesses'. He concludes that many employers still faced severe 'racial' constraints which had negative effects on the development of their businesses. He argues, however, that racism "is a force that employers manage rather than accede to." (1992:601).

With regard to education, there is evidence that members of ethnic minority groups are more likely to remain in full-time education between the ages of sixteen and nineteen than are their 'white' counterparts (Jones 1996). Ethnic monitoring has shown that South Asians were admitted to institutions of higher education in larger numbers than were the same age groups in the population as a whole. Those of Afro-Caribbean origin were represented by a percentage that matched their presence in the population as a whole (Mason 1995). It has been suggested that high rates of unemployment by ethnic minority youths might explain this higher rate of prolonged education. Jones showed that for those no longer in full-time education, 'white' men are generally more qualified than members of other ethnic groups. Bangladeshi and Pakistanis are the least well qualified (1996:36). Those of African Asian and Indian origin tend to be better qualified than 'white' people. Mason has pointed out, however, that one should not disregard the issue of continuing disadvantage. Pakistanis and Bangladeshis appear to be less qualified than other minorities, and Afro-Caribbeans are more likely to be in possession of vocational qualifications than those which are 'purely' academic. Also, despite higher levels of achievement, there is evidence of 'everyday racism' - for instance, as part of ethnic minorities' experience at school (Mason 1995:71-76).

Housing is also an area still characterized by patterns of disadvantage and discrimination. More than twice as many ethnic minority as 'white' households do not have self-contained accommodation (Mason 1995:89), and more Pakistani and Bangladeshi lack central heating (op. cit.:91).

Jones' re-analysis of the Labour Force Survey data and the census data reviewed have shown that the labour market experiences among Britain's ethnic minorities are increasingly diverging. The growth of a middle class of professional and managerial workers among some ethnic minority groups might suggest that the class structure of some groups is converging towards that of the 'white' population. According to Mason, however, the conclusion - as often arrived at by the political right - that "the success of members of some groups gives the lie to the claim that discrimination lies at the root of differences in achievement and opportunity between groups" (1995:124) should be treated with caution. He points out that marked differences remain in the performance of members of different ethnic groups and that those of Pakistani and Bangladeshi descent suffer in particular from the lowest positions in the labour market.

Moreover, the distinctive patterns of exclusion experienced by British Muslims - regardless of their class position - should also not be ignored.

*The German case* Similarly, in Germany the fashionable idea of multi-culturalism (Cohn-Bendit & Schmid 1992; Geissler 1991) has gained a higher level of awareness and acceptance by the majority. Despite these first signs of changes in attitudes, studies of the Turkish minority have shown how relative the improvement of subsequent generations' socio-economic position[23] is. There is evidence for some social upward mobility. Sen, for instance, has done work on Turkish entrepreneurs. According to him, in 1985, there were 22,000 enterprises run by the Turkish minority - a figure which has increased to 35,000 in 1992. This trend has contributed to the establishment of a Turkish middle class (in: Leggewie & Senoçak 1993: 27). Seventy-five% of these businesses are run as 'family businesses', which means that there could be similar problems as in the British context with regard to management and expansion (Ram 1992).

In educational terms, more and more children of immigrants complete their school education and thus, gain the necessary qualifications to get a good job training. This happens mostly at the level of *Mittlere Reife* (GCSE level). They still remain underrepresented in tertiary education (there are only 16,000 Turkish university students; Migration News 1996a) and secondary schools (only 22% of foreign youths attend these schools - 11% less than German youths; Mansel & Hurrelmann 1993:175), but they are over-represented in *Hauptschulen* (pre-GCSE level; school leavers are usually fifteen years old) and *Sonderschulen* (special needs schools). Hence, there seems to be evidence for "structural disadvantage" (Wagner, in: Leggewie & Senoçak 1993:106). Foreign youths are now increasingly interested in gaining professional skills as part of vocational training schemes, but a report quoted by Sen concluded that compared to 1984/85, foreign youths could improve their participatory quota in such schemes by only 1.3% (in: Leggewie & Senoçak 1993: 29). Almost double as many indigenous German adolescents than their foreign counterparts had been successful in finding a trainee post (Ausbildungsplatz) with the help of job centres (ibid.). Eighty-six% of the foreign youths under twenty years of age who are jobless have not learned an occupation (Migration News 1996a). A study undertaken by Wilpert shows that in 1985, "'foreign youths were two to three times more likely to be registered as unemployed than their German peers" (quoted by Collinson 1994:109). Moreover, almost 90% of those who were working occupied manual jobs and only 20% of those were employed as skilled workers (ibid.). This has not changed much: According to Mansel & Hurrelmann, foreign youths are five times more often unemployed or in unskilled jobs (1993:176). Since reunification, jobs have become even more scarce, and 'foreign' residents might find it even harder to find employment.

One of the main problems in Germany remains the legal aspect and thus, the fact that most labour migrants and their descendants do not have formal citizenship. Also, anti-discrimination legislation does not exist in a clearly defined and operational way as in Britain. Mansel & Hurrelmann (1993) summarized these aspects as the result of their report of a youth survey of the reasons for the increase in psycho-social stress in young foreigners growing up in Germany, undertaken during 1989 and 1990: There have been no differences in the evaluation of peer group interaction and leisure-time pursuits. However, the picture changed after the transition from school to work. Foreign adolescents were obliged to accept jobs with a lower social status and were frequently unable to realize their vocational options. They scored higher on emotional tension, and foreign girls had lower self-esteem than their German peers. The authors concluded that these findings are not particularly due to a low level of integration or to growing up in two different cultures. Daily discrimination in interaction with Germans, public administration, and the structures of social and legal inequality seem to be far more relevant. This is unlikely to change in the post-reunification period where huge socio-economic problems have created a climate of narrow nationalism with rising anti-foreigner sentiments and racially motivated violence.

For both countries, it can be said that the continuing terminology of 'race' and '*Ausländer*' also indicates social exclusion for subsequent generations to a greater or lesser extent. Furthermore, it should be noted for both countries that most of the recent studies mentioned in the more general section on substantive citizenship, such as the studies on racism and the media as well as on 'everyday racism', cover expressions of racism during the 1980s and early 1990s. Thus, they refer not only to first immigrants, but also (or even more so) to those generations born and brought up in Germany or Britain. This type of discourse in Germany, however, hides exactly this fact as these non-immigrant generations are always referred to (in the media, in political, and in 'everyday' discourse) as foreigners in the same way as their parents or grandparents.

As a result, it can be said that, despite differences in ethnic minorities' formal status, on the substantive level racism and nationalism in combined form continue to have exclusionary effects on ethnic or immigrant minorities to a lesser or greater extent in both countries.

The discussion of citizenship, however, does not end here as there is the European dimension to consider. The implications of the emergence of European citizenship for ethnic minorities in Germany and Britain are, therefore, subject of the next section.

## 6.6 European citizenship

The issue of citizenship has gained a new dimension with the finalization of the Maastricht Treaty - not only in terms of supra-nationality, but also as it involves scope for sub-national innovations. It is the aim of this section to investigate whether the European level offers any different provisions for ethnic minorities' citizenship or whether the nationally occurring effects of nationalism and racism are merely perpetuated. In this context, the issue of European citizenship functioning (or having the potential to function) differently as a mechanism for inclusion will be examined. In this respect, the developments at the European level are also of importance for future prospects.

### 6.6.1 Supra-national developments

With ratification of the Treaty on European Union (Maastricht Treaty), European citizenship as the "most important innovation" (Europe on the move 1993:15) has come into existence as stated in Article 8 of the above Treaty: "Citizenship of the Union is hereby established" (Council of the ECs & Commission of the ECs 1992:15). As citizenship is historically associated with nationality, the introduction of Union citizenship has special significance with political as well as cultural implications (Federalist 1993:3).

Until the Maastricht Treaty, the European Community did not assert any substantive list of entitlements for individuals living within its boundaries. The individual rights of Europeans implicit in the Treaty of Rome and the subsequent Single European Act were somewhat limited in scope and rudimentary political rights were introduced with the first election of Members to the European Parliament in 1979 (Welsh 1993). However, the minimal legislative competence of the European Parliament limited the emergence of a strong and coherent notion of Community citizenship (Closa 1992:1144). Welsh suggests that a rough idea of a European citizenship slowly began to emerge around two main practical realities: 1. the rights that the gradual completion of the internal market has granted to individuals regardless of (EC member-) nationality; and 2. the increasing need to delineate those individuals from citizens of non-member states (1993:27).

*Content of Union citizenship: Article 8* European Union citizenship as a relatively new concept in the Community sphere is laid down by Articles 8 to 8e of the Treaty on European Union which include the following elements:

- the right to free movement within the EU; the right of residence in any member-country of the EU;
- the right to vote and stand as candidate in *municipal* elections in the country of residence;
- the right to vote and stand as candidate in *European* elections in the country of residence;

- citizens of the EU in third countries have the right to the diplomatic and consular protection of the authorities of any EU member-state in that third country;
- citizens of the EU have the right to petition the European Parliament; citizens of the EU have the right to apply to an ombudsperson appointed by the European Parliament concerning issues of maladministration in the activities of the Community's institutional bodies with the exception of the Court of Justice (articles 8a to 8d).

Article 8e opens European citizenship up by setting out a procedure for the further development of citizenship should current rights need to be strengthened or new ones added. In this capacity, the Maastricht Treaty's conception of European citizenship has notably advanced from the Rome Treaty and Single European Act. However, the Maastricht provisions are also considered weak in certain respects (Closa 1992; Welsh 1993:25; Federalist 1993).

*Shortcomings* One of the shortcomings crucial to this thesis is the paradoxical situation that on the one hand, there is a separation between citizenship and nationality in that all EU member-state nationals enjoy a common European citizenship (in the formal sense). On the other hand, long term resident third-country nationals (as, for instance, the Turkish community in Germany) are not included as most of them are not nationals of one of the member-states. Thus, Welsh speaks of 'inherent exclusiveness towards non-EU nationals' (1993:25) and criticizes the concept of Union citizenship for its strong reliance on the framework of the nation-state. Similarly, Closa deplores that nationality of any of the member-states becomes the prerequisite for the enjoyment of citizenship (1992:1161).

The issue of nationality indeed remains a matter to be decided upon by each individual member-state as stated in the final declaration on nationality in the Maastricht Treaty (Declaration No. 2), using the following wording:

> ...the question whether an individual possesses the nationality of a Member State shall be settled solely by reference to the national law of the Member State concerned. Member States may declare, for information, who are to be considered their nationals for Community purposes... (European Union 1993:644).

Therefore, the character of Union citizenship, although "determined by the progressive acquisition of rights stemming from the dynamic development of the Union" (Closa 1992:1167), does not work as an inclusionary mechanism for non-European immigrants as such since national formal citizenship is its prerequisite.

*Provisions for third-country nationals?* The Maastricht Treaty marks the beginning of specific provisions for third country nationals within EC law. As described in Chapter Four, title II Article G inserts the new Articles 100c and 100d into the EEC Treaty which provides for the European Council (comprised of Heads of Government), on a proposal from the Commission, to decide which third country nationals will require visas. These articles, therefore, give the Community the ability to devise a common visa policy if it so wishes.

Title VI Article K establishes inter-governmental co-operation in the area of justice and home affairs, including rules regarding third country nationals crossing external borders and immigration policy as areas of common interest. 'Immigration policy' regards conditions of entry and movement of third country nationals, conditions of residence and employment. If the draft Convention on the crossing of external borders (see Appendix I) is ever finalized and passed, it will abolish internal visa requirements for legally resident non-EU nationals travelling to another member-state for a short period of time. So far, however, free movement of non-EU residents within the EU territory is not guaranteed (Fernandes 1992).

Overall, there is considerable *potential* for the implementation of provisions for third-country nationals. As yet, however, European citizenship does not offer any benefits for post-war labour migrants of non-EU nationality and/or citizenship. Thus, as denizens of Europe, they pay taxes and enjoy most social welfare rights, but cannot fully participate in political decisions via European elections or enjoy economic benefits provided by the freedom of movement. Under the Maastricht Treaty, as Garcia argues (1992:20), this group should have been given the right to participate in local elections, but so far this is only possible via naturalization - which Garcia regards as a discriminatory decision in view of the difficulty of the procedures involved in countries such as Germany, Austria, Belgium and Luxembourg. Moreover, Plender (1990:609) holds that the establishment of common rules relating to the immigration of non-EU nationals is necessary in order to achieve the objective spelled out in Article 3(c), namely the abolition of obstacles to the movement of persons between member-states.

As a result of the above explanations, European citizenship has not superseded nationality in much the same way as the European Union has not abolished the sovereignty of its member-states with regard to nationality/citizenship laws, although the Maastricht Treaty upgrades the condition of citizens with EU-nationality under Community law (Closa 1992). Welsh concludes that even during the post-Maastricht period, the decisive social and political status for individual Europeans has not been citizenship of the Union, but nationality in one of the member-states. Therefore, the European Union is, according to her, of intergovernmental character rather than supranational (1993:31).

*European citizenship for ethnic minorities in Germany and Britain* What are the implications of the above for ethnic minority communities in Britain and Germany? European citizenship as defined by the Maastricht Treaty applies only to citizens and/or nationals of EU-member-states. The implication for most of the ethnic minority groups from former ex-colonies in the UK is that they in fact enjoy *formal* EU citizenship in the same way as any other indigenous European person. This is different in Germany: Turkish long-term residents who are not naturalized (and most of them are not; see Beauftragte der Bundesregierung 1993a:166) cannot enjoy the freedom of movement nor any of the other provisions. Therefore, they are as much excluded on a European level as on a national. In addition, there is not only unequal treatment between Turkish immigrants and German citizens, but also different treatment of Turkish immigrants and residents of any EU-nationality - whereby the latter enjoy a more preferable status despite the longer periods of residence of the former.

In Britain, the situation is much more complex. For those members of the ethnic minority groups who are British citizens, they enjoy in theory the same rights associated with formal citizenship in Europe as every other indigenous person. There are, however, members of certain ethnic minority groups, such as the Indians, who are Indian passport holders (because India does not allow dual citizenship), but nevertheless enjoy full formal citizenship rights in the UK (such as, e.g., voting rights). For them, Europe creates a rather anomalous situation as they cannot take part in the freedom of movement in order to work in another European country, but they could be members of the European Parliament as they have the right to stand for any election in the UK (according to the President of the EU Migrants Forum, there is the example of an Australian MEP representing Britain). For British citizens of different ethnic background (blacks and Asians), another problem appears in practice when travelling to continental Europe: They have numerous experiences of being stopped and checked because they are not considered British[24]. On the basis of this experience of black and Asian UK citizens travelling on the continent, some organizations expect black and Asian Europeans to be more harassed than white citizens by random checks inside borders (Meehan 1993b:154). Ethnic minorities in Britain, according to King, "will in the future face comparative disadvantages in their ability to travel and work in Europe which will seriously affect their ability to live their lives as freely as their fellow citizens" (1993:4). Apart from the threat of being the "object of unwelcome attention from right-wing extremists", ethnic minorities "could also be the object of the interest of the police themselves, who may take him or her as an illegal immigrant or an illicit overstayer" (ibid.). These aspects indicate problems with the *substantive* side of European citizenship. In the case of Britain, the above explanations show that large parts of ethnic minorities enjoy the same formal European citizenship rights as the majority (at least in theory), but on the substantive level, the combined effects of nationalism and racialization might curtail their freedom of movement. It seems, therefore, to be the case that substantive European citizenship for ethnic minorities in Britain is similarly encroached upon as substantive citizenship on the national level. In Germany, the main problem which exists on the national level - i.e. the non-holding of formal citizenship - is exactly the same problem for most non-EU nationals on the European level.

The issue of European citizenship, however, does not only involve developments on the supranational level - as explained so far - but also on the sub-national level.

### 6.6.2 Sub-national developments: subsidiarity & the Committee of the Regions

The idea of the European Union as an ever closer union of the peoples of Europe by way of 'Europeanization' beyond national governments and the remote EC policy-making seems to have been of concern when the principle of subsidiarity and the clauses on the Committee of the Regions were included in the Maastricht Treaty (Taylor 1995:74). Both of those new elements, however, are not considered in the same way by each member-state. There seems to be a particularly divergent interpretation or motivation behind the inclusion of these elements in Britain versus continental Europe as suggested by Teasdale (1993) and Scott & Peterson & Millar (1994). This begs the question "what do subsidiarity and the Committee of the Regions mean".

*Subsidiarity* Subsidiarity, generally speaking, is the principle "that decisions should be taken at the lowest level possible" (The European 1992:34). This means that decisions (by parliaments, governments and other authorities) are to be taken as close as possible to the citizen, in other words, at the lowest level (i.e. local or regional authority). They are to be taken at higher levels (central government, the European Union) only if there is good reason (Europe on the move, 1992). The new Article 3b of the Treaty defines subsidiarity in the following terms:

> The Community shall act within the limits of the powers conferred upon it by this Treaty and of the objectives assigned to it therein. In areas which do not fall within its exclusive competence, the Community shall take action, in accordance with the principle of subsidiarity, only if and in so far as the objectives of the proposed action cannot be sufficiently achieved by the Member States and can therefore, by reason of the scale or effects of the proposed action, be better achieved by the Community. (Europe on the move 1992).

Subsidiarity, thus, appeared as the guiding principle to delineating the competencies of Brussels versus other administrative authorities, such as national states and regions. The debate between governmental and EU officials has centred upon the question to what extent subsidiarity provides a clear separation of responsibilities between the European Commission, the member-states and sub-national governments or other local authorities (Kersbergen & Verbeek 1994), and herein lies the difference in approach by each member-state. In Germany, for instance, subsidiarity is considered to be a guiding principle for federalism and thus, the Germans believed these two principles to be coterminous. The British government, on the other hand, sees them in opposition to federalism (Teasdale 1993) and the debate on subsidiarity in the UK has mainly centred upon how policy can be 'de-linked' from Brussels (Scott & Peterson & Millar 1994; The European 1992).

*The Committee of the Regions*  A further contrasting process of decision-making below the nation-state can be found in the emergence of the European 'Committee of the Regions'. Article 198A of the Maastricht Treaty states:

> A committee consisting of representatives of regional and local bodies, hereinafter referred to as the "Committee of the Regions" is hereby established with advisory status....The members of the Committee may not be bound by any mandatory instructions. They shall be completely independent in the performance of their duties in the general interest of the Community.

Article 198C adds:

> The Committee of the Regions shall be consulted by the Council or the Commission where this treaty so provides and in all other cases in which one of these two institutions considers its appropriate.

Hence, the Committee is comprised of representatives of regional and local authorities with only advisory power. The new consultative mechanisms, however, are viewed by Barber & Millns (1993) as capable of devolving more influence to sub-national governments. According to them, there are three main roles for local authorities: the implementation of European regulations, the enabling of the local economy to respond to opportunities and risks of the Single Market, and as co-ordinators of applications for the funding of local projects. The Committee is also a good forum for exchanging experiences and opinions on certain policies. It seems to Barber & Millns (1993) as if European institutions see local government through subsidiarity and partnership as more integral to the process of European government than some national governments do.

There is, however, again a problem with different approaches in different member-states. For countries like Germany with a long tradition of federalism and a strong position of regional independent decision-making, the establishment of the Committee of the Regions releases fears of its *Länder*  losing their power within the European structure. In the UK, by contrast, the national government attributes only a subsidiary legitimacy to local government and continues to deny it any form of constitutional recognition through such means as signing the European Charter of Local Self-Government (op.cit.). The high centralization of the British political structure - a process which has increased in the period of Conservative rule since 1979 - thus represents "a major 'democratic deficit' by comparison with other member-states of the EU, with the possible exception of Greece and Portugal" (Taylor 1995:74). The matter at issue, however, is not only local government's restricted constitutional status in the UK. Taylor argues that the central government has highly limited the elected local governments' power via a series of interventions in local affairs. In areas of direct service provision especially, local governments have lost many of their powers to non-elected and generally unaccountable quangos. How and to what extent the member-states will harmonize and standardize their traditional approach to regionalism is, therefore, still unclear. Taylor (1995) speaks of a 'quiet revolution' in local government in Britain and Barber & Millns (1993), too, view that re-organization of the British structure is necessary.

Generally speaking, the Maastricht Treaty created a Committee of the Regions as a step towards the recognition that sub-national governments have to be involved as a formal component of the EU decision-making process. In this way, the fact that people tend to identify most strongly with their close community (European Commission 1994) finds political recognition and renders the principle of subsidiarity concrete and operationable.

There are, however, problems with regard to the interpretation of these developments by national governments which means that the precise role of the Committee of the Regions seems to be very much a matter for future agreement. Also, there are other issues which need clarifying and improving. For this purpose, a campaign mounted by the national associations of local authorities in Britain with a clear set of objectives for the revision of the Treaty of Rome - planned as part of the IGC[25] - is said to include:

- a legally enforceable definition of subsidiarity;
- a legal basis for the principle of local government; and
- more power and independence for the Committee of the Regions (Taylor 1995:79).

*Implications for citizenship* These sub- and supra-national developments have very important implications for the issue of citizenship - in general as well as in particular with regard to ethnic minorities. The widely deplored democratic deficit existing at the European level seems to be compensated by the Maastricht Treaty's reinforcement of greater decentralization and subsidiarity. The 'European idea' - occasionally criticized for being elitist and technocratic (Taylor 1995) - could gain feasibility for the majority of

European citizens by confronting the basic problems of their everyday life in the form of a local dimension to citizenship.

Generally speaking, as part of the Committee of the Regions, regions could "learn from one another about practical problems and solutions" (Meehan 1993b:183) and they are linked "directly into European decision-making" (Smith 1994:3).

Co-operation of local authorities could also have positive implications for ethnic minorities. As Britain has the one of the most sophisticated legislation for the elimination of 'race' discrimination and has developed the most progressive 'race' equality policies at local level, its experience could be of great value for local authorities in continental member-states. One further objective for amendments to the Treaty of Rome, as proposed by the national associations of local authorities in Britain, is a legal base for EU work on racial equality (Taylor 1995). Moreover, the sub-national developments could benefit ethnic minorities probably to a larger extent than supra-national developments if, for instance, the subsidiarity principle dictated that racial equality be an issue for the 'regions'. Furthermore, co-operation of local authorities could also result in a more successful prevention of racially motivated violence[26] and also "everyday 'low-level' forms of harassment" (Collinson 1994:118) - issues which have a local dimension as noted by Oakley: "Such harassment is an effective means of maintaining racial boundaries at the *local* level...[and] of keeping victim communities subordinated." (quoted by Collinson, ibid.; emphasis added).

For third country nationals who do not have EU member-states' citizenship, this means an even more urgent need to be granted political rights at least on the local level. They should be able to elect and be elected as local representatives. Therefore, the provision of European citizenship which allows EU-nationals political rights at the local level should be extended to all long-term resident non-EU nationals.

## 6.7 Concluding remarks

It has been shown in this chapter that citizenship is the key indicator of inclusion into a socio-national community. Citizenship constitutes legal, economic, political and social practices which define social membership and which counteract social cleavages.

In this way, Marshall's concept of citizenship - which was the starting point of a general theory of citizenship - rightly becomes a method of social inclusion. Historically, in western Europe the concept of citizenship evolved from the city to the nation-state widening the circles of social inclusion. There are, however, signs of a reversal of this process. Ethnic minorities who are of non-European origin and whose presence in Europe derives from post-war labour migration are one group which experiences increasing social inequalities in terms of their legal status as well as in terms of social acceptance by the majority. Hall and Held (1989), therefore, seem to be right in claiming that one of the most important arenas in which issues of citizenship have remained virulent, is that of immigration and 'race'. The construction of racializing boundaries according to many-sided criteria of in- and exclusion belongs to the most important 'arenas of contestation' with regard to citizenship - a matter which was ignored by Marshall's concept (Yuval-Davis, in: Institut für Migrations- und Rassismusforschung 1992:220). I have argued, however, that racialization is not the sole factor responsible for exclusionary tendencies, but that nationalism is equally as important.

To demonstrate legal and social exclusion, it has been suggested that the concept of citizenship in the context of immigrants' settlement and their transformation into 'new' ethnic minorities should be sub-divided into formal and substantive citizenship. The emphasis for the former has been put here on the degree of ease with which citizenship can be acquired (i.e. provisions of dual nationality, naturalization, ius soli). Political and civil rights would follow as a matter of fact. The latter - substantive citizenship - covers social rights in the broad sense including housing, employment, and anti-discrimination policies. In this way, citizenship would not only involve a formal relationship with the state, but also a more substantive relationship with civil society. This sub-division does not only apply to national citizenship, but also to the European level.

As formal citizenship includes nationality/citizenship laws, this concept was also employed to illustrate the strong link to socio-legal membership being based on descent. Despite rather different histories of concepts of nationality and citizenship, a tendency towards ius sanguinis and thus the acquisition of citizenship being closer linked to nationality (i.e. ethnic descent) can be identified in both Germany and Britain, if not even throughout western Europe. Britain has departed from its very liberal position vis-à-vis non-European immigration by implementing immigration and nationality legislation which clearly racializes black and Asian immigrants. Although Germany has slightly improved the procedures of acquisition of citizenship, it has never moved away from its sole principle of ius sanguinis and still has one of the toughest regulations of naturalization - an area in which Britain has remained much more liberal.

Despite these differences, both countries have had their 'privileged immigrants' who were granted full formal citizenship rights without any restriction: the ethnic Germans and ex-GDR citizens in the case of Germany, and the Irish and (now mainly white) Commonwealth citizens in the case of Britain - a fact which implies, apart from any understandable historical reasons, national identity being closely linked to the identity as an 'ethnic group', or rather as a 'race', in both countries. This clearly has exclusionary effects on non-privileged immigrants or on those who have become stigmatized by changes within laws.

The above led to the following conclusions. First, on a *formal* basis, third country nationals in Germany cannot be described as citizens, but rather as denizens as suggested by Hammar (1990). In this respect, their position is clearly much worse than that of Commonwealth immigrants in Britain, although it has been suggested here that the latter has to do with very specific historical circumstances. With regard to *substantive* citizenship, post-war labour migrants in both countries suffered from their allocated position as either 'guest-workers' and *Ausländer* or as 'colonial subjects' and a different 'race'. Even for subsequent generations, their ethno-cultural background has been partly the reason for their less equal substantive citizenship status as opposed to the majority.

Secondly, it has been suggested that citizenship is more and more defined on the basis of ethnic origin and specific cultural criteria. Therefore, this might be referred to as 'ethnicization' of citizenship as the law, in defining citizenship, refers specifically to criteria which are, according to Heckmann (in: Bielefeld 1991) and Bös (1993), sociologically regarded as criteria of an ethnic group (such as common culture and origin). However, as 'origin' clearly carries the notion of 'descent' and 'blood-relatedness', the distinction between 'ethnicization' and 'racialization' is not seen here in such a clear-cut way. The argument was, therefore, that what is at stake should rather be referred to as exclusionary processes as the outcome of racialization *and* nationalism.

Thirdly, in a world divided into states, the separation of a 'people' from a 'non-people' seems to be inevitable. The formal mark of belonging to a people is the legal concept of citizenship. A certain relationship or link to the state is an important element of this concept. A genuine link is usually seen in birth or place of upbringing, however, this link could also be established via the social reality of residence and work-place (Franz, in: Institut für Migrations- und Rassismusforschung 1992). Therefore, it has been widely suggested that the idea of a 'new citizenship' (in a multi-ethnic/multi-cultural setting) should be recognized without consideration of nationality (Neveu 1989). For immigrants, citizenship through participation is not necessarily established on the basis of nationality, but rather residence (Withol de Wenden, in: Institut für Migrations- und Rassismusforschung 1992). Similarly, at the European level, a concept of citizenship is required which is also detached from nationality (Tassin, in: Mouffe 1992). The right of EU-nationals to vote in local elections in any member-state indicates the tendency towards the formation of a new community citizenship and that participation in the life of public institutions takes precedence over nationality (Withol de Wenden, ibid.; Tassin, ibid.). However, this right has to be extended to long-term resident third-country nationals. Thus, if citizenship is to remain the basic symbol of inclusion in the context of the complex composition of European societies, it has to be based on criteria of residence. This would not, however, solve the problem of substantive citizenship.

Fourthly, supra-national developments as the outcome of the Maastricht Treaty on European Union have not provided long-term resident third country nationals with any solutions to solve the kind of problems they have with regard to their full citizenship status at the national level in Germany and Britain. Sub-national developments within the European Union, however, indicate that national citizenship is not the only form of citizenship. The principle of subsidiarity and the establishment of the Committee of the Regions are phenomena which could have the general effect that all citizens participate more actively in local, national and European issues. Also, sub-national developments are regarded by Garcia (1994) as 'number one importance for identity formation', i.e. for the preservation of social and cultural identities at the local, regional and national level while developing a European identity simultaneously - a matter ethnic minorities, too, could benefit from. Overall, these subnational developments could have a positive impact on ethnic minorities' substantive citizenship by involving them actively in community matters and thus, creating mutual understanding.

As it stands now, however, citizenship in general (in law and in practice) conveys the effects of nationalism and racism to settled immigrants. This was shown with regard to access to formal citizenship (provisions of acquisition of nationality/citizenship) as well as with regard to substantive citizenship. I have also argued that equal formal citizenship as such can not work against the effects of racism and nationalism. The British example in particular has shown that immigrants' formally equal status is not necessarily recognized by civil society. It does, therefore, not provide a panacea against the power of racism and nationalism.

Substantive citizenship, which is only to a very limited extent made up of actual rights, is suggested here as being more or less equally affected by racism and nationalism in Germany and Britain. In this sphere, rights seem very much to be powerless. This does not, however, lead to the conclusion that citizenship - formal and substantive - cannot sufficiently work as a mechanism for inclusion. If formal citizenship was detached from nationality, it would function more inclusively. With regard to substantive citizenship, the 'solution package' would have to be much more complex and thorough. What has been particularly stressed here, however, is that *local* citizenship and *local* participation would enhance understanding and enable dialogue leading to compromises and negotiations of a basis on which social peace could be promoted and fragmented identities maintained.

Formal, but even more so substantive, citizenship status of immigrant 'newcomers' is often questioned by the 'indigenous' population. In the following chapter, therefore, the ways in which ethnic minorities' citizenship is affected by nationalistic and racializing attitudes on the part of the majority will be further investigated.

# Notes

1    Turner (1990) and Barbalet (1988) argue that it is not clear whether Marshall's theory in fact requires an evolutionary perspective.

2    It has to be pointed out that Barbalet and Young argue against this 'too homogeneous picture of Britain' in the context of class, and not ethnicity. It is, however, only the latter which is of concern here.

3    Marshall's concept of citizenship has been more extensively criticized in the context of gender inequalities by Anthias & Yuval-Davis (1992), Meehan (1993a), and Vogel & Moran (1991).

4    For a fully detailed historical account of British nationality and immigration law see Dummett & Nicol(1990).

5    This case "established that birth as a natural-born subject requires (1) that the birth occur within the bounds of the King's dominion and (2) that the parents owe obedience to the King at the time of the child's birth" (Guendelsberger 1992:388, footnote no. 40; see same page for more details).

6    The denial of civic rights on religious grounds for Jews, however, survived the Catholic Empancipation Act (1829) and the removal of those restrictions was not achieved until mid-Victorian years (Holmes 1979).

7    Under 1948 Act, "a person could become a British citizen or subject by virtue of being a citizen of a Commonwealth country." (Goulbourne 1991:96).

8    The title of this law is "Gesetz über die Erwerbung und den Verlust der Eigenschaft als preussischer Untertan sowie über den Eintritt in fremden Staatsdienst". In the second article, it says "Jedes eheliche Kind eines Preussen wird durch die Geburt preussischer Untertan, auch wenn es im Ausland geboren ist." (every legitimate child of a Prussian is a Prussian citizen via birth, even if it is born abroad) (Bös 1993:626).

9    It was only because of this federal citizenship system that Hitler, who had been a foreigner 'with a criminal record', could renounce his Austrian citizenship in order to be a candidate for president of the Reich. On February 1932, he was appointed senior administrative officer (Regierungsrat) of Braunschweig by one of his supporters who had shortly before become Interior Minister of Braunschweig. With this position, Hitler automatically became citizen of Braunschweig, and thus, citizen of the Reich (Engelmann 1991:23).

10    Wilpert rightly asks in this context: "Why then solidarity primarily with ethnic Germans? What about the Jews and the gypsies in the east who had to suffer as a result of the Second World War?" (1993:75, footnote no. 8).

11    See Ferstl & Hetzel (1990) for personal histories of *Aussiedler*.

12    The original version of Article 116 goes as follows: "Deutscher im Sinne dieses Grundgesetzes ist vorbehaltlich anderweitiger gesetzlicher Regelung, wer die deutsche Staatsangehörigkeit besitzt oder als Flüchtling oder Vertriebener deutscher Volkszugehörigkeit oder als dessen Ehegatte oder Abkömmling in dem Gebiete des Deutschen Reiches nach dem Stand

vom 31. Dezember 1937 Aufnahme gefunden hat." (Grundgesetz, Stand 1994)

13    As Italy, Spain and Greece had not been members of the European Community yet, the migrants from these regions had the same 'guest-worker' status as the Turks. However, in joining the EC, the situation has changed to their advantage - a matter which will be subject to more detail in the section on European citizenship.

14    The federal states of Schleswig-Holstein, Hamburg and Bremen passed a law granting local voting rights to 'foreigners' from 1991 onwards, but after intervention by the conservative parties (CDU & CSU), the Federal Constitutional Court ruled local voting rights for 'foreigners' out. In the official statement from 31.10.90, however, it appears as if the Court holds this matter to be a question of political will and not of legal interpretation of the Basic Law (Constitution) (Gottschlich, in: taz, 01.11.90; document by TGB 1988; see also Liegmann 1990 in a comparative perspective with western Europe). A survey undertaken by Sen & Karakasoglu in 1994 found that 83% of the Turkish respondents (of 601 of a total sample of 1412 foreign residents in Germany) and 67% of the ex-Yugoslav respondents (of 360) regard local voting rights as 'very important' or 'important' (the remaining foreign residents were EU-nationals who have local voting rights as a result of the Maastricht Treaty). Hence, there is a lot of interest among ethnic minorities to become politically active, even if only on the local level.

15    These are a number of articles collected during the period of 28 September 1994 to 31 January 1995 published by *die taz*. Headlines such as *Sechs Haftbefehle nach Kurden-Demonstration* (Six warrants of arrest after Kurdish demonstration; 30.09.94) and *Abschiebungen: Kanther bleibt hart* (Deportations: Kanther remains tough; 08.12.94; Kanther is the minister of the Interior) indicate the content of these articles.

16    Wilpert remarks in the context and in comparison with ethnic Germans from eastern Europe who can claim German citizenship as of right, that "an individual non-ethnic German may apply for citizenship and it may be granted to him/her. But, this is not his/her right as it is for a Volksdeutsch. It is the exception in the logic of a non-immigration country." (1993:73, footnote no. 7).

17    It has to be noted, however, that the empirical data in Essed's study stem from the Netherlands and the USA. Aspects mentioned by 'her' interviewees, such as racism at work - either from the part of colleagues or 'clients' - were, however, also mentioned by a number of authors in the British context (see, e.g., Burgess-Macey, in: Gill et al. 1992).

18    The infamous 'rivers of blood' speech was made by Enoch Powell in 1968 in Birmingham. It was characterized by extreme anti-black and anti-immigrant sentiments and "coined the phrase 'rivers of blood' referring to what would follow if we did not drastically reduce prospective black numbers." (Barker 1981:38).

19      Jäger, for example, refers to the empirical (interview) findings in his study as 'racist and nationalistic statements' (1993:291).

20      In the words of one interviewee in Modood et al.'s study on *Changing Ethnic Identities*, the difference between the experiences of the two main minority groups is that "they [the Afro-Caribbeans] were slaves, we were colonised..." (1994:96).

21      A more recent study by Tomlinson quotes the Swann Report (by the Department of Education & Science) as having recognized that the British school curriculum "was and still is in many ways influenced by the beliefs and values of a period of imperial enthusiasm and a final expansion of the British Empire." (1990:71).

22      An ever increasing population has been born in Britain. According to census data of 1991 (Owen 1993a:12), the figure is 46.8% .

23      One fourth of the seven million foreigners were born in Germany (Migration News 1996a).

24      The article in the Guardian of March 25, 1995, *Challenge to EU border scheme,* reports that the president of the EU Migrants Forum - with regard to the implementation of the Schengen agreement on March 26 - launched an action by which his members would be travelling within the EU by plane to test the new arrangements by refusing to show any travel documents. If there was any denial of entry, it would be taken to the courts.

25      Intergovernmental Conference; negotiations for amending the Treaty of Rome have started in July 1997.

26      See for example the chapter titled *A Local Response to Racial Violence* by Bowling and Saulsbury (1993).

# 7   Mass discourse

In this chapter, the viewpoints of the 'indigenous' population about nationalism, racism, and citizenship will be investigated. For this purpose, a number of social attitude surveys and opinion polls have been selected. These surveys and polls provide information on broad views held by 'the public' towards ethnic minorities and immigrants. It is precisely this high level of generalization of these surveys which allows the assessment of the conceptual link between racialization, citizenship and nationality in the wider perception of *civil society* at large.

I will first provide a brief review of selected polls and reports of social attitude surveys conducted in Germany and Britain. In the British context, these are aspects of the British Social Attitudes - a series of surveys produced annually since 1984 - and the Gallup political & economic index. The Gallup Organization conducts opinion polls mainly on behalf of newspapers and broadcasters with tight deadlines and budgets. The media use these polls in a rather "topic-specific" and "peremptory" way (Jowell & Airey 1984:4). The material produced over the years by polling organizations such as Gallup has been described as an "incomplete patchwork" (ibid.). This can be confirmed here: Racial discrimination, prejudice and nationalism are attitudes which have not been subject to more 'in-depth' attitude surveys.

In the German case, a number of IPOS studies, conducted on behalf of the Ministry of the Interior, were the main surveys consulted, as well as an independent survey by the *Zentrum für Türkeistudien*. Relevant Infas surveys and surveys conducted by the *Institut für Demoskopie Allensbach* - as summarized by Koch-Arzberger (1993) - are also included. They operate in a similar way as the Gallup Organization. The Commissioner for Foreigners' Affairs in Berlin published a number of surveys whose sample were an equal number of indigenous Germans living in the western part and the eastern part of the city (Ausländerbeauftragte 1990a & 1990b). Apart from the latter surveys and the survey conducted by the *Zentrum für Türkeistudien*, none of the remaining surveys has exclusively dealt with attitudes towards ethnic minorities. The IPOS studies and the reports on British Social Attitudes tried to repeat the same questions every year to show trends, but new questions were almost always added to each report. Because of the 'patchy' nature of these surveys and polls, the review sections are structured chronologically (year of publication) and by type of survey.

I will then comment on the findings with particular reference to the extent of 'racial' discrimination and acceptance of ethnic minorities or immigrants in both countries. Although as such not relevant to this study, aspects of future immigration or asylum seekers - which have tended to dominate the public debate on ethnic minority related issues - will be added to show that there is a link between public opinion and politicians' rhetoric - an issue which is subject to further exploration in the following chapter.

Also, the results of a number of Eurobarometer surveys which show trends in all EU-member-states will be reviewed. The last section deals with the findings of surveys which reveal attitudes about national identity.

## 7.1  Social attitude surveys and polls in the British context

### 7.1.1  The 1984 report

The first British Social Attitudes (hereafter: BSA) report in 1984 (Jowell & Airey 1984: 122-130) suggests high levels of awareness of racial discrimination amongst sections of the population as represented by the sample[1]. Around 90% of the respondents thought that there is prejudice against Asians and blacks, albeit as an attitude held by others and not as the respondents' own attitude[2]. When asked how they would describe themselves, around a third of the total sample thought of themselves as prejudiced against people of other 'races' who live now in Britain (Jowell & Airey 1984: 125). Asians were believed to experience slightly more 'racial' prejudice: 54% of the respondents perceived that there is 'a lot' of prejudice against Asians, whereas 50% thought the same for blacks. Only 6% of the respondents replied that there was 'hardly' any prejudice against Asians and 7% thought so in the case of blacks. On a personal level, asked how they would describe themselves, 35% of the respondents can be classified as 'prejudiced' or 'prejudiced-inclined', more so against Asians than against blacks. Sixty-four% thought of themselves as 'not prejudiced at all'. This means that more people perceived higher levels of prejudice in others than in themselves. As for party alliance, Labour voters (28%) were less likely than Conservative voters (46%) to describe themselves as prejudiced (op.cit.: 126).

The degree of social recognition or inclusion of ethnic minorities into British society was explored by two questions. The first tested what people would think if a suitably qualified person of Asian or black origin was appointed as boss over a white person. Again, more people perceived more prejudice in others than in themselves: Half thought that the population at large would object to an Asian or black boss, around 20% said they would object personally. The second question referred to cross-'racial' marriage: Over three-quarters thought that the population at large would object to an Asian or black marriage to a close relative, between 50% and 60% of them said they would object personally. These findings show that respondents made a sharp distinction between inter-'racial' contact in the workplace and in the family, both in their assumptions about other people's reactions and in their own reactions. The objection to a West

Indian or Asian person was greater in the context of family links than in the context of work[3].

The way in which existing prejudice translates itself into discrimination was tested by asking a question about job discrimination. Just under two-thirds believed that Asians and West Indians suffer job discrimination. The Race Relations Acts were supported by 69% and opposed to by 28%. The authors of this report, however, remarked that having told people that such acts exist, it was to be expected that a high proportion of the population endorsed the acts' existence (p. 129). Polls taken between 1967 and 1968 - before the introduction of the Race Relations Acts - found that such legislation was supported by only about 45% (Rose 1969). Since then, people seem to have become used to the idea of anti-discrimination legislation. And yet, a quarter of the 1984 BSA sample were still opposed to such a law. On the whole, opposition to a law against discrimination increased with age, and it was also greater among Conservative than Labour voters (Jowell & Airey 1984: 129).

As far as immigration and settlement are concerned, the 1984 report reveals that very few people supported the notion of more settlement by any group (choice was among Australians, New Zealanders, Indians and Pakistanis, EC-nationals, West Indians), but Australians and New Zealanders were more popular (15%) as potential immigrants than any of the other groups (p. 129). The proportions wanting less settlement were decisively anti-Asian and anti-black. The majority of respondents was also in favour of stricter controls of settlement of close relatives of those who have already settled in Britain (the ethnic minority respondents were the only group with a sizeable vote for less strict control of dependants). Conservative voters favoured stricter controls to a higher extent (62%) than Labour voters (49%) (op.cit.: 130).

## 7.1.2 The 1986 report

Two years after the 1984 report - a period in which racial incidents and reports of racial discrimination had received much media attention - the pattern of attitudes had changed only a little (Jowell, R. et al. 1986: 150). It remains the case that nine out of ten respondents believed that there is prejudice against Asians and blacks, but the proportion believing that there is "a lot" of prejudice against Asians has increased. It also remains true that just over a third of people admit to being racially prejudiced themselves. More Conservative party supporters are likely to describe themselves as prejudiced than supporters of the other main parties (ibid.).

## 7.1.3 The 1992 report

The 1992 BSA report states that between 1983 and 1991 only a very small proportion of British - fewer than one in ten - viewed their society as prejudice-free (Jowell, R. et al. 1992: 181). The percentage of those who answered that job discrimination existed against people of Asian and West Indian origin has risen from 60% prior to 1991 to 64% (ibid.). The authors of this report suggest that this does not necessarily mean that there was quantitatively more job discrimination, but rather that the perception of such discrimination has increased. In the 1992 report, a new question was added about the treatment of innocent 'black persons' or 'white persons' to be expected from the courts. Forty-four% of the respondents (and 58% of the small number of black and Asian respondents) thought a 'black' person was more likely to be found guilty of a crime they did not commit than was a white person (Jowell et al. 1992: 181-82). This indicates the level of criminalization of 'black' people in Britain. The question about how the respondents would describe themselves (as 'very prejudiced', 'a little prejudiced' or 'not prejudiced at all') showed that still almost a third of the sample admit to being either 'very prejudiced' or 'a little prejudiced' against people of other 'races'. Only a quarter of Labour supporters admitted to any degree of prejudice, compared with a third of Liberal Democrats and 40% of Conservative voters. This represents a further polarization of party difference since 1983.

Findings about the level of acceptance of a black or Asian person as a boss or as a marriage partner of a close relative did not change much in the 1992 survey. As opposed to as many as two in five people who would still mind, and half of those 'a lot', if a close relative were to marry a black or Asian person, there was relatively widespread acceptability of a West Indian or Asian boss. Around a third even of those who described themselves as non-prejudiced would mind a black or Asian marrying into their family.

Support for the 'race relations' policies pursued by successive governments in Britain (1. tightening of immigration controls; 2. introduction of anti-discrimination laws) has remained more or less firm. There was hardly any support for increased settlement, and slightly more respondents were in favour of less Asian immigration (62%) than immigration from the West Indies (58%). However, large majorities also supported the anti-discrimination law (76%) and the policy of helping those who have settled in Britain (62%)[4] (Jowell et al. 1992: 187).

*7.1.4 The 1995 report*

The BSA report of 1995 recorded a further progress in the shape of a drop with regard to the proportion of white people who would object to having a 'West Indian' or an 'Asian' boss. And yet, the proportion of people attributing similar egalitarian sentiments to others had scarcely changed since 1990, nor the proportion of the respondents (around half) who believed that the legal system treats black and white defendants equally (Jowell et al. 1995: 201). There has been a rise in the proportion who assert that racism in Britain is likely to get still more widespread over the next few years. The editors of this report commented on this that "one might have expected these responses as society actually becomes less racist in its attitudes and behaviour. We might then anticipate rather more public awareness of and sensitivity towards racism in Britain than had existed beforehand - which may be no bad thing." (op.cit.:202). This is underpinned by the strong support of the principle of anti-discrimination legislation (between two-thirds and three quarters of the respondents), although only around one in four people would implement the existing law 'more strictly'. There is also only a third who supported bringing in a 'special law against racial violence' (36%) (ibid.).

Apart from introducing 'tough' controls on immigration to Britain, recent years have also shown that Britain is among the least willing of the developed states to admit large numbers of refugees. The BSA report of 1995 tested the extent of public support for these policies. In 1990, 48% of the respondents were in favour of restrictions on political refugees as opposed to 44% in 1994 (op.cit.:203). Overall, the public seemed largely in sympathy with the government's general stance on restrictive immigration. The least welcomed were Indians and Pakistanis (60%), the most welcomed were Australians and New Zealanders (30%) - even more than EU-nationals with 40%. The attitude of 'colour first' and 'culture second' has, therefore, continued to influence responses: Settlers from Australasia, Western Europe and Eastern Europe would all, in principle, get a warmer welcome from the British public than would settlers from the Indian subcontinent, the Caribbean or Hong Kong. Although a shift towards 'softer' attitudes towards Asians and West Indians has taken place over the last eleven years, it has to be noted that this has coincided with a period of very low settlement by these groups - as rightly pointed out by the authors of the 1995 BSA report (p. 203). These two processes may, therefore, be linked: The more liberal attitudes towards ethnic minorities over the years may largely be the consequence of the steady reduction in the number of immigrants from these countries.

## 7.1.5  The Gallup polls

Findings from a number of Gallup polls testing broad social trends provide some more information on attitudes towards immigration and ethnic minority related matters. Sixty-one% of the sample in the issue of September 1995 (980 persons) supported the statement that immigrants should be encouraged to 'blend into British culture by giving up some important aspects of their own culture' and only 21% were in favour of immigrants maintaining 'their own culture more strongly, even if it means they do not blend in as well' (Report no. 421). The respondents disagreed or agreed in an almost 50% divide with the statement that 'Britain is a melting pot in which people of different countries combine into a unified British culture' (45% agree, 42% disagree, 13% don't know). In the issue of April 1996 (Report no. 428), most respondents (of a sample of 993 persons) saw Britain's future 'as a multi-racial society with tensions' (43%)

and a further third thought of it 'as a society where different groups live separately but with tension' (33%). The slightly negative view ('tensions') of the future of 'race relations' in Britain was also expressed in the BSA reports.

In terms of social contact, it is interesting to note that a clear majority of respondents in April 1996 replied that there are only a few 'coloured' people where they work or live (65%) and 21% even stated that there are no 'coloured' people at all. This means that two-thirds of the population have hardly any contact with ethnic minorities. The finding of 78% of the same sample stating that they thought of non-white people who were born in Britain 'as British' might be qualified by the fact that almost the same percentage of respondents has hardly or even no contact at all with 'coloured' people. Also, as mentioned above, 61% of the respondents in 1995 stated that immigrants should 'blend into British culture'. This could, however, also reflect that formal citizenship is no issue, whereas aspects of substantive citizenship (and thus the recognition of ethnic minorities in cultural terms) are an important part of a public debate. In other words, as far as the legal and thus formal status is concerned, ethnic minorities are considered as 'British', but culturally they are widely expected to assimilate.

The ongoing political debate about numbers of immigrants and asylum-seekers as well as the claim of large numbers being 'bogus' (see also following chapter) is somewhat reflected in public opinion. As found in the BSA reports, more people are against new immigration and think of the number of accepted refugees as too high (although the percentage opposing primary immigration is slightly higher than against asylum-seekers; there seems to be, therefore, more sympathy for political refugees). In the Gallup poll of September 1995 (Report no. 421), 26% of the respondents thought that most immigrants in Britain are 'illegal' as opposed to 55% who thought they were 'legal'. Asked about their views on the future (next decade), 58% thought that the flow of illegal immigrants will increase (25% thought it will stay the same and only 7% thought it will decrease). Half of the respondents believed that the country is 'losing ground' with regard to the 'problem of illegal immigration (20% thought it is about the same and only 12% thought there is any progress). In August 1992 (Report no. 384), a clear majority also disagreed with the statement that there should be 'a general amnesty for those asylum seekers who are presently living illegally in Britain' (40% disagree, 16% strongly disagree).

## 7.2  German opinion surveys

### 7.2.1  Trends prior to 1990

An opinion poll conducted in 1971[5] - before it was publicly accepted that most post-war labour migrants would be settling in Germany - found that

36% of the population thought that the presence of foreign workers poses a difficult problem (46% replied the presence was 'quite all right' and 18% were undecided). Asked about people's associations with 'foreign workers' in general (in terms of 'cons' rather than 'pros'), most (54%) perceived foreigners as 'loud', followed by 'not very clean' (41%), 'always after the girls' (38%), 'quick-tempered and often violent' (37%), 'cannot be trusted' (22%), and 'lazy' (11%) (Noelle-Neumann 1981). Most of these statements refer to cultural differences which were also found in an opinion survey in 1982 (conducted by *Allensbach* as quoted by Koch-Arzberger 1993): It was mainly the 'totally different behaviour' of foreigners which caught the indigenous population's attention. Sixty-nine% of the respondents thought so in view of the Turkish minority, 47% of the Italians, and 42% of the Greek.

In 1974 - one year after the official recruitment halt - half of the population had mixed feelings about foreigners (favourable and unfavourable opinions each scored 48%), and half of the population had never met any foreigners at all (Noelle-Neumann 1981). To assess the degree of 'racial' prejudice, respondents were asked in a survey conduced in 1975 whether they would sit next to a foreigner in a bus. Most said 'yes', but the least said 'yes' in the case of Turkish people. Asked whether they would invite a foreigner whom they know personally to their home for dinner, roughly half replied 'yes', but again most people said 'no' in the case of the Turks (42%; only 26% said 'no' to a Yugoslav). The questions whether people would like to have a foreigner as a neighbour or would like to see children of foreigners attend school with their own children were mostly answered with 'don't care' .

In the case of cross-national marriage, the 1975 survey (as quoted by Noelle-Neumann 1981) found that more than half of the German men would not have married a foreigner, and of those who would have, most would have married a Yugoslav, followed by an Italian, a Turkish, and least a black person. Women would have married a foreigner to an even lesser extent and 90% would not have married a Turkish man. There seems to be a distinctive dislike of Turkish people - one of the culturally most distant groups of immigrants in Germany.

In the survey of 1975, 42% of the respondents were of the opinion that foreigners should return to their country of origin, 37% would allow them to stay and 21% were undecided. A majority, therefore, still perceived foreigners as 'guests' rather than 'immigrants'. In terms of equal rights on the job, 57% thought that in times of crisis, foreign workers should be fired first. In 1975, 52% did not think that foreigners who had lived a long time in Germany should be able to participate in council or municipal elections, and 55% felt that foreign workers would become a serious problem in the future. Sixty-nine% even thought that German babies would be more intelligent than those of foreign workers (Noelle-Neumann 1981)!

Despite these signs of prejudice and 'racial' discrimination during the 1970s, Koch-Arzberger (1993) commented on the period of the 1980s that a generally hostile atmosphere against foreigners cannot be observed and that the agreement by the indigenous population with discriminatory statements vis-à-vis foreigners has rather decreased. She has, however, also noted that during this period the 'foreigner's issue' (Ausländerfrage) was not highly politicized and that the dominant picture of the 'foreigner' in the public's mind was that of a hard working person who kept a low profile in everyday life. Events in the more recent past, however, have resulted in a polarizing trend of attitudes towards foreigners. Issues relating to 'foreigners' invite people's views more than ever. Koch-Arzberger notes (1993) that it is difficult to say whether the increasing polarization of the public's opinion is related to objective perceptions of the situation (such as the number of foreigners) or to the politicization of this issue based on reports by the mass media. However, even the perception of numbers is not necessarily objective (this aspect will be returned to below).

### 7.2.2 The 1990 IPOS study

To show to what extent the above patterns of opinions have changed since the 1980s, I consulted four IPOS[6] social attitudes studies on current domestic affairs[7], conducted on behalf of the Ministry for the Interior (Innenministerium). The first of the IPOS studies (from 1990) points out that topics related to 'foreigners' living in Germany have gained importance in the public debate over the last years, ranging from promotion of inclusion (by granting voting rights etc.) to the more controversial debate about the number of asylum-seekers (p. 41). An important role was played in particular by the critical manner with which the *Republikaner* (extreme right-wing party) presented their 'foreigners policy' since 1989. This has, however, somewhat changed since re-unification as public debate has been dominated by other domestic issues relating to national-political developments[8].

Asked whether foreigners should be allowed to vote, the IPOS study of 1990 reveals that 80% replied that only those who have German citizenship should be allowed to do so (same percentage as in 1989) and only 20% of the respondents were of the opposite opinion (p. 42). There is a difference, however, between supporters of the Green Party and the other parties' supporters: Among identifiers with the Green Party, every second respondent thought that foreigners should be granted the right to vote, whereas among the supporters of all the other parties, the majority was against this (92% of the CDU/CSU, 74% of the SPD, 81% of the FDP and 95% of the *Republikaner*)[9].

With regard to the asylum law, most respondents in the IPOS study of 1990 - regardless of political alliance - were in favour of the right for political asylum (70% pro, 30% contra). Sixty-six% of the supporters of the *Republikaner*, however, were against this right. This right was mostly favoured by  supporters of the Green Party (91% of all Green supporters). Despite this generally positive reply on principle, 58% of all respondents would not grant this right to everybody, but wanted it to be limited to a certain number. This holds for most parties with the exception of the *Republikaner* (of whose supporters 45% would not accept *any* asylum-seekers) and the Green Party (of whose supporters 57% would accept 'anybody') (p. 43-44).

## 7.2.3 *The 1992 study*

In the 1992 IPOS study, the attitudes towards foreigners have hardly changed since the 1990 study. Asked whether they thought the number of foreigners living in Germany was 'all right' or 'not all right', a small majority of respondents in East and West Germany opted for 'not all right' (53% in the West, 51% in the East). Supporters of the SPD were split in almost 50% on this question, and 60% of the CDU/CSU supporters were against the high presence of foreigners. Acceptance was somewhat higher among FDP supporters, but much higher among the Greens (78% in the West) and the PDS[10] (78%). The *Republikaner* showed the least signs of acceptance: 83% of their supporters opted for 'not all right' (p. 80-81).

The next question in the 1992 IPOS study was whether the respondents thought that Germany's economy needs foreign workers or not. It seems as if most West Germans have become used to the presence of 'foreign workers' since the late 1950s as two-thirds positively replied that the German economy needs foreign workers. In the East, however, two-thirds of the respondents thought that this is not the case. It is suggested in this study that this has to be seen in the context of economic restructuring, rationalization of labour and high rates of unemployment as well as in the context of the little experience East Germans have had with the presence of foreigners[11](p.83-84). The respondents were then asked how much contact they have with foreigners at work or in the area where they live (p. 85). 30% (three out of ten) in the West did not have any contact as opposed to 70% who had. In the East this was exactly the other way round. Two results are particularly interesting in this context: In the East and West most supporters of the Green Party said they had contact with foreigners (and are the most liberal minded in this respect), and in the West most supporters of the *Republikaner* also said they had regular contact with foreigners (82%!). The latter, however, are comparatively the most hostile-minded. It seems, therefore, as if political party alliance or prior prejudice can have a greater influence on people's opinion about foreigners than actual contact[12].

The general opinion about asylum and the 'high' numbers of asylum-seekers has hardly changed between 1988 and 1992[13] (p. 86). The 1992 IPOS study includes the question whether the respondents thought that the asylum law is being abused (p. 93). In the East and the West, two-thirds of all respondents replied 'yes' and 68% thought that the Asylum law needs to be changed (supporters of the *Republikaner* thought so the most, followed by the CDU/CSU). Ninety% of those who did not find the asylum law 'all right' thought that the law was being abused. Seventy-four% of the SPD supporters replied that there is abuse, but only 66% wanted the law to be changed. Apart from a general agreement with the existence of the right for political asylum, the steadily increasing numbers of asylum-seekers (and the politicization of this issue!) seems to have led to the belief, that the law was abused and that 'political action' was necessary. Whether this indicates rising 'hostility towards foreigners' is difficult to say. The authors of the IPOS study suggest that since almost 50% of respondents thought that the number of foreigners was 'all right' and the majority thought that foreigners are needed by the economy, hostility might not be rising (p.97). However, it may also be the case that a 'shift in attention' has taken place from 'foreigners' to 'asylum-seekers', partly caused by political rhetoric. This rhetoric has pointed out the rising number of asylum-seekers by leaving settled foreigners largely aside (as a political issue which needed immediate attention).

## 7.2.4 The 1993 study

The IPOS study of 1993 pointed out that the 'asylum and foreigners' issue' was still perceived as one of the most important problems in Germany since October 1991 (according to research done for the *Politbarometer*). The increasing numbers of asylum-seekers as well as the rising attacks on foreigners around that time demonstrated the importance of this issue very well (p. 78). The acceptance of foreigners has, however, only decreased by one percent: 54% thought now that it is not 'all right' that so many foreigners live in Germany (in 1992: 53%). Less respondents in the West thought in 1993 that the German economy needs foreigners (62%) and in the East, this figure was again exactly the opposite (p. 81). The support of the asylum law in principle has decreased by two percent (72%; in 1992: 74%), but the proportion of those who thought the law was being abused has also decreased by two percent (p. 84).

A new question was included in this study about whether refugees are accommodated in the vicinity of the respondent's home and if so, whether this causes any problems (p. 89). Almost half of the respondents replied that there were refugees living in their neighbourhood, and 34% thought that this does not lead to any problems. However, the same phenomenon of party alliance and perception can be observed here as in the context of 'contact' (see above): many more identifiers with the *Republikaner* thought that they are confronted with refugees in their immediate environment and almost half of them thought that this leads to problems. It seems therefore as if acceptance is very much linked to subjective perception. Whether foreigners or refugees are regarded as a 'problem' seems to play an important role in this context.

## 7.2.5 *The 1995 study*

The 1995 IPOS study states that the issue of 'asylum' has lost a lot of its importance since 1993 as the result of the revised asylum law and the reduced numbers of accepted refugees (p. 1). It now seems as if the most important issue is the provision of jobs. Nonetheless, issues related to the presence of foreigners and asylum-seekers were still among the ten most important topics in domestic politics (p. 10-11). General acceptance of foreigners is said to have slightly increased by three percent: 48% of the respondents thought that the number of foreigners in Germany is 'all right' (1993: 45%). But nevertheless more than half of the population (52%) thought that this is not 'all right' (in the East even 54%) (p.84-86).

With regard to formal citizenship, in both the East (69%) and West (64%), most of the respondents did not support the facilitation of naturalization procedures (and thus, the acquisition of German citizenship) (p. 87). However, 54% in the West and 57% in the East thought that in future those who were born in Germany should be granted citizenship, even if one of the parents is not a German citizen (p. 88-89). This means that a slight majority would support the addition of the territorial component to the citizenship law. Supporters of the CDU/CSU were less in favour of the ius soli than supporters of the SPD and FDP. Identifiers with the Green Party were most in favour. Two-thirds, in the East and West alike, would reject the provision of dual nationality (83% even of CDU/CSU supporters, but only 46% of Green supporters) (p. 90). The replies to the issue of citizenship showed that the public largely supports the non-radical stance of the government in this matter.

## 7.2.6 *Other surveys*

The polling institute *Emnid* has conducted a survey in 1990 on behalf of the Commissioner for Foreigners' Affairs in Berlin. It found that only 39% of 'West Berliners' would invite a foreigner to their home or visit at his/her home and 32% of 'East Berliners' would do so (Ausländerbeauftragte, 1990b:12). This survey also reveals that indigenous Germans still shy away from closer relationships to foreigners: Only 25% of 'West Berliners' and 12% of 'East Berliners' would marry a foreigner (op.cit.: 13)[14].

Another way of testing the inclusion of 'foreigners' was done by the same institute on behalf of the magazine *Der Spiegel* in 1992 (quoted by Koch-Arzberger 1993: 20): Respondents were asked for their views on the idea of recruiting foreigners into the police-force[15]. 17% of the respondents thought of this idea as 'very good', 41% as 'rather good', 22% as 'rather bad', and 15% as 'very bad'. A clear majority (58%) was in favour. This high percentage could, however, be interpreted as a reaction to the numerous arson attacks on foreigners in Germany during 1991 and 1992, and thus, not as a fundamental, long-term change in attitudes.

## 7.3 Commentary

A comparison of the above social attitude surveys and polls conducted separately in Germany and Britain is not a straight-forward matter as the actual questions were not always identical in both countries, neither in terms of timing, nor in terms of content. However, a few general trends and phenomena can be observed. Thirty-five% of the British respondents have been identified as 'prejudiced' or 'prejudiced-inclined'. Fifty-two% of the German respondents thought the presence of foreigners in Germany is too high - which might be an indicator of prejudice. A study undertaken by the *Zentrum für Türkeistudien* (1995)[16] developed a scale to measure discriminatory statements and concluded that 25.1% of the respondents are 'prejudiced' and 47.3% 'prejudiced-inclined'. It seems as if respondents in Germany are more prejudiced, but the problem with the British surveys is that respondents were *directly* asked whether they thought they were prejudiced. In the German case, the level of prejudice was established *indirectly*. It can be assumed, therefore, that less British respondents described themselves as prejudiced than they might actually be[17]. There is also a difference between what people *state* that they are and how they *behave or act*. In other words, people might not be aware of their prejudices. Moreover, opinion polls and attitude surveys do not provide any information on group pressure and how the individual would act as part of a 'mass' (or crowd of people). More significant, therefore, might be the fact that more than half of the respondents in both countries object to a cross-'racial' or cross-'ethnic' marriage which shows a quite low level of acceptance on a personal level (moreover, in the British case, even a high proportion of those who claimed not to be prejudiced objected to such marriages!). There is also evidence that 'racially' or culturally more distant people are less welcomed (and less accepted). In Britain and Germany, Muslims seem to encounter in particular high levels of hostility, prejudice or 'racial' discrimination.

In addition, a European survey of 1995 established a 'xenophobia index' and concluded that 21% of the sample are very xenophobic, 27.5% xenophobic, 28% a little xenophobic and 24% very little to not at all (European Commission, Eurobarometer No. 42, 1995). Those percentages indicate a much higher level of 'xenophobia' compared with the surveys reviewed above. This might have to do with the definition of 'xenophobia' which is, unfortunately, not provided in the survey. The overall European attitude towards the *number* of immigrants residing in EU-member-states is, however, very similar to the nationally conducted surveys: 52% thought in 1993 that there are 'too many' non-European residents in their country (Commission of the European Communities, Eurobarometer No. 39, 1993).

In Britain, a lot of the questions centred upon ethnic minorities' substantive citizenship status: respondents were asked about their views on job discrimination on the basis of 'racial' differences, on the Race Relations Acts, and on criminalization of ethnic minorities. By contrast, questions put to German respondents dealt more with the formal citizenship of 'foreigners'. In both countries, the replies revealed that governmental policies were largely supported: i.e. the restrictive policies on future immigration and existing legislation (the anti-discrimination legislation as it exists in Britain; the naturalization procedures as they exist in Germany since the introduction of the 'child citizenship model': Most of respondents were in favour of the ius soli principle by rejecting dual nationality). It has also been suggested that slightly more liberal attitudes towards settled immigrants in both countries coincides with steady reduction in numbers of 'newcomers'.

Two observations are particularly interesting when comparing the selected surveys: in both countries, despite the described general trends, an increasing polarization of the various political parties' supporters seems to have taken place. Identifiers with conservative and right-wing parties are by tendency more 'anti-immigrants' than any of the other parties' supporters. In the British context, this was suggested as a phenomenon starting around 1983. It could, therefore, have to do with the rise in populism as promoted by the Conservatives under the government of Mrs. Thatcher (Clemens 1983). In Germany, the representation of the *Republikaner* in a few local governments has certainly had some impact on the CDU/CSU's move further 'right'. It must also not be forgotten that left-wing parties are aware of the support they get from ethnic minority groups. In Britain, the Labour Party began to respond to minorities' needs since elections are being more determined by marginal constituencies in which large ethnic minority populations hold the power of balance (Mason 1995:113); in Germany, most ethnic minorities would vote for the SPD if they could (Sen, in: Leggewie & Senoçak 1993; Sen & Karakasoglu 1994). The Green party is particularly popular among young Turkish people.

The second observation is that there seems to be a higher level of awareness, and an advanced understanding, of 'racial' discrimination in Britain, for instance with regard to job discrimination and criminalization. This must have to do with the existence of the Race Relations Acts. In Germany, by contrast, settled immigrants are still being seen much more explicitly as a 'problem' - already in the way in which questions were put in some of the surveys. In both countries, however, future immigration and the increasing number of asylum-seekers were similarly perceived as a 'problem'. Politicians' rhetoric of 'bogus' has, thereby, been taken on by respondents most of whom thought that the asylum law was being abused (as in Germany) or that a lot of immigrants were 'illegal' (as in Britain).

Overall, the surveys show that ethnic minorities do not enjoy an equal status with the indigenous majority in terms of citizenship - formally and/or substantially. The surveys reviewed above have linked this issue mainly to 'racial' discrimination. However, these surveys fail to address the issue of the differences between ethnic minority groups to a more satisfactory extent. Also, the issue of national identity has only indirectly been dealt with. In Britain, for instance, most people thought that immigrants should adjust to British culture, and in Germany 'foreigners' were perceived by fairly high percentages as not valuing what stereotypical Germans allegedly value (cleanliness, etc.; these surveys were, however, fairly 'old'). This issue needs, therefore, to be looked into in more detail.

## 7.4 Surveys on national identity

In this section, I want to discuss whether there is an association between a sense of national pride or identity which has exclusionary effects on ethnic minorities. A special international report as part of the British Social Attitudes series compared British and German levels of pride in their country (Jowell et al. 1989). West Germans are according to this report still conspicuously reluctant to express pride in being German. In 1986, only 20% of the German respondents thought of themselves as 'very proud' and 13% as 'not proud at all', as opposed to 53% of the British ('very proud') and 3% ('not proud at all'). This has changed however. A Eurobarometer survey of 1995 showed that although the Germans are still the least proud, the percentages of those feeling 'proud' were 45% and 'not proud' 35%[18]. For Britain, 81% opted for 'proud' and 15% for 'not proud' (European Commission, Eurobarometer No. 42, p. 67). Feelings of strong national pride are concentrated in the age group of 55 and over, and six out of ten EU citizens are reported as saying they are proud of their nationality either because this is seen to be a citizen's duty or because it is simply seen as 'something natural'. 'National identity' was also tested in connection to 'European identity'. In the six founder member-states is the highest proportion of respondents who say that they see themselves most of the time as 'Europeans' in addition to their nationality (and Britain is not one of those six). When all EU-respondents are taken together, 10% see themselves as 'European' first and then as a national of their country; 46% first as a national and then as 'European'; and 33% in terms of their nationality only. The UK is by comparison still the least European country, and the Germans have the highest figure for 'European first and then nationality' (15%). The answers to these questions are clearly related to those on national pride. Those who are 'fairly or very' proud of their nationality tend to identify themselves as such, while the less proud respondents tend to identify more with Europe, either additionally or exclusively.

The findings for 1996 reveal a further change with regard to the German data: Only 9% now think of themselves as 'Europeans first and then nationals', 43% as 'nationals' first and then European' and 38% as nationals only. There is, therefore, a remarkable increase in those who see themselves in nationality terms only. This must be related to post-reunification developments and an increase in confidence as a 'nation', but also part of an 'anti-foreigner' atmosphere in the light of huge socio-economic problems such as rising unemployment. The EU overall average in this matter is worse in 1996 than the year before (European Commission, Eurobarometer No. 44, 1996) which might be related to the increase in membership and the low European consciousness in the new member-countries (Sweden in fact has taken the place of Britain as the least European country in terms of identity). So, for whatever reasons, there seems to be increasing retreat to an emphasis on national identity. This trend might, therefore, indicate rising nationalism. On the other hand, high self-esteem does not automatically have to correspond with a feeling of superiority or degradation of others. However, with respect to more populist right-wing governments - at least in Germany and Britain - there might be rising nationalism at least among supporters of right-wing and conservative parties.

A survey conducted in the German context by the *Zentrum für Türkeistudien* (titled "The image of foreigners by the public") found that particularly among those people to whom national identity is a very important matter on a personal level there is the tendency to agree with anti-immigrant statements (1995:119). A relationship was, therefore, established by the authors between nationalism and racism. The data showed a strong correlation between total agreement with nationalistic statements and the characteristic 'prejudice-inclined' (20% of sample). For example, most respondents agreed with the statement 'Germans should have more rights' and most respondents emphasized the differences between foreigners and Germans based on the 'non-adaptability' of foreigners when asked for the causes of 'inter-ethnic' problems (however, more than one-quarter, 28.9%, saw the main cause for those problems in the prejudices and ignorance on the part of the indigenous majority - so, here again, a polarization can be noted). Overall, half of the respondents who identified with their nationality were classified as 'prejudice-inclined', followed by respondents who rather identified with the region they live in or who felt first of all 'cosmopolitan' or 'European' and who expressed the least anti-immigrant attitudes (op.cit.: 121-22). In terms of political alliance, the most who expressed rather 'nationalistic' and 'prejudiced' statements were identifiers with conservative and right-wing parties, the least nationalistic and prejudiced were supporters of the Green party. A similar survey could not be found for the British context, but as the previous section has shown that identifiers with the Conservatives were by tendency the most prejudiced and as the British Conservative Party is also well known for its nationalistic rhetoric (Gilroy 1987), it is assumed that a similar survey would have very similar results.

## 7.5 Concluding remarks

Ethnic minority and immigrant related issues appear in the surveys reviewed as quite controversial and seem to polarize respondents' views in both countries. It has also been suggested, that the replies to questions in public opinion surveys can be highly influenced by single or multiple events at a particular time and do, therefore, not necessarily indicate long-term changes in attitudes on the part of the respondents (Zentrum für Türkeistudien 1995).

Shortly after the infamous arson attacks in Mölln and Solingen, for instance, a survey conducted by the *Emnid* Institute on behalf of the magazine *Der Spiegel* in 1992 found that before the attack in Mölln, only 43% of the respondents disagreed with 'anti-foreigners' attitudes and phrases, but after the attack this percentage rose to 69. Another survey undertaken in Germany shortly after the attacks resulted in 70% of the indigenous respondents being in favour of granting the local voting right to foreigners which had been rejected four years ago by 72% of the respondents. The same is likely to be observable in the British case after incidents such as the Rushdie Affair or riots such as in Bradford in 1995. A short-lived increase in pessimism with regard to the future of 'race relations' in Britain - as identified in one of the British Social Attitudes surveys - for instance, has been linked to the riots in 1985 (Jowell et al. 1992). It might, therefore, be true that it is more plausible to assume that certain events have a strong influence on the responding behaviour rather than that there has been a sudden change in attitude. Hence, events can function as a 'shock effect' (Zentrum für Türkeistudien 1995).

The surveys reviewed show that with regard to general attitudes towards ethnic minorities, fluctuations are rather minor. Instead of seeing these fluctuations only as a result of events, however, Koch-Arzberger (1993) suggests that an increase in the agreement with more liberal or more discriminatory statements is linked to the level of politicization and politicians' rhetoric. It is, thus, questionable - as rightly observed by Koch-Arzberger - whether these fluctuations really mean a change of attitude or rather a change of conditions under which it is more acceptable to utter discriminatory or hostile remarks (or to even 'act' out intolerance through violence). A climate of more or less acceptability of anti-immigrant statements could again be created by politicians' rhetoric. If they depict foreigners or immigrants as a problem and if they show sympathy with anti-immigrant attitudes and depict them as 'justified', it is only to be expected that such views are taken on by the wider public.

On the whole, it can be observed that most respondents support governmental policies which underpins the hypothesis by the *Zentrum für Türkeistudien* (1995) that the language used by politicians in the context of asylum and immigration (which is then reproduced by the media) causes and stabilizes prejudices vis-à-vis foreigners and immigrants. This is, however, not only the case in negative terms: Politicians' rhetoric can also cause more liberal attitudes. This was shown in the case of major support for existing anti-discrimination legislation in Britain and the future willingness to accept the ius soli principle (albeit without the provision for dual nationality) by the German public.

Another proposition relevant in this context is that the asylum and immigration issue is used by politicians to distract from other, more important, but less easily solvable, socio-economic problems. In other words, the issue of asylum and immigration is made into a serious problem more or less deliberately to deter the public's attention from other socio-economic problems. Unemployment or the fear of potential unemployment, for instance, is often suggested as being the cause of racially discriminatory attitudes. Those attitudes are first of all directed against non-European immigrants and are expressed in many different ways (Zentrum für Türkeistudien 1995). This can be well illustrated in the German context: reporting on the results of a public opinion survey, Ms. Noelle-Neumann wrote in an article for the *Frankfurter Allgemeine Zeitung* of 8 November 1992:

> Economic problems and also resentments in the new *Länder* towards the West Germans are pushed into the background due to problems of 'floods' of asylum-seekers which then has the effect of uniting the East and the West. Under such circumstances, the worry that more conflicts between East and West Germans could break out becomes a minor issue. This remarkable result is hardly acknowledged by the public. (quoted by Zentrum für Türkeistudien, 1995:56; free translation)

More important than the actual socio-economic differences between the East and the West was the issue of the increasing numbers of asylum-seekers. This topic functioned, therefore, as a 'unity construct' to overcome social and psychological problems between the East and West.

In the British context, forthcoming elections have been suggested as resulting in increasing pandering to populism (Clemens 1983) and in the 'abuse' of the 'immigrant and asylum issue' (or the 'race card') in order to gain votes. Public opinion surveys seem, therefore, to be used to induce and accelerate political 'action' in a directed way, i.e. towards 'action' which is realizable. As the issue of immigration and asylum has gained increasing importance in political discourse in Germany and in Britain since the 1980s, if not even earlier than that in particular in the British context (Powell's 'river of blood' speech!), it seems that phrases such as 'bogus asylum seeker' and metaphorical references to numbers as part of argumentative patterns within political discourse have been reproduced as part of the wider public's opinion. These linguistic metaphors or phrases often depict the foreigner as a problem.

One issue which warrants caution when assessing results from opinion surveys is the aspect of personal contact with ethnic minorities. A study done by the *Leipziger Zentralinstitut für Jugendforschung*, for example, came to the conclusion that 50% of the respondents judge without ever having had any contact with 'foreigners'. In answer to the question of whom they think first when they hear the word 'foreigner', 48% replied 'the Turks' although no Turkish people lived in the former GDR (Zentrum für

Türkeistudien 1995). In the British context, a Gallup poll has found a similar phenomenon: Two-thirds of indigenous people have hardly any or even no contact at all with ethnic minorities. Interesting in this context - applicable to both countries - also is that there seems to be evidence that individual preference of a party can lead to differences in perception. In other words, if a respondent is a supporter of a right-wing party such as the *Republikaner* in Germany, this person is more likely to perceive foreigners in a more negative way than, for example, a supporter of the Green Party (IPOS 1993). Hence, increasing contact does not have to result in more acceptance and tolerant behaviour.

A typical German issue is that 'racial' discrimination and prejudice have often been regarded as a more serious problem in the eastern part since unification (Commichau 1990). The new surveys reviewed here, however, have shown that the East is not fundamentally different from the West (Zentrum für Türkeistudien 1995). The remaining differences result mainly from the fact - as pointed out in the surveys done on behalf of the Commissioner for Foreigners Affairs in Berlin - that in the East there has been less contact with foreigners at home and abroad.

On the whole, the above surveys and polls have shown that respondents are mostly concerned about members of ethnic or immigrant minorities who belong to the largest groups, who have come for economic reasons (whereby the public easily forgets that these people were originally invited to come to Germany and Britain as workers), and whose life-styles appear to be very different from indigenous peoples' customs or habits. Hostility, prejudice and 'racial' discrimination are, thus, not directed against *all* ethnic or immigrant minorities alike. This indicates that certain groups are racialized for certain purposes.

Public attitudes - as analyzed with the help of reports on social attitude surveys and opinion polls - show that there is a conceptual link between citizenship (formal and substantive) and nationality with racializing effects on ethnic minorities in both Germany and Britain. This link does, however, not appear in a clear and straight-forward way. People often display attitudes in contradictory ways. In particular racial prejudice and discrimination may be expressed on one dimension but not on another related dimension. This is less surprising on the proposition that attitudes can be inconsistent and that people rarely conform to tidy descriptions such as 'racist' or 'nationalist' (Jowell & Airey 1984:7).

At the same time, however, the majority of respondents (even if small in places) takes on views of immigration and ethnic minority related issues as expressed by the governing parties in Germany and Britain. In this context, it has been claimed that "what is most important about public opinion in a broader sense" might be "that people are willing to acquiesce in what a small set of leading individuals say" (Niemi 1983, as quoted by Margolis & Mauser 1989:3). In this way, public opinion needs to be treated essentially as dependent. Professional politicians play an important role as they draw "attention to the existence of problems and the merits of possible solutions" (Margolis & Mauser 1989: 309). Their rhetoric usually emphasizes values and goals, rather than facts or analysis, and it often consists of arguments in symbols or slogans that are misleading or incomplete (ibid.). However, it should not be forgotten that the public's opinion is highly polarized with regard to many, if not most, immigration and ethnic minority related issues. This and some of the other connections raised in this chapter will be further investigated in the following chapter.

## Notes

1    The sample in the British Social Attitudes Surveys consists of adults aged 18 and over who live in private households. The sample was selected with the help of the electoral register (twenty-six addresses in each of the eighty-eight polling districts). The 2,288 respondents were selected by a random selection procedure. Only 84 of those were members of ethnic minority groups and it is not clear which groups exactly they represent. Because of the small size and the non-identification of origin, special reference to their views has, therefore, to be treated with caution.

2    The precise questions asked were: "First of all, thinking of Asians - that is people originally from India and Pakistan, who now live in Britain. Do you think there is a lot of prejudice against them in Britain nowadays, a little, or hardly any?"; "And black people - that is West Indians and Africans - who now live in Britain. Do you think there is a lot of prejudice against them in Britain nowadays, a little or hardly any?" (BSA 1984:123).

3    This is also confirmed by the findings of a qualitative study (i.e. via in-depth interviews) conducted by Modood et al. (1994) in which ethnic minorities' thoughts and experiences on a variety of issues were tested. Some respondents felt that "on deeper and more personal levels barriers were put up" and that "acquaintance was permissible but 'serious' long term relationships were out of bounds" (p. 90). One respondent is quoted as follows: "They [white people] come in for a cup of tea, but that's as far as it goes. The day your son wants to marry their daughter it's a different story." (p. 90).

4    More precisely, 62% of the sample supported the statement "More or same aid to Asians and West Indians".

5    This opinion poll was conducted by the *Institut für Demoskopie Allensbach.*

6    The abbrevation stands for *Institut für praxisorientierte Sozialforschung.*

7    The sample in each of the four studies consists of persons older than 18 and includes only 'indigenous' Germans. In West Germany, 1546 respondents were selected and 1171 in East Germany.

8    A telephone survey (sample: 600 indigenous German youths aged between 16-25) done in 1990 on behalf of the Commissioner of Foreigners' Affairs in Berlin confirms this: Most Berliners thought that the

most important problem the Senate of Berlin should deal with is housing (53%), followed by traffic (43%), jobs (35%) and then 'foreigners' policy' (31%) (Ausländerbeauftragte 1990a:15) .

9    The same telephone survey mentioned in footnote 8 found that only 46% of the respondents are in favour of local voting rights for Turkish residents who are not naturalized (Ausländerbeauftragte 1990a:10). This survey does not include any information on party alliance of the respondents.

10    The PDS (Partei des Demokratischen Sozialismus) replaced the former SED and exists only in East Germany.

11    This is also confirmed by the surveys done in Berlin on behalf of the Commissioner for Foreigners' Affairs (Ausländerbeauftragte, 1990 a+b).

12    This is also supported by the findings in a study by the *Zentrum für Türkeistudien* titled "Das Bild der Ausländer in der Öffentlichkeit" (the image of foreigners by the public) (1995). In their qualitative study on 'Changing Ethnic Identities' (1994), Modood et al. have found that despite contact with one 'nice' member of an ethnic minority, the 'white' majority take this person as an exception and nevertheless hang on to their prejudices - as expressed in the following quote (by an Afro-Caribbean man): "Sometimes you will get all white people in a group and they hate black people, but you will be there and they will say 'you are all right' and it's because they know you so you are all right." (p. 67).

13    East Germans have only been part of the sample since 1990.

14    As opposed to the *Allensbach* surveys during the 1970s (Noelle-Neumann 1981), this survey does not make a distinction between the various groups of 'foreigners'. The sample consisted of 1,353 'East Berliners' and 1,505 'West Berliners'.

15 '    Foreigners' are largely excluded from employment in the police-force - as from most positions in the public service - based on their non-German citizenship.

16    This study was conducted in Dortmund in1994. The sample consisted of 263 persons older than eighteen and limited to indigenous Germans. The respondents were interviewed (45 - 60 minutes) whereby certain issues were addressed in an 'open ended' way to let the interviewees express their views in their own words. The results are said to be transferable to the context of other large cities of the same social structure as Dortmund.

17    A survey (1990a) conducted on behalf of the Commissioner for Foreigners Affairs in Berlin found a similar phenomenon as in the British case: When asked directly, the majority of respondents thought that other people are prejudiced, but only 24% thought of themselves as prejudiced.

18    It has to be noted that the Eurobarometer survey offered only two options ('proud' and 'not proud'), whereas the British Social Attitude survey had two more ('very proud', 'not proud at all').

# 8 Parliamentary debates on ethnic or 'racial' issues

Reports of a number of key parliamentary debates in Britain and Germany will be investigated in this chapter to provide an elite perspective on the effects of racism and nationalism on ethnic minorities' citizenship. Despite the fact that there has been a development towards more multi-ethnic or multi-'racial' discourse and practices in politics during the post-war period, racism and nationalism have not been eradicated in contemporary western Europe. As has been indicated in the previous chapter, politicians can undeniably be regarded as a crucial part of this problem (Miles 1989). There is, of course, a difference between some extremist right-wing parties which express their racist positions quite explicitly and the majority of the mainstream parties in most western European countries (European Parliament 1990). Most governments and mainstream parties actually distance themselves from explicit racist attitudes and practices (van Dijk 1993).

In this chapter, I will examine the definitions and language politicians use in formal speeches with regard to 'race relations' as well as the connections they make between the elements of racism (or racialization), nationalism, and citizenship. When taking a position on ethnic minorities or 'foreigners', politicians' assumptions about German and British society in terms of legitimate membership often reveal this connection. The focus will thereby be on the more subtle and indirect forms of 'white' dominance as expressed by elites operating on the basis of minimal consensus within society (van Dijk 1993). That is to say that the indigenous majority's dominance tends to be taken for granted since it is regarded as legitimate to treat ethnic minorities or 'foreigners' differently from the indigenous population in certain areas and situations (Hoffmann & Even, 1984). This consensus is tied into everyday language and comes to the surface as soon as issues related to ethnic minorities or 'foreigners' appear. The 'legitimately' different treatment of ethnic minorities excludes them partially from rights and liberties regarded as natural for indigenous people. On the basis of this consensus, political elites are involved in the reproduction of a system of ethnic or 'racial' dominance "in many apparently innocent and impeccable ways" (van Dijk 1993:59). Thus, the issues of immigration and asylum become subject to legislation in order to partially solve, or at least not to aggravate, unemployment, serious housing shortage, or for other 'good' socio-economic reasons. However, such legislation tends to affect immigrants from non-European countries more than any other immigrants which means that 'colour' and religion (in particular

Islam) become *the* issues of discrimination and racialization. This has implications for ethnic minorities' formal and/or substantive citizenship status.

The role of parliamentarians in all this is obvious: not only do their official statements reflect their party's position, but they are also well aware that their speeches will appear in the records and may be quoted in the mass media, which play an important role in linking elites and the public (Margolis & Mauser 1989; DISS 1992). Hence, politicians are fully responsible - politically and morally - for their verbal contributions which have an impact to a lesser or greater extent on media coverage and public opinion (Zentrum für Türkeistudien 1995). This is especially important in the context of 'race relations' "since the controversiality and sensitive nature of most ethnic topics require that the politicians be aware of what they can say and what should not be said." (van Dijk 1993:66).

## 8.1 Some general remarks on the debates

After having established which prominent debates expressing elite political views on immigration issues had taken place during the 1990s, a selection of parliamentary verbatim records was collected from the British House of Commons (Hansard) and the German *Bundestag* (Stenographische Berichte).  In the German case, these were the principal debates preceding the New Foreigners' Law of 1991 (Ausländergesetz) and concerning the call for dual citizenship for long-term resident immigrants. In the British case, ethnic or 'racial' affairs and related issues are not topics that are very often discussed in the House of Commons and most debates, therefore, centre upon immigration and asylum. Increasing focus has thereby been on the various measures to control the entry of refugees and other immigrants. The control of their numbers and of expenditure on social benefits has been debated by way of referring to the majority of asylum seekers as 'bogus'. The effects of the new immigration and asylum bill proposals on long-term resident ethnic minorities - in particular those from the Indian sub-continent - were of particular concern to the opposition parties. One exception to the debates which focused predominantly on asylum and immigration matters during this period was the 'Opposition Day' debate on 'Ethnic Minorities' on 9 June 1992.

The overall style of parliamentary debates in both countries is quite similar, characterized by much open aggression, constant interruption, derision, and protests against the respective parties[1]. In both countries, governments were formed by the conservative parties throughout the 1990s. In Britain, the governing Conservative Party debated against Labour and the Liberal Democrats; in Germany, the governing coalition of the CDU/CSU and FDP debated against the SPD, the Green Party (Grüne) and the PDS (successor of the former SED and represented in Parliament since reunification). In particular, the critical remarks and unconventional style of the latter two (such as the call for a 'Schweigeminute' - a minute's silence and the fixing of a banner to the lectern) usually led to furious reactions from the more conservative Right.

In Britain, the following debates have been consulted:
1.    debate on the Asylum Bill of 13 November 1991;
2.    debate on the Asylum Bill of 21 January 1992;
3.    debate on Asylum & Immigration of 2 March 1992;
4.    Opposition Day of 9 June 1992;
5.    debate on Asylum & Immigration Appeals Bill of 2 November 1992;
6.    debate on Asylum & Immigration Bill of 11 December 1995.

In the case of Germany, the following debates have been dealt with:
1.    debate on dual nationality for citizens of the FRG and GDR (Doppelstaatsangehörigkeit für Bürger und Bürgerinnen der BRD und DDR) of 8 November 1989;
2.    debate on the Bill for Amendments to the Foreigners' Law (Entwurf für ein Gesetz zur Neuregelung des Ausländerrechts) of 9 February 1990;
3.    debate on the same Bill of 26 April 1990;
4.    debate on the Bill for the Facilitation of Naturalization and Acceptance of Dual Nationality (Entwurf eines Gesetzes zur Erleichterung der Einbürgerung und Hinnahme der Doppelstaats-angehörigkeit) of 29 April 1993;
5.    debate on the Bill for Amendments to the citizenship law (Entwurf eines Gesetzes zur Änderung und Ergänzung des Staats-angehörigkeitsrechts) of 11 November 1993;
6.    debate on SPD Bill for the Facilitation of Naturalization and Acceptance of Dual Nationality of 28 April 1994;
7.    debate on the same SPD Bill of 9 February 1995.

In all the quotes, I have chosen remarks by major proposers of bills and opponents (all of whom elected Members of Parliament). The quotes from German debates appear here in free translation.

## 8.2  The German debates

### 8.2.1  *Ausländerfeindlichkeit and racism*

Dr. Burkhard Hirsch (FDP) remarked that "hardly any other political topic divides public opinion more than that of the correct 'foreigners' policy." (9 February 1990, p. 15031) - and this is also the case among parliamentarians of the various parties[2]. One of the areas of differences is the approach politicians take to the terms of *Ausländerfeindlichkeit* and racism. None of the established parties (CDU/CSU, FDP and SPD) used either of the two terms *explicitly* in all of the above mentioned debates. In a debate on amendments to the existing Foreigners' Law, the Home Secretary in 1990, Wolfgang Schäuble, only mentioned the positive version of *Ausländerfeindlichkeit* when insisting that German society has been *ausländerfreundlich* (friendly towards foreigners) and that it would remain so in the future with the help of the proposals for a new Foreigners' Law (9 February 1990, p. 15023). There are, however, a number of ways in which parliamentarians' hostile, or racializing, rhetoric - albeit expressed implicitly - can be pinned down conceptually. Even in their criticism of the government's policies and in their demands for more radical advances in naturalization and citizenship law, members of the SPD and FDP expressed the discriminating effects of the existing laws and the new proposals by using terms such as 'exclusion' and 'lack of participation'.

Only members of the Green Party (Grüne) and the PDS explicitly referred to 'racism' in the course of the debates.

> We don't need a further Foreigners' Law whose expression and driving force is a racist attitude which declares certain people as a risk on the basis of their nationality and devalues them by denying them elementary human rights. (Trenz, Grüne, 9 February 1990, p. 15034)

The same MP argued in another debate that the present law as well as the proposals for the New Foreigners' Law would encourage 'routine racism' and the scapegoating of immigrants and refugees, and thus would make foreigners responsible for increasing social problems in the post-reunification era (26 April 1990, p. 16288). She referred to a number of proposals (such as restrictions on family unification) as 'institutional racism' (p. 16289) which was perceived as a provocation by members of the governing coalition and led to the following reaction by Dr. Hildegard Hamm-Brücher (FDP):

> ...a chill ran down my spine when our colleague, Ms. Trenz, said this bill was a form of institutional racism. As the older ones among us had to live under institutional racism for twelve years, Ladies and Gentlemen, I beg you, and in particular our younger colleagues, to show respect for these terrible experiences and not to introduce such concepts into our everyday political business. (26 April 1990, p. 16295)

Here, reference is clearly made to the Nazi-period during which, undeniably, an extreme form of institutional racism existed and which is believed to warrant the concept of racism being treated as a taboo in the post-1945 period. In this view, the contemporary approach to, and treatment of, ethnic minorities and immigrants cannot be racist. The use of the term itself is experienced as a moral accusation, never as a factual description of the situation - and Trenz justified her previous remarks on similar lines:

> I have been criticized for having used the word 'racism'.... Racism is a word that always provokes outrage here in the German *Bundestag*. Racism does not always have to be homicidal. Racism is a word which, for instance, is normally used in France. In the Federal Republic of Germany....I am not allowed to mention it....According to its definition, racism merely means that people are being evaluated,devalued and discredited on the basis of their different nature, their different nationality, etc. That is exactly what happens in this bill. That is why I said it. (Trenz, Grüne, 26 April 1990, p. 16298)

Despite the reluctance to use the term 'racism', there is, however, a general understanding among the opposition parties that the proposals for a New Foreigners' Law do not abolish the distinction between peoples of different cultural and phenotypical backgrounds and that this distinction's main function is the maintenance of particular power and material relations. There is, therefore, an implicit understanding of racialization. This also becomes clear in the way in which the need for a new type of collective identity and the demand for full citizenship rights for settled immigrants has been debated (see also below). By avoiding the explicit use of that term, however, contemporary forms of racism are being mitigated or even denied.

The classification of peoples into the different categories of 'citizens' or 'residents' has not only appeared in the debates as a matter of *Ausländerfeindlichkeit* or racialization, but also as a sign of nationalism.

> We will not support a single line...of this proposal which is founded on the classification of people by means of ethnic criteria (völkische Abstammungs-kriterien) and which tries to gloss over the government's planless immigration policies with the help of *nationalistic* pathos. (Trenz, Grüne, 26 April 1990, p. 16289; my emphasis)

> In view of the *nationalistic* and restorative tendencies in our society, in view of assaults on foreigners and arson attacks, and in view of *racist* aberration...the delaying of reforms of the citizenship law has to come to an end. (Weiss, Grüne, 28 April 1994, p. 19411)

In the above quotes, both nationalism and racism are perceived as being on the rise (probably since reunification) and as affecting immigrants in a negative way. This could be interpreted as an elite view, on similar lines as done by Bauman who claimed that nationalism is the 'racism' of the intellectuals (1992:675). One way of counteracting these negative effects for 'immigrants' would be a re-definition of Germany's concept of membership.

### 8.2.2 *Collective identity*

There are a number of elements - based on minimal consensus - which constitute collective identity: the image a society, or nation, has of itself; common values; and the collective upgrading and depreciation of groups of people (who are usually outsiders, i.e. 'the other').

Images a society or nation has of itself include all those elements which are perceived as 'normal' and 'natural' to the indigenous majority. These images tend to be founded on positive values, but they become negative when contextualized with 'the other' (Hoffmann & Even 1984). The then Minister of the Interior, Wolfgang Schäuble (CDU), said the following in his introduction of the Bill for a new Foreigners' Law:

> One of the traditional values of the occidental society is tolerance vis-à-vis different life-styles. (9 February 1990, p. 15023)

As residents in Germany, foreigners and their 'different life-styles' are, however, often perceived as a threat or a problem - either on the basis of the length of their residence or their numbers. Schäuble's statement, therefore, seems to apply to foreigners who come to Germany only as 'guests' and return at some point, but not necessarily to the context of permanent settlement. As opposed to the above quote, it is often pointed out that the existence of 'foreigners' constitutes a danger to German national identity because the indigenous majority will become a minority in its own country.

> The less we rob the Germans of their feeling that they can live in a nation [Heimat] of Germans in the future, the more openly they will welcome and accept foreign residents. The more we convey to the Germans the feeling they will live in a ...fluid multi-ethnic society tomorrow, the more hostile they will act towards foreigners. (Gerster, CDU/CSU, 9 February 1990, p. 15035)

Here, clear fear of *Überfremdung* [3] is expressed and thus, an indirect reference to numbers of foreigners - and in particular those who originate from distant cultures. Moreover, the speaker, Gerster (CDU/CSU), indicates in this excerpt sympathy with hostile reactions on the part of the majority. The numbers of foreigners play an important role as there is the general perception of "limits to the ability to integrate and the willingness to integrate" (Schäuble, 9 February 1990, p. 15023). However, not all foreigners are perceived as such a threat.

> We receive them [East Germans and ethnic Germans from Eastern Europe]
> in our midst as Germans among Germans. (Chancellor Kohl, CDU, 8
> November 1989, p. 13013)

> All borders are open to [East] Germans and ethnic Germans.....The fact
> that national and ethnic minorities belong to this country....is usually
> ignored.... (Trenz, Grüne, 9 February 1990, p. 15033)

There seems to be consensus about the 'naturalness' with which
East Germans and ethnic Germans are incorporated as 'Germans' into
German society. However, opposition parties deplore the fact that long-
term settled immigrants are excluded from this collective identity which
thus gains an ethnic/racial character. The negative depiction of certain
foreigners has been criticized by a number of parliamentarians. The
following two quotes illustrate the clash in approach by Conservatives
and the SPD:

> [In addressing Manfred Kanther, the Minister of the Interior] Why do you
> make statements about Muslims which almost always imply that these are
> people we have to fear? (Däubler-Gmelin, SPD, 9 February 1995, p.
> 1232)

> Will the Federal Republic of Germany be able to get rid of violent
> foreigners or foreign drug dealers, if they possess dual nationality?
> (Marschewski, CDU/CSU, 28 April 1994, p. 194060)

These quotes show that some foreigners are in particular seen as
a threat to national identity on the basis of their religion (mainly
Muslims, i.e. Turkish people) or as potentially violating law and order.
There is a tendency to criminalize certain groups of immigrants and
thus, to depreciate them.

A further aspect of collective identity are common values. As
opposed to the opposition parties which relate common values mainly to
constitutional aspects ("We should concentrate on our central
constitutional values", Däubler-Gmelin, SPD, 9 February 1995, p. 1230),
the governing CDU/CSU adds rather diffuse ideas to these values as
expressed in the following:

> ...citizenship is the expression of the fundamental relationship between
> social and legal membership. ...Citizens' rights and duties are ....the most
> integral part of our state and our democracy. There is one reason for this:
> as history has taught us, every nation [Volk] is a *Schicksalsgemeinschaft*
> (a community sharing the same fate). (Schäuble, CDU/CSU, 29 April
> 1993, p. 13199)

The above statement shows how the speaker focused on a positive approach to a certain understanding of German society and life within it rather than on an explicit approach towards foreigners. Schäuble attempted to separate the assessment of foreigners as people of different cultures from the legitimate membership in German socio-national community. He has thereby ignored the fact that two-thirds of all foreign youths have meanwhile been born in Germany and that in everyday language, the term 'foreigner' has ceased to mean exclusively members of other nation-states, but that it is also used to refer to certain ethnic minorities in German society. In doing so, Schäuble holds on to the 'old' image of Germany not being a country of immigration and settlement. The opposition has very different thoughts about this:

> We make a clean sweep of the life-long lie of our country, namely that it has never been a country of immigration. (Schröer, SPD, 9 February 1990, p. 15030)

> We are de facto a country of immigration. We have to realize that. Not only by putting it in nice phrases, but by adapting this reality to our legislation. (Sonntag-Wolgast, SPD, 11 November 1993, p. 16274)

In this way, members of the opposition show the contradiction between the traditional image of German society and the existence of fairly large numbers of long-term resident 'foreigners' within this society. By referring to Germany as a country of immigration, or a multi-cultural/multi-ethnic society, the traditional image is not adjusted to reality (as attempted in the CDU/CSU rhetoric), but reality is adjusted to the image of German society.

Furthermore, the CDU/CSU arguments mostly come from the point of view of the indigenous majority. Rarely is the position of foreigners taken into consideration from the foreigners' perspective. It is the Federal Commissioner for Foreigners' Affairs who points out the dilemma young foreigners are facing:

> [about the situation of foreign youths] Many of them are in a contradictory situation. ...Part of these contradictions is that on the one hand, they are brought up in a democratic country and are educated at school to be responsible citizens....on the other hand, they experience that they cannot take part in elections. The image which they have of themselves - namely: "we live like German youths" - does not correspond with the image that others have of them. ...On the one hand, it is demanded of them to integrate, and on the other hand, they stumble again and again against the limits of [this interpretation of] integration. (Schmalz-Jakobsen, FDP, 11 November 1993, p. 16277)

It is, therefore, not only the indigenous majority which seems to have problems with its (traditional) image and reality, but the immigrant minority too - with the crucial difference that the latter are excluded from citizenship on the basis of these wrong perceptions.

### 8.2.3 *Citizenship and nationality*

In particular the debates about the facilitation of naturalization procedures by allowing for dual nationality make very clear that the CDU/CSU's understanding of citizenship is strongly linked to nationality - as for example in the following quote:

> [Explaining why he is against dual nationality] "For me, to be a German citizen means to accept this country with its advantages and disadvantages, to identify with the past and the present, with our history. For me, to be a German citizen means to belong to this *Schicksalsgemeinschaft* (community sharing the same fate), which one cannot join or leave as one pleases. " (Marschewski, CDU/CSU, 28 April 1994, p. 19407)

Resulting from this, Erwin Marschewski explains the CDU/CSU policy position:

> In the context of the comprehensive reforms of the citizenship law, we will adhere to the principle of descent (Abstammungsprinzip)." (28 April 1994, p. 19408)

The member of the SPD, Dr. Cornelie Sonntag-Wolgast, rightly commented that this term 'community of fate' describes a society "to which foreigners do not belong" (9 February 1995, p. 1219). A member of the Green Party, Konrad Weiss, referred to this term as "typically German" because it actually is about "German blood". He demands a "modern citizenship law" which allows that those "who want to be German, can be German" (28 April 1994, p. 19411). Here again a clash can be observed between the traditional image of a community of descent (as adhered to by the CDU/CSU) and the reality of a country which has become the new home of fairly large numbers of immigrants.

German citizenship in its legal sense is, of course, not totally exclusive as naturalization is possible. There are, however, different views on the requirements. A member of the Green Party criticized the CDU proposal for a new Foreigners' Law on the grounds that it means effective facilitation

> only for the third generation whose ties with the country of their parents' origin have totally - I quote - "been severed". (Trenz, Grüne, 9 February 1990, p. 15034)

The requirement of 'severing ties' with one's country of origin can be interpreted as a definition of 'integration'. The CDU/CSU is of the opinion that naturalization presupposes integration (Schäuble, 29 April 1993, p. 13199) and even more so, there is the view that granting German citizenship is not only the precondition for integration, but "the evidence for its success." (Kanther, Minister of the Interior, CDU/CSU, 9 February 1995, p. 1220). As opposed to this definition - which again entirely comes from the indigenous majority's point of view based on a definition of 'integration' which is very close to 'assimilation' - the opposition parties developed an understanding of integration which takes into account that immigration is a long-term process that requires "mutual recognition" (Sonntag-Wolgast, SPD, 9 February 1995, p. 1219).

> We don't demand that [foreigners] tear down all bridges. For us, naturalization as of right does not presuppose 'mastering' the German character. (Sonntag-Wolgast, SPD, 28 April 1994, p. 19405)

The opposition parties define citizenship as separate from nationality. For them, it is crucial to provide immigrant minorities with the necessary legal changes which give them the status and the feeling to be "a responsible citizen of this state" (Schmalz-Jakobsen, FDP, 29 April 1993, p. 13202). They have to be able to participate as fully recognized citizens, and not only by way of 'duties' such as tax-paying - as summarized by a member of the SPD:

> It is about mutual recognition and the living together of people of different origin. The immigrants who have resided here for a long time, should be able to feel at home and recognized, not only as tax-payers, as 'stopgaps' in the labour- market, as providers of our pensions, but also as partners who are able to participate fully in the political and social formation of the will of the public. (Sonntag-Wolgast, SPD, 28 April 1994, p. 19404-405)

The emphasis in all of the German debates is clearly on the formal status of long-term resident immigrants and their children. But there is also appreciation of a substantive side to citizenship, albeit the CDU/CSU uses this as an argument against dual nationality. The opposition parties, similarly believe that formal equality will not eradicate verbal or physical assaults on people of non-European origin. However, they also think

> that the 'hopeless' [die Unverbesserlichen] among us might not so easily utter the phrase "they take our jobs and flats away", when they learn that the 'foreigners' are citizens in legal terms. (Sonntag-Wolgast, SPD, 29 April 1993, p. 13208)

The opposition parties are clearly against the treatment of immigrant minorities as "second-class citizens" (Weiss, Grüne, 29 April 1993, p. 13203) and demand their full equality with ethnic Germans who migrated from Eastern Europe and in whose case "dual nationality is tolerated and accepted" (Cem Özdemir, Grüne, 9 February 1995, p. 1236). The latest amendment of the Citizenship Law by the so-called 'child citizenship' model has not satisfied the opposition parties. The Minister of the Interior, Manfred Kanther (CDU/CSU), described this new model as "an alternative to the concept of territorial rights [ius soli] and to the general acceptance of multi-nationality" (9 February 1995, p. 1223) - a compromise which has, according to the Federal Commissioner for Foreigners' Affairs who represents the coalition-partner FDP, not been "the FDP's baby" (Schmalz-Jakobsen, FDP, 9 February 1995, p. 1227). This amendment has been criticized for not providing immigrants with "equality", but for pushing foreigners into a further "special law" instead (Jelpke, PDS, 9 February 1995, p. 1229).

## 8.3   The British debates

### 8.3.1 Racism

The British debates show a more straight forward use of the language of 'race' and 'racism' to the extent that some parliamentarians refer to each other as 'racist', but overall - as in the German case - there are differences between the governing Conservatives and the Opposition parties with regard to their general rhetoric and content of their statements. Those parliamentarians who represent the Conservative Parties usually deny the allegations that aspects of the Immigration and Asylum Bill have racist implications and that their way of responding to the phenomenon of asylum seeking is in any way "racialist" (Kenneth Baker, Home Secretary, 13 November 1991, col.1085). When comparing the British situation with continental Europe, they come usually to the following conclusion - as expressed by the then Home Secretary - that

> [we] have been working at improving race relations in Britain for over 30 years, under successive governments. Some of the speeches by politicians of all parties on the continent in recent months would be simply unacceptable from a politician in Britain. I draw some comfort from that fact, because it reflects our maturity with such matters. (Baker, Home Secretary, Conservative, 13 November 1991, col. 1083)

There is certainly some truth in the claim that Britain is well advanced in its anti-discrimination legislation which does, however, not mean that racism as such is eliminated. When it comes to rhetoric,

British politicians are not far off their European counterparts - as rightly remarked by two parliamentarians;

> We have heard in what I can only describe as the intemperate rantings of the hon. Member of Welwyn Hatfield (Mr. Evans) what the extremists - the hardliners in the Tory party - really feel about foreigners.....The hon. Gentleman's speech might more appropriately have been delivered at a National Front rally. (Watson, Labour, 13 November 1991, col. 1132)

> [The] decline of the National Front owes more to the swamping speech of the former Prime Minister which led to members of the National Front leaving in droves to support the Conservative party, than to any immigration or asylum policy. (Austin-Walker, Labour, 2 November 1992, col. 94-95)

The above statements might represent a somewhat provocative and exaggerated picture of the Conservative rhetoric style. Nevertheless, it can be observed that the governing party's racializing discourse is mostly embedded in a rhetoric of 'fair, but firm', the 'bogus asylum seekers', 'law and order' and the never ending 'numbers game'.

> Good race relations are heavily dependent on strict immigration control. Race relations in Britain are not perfect - they could be better - but they are better than they are almost anywhere else in western Europe or north America. One reason for that is that our host population feels comfortable with a system that restricts to manageable numbers the influx of people from overseas. (Clarke, Home Secretary, Conservative, 2 November 1992, col. 21)

> Race relations in Britain are much better than in many other European countries, but we have to tread carefully to ensure that they stay so. Above all, we must act in a way in which prejudice is not fanned, and people must not be led to believe that immigration is out of control. It that happens, racial tension will rise, and the whole country will be the loser. (Howard, Home Secretary, Conservative, 11 December 1995, col. 711)

Firm immigration controls are regarded as the prerequisite for 'good race relations' (Layton-Henry 1992). This means that the presence of immigrants is seen as the cause for 'bad race relations'. The above quotes, thus, imply that in the light of increasing immigration, rising 'racial tension' would be a natural and 'understandable' outcome. As much as in the German case, therefore, the Conservatives in Britain mainly focus in their rhetoric on the indigenous majority's point of view and the general public's minimal consensus on the issue of immigration.

In doing so, they convey to the wider public that their attitude is fully acceptable.

> The Government want to protect genuine refugees and will work for solutions to their problems, but domestic asylum policy is only part of that process. To achieve the wider objective, it is essential to preserve public sympathy for refugees - and public confidence in the fairness and firmness of our determination system is crucial to that. (Baker, Home Secretary, Conservative, 13 November 1991, col. 1094)

Being depicted as 'firm, but fair', this rhetoric hides the fact that the proposed Bill's main purpose is to keep black and Asian people out of Britain. By referring to the 'public's confidence', the Conservatives pander to populism and the anti-immigrant sentiments within the wider public - an aspect taken up in the following quote:

> Reference has been made to the rise in racism, particularly on the continent. We should not pander to that racism. We should condemn it and remember that immigration is not the cause of racism. Immigration is simply an excuse for racism. (Darling, Labour, 13 November 1991, col. 1164)

This statement makes clear that it is not the immigrants as such who are to be seen as the cause of racism, but that racialization takes place in connection with wider social problems for which immigrants are not responsible.

> Racism and fascism are on the increase in Europe [including Britain] because the ingredients on which they feed are present: unemployment, poor housing and poverty. ...such elements have little to do with immigration controls, which are entirely independent of those who feed on people's fears and turn understandable concern into prejudice by pandering to the worst of those fears. (Darling, Labour, 9 June 1992, col. 194)

> I am concerned that a pattern is emerging of black and migrant communities being blamed for the economic failures of the countries in which they happen to be living. That blaming process....cannot be separated from the arguments about the position of refugees and asylum seekers. There is a serious and sustained attempt to deflect the failures of capitalism.... (Simpson, Labour, 2 November 1992, col. 100)

Interesting are the Conservatives' rhetorical tactics aiming to hide the fact that their proposed Bill includes racializing elements.

> Differences in race and colour matter a great deal less in Britain than they did, but numbers matter very much indeed. They matter regardless of race

and colour; they matter because this is a relatively crowded island;...they matter because of the importance of keeping our communities, diverse as they are, together as Britons. (Baker, Conservative, 11 December 1995, col. 740)

Concern for 'numbers' is claimed as replacing 'concerns for race and colour'. Implied is that the British are not anti-immigrant or 'racist', but legitimately worried about their overcrowded country. Again, it is hidden here that the 'concern for numbers' is dealt with in the new Bill by refusing  black and Asian people entry into Britain.

A further rhetorical tactic of the Conservatives is their repeatedly stated aim to crack down on 'bogus applicants' which they have mentioned in connection with phrases such as 'flooding' and 'waves of immigrants'. In doing so, they blatantly generalize and give the wrong impression to the public about immigrants.  This rhetoric has, therefore, been rightly criticized as "a thinly disguised campaign of racism" (Maclennan, Liberal Democrats, 2 November 1992, col. 54) and as treating "all asylum seekers as a guilty group" (Watson, Labour, 21 January 1992, col. 257).

Concern has also been expressed about cultural dilution.

If I am concerned about the cultures in the town that I represent,  which have changed so much over the past few years because of so many activities, then I admit to being a racist. (Carlisle, Conservative, 13 November 1991, col. 1133)

It is acknowledged in this statement that colour does not have to be the only element of racism, but culture as well. By admitting so openly to be racist (despite the word 'if'), however, John Carlisle conveys that his concern is understandable and natural, and thus legitimate. Cultural concerns could also be interpreted as elements of nationalism, and elsewhere Carlisle said that he stands "purely on the basis of being nationalist" when asking for the protection of his community by keeping the numbers of immigrants down (2 March 1992, col. 57). The co-existence of nationalism and racism is, therefore, evident in this quote, too.

### 8.3.2 *Positive self-representation and collective identity*

References to positive values and characteristics are made for a number of purposes: 1. they can represent collective identity of the whole 'nation' on the basis of minimal consensus, 2. they are used to show that certain parties have better principles than other parties (opposition to the opponent); and 3. they are used to defend policies.

The following statement makes clear reference to the whole national collectivity.

[G]ood race relations....require a sense in the host community that the law of reason is being applied to the level of immigration and the degree of assimilation or integration that is thus required. (Brooke, Conservative, 11 December 1995, col. 723)

It is implied here that British people's concern for increasing numbers of immigrants is guided by 'the law of reason'. Being reasonable is, therefore, part of the British character and justifies the concern for high numbers. By using the term 'law', this fits into the populist 'law and order' rhetoric of the Conservatives.

We shall represent legislation that will be fair to the genuine applicant - fair to everyone indeed - but the system will be governed by the rule of law. (Clarke, Home Secretary, Conservative, 9 June 1992, col. 162)

The Conservatives 'sell' their proposals by claiming to pursue 'firm, but fair' policies within the 'rule of law', and thus, make the general public feel good about taking these concerns on. They point out that these policies are part of their party's principles and that they are, therefore, to be preferred to the opposition by saying that the Labour Party "represents a weak policy. [Whereas] we represent a strong policy." (Baker, Home Secretary, Conservative, 13 November 1991, col. 1106).

Another element of positive self-presentation in the debates is the recurring reference to the British tradition of tolerance.

Historically, the United Kingdom has been tolerant of asylum seekers. The public have always felt that they should tolerate those who have faced harder circumstances than their own and who have been forced to leave their country of origin. We should applaud such tolerance, which has always been a fact of life. However, it has been subject to enormous strain in the past seven years because of the number of asylum seekers who have been proven bogus. (Duncan Smith, Conservative, 2 November 1992, col. 52)

We have a long and honourable tradition in the United Kingdom of offering political asylum to those who flee to this country from their country where they face individual persecution...The Government intend to uphold that fine tradition. (Clarke, Home Secretary, Conservative, 2 November 1992, col. 21)

Britain has a proud record of giving refuge to those fleeing genuine persecution, but we cannot ignore the fact that our procedures are being abused. (Howard, Home Secretary, Conservative, 11 December 1995, col. 699)

Phrases such as 'historical', 'long and honourable' and 'proud record' all imply that Britain has always been a tolerant country. The myth of this claim has, however, been uncovered by the work of Colin Holmes (1991) in his historical account of reactions to immigrants and refugees since 1871. By implying that "Our party, Our country, Our people, are humane, benevolent, hospitable, tolerant and modern" (Van Dijk 1993:72), however, politicians open their rhetoric line for negative 'other' representation. If 'we' are the 'good ones', then 'they' must be the 'bad ones'. This in fact happens in the British debates which centre upon the 'bogus' nature of immigrants and asylum seekers. Ethnic minorities' marriages are described as 'arranged' (and thus, not the result of a 'love relationship'), therefore they are subject to suspicion by the immigration authorities who operate with the help of the 'primary purpose rule' - a fact highly criticized by the Opposition.

> In the official mind the arranged marriage is confused with a bogus marriage. ....The primary purpose rule by which applicants who wish to join their wives in Britain are judged is intellectually absurd and morally indefensible. (Hattersley, Labour, 9 June 1992, col. 156)

Overall, a clearly negative depiction of the immigrant and asylum-seekers can be observed, partly based on their criminalization[4]. This has been regarded by the Opposition on numerous occasions as having negative effects for settled ethnic minorities.

### 8.3.3 Discriminatory effects for ethnic minorities

As opposed to Germany, 'racial' discrimination in Britain is mainly to be identified with regard to substantive citizenship, as most ethnic minorities enjoy an equal formal status as citizens. This becomes clear in Roy Hattersley's introductory speech on Opposition Day about Ethnic Minorities:

> [He begs] that this house recognising that the ethnic minorities within British society receive less than their fair share of national resources and remain victim of discrimination and prejudice, calls upon the Government to introduce and implement policies which initially reduce and eventually eliminate the disadvantages which are suffered by these British citizens. (Hattersley, Labour, 9 June 1992, col. 149)

Although formally British citizens, Hattersley claims that ethnic minorities "are denied the full rights of British citizenship" (9 June 1992, col. 149). This is based on many facts, according to Hattersley, such as: the denial of bail for 'black' defendants in circumstances in which it would be granted to 'white' suspects; rejection of highly qualified black and Asian job applicants for no other reason than their racial origins; and the unemployment rate among 'black' males which is twice as high as among 'white' males. In particular Muslims and Sikhs are regarded as "permanently condemned to second-class status" in terms of their substantive citizenship (Hattersley, 9 June 1992, col. 151).

Despite the fact that ethnic minorities enjoy full formal citizenship rights,

> there is a tendency by officialdom when confronted with a black, brown or yellow face to suspect that the person is not a genuine British citizen and to require him to prove his status. (Hattersley, Labour, 9 June 1992, col. 155)

The idea of nationality and citizenship being identical seems, therefore, to be still present in the attitude of some parts of the indigenous majority .

The Conservative Party interpreted the statistical evidence in a different way when suggesting that

> [t]here is a large and successful Asian entrepreneurial and professional middle class. ...We need a stronger black middle class (col. 169)....Many people from all minorities are rising in the professions (col. 170). (Clarke, Home Secretary, Conservative, 9 June 1992)

The Opposition used the figures to support their claims that "low numbers in professions" and the high numbers of black and ethnic minority inmates "demonstrate institutional racism" (Abbott, Labour, 9 June 1992, col. 172). So, in some respects there have been improvements, but they are not entirely satisfactory to all members of Parliament. Jim Lester (Conservative), for instance, explained that the numbers of ethnic minority recruited into the police force have risen, but that more should be represented "in the magistracy, as barristers, judges and at all levels of our legal system." (9 June 1992, col. 188). Only in that way can it be assured that the special privilege of living in Britain is exercised by all citizens.

There is also the issue of racially motivated "harassment, abuse and often violent attacks" which are the "daily experience of many black citizens." (Austin-Walker, Labour, 9 June 1992, col. 189). This shows that certain sections within the majority do not recognize ethnic minorities as equal. Moreover, this also means that apart from indirect racial discrimination, there are instances of direct racial discrimination in the form of physical attacks and abuse.

As ethnic minorities' issues are rarely debated in the House of Commons, most of the debates from which quotations have been chosen in this chapter centre upon the Immigration and Asylum Bill. Although this Bill is mainly about restricting new immigration and the number of asylum seekers, it has been criticized as having implications for settled ethnic minorities, too. The Bill has been described by various members of the Opposition as "stirring up racist feelings" and thus, as having "repercussions on the general attitudes to the black population in the United Kingdom". (Hoey, Labour, 13 November 1991, col. 1144). The proposed restrictions on housing and the crackdown on illegal workers were also seen as having negative effects for settled ethnic minorities.

> The boss of the firm will immediately cross out from the list of applicants all the people whom he or she thinks might possibly be bogus asylum seekers or illegal immigrants. The people crossed out will not be called Howard and Hattersley: they will be called Khan and Patel. I do not suggest for a second that in doing so that employer would be intentionally racist. However, he would be doing what so often happens in this country. Without wishing to and almost without knowing, he would be discriminating against one section of the population. (Hattersley, Labour, 11 December 1995, col. 729)

One member of Parliament even referred to this situation as "job apartheid" (Henderson, Labour, 11 December 1995, col. 788) - a provocation which could have resulted in outrage in the same way as Trenz's (Grüne) reproach of 'racism' received in one of the German debates. But this did not happen. Another important issue of concern for settled ethnic minorities is the separation of 'bogus' and 'genuine' visa applicants. This was claimed to affect black and Asian citizens' right "to be visited by their friends and families" (Hattersley, Labour, 9 June 1992, col. 154).

All of these criticisms relate to ethnic minorities' substantive citizenship as racial discrimination in the British context mainly takes place in connection with substantive rights and liberties.

## 8.4 The European level

In the selected German and British debates, the European dimension of ethnic minority related issues has also been mentioned - albeit not in a comprehensive way, as these debates dealt with amendments to *national* laws.

Opposition parties have deplored the creation of "a Fortress Europe, so that the European Union can turn its back on those who are seeking refuge from violence, from persecution, from war, and from torture." (Madden, Labour, 21 January 1992, col. 278). Concern has also been expressed in both, British and German debates, about the status of non-European long-term residents in countries such as Germany where they usually do not have formal citizenship rights and can, thus, be "denied the status of free movement throughout the European Community." (Godman, Labour, 2 March 1992, col. 27). By not extending European citizenship rights to non-European settled immigrants, the Community has been criticized for "creating an underclass" (Corbyn, Labour, 2 March 1992, col. 63). In the British debates, this was mainly seen as a problem for "immigrant workers long domiciled in...France or...Germany" (Godman, 2 March 1992, col. 27) and not for ethnic minorities residing in Britain. In Germany, too, concern was expressed about preferable treatment of EU-nationals as a result of the Maastricht Treaty (in terms of granting local voting rights) by excluding long-term resident non-EU nationals from these provisions (see, e.g., Däubler-Gmelin, SPD, 29 April 1993, p. 13196). This has led an MP representing the SPD to claim that

> one could regard the privileges for EU-nationals as a form of discrimination of the remaining permanent foreign residents - such as the approximately 1.9 million Turks - in the FRG. (Andes, 28 April 1994, p. 19413)

The lack of formal citizenship is, therefore, recognized as a problem not only on the national (German) level, but on the European level, too.

Despite being formally recognized citizens, ethnic minorities in Britain might also encounter problems in the form of a clash between their formal rights and their substantive liberties on the European level.

> [T]he Maastricht Treaty....will create problems for people from black and ethnic minority communities. The Act is supposed to allow free movement of people, but we know that, because of racism, people are not being allowed to move freely around Europe. They are being stopped on the borders and on the streets of European cities and asked to produce documents, purely on the basis of the colour of their skin. (Grant, Labour, 9 June 1992, col. 183)

Definitions of European citizenship are thus not only legal issues, but also issues of identity. This has been mentioned in the German debates, too. A member of the Green Party, for instance, has criticized the positive evaluation of the collective 'European' majority by depreciating 'the [non-European] other':

> What kind of Europe do we want?...In this Europe, where new definitions are being preached, the collective depreciation of social groups which are not European, are reinforced. ... A social civil war is stirred up between Europeans and non-Europeans. A Europe where Arabs, Asians and Latin-Americans are stigmatized - such a Europe...is not open as long as it reduces its *Ausländerfreundlichkeit* (friendliness towards foreigners) to Europeans. (Menenes Vogl, Grüne, 26 April 1990, p. 16277)

As a result, it appeared in the debates that ethnic minorities' formal and/or substantive citizenship is negatively affected on the European level, too, on the basis of racialization and traditional images/identity on the part of the majority as 'white' and 'culturally homogeneous'.

## 8.5 Concluding remarks

The tendency - starting around 1980 - of rendering immigration issues increasing importance in political discourse (Zentrum für Türkeistudien 1995) has not ceased during the 1990s. Parliamentary debates in both countries, Germany and Britain, have played an important role in this.

The selected parliamentary debates in both countries have shown that the reproduction of racism is a complex process and often appears in connection with nationalism. What happens in political discourse is not simply a matter of imposing a dominant ideology of 'white' supremacy. On the contrary, as van Dijk has rightly remarked, "contemporary ethnic-racial attitudes and practices are usually much more sophisticated and even contradictory" by incorporating "general egalitarian and humanitarian norms and values" (1993: 113). This is mostly done in a subtle and indirect form by focusing on positive self-presentation. The purpose often is indirectly to hint at negative construed properties of other groups of people.

Moreover, political discourse on immigration and asylum policies seems to be largely polarized. This shows that ethnic or 'racial' dominance is not absolute, but rather that "different elite groups and subgroups may be variously involved in the reproduction as well as in the challenge of dominance" (van Dijk 1993:113). This polarization has become especially clear in the German case where the majority of conservatives hold on to the claim that "Germany is and cannot be a country of immigration from countries outside the European Union", whereas a minority of Green party members is in favour of an 'open door' policy (Kulluk 1996:302). The SPD, the majority of the Green Party, and some members of the FDP represent a third, and more realistic, position: they press for the improvement of the legal and socio-economic status of current immigrants with long periods of residence. The Greens and the regional SPD groups do not demand citizenship of origin to be given up at any point (Kulluk 1996; Cohn-Bendit & Schmid 1992) - which represents a more radical policy than the new 'child citizenship' model which includes 'toleration' of dual citizenship until immigrant children come of age.

In Britain, the polarization of the parties is not quite as evident as the Conservatives and Labour are both against an 'open door' policy and the reduction of 'bogus asylum seekers'. They disagree on measures for ascertaining and defining 'bogus applicants' and also on the general effects this has on settled ethnic communities. Members of the Labour Party are in general more concerned about racial discrimination with regard to ethnic minorities' substantive citizenship. Both parties recognize the diversity of ethnic minorities' experience and socio-economic position in British society, but Labour is far more critical of remaining areas of evident racialization (such as the criminal justice system) and the shortcomings of European citizenship. The polarization of political parties in Germany and Britain is reflected in public opinion, as illustrated in the previous chapter. And yet, on the whole, public opinion reflects the power position of the governing parties as the majority - at times overwhelmingly, at times narrowly - holds the same views as the conservative parties in both countries.

Overall, it can be observed that there is a more advanced understanding of racism and its indirect effects on ethnic minorities' citizenship in Britain. This has to be linked to the fact that formal citizenship is not an issue in the British context and that comprehensive anti-discrimination legislation exists. By contrast, political discourse in Germany centres upon formal citizenship. However, the governing Conservatives in both countries make use of similar populism and dangerous rhetoric about immigrants, foreigners, and asylum-seekers by negatively stereotyping these groups in association with crime and 'bogus' (Husbands 1994) - dangerous as this rhetoric tends to result in blatant generalizations about ethnically or 'racially' different people in general and thus, can have negative effects for settled migrant communities (in particular on their substantive citizenship). This type of rhetoric has been described in both countries by the opposition as 'pub talk' (Hattersley, Labour, 2 November 1992, col. 48; Sonntag-Wolgast, SPD, 28 April 1994, p. 19405-406; the German equivalent is 'Stammtisch'). Thus, despite national differences in content and use of terminology, the prevailing political discourse in both countries is remarkably similar as to rhetorical and argumentative strategies of legitimation, rationalization and persuasion - as also observed by van Dijk (1993). References to positive self-evaluation and depreciation of 'others' are thereby signs of racialization and nationalism.

These strategies in German and British parliamentary discourse can also be interpreted as constituting an 'us' and 'we' pattern: 'we' are above all suspicion with regard to racism and nationalism as opposed to 'them', the political opponent. It is thereby arguable to what extent left-wing parties are genuinely more liberal and free of a sole interest in securing votes (a criticism made against the Conservative Right). In both countries, the asylum issue has shown a 'change of heart' of the Left (SPD and Labour) and thus, a move towards 'the right'. The example of the asylum laws shows that "at the end of the day, it is the professional politicians who decide often ignoring the considerations and the recommendations made during hearings and motivated solely by securing maximum success and their own power in the next election."

(Kulluk 1996: 313). And yet, it cannot be denied that left-wing parties are perceived as being more concerned about ethnic minorities' interests (Sen & Karakasoglu 1994) and that the right-wing parties tend to use a more populist rhetoric than their left-wing counterparts[5].

Kulluk comes to the conclusion that "rethinking and restructuring of political discourse in ways which could contribute further to the projects of 'citizenship in Europe' and open, transnational citizenship, cannot be left primarily to the professional politicians." (1996:318). Her suggestion that "it calls for the active efforts of both the immigrant and the German [and British, N.P.] populations" (ibid.) leads to my conclusion as explained in chapter Six: that this is best done by way of local citizenship.

This chapter has shown that the symbiotic relationship between nationalism and racialization appears in parliamentarians' rhetoric, expressed in positive self-presentation of the indigenous majority by (mainly culturally) depreciating ethnic minorities. The views of representatives of ethnic minorities' pressure or interest groups on these issues will be the subject of the following chapter.

## Notes

1       This is the case when *reading* the transcribed debates. It is a different matter when actually listening to the debates: in Britain, there is far more 'noise' (laughter etc.) than in Germany.

2       Hidir Çelik came to the conclusion in his work on media coverage of the 'foreigner' issue (Ausländerfrage) between 1980 and 1990 that the policies proposed and/or pursued by the SPD, FDP, and CDU/CSU were characterized only by minor differences. Having read the key parliamentary debates during the 1990s, however, I can not support this view - at least with regard to *verbal* articulation of the SPD's policy demands or proposals (and some members of the FDP) as opposed to the conservative Right.

3       There is no perfect equivalent of this expression in the English language. 'Foreign infiltration' is what the dictionary has to offer, but 'swamping' comes much closer. *Überfremdung* is politically loaded - and so is 'swamping' since the Thatcher-era.

4       The aspect of criminalization has been debated by the Opposition in particular with regard to fingerprinting of asylum seekers.

5       A fact which Clemens (1983) has underpinned by empirical evidence in his work on the Conservatives' electoral success in 1979 and the move towards populism in British politics since then.

# 9 The Interviews

Having reviewed most of the relevant academic literature, I wanted to find out the way in which the theories I had read and my own thoughts about them - as outlined in the chapters Four, Five, and Six - match up with the opinion of organizations who are actively engaged in improving 'race relations' in Germany, Britain, and on the EU level. In addition, having identified some common trends regarding general public attitudes and patterns in parliamentarians' discourse regarding immigration and ethnic minority related issues in Germany and Britain, it was also of interest to find out whether the selected organizations made any reference to these attitudes and politicians' rhetoric.

The objective of this chapter is, therefore, to explore the views of lobby groups and governmental or semi-governmental organizations working in the 'race relations' field (or Ausländerarbeit - the German equivalent) concerning the three main issues of interest here: racism, nationalism or national identity, and citizenship. The issue of the extent to which nationalism and racism affect (in a combined form) immigrants' citizenship status and the extent to which the concept of citizenship could minimize these effects, and thus function as a mechanism for inclusion, has so far not been explored by empirical research. Therefore, in their capacity as experts and opinion leaders influencing policy-makers by lobbying and as general campaigners for issues of their concern (aimed at 'the public'), the thoughts and ideas of the interviewed representatives of selected organizations are regarded as very useful for the understanding of the interrelated workings of racism, nationalism and citizenship.

The proposing of actual policies is an area only a few of the selected organizations engage in. More importantly, though, as most of them are involved in grass-root work or have strong links to grass-root organizations, they are familiar with ethnic or immigrant communities' concerns and needs. If not directly active at grass-root level, they offer personal advice to single members of ethnic communities in matters of integration/inclusion and are, therefore, in one capacity or another an important source from which to find out the nature of the 'dimensions of welcome' - to use Husbands' words - within British or German society. Thus, the interviewed groups were also expected to express their satisfaction or dissatisfaction with available policies of inclusion as well as their demands for future improvements.

The interviews were expected to yield information with regard to the main arguments developed in the previous chapters, i.e. the argument for

1.  a symbiotic relationship between racism and nationalism and its impact on citizenship as reflected in the close link of citizenship and nationality

in law (state level) as well as on the level of acceptance or rejection of the ethnic/immigrant minorities by the indigenous majority (i.e. within civil society);
2. a conception of citizenship which is a) sub-divided into a formal and a substantive notion to grasp conceptually the difference between the legal status and a wider social status; and b) three-layered.

This should allow the assessment of the inclusionary powers of such a conception and its usefulness as a mechanism to resist the power of racism and nationalism.

As for a three-layered conception of citizenship, these groups' awareness of developments on the European level and their understanding of European citizenship will be identified (or similar notions within their common sense thinking) with the implications for the emergence of a new type of (sub-national and/or supra-national) citizenship. Therefore, the interview replies were analyzed according to the additional question whether the EU has made or might make any difference to national citizenship regarding the minimization of the powers of racism and nationalism.

The structure of this chapter follows the structure of the previous chapters in that there are three main sections on racism, nationalism/national identity, and citizenship. The order of appearance was different during the actual interviewing (see Appendix IV) as the interviews began with the issue of national identity/nationalism, followed by the issue of racism and then by the issue of citizenship. The thought behind this was that in the actual interview situation, it was tactically viewed as better not to start the interviews with the controversial and 'touchy' issue of 'racism' (which is maybe more the case in Germany than in Britain), but rather with national identity. However, to maintain the same structure and line of argument, the sections of this chapter will follow the order of the previous chapters.

## 9.1 Racism

In this section, the objective was to explore the variety of the selected groups' views on, or definitions of, racism and the consequences or limitations for immigrants' citizenship. For this purpose, the questions focused on: 1. whether the interviews conveyed the idea that racism exists in German and British society (and if so, how); 2. whether the interviews expressed the notion of racialization and racisms (or similar notions in their common sense thinking), i.e. different racisms across time and space in terms of target groups and articulation; and 3. whether they yielded any evidence for the argument of a symbiotic relationship between nationalism and racism.

As a reminder, in Britain, five organizations were interviewed: one semi-governmental organization which is in charge of monitoring the workings of the Race Relations Acts; and four non-governmental groups (one of which is run by and mainly for the Indian community; the remaining three engage in all sorts of lobbying and consciousness raising activities). In Germany, seven organizations were interviewed ranging from two federal-state institutions (one of which is directly involved in policy-making) to five lobby groups (three Turkish groups, two established by indigenous Germans). On the European level, the EU Migrants Forum was interviewed as it is the only 'pan-European' lobby group.

### 9.1.1 The British organizations

*General definitions* The *existence* of racism in general was not disputed by any of the interviewees. However, there were differences in their views on its broad definition - a fact which could have to do with the different nature of each organization's 'field of activities'.

The head of a voluntary organization which mainly engages in public campaigning without any policy-making power thought of racism as:

> ...[P]rejudice plus power. ...And a lot of politics....It is about power, it is about systems of control...It is the system of capitalism also. (Int. 3/B)

In this definition, two different dimensions of racism are combined: 'prejudice' as an individualistic notion and 'system' as an institutional or systemic form of racism. This rather simplistic 'prejudice & power' view could be interpreted as reflecting the type of activities this organization is involved in, which seems to require a rather symbolic, challenging and rhetoric language (i.e. persuasive speech rather than the reflection of 'objective' reality). The 'prejudice & power' definition might, therefore, function as a 'catch-phrase'. Such a broad view could also hardly be translated into actual policies - an area outside this organization's capacity.

A different view, however, was expressed by the director of another voluntary organization whose main objective is to publish research type of literature on 'race relations' matters and related issues. In the interviewee's own words, this organization is "in principle interested in philosophical issues." There is, therefore, no need for a 'catchword' type of definition and the involvement in research seems to result in a more complex definition:

> I have a view of racism itself as a complex set of interactions...There is a whole range of things and I do not want to say the one thing is more important than another. I rather speak in terms of a package...And I think if one did say this is the thing and in fact only this, then that is what is mostly called tokenism...when we criticize things for tokenism, what we

often mean is that something which is good in itself ....has been split off from other things..... (Int. 1/B)

The distinction between 'catchword' and 'complex' definitions can be made for all the interview replies. Most of the non-governmental lobby groups expressed a 'prejudice & power' view (with the exception of the above quoted group), whereas the semi-governmental organization had a far less simplistic approach to the definition of racism.

Despite this distinction, the ideas on racism merged when they were applied to concrete situations.

*Concrete manifestations*  The interviewees referred to a range of elements as reflecting racism: attitudinal, structural and discursive elements. Taking them all together in "a complex set of interactions", they present racism as all-pervasive in British society.

> Racism....really, that is from just name calling or graffiti to...deaths. Extreme levels of prejudice played out in that way [are] mainly in housing. Black people have the worst housing, education, social services, employment. Black people are more likely to be unemployed than their white colleagues. And there is racism within the state, the police or the judiciary, the criminalization of young black people - in all forms of life racism...raises its dirty hand... (Int. 3/B)

The attitudinal elements, according to this view, cover verbal abuse and physical violence. This form of racism is also reflected in the social structure, i.e. in the area of housing, employment, health etc., and as part of the control machinery of the state. These elements were mentioned by other interviewees as well (5/B; 2/B).
One interviewee added another type of element - discursive racism.

> In particular, if I look at the effects - the unemployment figures, for example, I would say they measure racism. Figures from health, figures from housing, education, achievement - there is a whole range of things which represent structural racism. In terms of discourse as distinct from structure, [there is] the discourse of the extreme right-wing party....but also the more coded discourse of the tabloid press and *The Times* and *The Telegraph,* I would mention.... (Int. 1/B)

The first quote stems from the same interviewee who defined racism as "prejudice & power" which is clearly of a rhetoric nature. But when looking at the elements mentioned as concrete reflections of racism, they are as 'complex' as the elements mentioned by the second interviewee (who described racism straight away as a complex phenomenon). There is consent among all the interviewees that racism is reflected at all levels of (British) society and that it is manifested in a variety of ways. This is underpinned by the many different types of research done on racism in the area of housing (Rex & Tomlinson 1979), employment (Brown 1984), racial violence (Gordon 1990), state structure (Gordon 1993), criminalization (Gordon 1992; Gilroy 1987), education (Gill et al. 1992) and health (Skellington & Morris 1992) as well as discursive racism (van Dijk 1993). There is, therefore, plenty of empirical evidence underpinning this view of racism as existing within many institutional spheres as well as the discursive realm.

*Articulation*  All interviewees agreed that contemporary forms of racism are less expressed in biological terms and more culturally. It was, however, not suggested that a biological way of thinking has completely disappeared from people's minds. This means that Barker's notion of a 'new racism' (1981) or Balibar's notion of a 'culturalist racism' (in: Balibar & Wallerstein 1991) focusing on cultural differences was similarly expressed by the interviewees. At the same time, however, Mason's belief that the 'old', i.e. biological racism, has not completely 'died out' (1992:23) was confirmed by most of the interviewees.

> ...As for articulation - overtly, most certainly, there is much less discourse of a biological difference, though I think that has not disappeared, it is just beneath the surface...there are still metaphors or words which imply biological belief...But I do not think that any educated person will still maintain and expand a biological basis for racism. They would still expand the belief that any country should be culturally as homogeneous as possible. (Int. 1/B)

It is interesting that this interviewee mentions education as one criterion for the way in which racism is articulated. An educated person would 'wrap up' racist thinking in cultural explanations - a statement which shows clearly how close this cultural type of racism is to nationalism. In other words, the belief that a country "should be culturally homogeneous" could very well be read as a nationalistic idea. The view that in particular educated people express their racist views in cultural terms is also suggested by Bauman who defines nationalism (i.e. cultural explanations) as the racism of the intellectuals and racism as the nationalism of the masses (1992:675).

This aspect of education could also be the reason why another interviewee thought that, from a personal point of view, racism "is less articulated than ever before". And yet, when it comes to his professional experience (as senior information officer in a semi-governmental organization which monitors the workings of the Race Relations Acts), he qualified this statement:

> When we get involved in race discrimination cases, we continue to find a - I mean I could show you piles of cases which we have taken to courts

when black workers going to a factory are abused, assaulted in a way in which somebody like me who never experiences it would assume this is gone. But no, it is alive. (Int. 4/B)

The view that racism is "less articulated than ever before" might, therefore, refer to the interviewee's private environment with people who are as well educated as he is. However, when it comes to cases revolving around racial discrimination, the open and blunt type of racism seems to be very much alive. Hence the kind of conclusion the interviewee arrived at:

I do not think, the roots [of racism] have changed. The expression of it may have changed. There is no doubt that English people have different layers of prejudice. (Int. 4/B)

Not only might predominant expressions of racism have changed depending on different historical periods, but also the main target groups.

*Target groups*  As for target groups of racism, some interviewees mentioned different historical periods during which certain groups suffered most from racist attitudes. The notion of racisms (Hall 1978b) and racialization - in particular the idea that not only people of colour can be racialized (Miles 1982; Small 1994) - was, therefore, touched upon.

If we look at British history, the main target groups of racism earlier in the century were Jewish refugees from eastern Europe settling in Britain. (Int. 5/B)

The victims have included Jews, of course. And to a certain extent - we have just published a report on that  - gypsies, but less than on the continent. The Irish in the 19th century - but lots of Irish people maintain that at the present time. (Int. 1/B)

Although Irish and Jewish people have not ceased to be victims of racism, post-war labour migrants seem to be the main target groups in today's context - in particular immigrants from Asia, as explained by one interviewee:

I think a lot also depends on economic [circumstances] - well, say in that group [the Asians], the Bangladeshi community came here latest, has been here in an economic recession and has been less able to move on economically and therefore, is still stuck in a much more dangerous position than, say, some people from India... (Int. 5/B)

'Lateness' of arrival, length of residence and socio-economic conditions are seen here as decisive for the different degrees of racism the various groups of immigrants suffer.

*Origin and sources of racism*  There was the predominant view among the interviewees that the 'economy' is one important source of racialization processes, i.e. as a 'system' (capitalism) which creates circumstances under which racism flourishes (such as in times of a recession). The media and political parties were largely seen as playing an important role in creating an 'anti-foreign' climate in which immigrants are blamed for socio-economic problems. In this way, most interviewees established a macro and micro level of racism suggesting that the roots of racism are lying very deep.

> I think it is an alliance between the media and the parties....It is undoubtedly the media, daily conversation...education....Those are the three biggest places, I think, where the world is - as the phrase is - constructed on a daily basis. ..A view of the world is maintained. (Int. 1/B)

The term 'maintain' is highly suggestive of 'tradition' and the passing on of fairly unchanged ideas. This can, therefore, certainly be interpreted as referring to deeper historical roots of racism - an aspect which the same interviewee expressed more clearly elsewhere:

> I think political parties respond to forces and use these forces....forces in society, the forces in civilization. And the political parties do their best to respond to this and to claim that they can do something about it. (Int. 1/B)

The role of politicians and the media are understood here as crucial 'sources' of racism in the 'micro level' context, but it is also suggested that there are deeper forces within society as a whole. It is, therefore, probably better to refer to the role of politicians and the media as 'triggers' of something which already exists in the midst of society.
   The idea of 'deeper roots' was much more explicitly expressed in reference to history by the following interviewees (the first being a member of an ethnic minority, the second being a member of the majority):

> [Where do racist ideas originally come from?]  "It is from society...It is based on history. (Int. 2/B)

> From our past....We have been in competition with other nations, we have dominated - our peoples have dominated other nations for so long. It is part and parcel of our way of thinking...It is there, it has been passed on from one generation to another one...[Thus] [r]acism appears to be at every level. (Int. 4/B)

This shows quite explicitly how racism has become an almost inevitable part of British society. The latter quote also expresses the idea of racism being rooted in imperialism and colonialism (a racist attitude was developed by dominating other peoples). This leads to the depiction of racism as being linked to the formation of an identity as a (superior) 'race' or an identity as a dominating nation vis-à-vis the inferior and dominated 'Other'. It might, therefore, not be too far fetched to interpret this quote as indicating a symbiotic relationship between racism and nationalism.

### 9.1.2 The German organizations

*Racism - a taboo?* For German organizations, the first question was why there is a general recognition of the existence of 'hostility towards foreigners' (i.e. in the media and political discourse) but a reluctance to refer to this phenomenon as 'racism'. All interviewees (members of the majority as well as Turkish minority) thought that the Nazi-past has something to do with this. But there were differences among the interviewees with regard to their personal opinion and further explanations about the influence of the past on the contemporary context.

> Racism - that was always murder of Jews. (Int. 8/G)

> The term 'race' has become a taboo because of the 'race policies' of the National Socialists. Therefore, it is difficult for us to talk about it because it is the instant reminder of these absurd 'race policies' aimed at extermination. (Int. 2/G)

The experience of extreme racism during the Hitler-era has obviously left its imprints on today's general understanding of racism which is first of all seen in the context of anti-semitism and genocide. Because of racism's "direct historical connection with Hitler", there is the wide-spread belief in Germany that "Hitler is done with since 1945, therefore racism does not exist anymore" (Int. 1/G). But what are the interviewees' personal or organizational opinions?

> The fact that 'hostility towards foreigners' is more talked about in every day life, might also be an avoidance of the issue, but it has also got to do with the fact that the recruited foreigners are referred to. It is not so much about 'race', but that they are non-Germans, whereas....Hitler placed 'race' in the foreground. There is a 'race problem' ...when it is about blacks and whites, namely German blacks or Afro-Germans...and white Germans. In this case, *I would explain* the problem as racism.... (Int. 1/G; emphasis added)

This interviewee believes that because the 'targets' of contemporary hostile attitudes include the recruited labour migrants (i.e. former guest-workers), the terminology of 'race' is not applicable. According to her, labour migrants are thought of as 'non-Germans' in a cultural sense, whereas Hitler's racist ideology and policies were clearly based on biological explanations about the differences between Jews and Gentiles. Interestingly, the same interviewee would use the terminology of 'racism' in the contemporary context of 'Afro-black' and 'white' relations which shows a predominantly biological understanding based on phenotypical criteria, such as the colour of the skin. Differences based on culture are not viewed here as racist. Thus, the distinction between 'new racism' in culturalist terms and 'old', pseudo-scientific racism - as argued for  by Barker (1981) and others - is not reflected in this statement at all. On the other hand, there is the hint that the official denial of 'racism' could also be a matter of avoiding the issue - an aspect another interviewee mentioned in a similar way:

> [The reluctant use of 'racism'] is also about the bad image abroad. ...Seiters, the [then, N.P.] Minister of the Interior, was standing there in front of the burning house in Rostock[1] and said that this damages our image! And if you admit that racism exists, it sounds even worse than hostility towards foreigners....*I think* it has got a lot to do with playing down. (Int. 3/G; emphasis added)

There seems to exist particular pressure - based on recent history - on Germany with regard to its international standing. Parallels to its Nazi-past are drawn quickly by other countries, conveying that Germany 'relapses' into Nazi practices. This might indeed be a reason for the (official) attempt to 'play down' the seriousness of recent arson attacks by avoiding the terminology of racism. This aspect was also mentioned by the following interviewee:

> It is clear that the importance of events in Germany - Solingen, and before Mölln or Rostock - meet a stronger echo within the world public than if it had happened anywhere else. That has got to do with the German past. (Int. 1/G)

Although the past has certainly something to do with the reluctant use of the terminology of 'racism' in the contemporary context, most interviewees did not express the thought that there might be some sort of continuity and 'racist tradition' within society at large. Kalpaka & Räthzel's view of racism - as an 'issue of historical connection' (Frage nach historischer Verbindung; 1990:18) - does not find any equivalent interpretation among most of the interviewees. Only one of the respondents expressed this idea quite clearly. Her view also summarizes very well the prevailing attitude towards 'racism' in Germany:

> There are certainly differing opinions [on whether hostility towards foreigners or racism is the 'correct' terminology]...In politics, it has been maintained for a long time that there is no racism at all in Germany, because we lost our colonies during the First World War. ...Racism is

perceived as a negatively discriminating attack on (Afro-)black people by whites...And that leads to the fact that the term racism must not appear. However, it is individualized by saying "hostility towards foreigners". Moreover, it was made clear in politics that Germany was not a racist country...and the term 'hostility' was [used] as an individual matter [in the sense that] there are only individual 'nut cases' who are hostile towards foreigners. But a general climate, for which the term racism is much more suitable [in my opinion], does not exist. This is the point, why the term is not used, because it is generally denied that something like that exists...*I personally think* that racism does exist collectively in such a society - you can see it institutionally...And it is also in our minds....at least since colonialism it has been in our minds. (Int. 4/G; emphasis added)

This view refers to the issue that the term 'hostility towards foreigners' characterizes an individual attitude, implying that only single persons are responsible for hostile 'activities' (Bhavnani 1993). Another interviewee (Int. 2/G) expressed such an individualizing interpretation as her own opinion of racism. She actually believed in the so-called *'Einzeltäterthese'* (single perpetrator thesis). This understanding, however, does not describe a general climate as expressed by the interviewee in the above quote (Int. 4/G), who viewed racism as resulting from a long history beyond the Nazi-era, including Germany's involvement in colonizing other countries. Therefore, this interviewee seems to have a view of racism as an inevitable logic within all levels of German society (collectively and institutionally). This could further mean that there is an implicit understanding of historically different racisms and racializing processes.

The distinction between 'hostility towards foreigners' as an individualistic notion and a general 'climate' reminds of the distinction made by the British organizations between 'prejudice' and 'systemic' forms of racism.

The view of racism being connected to Hitler's 'race policies' or to the colonial context of 'black and white' relations - meaning that in the contemporary context of Germany, it is 'hostility towards foreigners' as a sole individual matter which exists - was expressed by the interviewees 1/G and 2/G. They both work in the same semi-(state)governmental organization (one as the head, the other one as the senior information officer). This could stem from the fact that the head of this organization was a former CDU member of the city-state parliament. Her general political views are, therefore, likely to be similar to those of the Conservatives - the main party denying any contemporary (German) forms of racism[2] - and this organization's approach to the issue of racism seems to be influenced by these views.

The understanding of racism as a general climate rooted in history, as expressed by interviewee G/4, on the other hand, might reflect the fact that this department was created by the Green Party. Also, the interviewee - the head of this department - has never been a politician herself, but has worked in grass-root organizations for many years. Her knowledge of 'ethnic minority issues' based on her long-term grass-root activism and her personal history (born of a 'mixed' couple, married to a 'foreigner') might have led to the recognition that racism exists at all levels of society.

The acknowledgement of racism on official or political level is mentioned by one interviewee as coming slowly to the surface - albeit in the limited context of the city-state Hamburg.

> [N]ow, for about five years, the term 'racism' is likely to be used in the new guidelines for the policy on foreigners of the Senate [state-city government of Hamburg, N.P.]. In this way - I don't know whether consciously - [something has changed]. (Int. 8/G)

This changed official approach to racism might be the result of the successful campaigning and 'educational' work of this organization which concentrates on Hamburg and the policies of its state-city government. Also, the party in power has for a long time been (and still is) the SPD, many of whose members and MPs - in contrast to the CDU/CSU - do not deny the existence of racism in contemporary Germany.

*Articulation and elements*  As for the question of how racism is articulated, the issue of the difference between a more subtle, culturally based definition and a cruder, biologically based expression was mentioned by those interviewees who did not minimize the existence of racism in the contemporary context. Most of them thought that 'culture' is predominantly used today as a criterion to distinguish between peoples, but there are slight differences in their views on the extent to which biological thinking is still alive.

> [Racism is linked with] ethnicity and culture. This is  now new racism. [Biologically based racism] exists only within the right-wing extremist scene...But it is also difficult when an Afro-black person marries a white person. This is somehow biologically explained...[With a Turkish person it is] the religion which does  not fit in.  (Int. 8/G)

> ..Religion plays a role....but biological factors, I think, play still a hidden role in Germany society.  (Int. 6/G)

> There is one dominant culture and others. It is more cultural. Biological - nobody  dares to mention that anymore...I think that has gone. Or it only appears latently...I maintain that there is a hierarchy of cultures in the minds of people.  (Int. 4/G)

All these statements suggest that 'biology' has not disappeared completely from people's minds and most interviewees suggest a co-existence of cultural and biological expressions of racism. This reminds us of the 'British' interviews which similarly referred to what has been termed 'new racism' (1981) by Barker (i.e. culturally-based) by denying the 'death' of biological forms of racism. It seems to depend on the recipient of racially motivated discrimination (Afro-black or Turkish) and the social group involved in discriminating (such as right-wing extremists). Important is that - no matter whether it is on biological or cultural grounds - distinctive boundaries are drawn between indigenous Germans and ethnic minorities which are supposed to demonstrate that the latter 'do not fit in'. Moreover, it seems that these boundaries have the tendency to be based on a hybrid or a link of racism and nationalism as expressed by the following interviewee:

> ...[It] has turned out that this [rejection of Turkish people] is clearly based on or is substantiated by 'Germany for the Germans'. The non-Germans, the foreigners, the other ethnies, don't belong here. They should disappear. (Int. 7/G)

The slogan 'Germany for the Germans' has frequently appeared since reunification. It is referred to by this interviewee as a clear sign of racism. However, it could also be interpreted as a sign of nationalism (other commentators, such as Oberndörfer, 1993, related this slogan to rising nationalism since reunification). In any case, the aim is to draw boundaries between Germans and foreigners, whereby the latter are not seen as legitimate members ("they don't belong"). Nonetheless, it is suggested here that this interviewee's view demonstrates an understanding of racism which is not clearly distinguishable from nationalism.

As for concrete racist elements in Germany, in the replies of many interviewees the emphasis was put on the nationality/citizenship law (Int. 5/G; 7/G; 8/G) - a matter which will be returned to in more detail in the sections on national identity and citizenship.

*Target groups* A few interviewees mentioned that there is a hierarchy of 'foreigners' which indicates that the sole factor of being 'foreign' does not necessarily result in racism - an idea mentioned by authors such as Forsythe (1989). For instance, western Europeans (in particular EU-nationals) and North Americans are not necessarily perceived as foreigners. One interviewee also observed

> in Berlin the following phenomenon: Japanese people are regarded as western Europeans without any problem, although their culture...is so different...It depends on the social and economic position of the respective non-whites...Therefore, I think racism also has a lot to do with the social position of the minority. (Int. 1/G)

This view could also function as a critique of the terminology of 'hostility towards foreigners' which is seen by many commentators as referring to *any* group of foreigners (which is obviously not the case). The sole factor of being from a different cultural background, therefore, does not have to result in racism. Rather, certain socio-political processes are involved. This links up with the notion of racialization as a social process of constructing boundaries between ethnic minorities and the majority (Small 1994). Although the interviewee did not explicitly come to this conclusion, she gave another example which fits this notion:

> [B]efore the Wall came down, the Vietnamese in West-Berlin wereconsidered the best integrated group among the foreigners. But they had something very special: they were so-called boat people who came to Germany as *Kontingent-Flüchtlinge*[3]. And from the very first day they had a secure status and received certain 'starting aids' from the state. After the fall of the Wall, the ex-GDR citizens claimed that the Vietnamese, the contract workers, were not integratable. The main difference between those Vietnamese was...that in East-Berlin, the contract workers were accommodated in hostels, they were controlled and there was an absolute 'contact barrier' to the 'normal' German population. And therefore, they did not have the opportunity to learn German. (Int. 1/G)

This example illustrates that the sole fact of being from a very different cultural background (here: Vietnam) does not have to result in low degrees of integration or in the view of 'cultural incompatibility'. It is rather concrete immigration (integration) policies which help 'foreigners' to be generally accepted. The non-existence of such policies could result in racist attitudes and practices on the part of the majority. The active role of the government is, therefore, very important. This somehow shows that racism is not a 'natural' reaction to culturally distant people, but rather a political and social process - a phenomenon which is best grasped by the concept of 'racialization'.

*Origin and source* In every day life, governments and politicians were seen by many interviewees as being immediately involved in spreading racist ideas. The role of the media was also emphasized in this context. The role of politicians was suggested as reinforcing racism for their own ends, i.e. in order to catch votes and to appear competent with regard to solving socio-economic problems. This links up with the theme of 'crisis' and the increase of anti-foreign propaganda claiming that the solution is 'to get rid of immigrants'. One interviewee explained the relationship between 'crisis' and the racializing role of the media and politicians:

> The media surely play a role...When [news] is about foreigners, the impression is enforced that there is a direct link between the presence of foreigners and e.g. crime...I cannot make a clear statement concerning the government. [But] we are here in the middle of an enormous phase of radical change, and [the problems which are related to unification] are not

openly debated, because nobody knows the solutions. Thereby the atmosphere against foreigners is indirectly enforced.....There is no difference between the parties. (Int. 1/G)

Other interviewees, however, thought that the reason why politicians and the media pick foreigners as scapegoats has deeper roots. In particular politicians are suggested as having a 'trigger' role.

> I think these things are passed on. Passed on from generation to generation. And we underestimate the unspoken messages....Politicians and the media are also responsible..Young people only do what is already going on in the midst of society....It [racism] exists in one part of this society and latently in many more parts, and children are aware of that....And there, something has snapped. A break of taboo, and those [politicians] who always wanted to get through try to get ahead. ...I regard 'big politics' as the trigger. (Int. 4/G)

> It is passed on from mouth to mouth...It was passed on from generation to generation. (Int. 6/G)

These statements carry the connotation of 'history' and the deeper roots of racism within society and thus, support the view of racism being an inevitable logic within German society - as similarly expressed by the 'British' interviews. The notion of a 'macro' and 'micro' level of racism is, therefore, indicated by the 'German' interviewees, too, whereby politicians and the media are seen as responsible for supporting and even aggravating a generally racist climate.

*Ausländer* As a specifically 'German' issue, the interviewees were asked for their opinion of the term *'Ausländer'*. In particular those who were members of the Turkish minority rejected this term completely by calling themselves "immigrants. But this does not actually apply to those who were born here." (7/G). For the non-immigrant generations, it was strongly felt that only a term which reflects their belongingness is appropriate.

> We are not *Ausländer* anymore. I do not use this term at all. We are *Nicht-Deutsche* (non-Germans). (Int. 6/G)

> For me, the term minority does not exist in this way. And also the term non-German citizens or foreign fellow-citizens does not exist. ..For me, we are immigrants and I refer to the younger generations as *neue Inländer...Inländer* of Turkish or Yugoslav background. (Int. 5/G) [neue Inländer - new 'insiders'; Inländer is the opposite to Ausländer]

Whatever the preferred choice of the organization or individual - the main message of the suggested alternatives is that these people have become new ethnic minorities, i.e. established parts of German society. However, there is still the problem of their legal status as most of the Turkish immigrants are legally still defined as *Ausländer*. This aspect was referred to by two interviewees (members of the majority):

> I know of people who use the term *Ausländer* because it is a legal fact. So, from this perspective they say: legally, we or they are *Ausländer* and one should not try to pretend [that they are not]...and others say that the reality is that they have been living here for 20, 30 years and have, therefore, settled [for good]... (Int. 8/G)

> We have stayed with the term *Ausländer*...I think that the content has to change. The change of a term alone does not improve anything. (Int. 3/G)

These views clearly show the discrepancy between being legally defined as *Ausländer*, but being socio-culturally *Inländer* (as a result of long periods of residence, birth and/or upbringing in Germany). The choice of terminology, therefore, becomes a matter of which 'reality' each organization (or individual) wants to emphasize.

The insistence on calling settled immigrants in Germany *Ausländer* to highlight their legal situation links up with the suggestion in Chapter Four as to what the best solution to this terminological dilemma could be: a change in law (i.e. the easing of the acquisition of citizenship) and thorough inclusionary policies. As it stands at present, the interviewed organizations showed a very pragmatic approach to this dilemma. Depending on the type of 'activity' (in a speech or in a piece of writing), on the purpose at the moment of usage (educational, challenging), and on the 'addressees' of the 'activity', most organizations are compromising in order to achieve the best result.

### 9.1.3 The EU Migrants Forum

*Definition* The official definition of racism of the EU Migrants Forum is laid down in the introduction to its *Manifesto Against Racism*[4] where it is stated that racism is not so much the expression of individual people, but more so "that of masses". Furthermore, racism "is no longer the mere and appalling expression of rejecting other people's colour of skin, but a differentiating expression of non national cultures" (Manifesto, p. 1). This definition is applicable to every ethnic minority group and to every country's immigration history and thus reflects the Forum's structure as an organization which represents the various ethnic minorities in all EU-member-states. In this approach, racism is not only based on colour, but also on culture and (alleged) national differences which links the issue of racism to the issue of nationalism, implying that the boundaries between those two are not that clear.

*Origin and purpose*  The general existence of racism within the EU is not disputed by the interviewee who believes that the

> European society which is now being planned is based on racism...Historically, ...racism is endemic in the European society to a greater or lesser extent according to the country.

Racism is here viewed as being deeply rooted in history. This could be interpreted as suggesting that racism is an inevitable logic within western European societies because of that long tradition.  As for the purpose of racism, it is viewed by the interviewee as

> ...a weapon which the institutions are effectively using against us [the ethnic minorities]. ..They [officials, politicians] are using racism as a weapon in order to....consolidate the white man's position.

Being used as a 'weapon' means that racism is a purposeful construct rather than a matter of biological facts, and thus, a link is made here to Small's notion of racialization. Furthermore, the expression of 'the white man's position' seems to refer to the era of colonial expansion and imperialism as well as economic exploitation. There is, therefore, a link between historical and systemic processes involved in racialization. The Migrants Forum's definition of racism is, thus, 'complex' and pervasive within society rather than the expression of individuals.
  As western European countries have similar histories and systems, the European Union as a whole is likely to be influenced by this.

*European racism and racism in Europe*  As a European issue, racism is viewed by the interviewee as a two-dimensional phenomenon: 1. as an institutional problem of the EU as a whole, in that it created provisions for EU-nationals by not including long term resident non-EU nationals; and 2. as a common problem within each individual member-state, partly triggered by the generally worsening economic climate. The theme of 'crisis' is indicated here, and the politicians are again seen as mainly responsible for using immigrants as scapegoats.

> Racism is thriving...because of the present economic climate. The politicians without  exception in all countries...are pampering to the lowest  instinct of the constituents...They are looking at us [immigrant minorities] as a problem, not as an opportunity. They are talking about immigration, and not about integration.

The interviewee refers to the fact that EU policies (as a result of 'co-operative talks' as part of the pillar structure) do not include integrative measures but revolve mainly around immigration issues such as 'external border controls' and visa requirements (see Chapter Three). This has negative effects on settled minorities because in this context, they are depicted as 'problems' and not 'opportunities'.

Certain differences with regard to anti-racist policies within every member-state are, however, acknowledged - in particular those based on the effectiveness of anti-discrimination legislation. According to the interviewee, some sort of legislation exists in every member-state with the only exception of the Republic of Ireland. However, not every country applies its legislation and not every legislation is as effective as the British.

> [I]n this country [UK] because they have got a Race Relations Act which they have generally tried to implement, overt racial discrimination is practically eradicated...But what is happening, is what I call 'lace curtain racism'...'Lace curtain racism' is how to say 'no' to a person of colour or race without being proven that I am racially discriminating against him. So...you cannot prove it.

This statement shows that the interviewee recognized that, although anti-discrimination legislation has some impact on the minimization of racism ('less overt'), it does not result in the complete eradication of racism. It rather re-appears in other forms ('lace-curtain' racism). This could be interpreted as referring to the 'endemic' or inevitable nature of racism.

*EU-action?* On the institutional basis of the EU as a whole, the Migrants Forum confirmed that competence in the 'race relations field' does not exist.

> [T]hey [the officials, politicians] kept two things out of the Community control: immigration and race.

One of the important initiatives of the Forum as a response to the Maastricht Treaty and its failure to enable EU-wide activities in the 'race relations field' is the above quoted *European Manifesto against Racism*. In this Manifesto, the Forum calls upon the member-states to review or abrogate "legislation of Union Member States which could include non-egalitarian measures between migrants and native persons and would express a latent institutional racism" (p. 2) and to actively support 'the Starting Line'[5]. Furthermore, the powers of the European Parliament should be extended "in terms of controlling governments in the implementation of anti-racist legislation" (p. 3).

So far, the Manifesto has not been very successful and is unlikely to be so in the near future for various reasons mentioned by the interviewee: 1. because countries like Germany impede any progress by denying the existence of racism and by not acknowledging an official status to minorities ("In Germany, when I saw Eduard Lintner [Permanent Under-Secretary, CDU/CSU, N.P.] he said: 'No, [racism] does not exist.' These were his words."); 2. because of the present economic climate, and

3. because of general elections in the member-states during which the "race and immigration card" was used which is viewed as most likely to be continued in forthcoming election campaigns, although the Forum had made an appeal to all politicians to publicly denounce doing so. The interviewee's comment on their success so far, therefore, was:

[W]e have lost our European Manifesto of Racism.

### 9.1.4 Commentary

The interview data in this section show that different historical backgrounds of racialization in Britain and Germany have resulted in different understandings of 'racism' - officially and partly also by the organizations.

In Britain, a clear distinction can be made between a 'catch-phrase' type of definition and a 'complex' definition of racism. When those two definitions were applied to concrete situations, however, they merged resulting in a concept of racism seen as a structural, behavioural and discursive device present at all levels of society. This is reflected in the official recognition of racial discrimination in the Race Relations Acts. Racism was understood by most of the interviewees as existing on a macro and micro level, whereby the main target groups as well as prevailing articulation of racism differed. I have suggested that the two broad definitions of racism ('prejudice plus power', 'complex set of interactions') do not seem to reflect anything else but the organizations' different fields of activities and/or levels of influence on actual policy making.

In Germany, the interview replies showed that racism is officially denied by the Conservative government and many other politicians, as well as on policy-level, underpinned by the absence or non-application of anti-discrimination legislation - partly on the assumption that racism only refers to anti-semitism and genocide[6] and thus, to a particular phase in Germany's historical experience, or to a colonial context of 'Afro-black and white' relations. There seems to be a preoccupation with the definition of racism in terms of the National Socialist ideology and 'race' policies[7] with the reverse effect that racism is treated as a taboo term in the contemporary context. Not only on official level, but in the 'German' interviews, too, references to this particular era were predominantly made when defining racism. This understanding is quite limited as it ignores other historical processes of racialization during the colonial and expansionist period and thus, ignores the racialization of, e.g., eastern European peoples (Burleigh & Wippermann 1991; Herbert 1986). Many of the interviewees, however, disagreed with this official view (most of them were members of an ethnic minority) and acknowledged the existence of racism in contemporary German society.

The official line in Germany - supported by two of the interviewees (1/G; 2/G) - shows a limited understanding of racializing processes at the state level, as well as within civil society. The denial of racism is equated with the common usage of the terminology of *Ausländerfeindlichkeit* (in political, media and academic discourse), reflecting an individualizing understanding of 'hostile' attitudes. The non-existence or non-application of anti-discrimination legislation is one of the consequences, another could be that such an individualized 'hostility' might be regarded as resistible, or even eradicable, as it is not perceived as existing at all levels of German society. The British interviews, on the other hand, conveyed a clear understanding of racism as ineradicable and all-pervasive - an idea the EU Migrants Forum supported.

In Britain and Germany, all of the interviewees who recognized 'racism' as the cause for anti-foreign practices believed that cultural expressions of racism prevailed over the biological. However, biological explanations or views were not regarded as 'extinct', but rather as co-existing with cultural explanations - albeit not to the same extent or not with the same outspokenness. Furthermore, the idea of deeper historical and systemic roots of racism support my argument that the emphasis should rather be on the historical processes and purposes involved in distinguishing between 'insider' and 'outsider' (see Chapter Four). This also links up with the idea that racism is an inevitable logic within German and British society - or in (western) Europe as a whole, as claimed by the EU Migrants Forum.

Despite this notion of 'inevitability', politicians in particular, as well as the media, were regarded by most of the interviewees (also by the EU Migrants Forum) as having a crucial role in 'triggering' stronger anti-foreign sentiments and the rising outbreaks of violence within sections of civil society. The influence of political discourse on public opinion - as demonstrated in the previous two chapters - is, therefore, confirmed by the interviewees. This is also supported by authors such as Jäger and Cohen. The latter refers to influential (governmental) politicians in Britain as 'open frontier guards' (1994:200), the former calls German politicians' rhetoric *'BrandSätze'* (1993)- a linguistically brilliant creation (*Brandsätze* actually means 'arson attacks'; but *Sätze* can also mean sentences; this term, therefore, refers to people who 'set fire' by their rhetoric) - as they influence the way how the public expresses its opinions on the presence of foreigners.

On the European level, the argument for a distinction between European racism and racism in Europe (as made in Chapter Four) was implicitly underpinned by the EU Migrants Forum.

The effects of the different understandings of racism as well as the general relationship between racism and nationalism will be further explored in the context of national identity.

## 9.2 National identity and nationalism

The aim of this section of the interview was to document the meaning of 'national identity' as defined by law (in nationality terms) and as perceived within civil society. To do so, the questions were to explore the following aspects:

1. which points of reference are chosen to represent British or German national identity;
2. where do these definitions originate from (i.e. who or what has the authority or power to define);
3. do these definitions include immigrant/ethnic minorities?

### 9.2.1 *The British organizations*

*Subjectivity*  This section began with the general question "Do you think British people have a sense of national identity?". Most of the replies of interviewees who were members of the majority referred to an individual understanding, and there did not seem to be an easy and straightforward answer to the essence of Britishness in general. Thus, most of the replies from members of the majority indicated that on a personal level, the issue of national identity is a very subjective matter.

> I suppose if you ask 50 people, they all say something totally different. (Int. 5/B)

> I think, it is contested of course.  (Int. 1/B)

For ethnic minorities, however, 'being British' refers first of all to citizenship, i.e. the holding of a passport, and national identity is defined in cultural or historical  (or maybe even in political) terms. One interviewee explained:

> What does British mean?  I have got a British passport. [But] I see myself as an African and that is my  nationality....It [also] depends on whom you speak to.  (Int. 3/B)

According to this view, it is also a very personal question as to how ethnic minorities define their own national identity. 'Being African' seems to refer to this particular interviewee's cultural and historical background. This could also be read as a political statement of the head of an organization which represents members of ethnic minorities, i.e. as a response to racism within, and non-acceptance by, British society which results in a reverse orientation back to the minorities' ethnic roots. In this way, the statement 'being African' could be interpreted as 'ethnic identity' rather than 'national identity', as it derives from the position of an ethno-cultural *minority*.

'Britishness' is suggested here as meaning first of all (formal) rights attached to citizenship of the country of residence, but it does not seem to have an explicit cultural meaning. This was further expressed by the same interviewee as follows:

> [I]n terms of how I conduct myself, my sense of history, my experience and so on, I certainly would not describe myself as British even though I argue strongly for a multi-cultural Britain and even a multi-cultural Europe.  (Int. 3/B)

'National identity' appears here as an issue which is linked to personal history and experience - an aspect which leads to the question about the elements generally viewed as demonstrating 'Britishness'.

*Boundaries and source*  The next questions referred to the content of national identity as predominantly claimed and who or what the source of these ideas is. It appeared in most replies by members of the majority that the way in which Britishness is perceived can be a question of political alliance. Precise ideas were suggested as coming from the right-wing conservative political angle, promoting a 'narrow' understanding of national identity in the sense that "far fewer things are defined as British" (Int. 1/B):

> They are things connected with authority.  So, the Royal family, for example, and the symbols around that. English literature, Christianreligion, authority generally....Conservative politicians such as Michael Portillo hint in a coded way about what distinguishes British identity from foreigners. We ought not to criticize anything British using foreign models or examples or implying that foreigners are anyway better or have solved problems better....so that we have things to learn. So there was a defiant view of all foreigners...  (Int. 1/B)

The distinction from foreigners is explained here as the (main?) purpose of defining national identity in clear (i.e. narrow) terms. Points of reference are thereby institutional symbols such as the monarchy, cultural symbols such as English literature and the Christian faith - elements named by other interviewees as well (Int. 4/B; 5/B).

Right-wing/conservative claims as the source of clear ideas about 'Britishness' appeared in many interview replies which seems to be the case for two reasons: 1. the Conservatives have been the party of government for a long time; 2. the 'right' is usually seen in connection with the promotion of a 'narrow' (i.e. 'ethnic') type of nationalism  (Goulbourne 1991; Gilroy 1987).

Many interviews implied that there is a (right-wing) notion of national identity as defined vis-à-vis 'the Other' (distinction of British identity from foreigners), whereby 'the Other' is depicted in a negative way (defiant view of all foreigners). This links up with what has been described as the "formation of national identity vis-à-vis the Other" (see also Cohen 1994; Colley 1992), whereby one's own national group is regarded as superior. In this way, national identity becomes a matter of (positive) self-identification. Apart from institutional and cultural symbols, another point of reference said to be chosen by individuals representing the Conservative Party, which illustrates this point, is a particular key moment or period in history: imperial Britain.

> Margaret Thatcher based much of her ideology on a traditionalist, backward looking view of British nationhood. She called on the small-town chauvinism of England...the imperialist, racist, chauvinistic prejudices that are still very strong in much of middle England. That sense of a desire to be a great nation again. (Int. 4/B)

> [There is the] Thatcherite discourse [on] 'make Britain great again'... (Int. 1/B)

The reason why this particular historical period is chosen for national identification is explained by interviewee 4/B with the fact that "there is not that sense of challenge to our past [as in Germany]". Identity as a 'great nation', therefore, derives from a particular understanding and perception of British/English history. An additional explanation could be the desire of the government to reshape national identity during a period of prolonged recession and rising unemployment. In such a moment of 'crisis', 'old' values and symbols are revived.

Imperialism is not the only impersonal historical period or element chosen for a positive image of collective identity. Among others, it is, however, an important period which also resulted in self-identification as a superior 'race' - as expressed by the following interviewee:

> ...[T]here is a lot of subconscious racism in Britain in assuming that they have been around for an awful lot of time, we are the mother of democracy, the British Empire brought civilization to the rest of the world. A lot of that background is in many people. (Int. 5/B)

As mentioned above, the source of a clear definition of national identity is claimed by most of the interviewees to be the party of government, whereby individual names such as Margaret Thatcher, Michael Portillo and Norman Tebbit were mentioned. There are, therefore, individuals who are perceived as having great definitional influence (referred to by Cohen, 1994, as 'open frontier guards').

Moreover, these individuals are not only interested in distinguishing 'British' from 'foreign', but "what [they] are talking about is London dominating England dominating Britain." (Int. 4/B). There seems to be an element of cultural domination by the English and, therefore, an exclusive element of national identity vis-à-vis 'insiders' such as the Scots, the Welsh and the Irish people, as well as vis-à-vis 'outsiders' ('imperialist, racist, chauvinistic prejudices'). 'Britishness' seems, therefore, to be a definition for 'Englishness' (in this narrow Conservative view).

As for drawing boundaries along the blurred notion of 'racial' and national identity, it is, however, not only the party of government or any other politicians who are seen as influential in promoting these ideas, but also the print media, as explained by this interviewee:

> Some terminology...- a word like stock -...is a metaphor from the language...[of] breeding animals. ...It is sometimes used in the mainstream press, in *The Telegraph*, people of British stock, people of Bangladeshi stock, implying that there is actually something genetic and racial in human beings. (Int. 1/B)

The multi-'racial' composition of contemporary British society seems to be depicted by much of the mainstream press and many members of the government as negative. The role of the prime minister is thereby seen as powerful in shaping the general perception of a socio-national community.

> [F]or eight years, Margaret Thatcher never made a speech about race relations. From 1979 to 1986 she never made a speech about race relations. An amazing achievement for a prime minister of a multi-racial society where there were race riots, where there is race murders, where there is the most awful problem of race discrimination. She never once made a speech about it. (Int. 4/B)

In times of 'racial' conflict and rising 'racial' discrimination, a clear statement by the prime minister recognizing the fragmented identities of contemporary Britain is regarded by this interviewee as helpful to 'de-narrowrize' (and 'de-racialize'), and thus broaden, British national identity to make it more inclusive. This could help to improve the relationship between the indigenous and immigrant parts of the population.

*National identity in legal terms and as perceived by civil society* The official recognition of immigrants as part of the 'nation' could help to promote their acceptance by civil society at large - an aspect authors such as Wrench & Solomos (1993) and Gilroy (1987) refer to when claiming that there is a discrepancy between legal belonging (nationality in legal terms, i.e. citizenship) and cultural belonging (national identity). Although post-war labour migrants and their descendants are legally full members of the British 'nation-state', they are not necessarily perceived as such by sections within civil society in terms of identity and cultural belonging. One interviewee (a member of the majority) refers to this aspect:

In Britain, the prejudiced white person has a view of what is British or English, but that is not coterminous with who has got the *right to be British*. So, you can go to the East End of London and you can hear the racists and the fascists screaming abuse at the Bangladeshi, but the Bangladeshi will be walking into the polling booth to vote for the local members of Parliament. And while the BNP person does not see their Asian neighbour as being one of us or being British..., in terms of political rights, they are - which does, I think, quite transform the power relationship. (Int. 4/B; emphasis added)

It might be arguable how strong the influence of the 'ethnic vote' on British politics in fact is (and thus the 'power relationship'), but the point that nationality and citizenship are not necessarily coterminous is very interestingly put here (and reminds of the statement above made by a member of an ethnic minority): 'Being British' can, according to this view, be explained in terms of cultural belongingness (that is why the BNP person does not recognize an Asian immigrant as British) or in terms of formal citizenship (and thus, including political rights such as voting). The latter is seen by the interviewee as crucial in the sense that no matter how much racism there is (within civil society), the immigrant has the legal right to stay and can also be politically active. Although national identity is perceived by certain sections of civil society as exclusive, in legal terms immigrants are included. The emphasis could, however, be put differently, i.e. that moments of racism and nationalism within civil society have exclusionary implications for immigrants *despite* their legal equality.

Furthermore, the above interviewee's view ignores the gradual link between nationality (in an ethno-cultural sense) and citizenship, as established by immigration acts since 1962 and by the British Nationality Act of 1981. This ignorance might be based on the fact that large parts of the post-war labour migrants are not directly affected by these acts. It is recognized, however, that the link between nationality and citizenship exists within the perception of civil society - as expressed by a member of one of the ethnic minorities:

The British people still recognize those who migrated to [this] country over the last 50 years by their colour, by their religion...One of the difficulties [the ethnic minorities] are facing in this country is that in spite of the fact that they have taken up British citizenship,....the way they contribute towards society...is not fully recognized in nationality terms. Therefore, there is this idea 'perhaps they are not loyal to this country'. That is rubbish, because the second generation has not got another country...There are....difficulties because of the initial attitude in this country because of the past historical...perception of the ethnic minority communities who came from former colonial countries. (Int. 2/B)

Reference to non-recognition in 'nationality terms' means here in 'terms of national identity'. The last remark in this quote links post-war labour migration to the type of society Britain used to be - namely colonial - and the perception of immigrants' position in such a society. This refers to the particular difficulties the first generation of immigrants had in their role as 'ex-colonials'. Their children seem to suffer from this 'inherited disadvantage', despite their birth or up-bringing in Britain, and are still not regarded as parts of the 'nation' - or at least not to a satisfactory extent, as felt by the above interviewee. Therefore, the above quote expresses the same idea that being British in the legal sense does not necessarily correspond with being British in cultural terms, as perceived by influential sections of civil society.

Racist attitudes among sections of civil society are also viewed as preventing immigrants from identifying with the socio-national entity of Britain.

> I think when things like that happen [racist attacks and abuses] I think...the less they [black people] feel British. (Int. 3/B)

It can be said, therefore, that racism too functions to draw boundaries between the majority and ethnic minority populations and makes the latter feel not accepted as legitimate, equal members. Thus, racism and nationalism (as the source of an ethno-cultural identity) are suggested to exist in a combined form, with both having exclusionary effects on ethnic minorities.

*Recognition as belonging*   The notion of 'belonging' - being a key feature of collective identity - was further explored by asking whether cultural contributions and/or particularities of ethnic minorities are adequately recognized by, and whether ethnic minorities are 'visible' or 'invisible' parts of, the British socio-national community. The head of a voluntary organization - a member of the majority - expressed his opinion on this matter:

> Well, to answer that it is helpful to have a yardstick, both in time and place. In some ways we are worse than - in time - than ten years ago. It has got worse in terms of British identity...But...[as for] the recognition of pluralism, with other respects there are advances in time...There are...MPs in the House of Commons in both the main parties who are black - well, there is one in the Tory Party and five in the Labour Party. ...That would have been unthinkable a few years ago. Well, six MPs is not enough. Ten years ago [however] people would have said there is no way that by 1994 there would be as many as six....In the youth culture...my impression is that teenagers are creating a new culture which is much more pluralistic because of the presence of the black and Asians.

..We have to look in comparison. Comparatively to ten, fifteen years ago, they are far more visible in public life and in popular culture. (Int. 1/B)

'Youth culture' appeared a few times as an area of 'improvement' which could be interpreted as supporting the argument (as explained in Chapter Six) that imperial attitudes on the part of the majority are vanishing among younger generations who were born and brought up after the break-up of the Empire. This could also have to do with a generally higher level of recognition by younger generations because they are used to the long-term "presence of the black and Asians". Again, length of residence appears here as an important factor.

Another area which is supposed to demonstrate general recognition of ethnic minorities is sport. This view was expressed by two representatives of the majority, one of whom explained:

Afro-Caribbeans are probably the most dynamic and forceful influence...in sport. There is no doubt that in big parts of sport now, the presence of black sports figures ...is very important... There is this picture of Linford Christie and suddenly it is the Union Jack and he is us....there is no doubt that that has had an impact on [people]. It could not have happened thirty or twenty years ago. (Int. 4/B)

This view, however, shows a rather stereotypical, if not racializing, way of thinking about black athletes.[8] Moreover, if they are indeed accepted as legitimate members of the national community on the basis of winning championship titles and Olympic medals, it should be rather assumed that this kind of acceptance is based on the positive image of 'winning' and 'strength' or 'power' and thus, suits any national identity.

In the context of other professions, it is admitted by the same interviewee that, although ethnic minorities might be rather successful in (certain) sports, it is

less so in business and academic life. The professions in Britain are still very, very white...Academia is still very white...[and] the upper reaches of medicine...The further you go up, the whiter it gets. (Int. 4/B)

Although the existence of a few black and Asian MPs has been described above as an improvement, a member of an ethnic minority does not quite agree with this. He would like to see more blacks or Asians in ministerial or administrative key positions - such as in foreign affairs, defence and the civil service - as in those areas "the loyalty of the person...can be tested, whether the person is trustworthy to be given a position in [e.g.] the foreign office." (Int. 2/B).

With regard to professional life and representational key positions, and thus as part of the higher levels of decision-making, the degree of recognition of ethnic minorities as part of the British 'nation' does not seem to be satisfactory. It has been acknowledged, however, that there is a slow "process of developing a multi-cultural, multi-religious society" (Int. 2/B) and it is again among the younger generations, that the level of acceptance seems to be higher - as experienced by one interviewee (member of the majority):

> Undoubtedly things have changed enormously in my life-time, the whole atmosphere. The part of London where I live in,....there is this little sort of town centre, and you can walk through the town centre late at night and there are black and white young people together,.., black boys and white girls. Now, twenty years ago that would never have happened. Now it happens and it is not commented on, nobody looks, nobody is surprised, it is acceptable....Particular[ly] among young people...that open stark prejudice as an overwhelming prejudice within an age group, I think, that has gone. (Int. 4/B)

All interviewees agree that there has been improvement to some (albeit not necessarily to a satisfactory) extent with regard to general recognition and acceptance of ethnic minorities. This might be the result of their length of residence and younger generations being more used to a multi-'racial'/ethnic society than older generations. This could also partly have to do with anti-discrimination legislation and equal opportunity provisions.

As the very first quote in this section (d) indicated, however, in terms of 'identity' the situation has rather become worse which stands in direct connection with the claim by many interviewees that nationalism has been on the rise (see also section f). Therefore, the statements in this section could be interpreted as supporting the idea of a discrepancy between legal recognition (by nationality laws and 'Race Relations' legislation) and social recognition (by civil society). And yet, a generational shift towards a kind of new type of identity cannot be denied.

*Post-conventional identity* Both, interviewees representing a minority and the majority, are aware of positive changes - albeit very slowly - towards multi-culturalism or ethnic pluralism. This means that a new type of collective identity is slowly emerging.

A further 'boost' towards this change seems to have been given by the successor of Prime Minister Margaret Thatcher as explained by an interviewee who works for a non-voluntary, semi-governmental organization:

> When John Major came, he adopted a completely different approach...He made a major speech in September 1991 which repeated our [the organization's] view on that question...He said: "We value people for their differences. Britain is a multi-racial, multi-cultural, multi-ethnic society. We have unity in diversity in which we value the fact that we have as part

of our society people who are different.".....[This is] not necessarily the majority opinion in government, but it certainly is very strongly his opinion and..that has helped...The principle idea that we can be different and yet all be part of the same [collective, N.P.] identity has come on to the platform. (Int. 4/B)

This statement seems to suggest a certain move towards what has been described as post-conventional identity de-linked from the necessity of common ethnic or 'racial' roots (see Chapter Six). This could also be interpreted as promoting the idea that cultural identity as part of nationality should not be the decisive element of a collective identity. So far, however, this idea has just appeared "on the platform" which means that this understanding has not (yet?) penetrated most sections of civil society.

*European identity* New developments with regard to identity formation might also be under way as part of the European integration process, of which European identity might be a result. Therefore, the question whether national identity is nowadays still an important issue was asked. The replies stated that the nation-state as a source of collective identity is still very strong, and one interviewee thought that national identity is not only still "extremely important", but also that "it is even becoming more so." (Int. 1/B) as nationalism is on the rise (of which a more emphasized national identity is the outcome). Various crises have triggered this increasing nationalism: 1. a general political crisis in the West since the collapse of the Soviet Union and the end of the cold war[9]; 2. the economic crisis; and 3. the crisis with regard to Britain's transition from the Common wealth to Europe. In other words, it is

certainly the increasing closeness of Britain in Europe that is [resulting in] increasing nationalism in this country. ...Very, very few people have ever learned foreign languages or felt European. There has been a general suspicion and mistrust rather than a sense of 'we are Europeans'. (Int. 1/B)

The thought that there is a rather weak feeling of being European among British people is supported by empirical evidence as the result of an European survey on that matter: Britain ranked last among EC-member states with regard to the development of a European identity (see Chapter Three). So, political as well as economic crises are suggested here as causing narrow nationalism and a reinforcement of national identity preventing the development of a post-national, i.e. European, identity.

And yet, there are signs that a 'pan-European' identity (in the west) exists which, however, seems to be exclusively 'white'. Politicians are again viewed as very powerful in this definitional process. They support nationalistic tendencies by putting the blame for any crises on foreigners or immigrants and "the solution is partly to get rid of foreigners." (Int. 1/B).

Politicians are seen as a highly influential source in drawing boundaries between indigenous Europeans and those who are regarded as not belonging - as expressed by one interviewee:

> There is a real danger [that European identity is as exclusive as national identity]. Some discourse about Europe is coded discourse for white, and again there is an element of Christianity. Mrs. Thatcher in her famous speech called the Bruges speech....spoke of what we Europeans have in common is that we civilized the world. That was the phrase. And that is quite strong.  (Int. 1/B)

As on the national level, an exclusive type of European identity seems to be promoted. The element of Christianity, for example, had also appeared in one of the replies on the essence of national identity. This type of exclusivity based on religion has been of great concern to authors such as Senoçak (1994) and Said (1995) with regard to anti-Islamic attitudes in (western) Europe.

In some respects, European identity seems to work in an even more excluding manner for ethnic minorities in Britain than national identity, as expressed by two members of ethnic minority groups:

> What is European identity actually? .... I am a British citizen. Germany, France, Holland, Italy - are they prepared to accept me? They are not. [If[ I entered the country on the border,.... they would still stop me because of my colour....So their identity is totally a false identity for us. (Int. 2/B)

Here, the problems revolving around border controls, freedom of movement and 'Fortress Europe' are touched upon (as explained in Chapter Three). This quote also describes the fear that 'black' British citizens (nationals in legal terms) are not recognized as such by 'continental Europe' and thus, the fear of having to put up with being 'hassled' at intra-European borders. This demonstrates a clash of identity in legal terms and cultural identity within a wider European civil 'society' - as an outcome of common European policies.

In contrast to the replies of members of the majority, who relate the problems in developing a European identity to elements such as economic and historical crises resulting in rising nationalism, interviewees from the ethnic minorities relate the difficulties with their identification with Europe more to concrete policies such as border controls, visa policies and the creation of 'Fortress Europe'. Although most of these policies are actually aimed at preventing new immigration, settled minorities feel that these policies have a negative impact on them. Therefore, it cannot be denied that restrictive European immigration and visa policies are likely to have stigmatizing effects on settled ethnic minorities and might prevent them from feeling part of Europe.

Thus, although representatives of ethnic minorities argue that "we are black Europeans as well" (Int. 3/B), the EU as an institution is described by two organizations in particular (non-governmental; headed by members of an ethnic minority) in very negative terms - as expressed by one of them:

> For the black community, it [the EU] is a nightmare....which has just been anti-black....Every time they [EU-officials] looked at immigration it has been in a negative and hostile way. So, I am afraid that is the context in which the black community views Europe. We see it as a very difficult, a very hostile environment. (Int. 3/B)

This very radical and negative view of the EU must be rather an expression of this organization's rhetoric than the description of 'objective' reality. It cannot be denied, however, that on the whole, there seems to be a problem with European identity for both the majority as well as for the ethnic minorities. The latter, however, see themselves excluded on the basis of EU policies and racist attitudes, as well as rising nationalism. It does, therefore, not seem to be too far fetched to claim that European identity - as far as it exists - conveys the problems ethnic minorities have with being excluded from 'national' identity. If identification is problematic on the national level, it is even more so on the supranational level.

*Different levels of identity* The problem with European identity might, therefore, have to do with its remoteness and the fact that there are other levels of identity which are felt to be more feasible. One member indicated this from the ethnic minorities' point of view:

> If you had the opportunity to go to Liverpool or Tottenham or Brixton or so on, you will see that there is a large black community, a large number of unemployed, poor housing etc. etc., in which they are alienated from local councils, never mind national governments, never mind [the European Union]. All that seems to be totally irrelevant to them because of their reality of pressure, racism and bad housing, bad education. That is the reality. (Int. 3/B)

From the point of view of the majority, there is a similar statement referring the difficulties of identification to unemployment. A third of the white working class is said to have had a "corporate identity as coal-miners, as railway workers, as dockers" - areas which suffered from huge job losses. Therefore,

> if you..go to the communities where these people were, you find a sense of loss of identity which can be catastrophic...Suddenly, within a generation, that just vanishes. And these people now have no work, no sense of identity, no location in the world at all. (Int. 4/B)

There are various ways of interpreting the above statements, but what they indicate for the purpose here is that identity is formed for many first of all on a local basis in relation to the familiar working and residential environment. Apart from having a national identity, let alone a European, the local or regional level of identity is also very important, if not even most important. A feeling of 'belonging' seems to build itself from a local to a national to European level. Any problems of racism and nationalism should, therefore, also be dealt with on the local level. This links up with future developments of the Committee of the Regions and the notion of local citizenship - a matter which will be returned to in the section on citizenship.

### 9.2.2 The German organizations

*Subjectivity* Similarly to the British interviews, 'national identity' in general was viewed by those interviewees who are members of the majority as difficult to define in an objective way. It was even questioned "whether it is possible to speak of an objective [national] identity" at all (Int. 3/G). It was referred to as a "catchword", a "sponge" which can absorb a lot" (Int. 2/G). Furthermore, one interviewee strongly expressed her doubts with regard to the existence of a collective type of identity in cultural terms:

> It is not possible to say "*the* Germans" or "*the* Turks" - this consists of many identities.  (Int. 8/G)

On a personal level, the interviews with members of the majority showed that the notion of 'national identity' is not clearly definable and, therefore, a highly subjective matter. However, when approached from a general rather than from a personal perspective, national identity can be pinned down. This was similarly expressed in the 'British' interviews, but there is one particular  German problem with national identity at the time of pre- and post-reunification.

*Identity crisis* When asked whether reunification has made any difference to a *generally* promoted idea of national identity, there was wide consent among the interviewees (of both, majority and minority) that West Germany had certain identity problems before reunification in 1990 and that this situation has somehow changed since then, in both the eastern and western part. Most interviewees thought that before reunification, national identity was "no subject" (Int. 3/G), it was "never talked about" (Int. 5/G) or at least "did not play an important role" (Int. 4/G). This was explained by reference to Germany's experience with extreme ethnic nationalism during the Hitler-era and also by its special post-war situation as a divided country located at the immediate border to the East Bloc. A member of the Turkish minority expressed this very well:

A distinction has to be made between what national identity has meant in West Germany before and after unification. The German identity had surely suffered from its past, and when you came from outside, you could notice that the Germans in the West had a distance towards their nationality or identity. This had without doubt to do with the Nazi-past. (Int. 1/G)

The process of reunification, however, has brought vast socio-economic and political changes resulting in a wide-spread feeling of insecurity. Rising nationalism is said to be the response to this new situation.

I think [nationalism] also existed before [reunification], only now, [nationalism] is reinforced through the socio-economic crisis,...., through the disintegration of family structures...Radical changes are happening at the moment resulting in an identity crisis for many. (Int. 8/G)

As a response to such a multi-layered crisis, nationalism is rising, usually entailing a stronger focus on national identity by emphasizing common ethnic (or racial) roots. This is believed by some interviewees (members of the Turkish minority) to have had an impact on the immigrants too.

Unification - that was a turning point for us [the immigrants] too. Before the *Wende* [political and social changes, N.P.] we have never asked ourselves, whether we should stay or leave. Now, we ask ourselves whether we *can* stay..... (Int. 6/G)

It seems, therefore, as if the particular political and socio-economic changes caused by reunification have resulted in the drawing of clearer boundaries as to who belongs and who does not.

*Boundaries* The reunification process is suggested by many interviewees as having triggered rising nationalism and a re-definition of national identity with a stronger ethnic connotation. One interviewee explained these changes:

I think that the question of national identity has grown since unification, that this question did not play an important role before, because the West Germans were doing well materialistically. In a way, they had established themselves behind the Wall....By unifying both German states, a massive process of social sharing has been set off. This is the main reason for me: [This process] has automatically started this exclusion - why do I want to participate in the first place and you only second? - and from this developed: "Yes, I am German and that is why we belong together, and the foreigner shall not get anything." ....With this social sharing, huge legitimation problems have emerged and they help to re-establish old ideologies - suddenly we are a nation, we have got a national identity, whatever it is..... (Int. 4/G)

The phrase 're-establishing of old ideologies' implicitly indicates a link to historical continuity. The idea of the 'nation' is supposed to link both Germanys. This leads to an ethnic definition of national identity.

Furthermore, the theme of economic crisis appears very clearly here. Before the Wall came down, post-war Germany avoided the issue of national identity as a result of its past, by hiding behind its economic success - a phenomenon which has been termed *Wirtschaftpatriotismus* (economic patriotism) by Weidenfeld & Korte (1991). The newly arisen situation of 'social sharing' with the poorer and much more underdeveloped East is seen in the above as the link between reunification, rising nationalism and exclusion of 'foreigners' (i.e. the boundary drawing between 'us' and 'them'). The socio-economic problems created by unifying East and West Germany have triggered a battle for a piece of the 'cake' and there is a need to define who is a legitimate claimer of a piece. As a common denominator, national identity is near at hand - and the 'losers' are the immigrants and their children.

In addition to economic problems, in the former GDR

...a value system has been declared null and void. Therefore, only national identity remained about which there could have been no doubt, because one was born in Germany, one spoke German and one was of *German ethnic origin*. This was the only thing people could hold on to. (Int. 1/G; emphasis added).

Boundaries are drawn on ethnic lines, i.e. in terms of descent. This involves a notion of biology and hence, the identity as a 'nation' is not far from an identity as a 'race'. Both concepts are very closely linked as, for example, reflected in legal terms.

*National identity in legal terms* The quick 're-establishing of old ideologies' has probably been facilitated by the legal and discursive link of citizenship and nationality, i.e. that there does not seem to be an understanding of a concept of citizenship separated from nationality. The 'meshing' of those two concepts was explicitly mentioned by two interviewees (members of the majority) who said that they are used "interchangeably" (Int. 3/G; 4/G).

Among members of the Turkish minority, there is, however, awareness that both concepts do not mean the same - at least in theory:

Citizenship [i.e. nationality in legal terms, N.P.] is clearly a declaration of belief in the social order, the constitution, the institutions of the country, so that there is a certain common ground for action, whereas nationality has as its background *ius sanguinis* and reminds one very much of the 19th century. ...It is therefore - how can I say? - a backwards oriented term. (Int. 1/G)

Here a clear distinction is made between citizenship based on residence and nationality in the sense of blood-relatedness (ius sanguinis). The former is described as collective identity, based on common socio-political institutions and concepts, whereas nationality is viewed as an historical phenomenon which is somewhat inappropriate in the contemporary context.

From the point of view of another Turkish interviewee, the difference between both concepts is also very clear:

An immigrant who has got German citizenship..... has not got German nationality. Citizenship is...a passport...[and] the passport is important when it is ...about legal equality. (Int. 5/G)

Here, citizenship is clearly viewed as a decisive element for (legal) equality. Nationality has actually nothing to do with citizenship rights. However, this matter is said to be treated differently by German law. Two views of members of a minority:

Here in Germany, it is associated.... that being a German citizen means at the same time to be a German national. This means - and the naturalization law explains it in detail - that you have to prove allegiance to Germanness. (Int. 7/G)

For me, the citizenship question is one of the most decisive.... The ethno-national element which is embodied in the citizenship law and which is constantly reflected in our [governmental] policies.. - this is exactly the element we have to get rid off. (Int. 4/G)

Here, the demand to de-link nationality and citizenship is explicitly expressed. This issue gained topicality in 1991 when the Federal Constitutional Court ruled out the possibility for long-term resident immigrants to vote in local elections on the basis of Article 116 of the Constitution (the Basic Law) which says that "political power emanates from the people [Volk]" (Basic Law, paragraph 20 II) whereby 'people' was interpreted as 'Germans' and thus, a clear link to 'blood-relatedness' was made (Karpen 1989). Comments on that by two interviewees (members of the Turkish minority):

Yes, everything emanates from the people. Article 116....It is always justified by saying that you have to prove allegiance to the state, the history and Germanness...A person in the fourth generation will say "I am

> also *Volk* [people]" ...[So] it is a question of ...how *Volk* is defined. Is *Volk* defined nationalistically...homogeneous or...multiculturally heterogeneous? (Int. 5/G)

> In the Basic Law, it says 'the *Volk*'. What is 'the *Volk*'? *Volk* is, or members of the *Volk* are, those who fulfil their duties as citizens ... We [the Turks] are *Volk* too ... We are not German, but we are *Volk*, because we too fulfil our citizens' duties ... The basic Law [however] does not define citizens, but Germans. (Int. 6/G)

The prevailing juridical interpretation of the 'German people' as laid down in the Constitution has a clear racial connotation. In its link to citizenship, the notion of *Volk* works in an exclusionary way for immigrant minorities who view themselves as unjustly excluded from this definition of *Volk* in spite of their long-term residence and their fulfilment of citizens' duties (in particular the last quote seems to express the implicit notion of 'no taxation without representation').

The linking of nationality and citizenship in German law would not be quite so strongly criticized if naturalization procedures were fairly easy and if there were better immigration/integration policies. A view on this issue was expressed by the chief executive of a local government department who used to work many years in grass-root organizations:

> For too long West Germany has not taken into consideration any processes of change in the area of migration...It was realized too late [by the government] that, if I want to integrate these people, that doesn't just mean that they don't stand out, but if I want them to participate, if they should identify themselves with the nation or republic, with this state - and this is our common ground. ....- you can pray how you want, that is not important - that [opportunity] was missed by not offering them citizenship and political participation..... (Int. 4/G)

An important aspect for developing collective identification is seen here in terms of citizenship and political participation. Citizenship is, however, based on nationality and since it is not easily to be acquired for immigrant minorities their ability to reallocate their identity to the new country of residence is hindered. For immigrant minorities, therefore, the issue of national identity in its legal sense is of great importance, as it is tightly linked to formal citizenship.

Aspects of nationality in the legal sense, such as the ius sanguinis principle and the prevailing interpretation of the *Volk* , were regarded by many interviewees - members of the majority as well as minority - as racist because of their link to blood-relatedness (Int. 7/G; 8/G; 5/G). In legal terms, therefore, there are clear signs of an understanding of collective identity which is based on racism. Such a legal definition is likely to have an impact on social recognition.

*Legal and social boundaries: Do immigrants belong?* The legal interpretation of taking 'citizens' and 'nationals' as identical is suggested by some interviewees to have had a profound influence on the socio-cultural interpretation of who is a German in the same ethnic/racial terms and thus excluding immigrants.

> What is still in the minds [of policy-makers] is...the foreigner as an alien object, as 'enemy of the state', as endangering...And this is how [the foreigner] is presented in the media, in politics, theForeigners' Law describes him as such....This is the stranger who has got to behave properly, but he remains defined as a stranger because he is called 'foreigner' (Ausländer), he is not an 'immigrant' as in other countries...And this impedes these people from identifying themselves in any form with this republic. (Int. 4/G)

The terminology of 'foreigners' as applied by policy-makers in legislation is taken on by sections of civil society. This reflects the low level of inclusion of immigrant peoples and their non-belongingness to the socio-national community as a whole. Most of the interviewees emphasized that this is a particularly serious problem for subsequent generations who do not regard themselves as 'immigrants' but as a firm part of the population, raised or even born in Germany.

> The second, and more so the third, generation - for them, a perfidious situation emerges. They actually identify with this country. But every day they feel, and this is said and shown to them by their exclusion from lots of things, that they nevertheless do not belong....Those who were brought up here, whose country this is and at the same time is not - they come into conflict, and this results in resentment. And this is becoming dangerous. (Int. 4/G)

The situation in which the majority society treats settled ethnic minorities as 'foreigners' - in the legal as well as in the social sphere - and in which non-acceptance of ethnic minorities is based on an exclusionary understanding of the majority's 'national identity' can result in a kind of 'vicious circle' as explained by one interviewee (member of the Turkish minority):

> The question is not, do I feel German or Turkish, the question is simply, how am I accepted by society? And...a very normal reaction from the younger generation partly [is], the more I am excluded from society, the more there is the tendency to look back.....to one's own nationalistic feelings and values. And Germany stirs this up by making the *social sphere* hardly accessible for the young generation. These adolescents do not feel that they belong because they are forced to come under

> regulations of a *Foreigners' Law*...I think this state produces a 'foreigner syndrome' which does not actually exist anymore. (Int. 5/G)

The statement of there being a tendency to search for their "own nationalistic feelings" brings one back to the section on the 'British' organizations where I suggested that the term 'their own nationalistic feelings' should probably be rather replaced by 'ethnic identity' as the context is again the position of an ethno-cultural minority.

The perception of immigrant minorities as 'foreigners' is, according to the above interviewees, clearly reflected in a combination of legal and socio-cultural exclusion. The latter is also seen as partly caused by racist attitudes which have become a particular problem in the form of racially motivated violence and attacks (such as the infamous incidents in Mölln and Solingen ) - on the rise since reunification. In this sort of climate, the lack of any signs - in the form of verbal statements or, more importantly, legal actions - from politicians in general and the government in particular, seems to have had devastating effects on the immigrant population. One interviewee (member of the Turkish minority) explained this:

> Sections of the [Turkish] community have considered themselves as an integral part of this society. For them, it [unification] was a shock. I would say...it was actually the political signal which we [the Turks] had expected in those sensitive moments, which we did not get. And this was a rather strong 'stab in the back'. And the question arose "Where does the police stand? Where does this state stand...and where..the monopoly of power...?" (Int. 5/G)

This statement seems to suggest that until reunification, the Turkish minority assumed they had become an established part of German society. The unification process, however, somehow made them realize how little they are actually recognized as belonging - legally as well as by civil society - despite their long periods of residence or even birth in the country.

One section of civil society regarded by many interviewees as being important for the promotion of immigrants' belongingness is the media. Here, a tendency to present immigrants only "via crises" (Int. 8/G) is perceived, such as the arson attacks, or to present them "as a problem" (Int. 5/G). The immigrants are said to appear in the media only as part of the relationship 'foreigners and indigenous people' and never "as Germans. They are not invited as Germans." (Int. 8/G). Thus, they do not seem to be recognized as an integral part of German society which is not regarded as a multi-ethnic or multi-cultural society. This could also mean that signs of post-conventional identity, if existing at all, appear very faintly in Germany. How about supra-and sub-national identity?

*Post-national identity. Supranational (European) identity.* On the inter-personal level, it seems as if the ethnic (or racial) interpretation of national identity is conveyed on the European level, as expressed by one interviewee (member of the majority):

> I think, there are few [people] who would not regard a French person almost as a German or an English person when compared with [feelings towards] Moroccans or Tunisians or black Africans. There is a stronger common identity. (Int. 3/G)

This is similarly viewed by a member of the Turkish minority:

> There are two types of foreigners. There are the European foreigners, and those are not perceived as foreigners. They are not called 'foreigners'...It is those who were recruited [as 'guest-workers', N.P.] who are mostly referred to as foreigners. (Int. 1/G)

This indicates a situation which Castles describes as follows: "By the late 1980s, there appeared to be a much higher degree of social acceptance of intra-European migrants, which contrasted with strongly exclusionary attitudes towards immigrants from the south and minorities who were phenotypically different." (1993:26). The reason for this might be a generally positive attitude towards membership in the European Union and the freedom of movement. This positive attitude might derive from the past two wars in this century and the strong desire to live in peace with the immediate neighbour countries (George 1991). Another reason, however, might be that western Europeans are regarded as culturally closer - an aspect which had been mentioned by a 'British' interviewee in the context of Thatcher's Bruges speech. This hints at a European identity based on the image of indigenous 'white' Europeans. The word 'European' seems to be associated with indigenous French and English etc., but not with Turks, Algerians, Asians, Afro-Caribbeans and any other residents of non-European background. Thus, European identity seems to be as much flawed by a racial interpretation as national identity.

*Sub-national identity* Apart from being a source for some sort of 'Pan-European' identity, the European Union - by establishing the Committee of the Regions - might support or revive a further layer of identity. The question here was whether national identity will be replaced altogether by these developments.

> I think, all this is going to happen at the same time. People naturally see themselves as belonging to the environment in which they were born, the city to which they belong. And at the same time [there is] a feeling for the responsibilities of a nation within a larger Europe and at the same time a

feeling as a European citizen. Which ever is more emphasized, I think, depends on the individual. (Int. 2/G)

European developments, according to this view, seem to be less a question of 'replacement', than of 'addition' in the sense that there are different layers to collective identity. It seems to be a personal matter as to which layer is more pronounced. Some of the other interviewees, too, expressed this idea of an *additional* European identity whereby the other layers do not cease to exist.

*Legal and socio-cultural boundaries*  For ethnic minorities, there is a similar problem on the European level as on the national level: without citizenship rights, it is difficult for them to develop a sense of belonging and identification. They might consider themselves as Europeans, but this is not reflected in their European citizenship rights as opposed to EU-nationals, despite the latter's shorter periods of residence - conditions which are viewed as racially discriminatory and exclusionary. Here the opinion of a Turkish organization on this matter:

> Within the EU, there are many immigrants who have not got EU-citizenship...That means for them a further internal discrimination....Why should the others [non-EU nationals] who have spent a much longer period of their life within the EU be discriminated against?...We [the third country nationals] are also part of Europe.  (Int. 5/G)

The hope by some interviewees that phenomena such as nationalism, which prevent ethnic minorities from identifying with the socio-national collectivity, would be minimized by developments on the European level, have not yet been realized. The head of an organization representing Turkish people in Berlin put it as follows:

> I always thought the EU would save us from nationalism...But now I realize what it looks like, in Italy etc. This has changed my opinion about the EU. I no longer believe that the EU is a good union, a humane union...It continues to be an economic power, but not a union for human rights. ..We [the Turks] consider ourselves Europeans, but these issues [of nationalism] have suddenly appeared...As long as there is no answer to that, it is not possible to identify with the EU...I can personally, for myself, feel European, but I cannot identify with the European idea. (Int. 6/G)

Therefore, the exclusionary tendencies of national identity do not seem to be solved on the EU level, but rather perpetuated, as "it is again the same identity of the indigenous majority and the ethnic minorities are not made part of it." (Int. 6/G)

### 9.2.3 The EU Migrants Forum

*Rising nationalism*  The president of the EU Migrants Forum felt (in a similar way as it was expressed by many 'British' and 'German' organizations) that nationalism has risen within each EU member-state despite - or maybe as a reaction to - further European integration. The present economic climate is seen as the driving force for protectionist 'narrow' nationalism, as well as politicians who "pamper to the lowest instincts of the constituents." In other words, there is a tendency to draw tighter boundaries along 'racial' lines and to make 'foreigners' responsible for socio-economic problems. This has exclusionary implications for ethnic minorities.

*European exclusion of ethnic minorities?*  A distinction has to be made between exclusion based on policies and practices of the European Union as a whole and exclusion as the result from policies and practices among all member-states. The existence of the EU Migrants Forum as such already indicates that inclusion into the EU is not satisfactory.

The Migrants Forum is aware of the different levels of inclusion of the various ethnic minority groups in each member-state. This is seen as posing various problems with regard to identification with Europe. For example,

> Germany is entirely different from Britain in as much that the German constitution is racially discriminatory...They would not accept the legal resident non-Community citizens as part of the Community. They still insist on calling them 'foreigners'. They make it very hard for them to become naturalized. They have no arrangements for dual nationality. Their thinking is still very much pre-war thinking about German blood...

The strong link between nationality and citizenship in German law is seen here as hindering the formation of national and European identity. There is, however, awareness that this link does not only exist in German law, but that more EU member-states have moved towards stricter nationality laws and away from sole ius soli - a tendency which shows a generally more 'racial' understanding of national identity.

> [Is there a general tendency in the EU to move more towards blood-related laws?] "Yes, indeed."

The main reason for this shift is again seen in the present economic situation and the attempt by politicians to find solutions and to gain votes.

> [This shift is happening] in order to get political votes, in order to get power...They [the politicians] are showing the white electorate 'we are getting tougher with these people' so that they can win the votes. That is

> what they are after...That is where racism and xenophobia increase....They are preaching narrow nationalism and that effects us [ethnic minorities]. And therefore, ...people see us as a problem.

In view of the above, there is a common tendency among EU member-states to define collective identity more narrowly. The formation of an European identity is, therefore, rendered difficult for ethnic minorities. There is an indication that the main reasons for this encompass both nationalism and racism. Both are on the increase as a reaction to socio-economic crises re-inforced by politicians' vote-winning rhetoric. Being scapegoated for these socio-economic problems, ethnic minorities are the main victims of racial nationalism. One way to counteract the force of nationalism could be to promote the equal existence of multiple layers to collective identity.

*Different layers of identity* National identity as such is not at all seen by the Migrants Forum as something which should be abandoned altogether in favour of European identity.

> What the ultimate objective is, is that everyone should get into the European way of life without losing their national identity and that is quite possible. ...In some countries, like in this country [UK], they have distorted the word 'federalism'. Federalism means that each state will keep its identity without losing their national identity. But within that, there will be a European Union. Therefore, the national identity will never be lost...The example is Germany itself:...[T]he Bavarians are very, very independent minded, but they still are essentially German. And that is exactly what will happen on a much larger scale.

This expresses the same understanding of different layers of collective identity as in the case of some 'German' organizations. European identity is not regarded as a replacement, but as a supplement. This also shows that the Migrants Forum has adopted the German understanding of 'federalism' (see Chapter Six for details).

However, as it stands at present, rising narrow nationalism works against the development of the European 'identity layer'. Politicians are again seen as a major influence, in particular "[t]hose people who are Euro-sceptics, they are distorting the real Europe".

### 9.2.4 Commentary

Immigrant or ethnic minorities define 'being British' or 'being German' with the holding of a passport, i.e. with citizenship and thus, a legalistic notion. They relate their own 'national identity' to their countries of origin ("I am Turkish") which can be explained as a response to 'racial' and nationalistic exclusion in their country of residence[10] . This might also have a political

("I am black") or politico-historical connotation ("I am African"). It was suggested, therefore, that this identity should be seen as 'ethnic' rather than 'national'. For immigrant minorities, the distinction of nationality (or ethnicity) and citizenship appeared to be important.

In particular in times of rising nationalism (which is widely regarded as a response to socio-economic crises), most interviewees strongly believed that influential sections within civil society were responsible for a clear definition of the essence of national identity. The media were seen as particularly powerful in Britain and Germany. Right-wing and conservative parties were viewed as promoting narrow nationalism and thus, a 'racial' definition of collective identity. Although all of the interviewees rejected this kind of narrow definition personally, they could not deny its strong influence. The right-wing notion of national identity tends to revolve around a negative image of the 'Other' and around culturally exclusive elements. The way in which 'Britishness' or 'Germanness' is interpreted, thus, appeared in the interviews partly as a matter related to political alliance. This connection was similarly established in chapter Seven (on 'mass discourse') and Eight (on parliamentary debates).

In both 'German' and 'British' interviews, the link between nationalism and racism appeared in a number of contexts. Socio-economic crises, for instance, were suggested as not only having resulted in rising nationalism, but also in racism. Thus, boundaries between 'insiders' and 'outsiders' are not only drawn on ethno-cultural lines, but also based on the distinction between 'races'. This was seen as reflected in the legal understanding of nationality in Germany. The elements on which the German nationality/citizenship law is based - such as the ius sanguinis principle, the interpretation of *Volk*, the harsh naturalization procedures - were implicitly regarded as indications of national identity blurred with the identity as a 'race'. Moreover, some interviewees perceived the narrow definition of national identity as rooted in the same historical periods as it was stated with regard to racism: The 'British' interviewees referred mainly to colonialism and imperialism, the 'German' interviewees to pre-war thinking about blood-relatedness - which certainly means the Hitler-era, but could also include the whole period since the creation of the German nation-state (in 1871). This suggests that there is a link between national identity and identity as a superior 'race'.

In Britain, the link between nationality and citizenship is not so much recognized in legal terms, as most post-war immigrants and their children are legally British. In both countries, however, this link was seen as existing within civil society. This means that there is a discrepancy between the legal understanding of 'Britishness' and its perception within the wider public. In Germany, there is a continuous understanding of immigrants as 'foreigners' (and thus, 'outsiders') in legal as well as social terms.

In Britain, the notion of a post-conventional identity based on citizenship detached from the notion of nationality (i.e. common descent) was implicitly touched upon by few members representing the ('white') majority. Among members of the ethnic minorities, however, the necessity of a stronger development of such an identity was more explicitly expressed as a result from their own experience of immigration. The 'German' interviewees showed that multi-culturalism/multi-ethnicity has not yet reached the level of Britain. Elements such as a 'mixed' youth culture were not mentioned at all.

Supra-national, i.e. European, identity appeared as an aspect most of the interviewees did not have too much to say about. This could be related to the 'remoteness' of European issues to people's everyday lives. Another reason could be the 'newness' of developments on the European level. The EU Migrants Forum and some of the 'German' and 'British' organizations thought of supra-national identity not as a replacement for national identity, but as a supplement. The idea of different layers of collective identity - i.e. local/regional, national and European - was more explicitly expressed by 'German' interviewees which must be related to Germany's long tradition of (politically and culturally) fairly independent *Länder* .

It was widely viewed that ethnic minorities have an additional problem with European identity. For them, it functions to exclude for two main reasons: 1. as the outcome of a predominantly 'white' definition (cultural identity); 2. as the outcome of certain EU policies (border controls; refusal of EU-citizenship to non-EU nationals).

By depicting the issue of national identity as related to nationality in its legal sense and as an expression of cultural belongingness, all of the interviewees - more or less explicitly - linked this issue to citizenship in a formal (legal) and substantive sense.

## 9.3 Citizenship

The main objective of the questions in this section was to find out the way in which the interviewees viewed the citizenship status of immigrant minorities affected by the relationship between nationalism and racism - in a formal and/or substantive sense. Further, Husband's 'dimensions of welcome' were explored by questions about anti-discrimination and related legislation. The interviewees were also asked about the meaning of European citizenship and the potential of the Committee of the Regions.

### 9.3.1 The British organizations

*Formal equality and its historical connection*  None of the interviewees denied the formal citizenship status enjoyed by post-war labour migrants and their children. The specific historical circumstances which resulted in legal equality of those immigrants from former British colonies were pointed out in particular by two interviewees (both members of the majority). They both referred to 'common subjecthood' of all peoples residing within the British Empire:

> We were *subjects* to the Queen...The Indian peoples living in our Empire in India were subjects of the Queen in exactly the same way that my ancestors in this country were subjects to the Queen...Therefore, when immigration started in a substantial way from Commonwealth countries immediately after the war, the people coming here had the same rights that I had. (Int. 4/B; emphasis added)

> Well, before 1948, I mean, everybody from the Empire was a British subject..... (Int. 5/B)

Common 'subjecthood' has resulted in equal formal citizenship of ex-colonial immigrants and indigenous British people. Subjecthood did not mean belonging to and participation in a socio-national community, but clearly defined loyalty and duties to the monarch (Dummett & Nicol 1990). The concept of citizenship, by contrast, emphasizes the combination of rights and duties - with rights being a very important part of it. The friction between these two concepts emerged when the first immigrants actually made use of their 'freedom to move' within the Empire after the war.

Nonetheless, equal formal citizenship has derived from the specific context of subjecthood under the British Empire, and thus

> ...a loophole [was left]...through which these immigrant groups could enter political life on the basis of complete equality with people living in this [Britain] country. (Int. 4/B)

The decisive point made by interviewee 4/B and 5/B is that immigration to Britain did not result *in general* in an equal formal citizenship status, but that only ex-colonial peoples enjoyed this special 'treatment'. It was these specific colonial ties and the concept of subjecthood which provided the immigrants from the Indian sub-continent and the Caribbean islands with this quite unique legal status when compared with immigration to most of continental Europe.

Moreover, the phrase 'complete equality' in the above quote is rightly put in the context of political rights (such as voting rights) and thus, formal citizenship. This could mean that in the context of substantive citizenship, 'complete equality' does not exist.

*Substantive citizenship* As the outcome of these specific historical circumstances, most ethnic minorities in Britain enjoy full legal equality in formal terms, but it is acknowledged by the interviewees that this somehow does not mean fully equal citizenship in general. Racial discrimination is seen as affecting immigrants' social (in a broad sense) citizenship. Therefore, the question whether ethnic minorities are fully equal citizens in Britain was answered by two interviewees, whose organizations mainly deal with legal matters (the former mainly in the area of immigration, the latter in the area of anti-discrimination legislation), as follows:

> In law yes, but in fact, there is discrimination.... (Int. 5/B)
> There can be none of these sort of barriers [to formal citizenship]. However, they [the immigrants] continue not to share full citizenship in practical terms...If you look at the statistics, social deprivation, all the statistics show that they are worse off. Wherever you look. For housing, higher unemployment, poorer health... (Int. 4/B)

These quotes show that there is an implicit understanding of the difference between formal and substantive citizenship. Important to notice is that the elements illustrating inequality on the substantive level are identical with elements mentioned previously as concrete situations of racism. There is this whole range of areas in which ethnic minorities' substantive citizenship status is encroached upon - such as housing, the employment situation, education, criminalization, depiction in the media etc. Some of these elements did also appear in the replies on the exclusive tendency of 'national identity' (as the outcome of 'narrow' nationalism). This shows, therefore, that inequality on the substantive level is the result of the combined effects of racism and nationalism. Hence, one interviewee (member of the majority) concluded that

> [t]hey [immigrant minorities] are second class in terms of their social experience in our society. (Int. 4/B)

As for the roots of this unequal substantive citizenship status, one interviewee explained that they are

> ...a result of inherited disadvantage. Because they [the immigrants] come lower on the socio-economic scale. (Int. 4/B)

The notion of 'inherited disadvantage' in this quote can certainly be interpreted in a similar way as done by Rex & Tomlinson (1979) and Goulbourne (1991), i.e. as a residue from imperial Britain and the roles which immigrants were to fill in such a colonial society. Their socio-economically lower position was related to a feeling of superiority on the part of the majority resulting in racist and nationalistic attitudes.

Meanwhile, however, the Empire is a matter of the past and might have lost its impact on attitudes among younger generations. This could mean that the substantive status of ethnic minorities has improved.

*Improvements towards further equality?* The notion of 'inherited disadvantage' is expressed differently by Vogel's notion of 'late coming'. She suggests that the specific disadvantages these groups suffer are typical 'problems of latecomers' as they often lack resources that are necessary to make full use of citizens' entitlements (in: van Steenbergen 1994). 'Late coming' also entails non-belonging and non-acceptance by civil society which might, however, have changed for subsequent generations born in Britain. Therefore, in a similar way as suggested in the section on national identity, it was said by some interviewees that there have been certain improvements. An increased level of acceptance of ethnic minorities on the part of the majority has had a positive impact on minorities' substantive citizenship. With regard to racial discrimination, the fact that Britain has implemented anti-discrimination legislation was also regarded as having improved minorities' citizenship status. One interviewee (a member of the majority) expressed his opinion on this matter:

> I think it [anti-discrimination legislation] has made some [difference]. Yes. It has not removed discrimination in housing or unemployment, but it certainly had an impact.   (Int. 1/B)

It is indicated here that this type of legal remedy is not sufficient to minimize, let alone eradicate, all forms of racism - as stated by another interviewee (a member of an ethnic minority):

> Though we argue for legislation, we always say that legislation is not a panacea to rid ourselves of racial attacks and racial violence.   (Int. 3/B)

Racially motivated attacks and violence could be interpreted as a sign that sections within civil society do not recognize ethnic minorities as 'belonging', and thus there is a discrepancy between minorities' equal formal status and how this is perceived and 'translated' into an equal social status by civil society. In substantial terms, therefore, certain sections within civil society do not perceive ethnic minorities as equal members of the socio-national community in every respect and express this in all sorts of 'racist' ways, ranging from verbal to physical abuse.

*Other legislation* There are other types of legislation which seem to have racializing effects and thus a negative impact on the social position of former ex-colonial immigrants and their children: restrictive immigration laws (in particular the 'primary purpose rule'[11]) and the Nationality Act. Despite theoretically equal political, civil, and social (narrow sense) rights, the latter is viewed by most interviewees as encroaching on ethnic minorities' ability to acquire British citizenship - as expressed by the following interviewee:

> [t]he Nationality Act..... has lots of restrictions...It does discriminate...[Therefore], in the eyes of the law, they [ethnic minorities] areless equal.  (Int. 2/B)

Although the British Nationality Act of 1981, as mentioned in Chapter Six, does not have direct implications for post-war labour migrants and their children, it is viewed as discriminatory and as sending out a message "that there is something wrong with these people" (Int. 5/B). By implementing ius sanguinis, the formally primary rule of ius soli was given up - a fact deplored by some interviewees. The introduction of ius sanguinis could also be seen as racializing - but none of the interviewees explicitly mentioned this aspect.

*European citizenship*  Most interviewees (in particular those who are members of an ethnic minority) recognized the complexity of issues revolving around ethnic minorities' citizenship when approached from the European point of view. The issues raised by the interviewees allowed the same distinction into formal and substantive citizenship as on the national level.

*Substantive citizenship*  The formally equal citizenship status enjoyed by most blacks and Asians in Britain seems to meet practical (and thus, substantive) problems in the context of the European Union. A member of an ethnic minority expressed his view on this matter:

> I mentioned the free movement campaign...even if [blacks did regard themselves as fully equal citizens], their movement  would be restricted, they are stopped and harassed...*Theoretically,* I can get up tomorrow and get a job in Germany...*In practice*, there is a racial side to it and that prevents black people from being full [European citizens]...    (Int. 3/B; emphasis added)

Elsewhere, the same interviewee continues:

> Even though I am a black citizen, when I want to travel, I will  be stopped, searched and harassed. My citizenship will be questioned. That is our [ethnic minorities'] experience.  (Int. 3/B)

These quotes refer to problems which also appeared in the section on national identity in connection with the crossing of intra-European borders, as well as to the issue of identity in general. Not only do 'blacks' tend to be excluded from national identity, but also from the identity as citizens - a matter which indicates that these two concepts are not necessarily separated in the ('white') majority's everyday understanding (i.e. 'nationality' and 'citizenship' tend to be enmeshed). In the way in which this concern is expressed in the above quote, however, it sounds almost like a matter of fact that every 'black' British person will always have his/her citizenship questioned. This again is a rather provocative and rhetorical way of expression, but this matter must nonetheless be taken seriously. Such problems have also been mentioned by other commentators as part of ethnic minority members' experience (e.g. King, 1993; see also Chapter Six). Furthermore, 'a racial side' is mentioned by which the above interviewee seems to suggest that black and Asian British citizens are likely to experience racism when trying to apply for a job in another member-state. This could refer to the fact that there are differences in continental European anti-discrimination laws which are not directly equivalent to the British 'Race Relations Act'.

*Formal citizenship* In addition to these substantive types of problems, formal citizenship can also become a problem in the European context - as explained by the following interviewees (the former a member of an ethnic minority, the latter a member of the majority):

> And moreover, the Third World citizens,...those who have not given up their own nationality, but [who have got all rights in Britain, N.P.]...they have no freedom of movement...So this is false for us...It is like a ...closed community. (Int. 2/B)

(The interviewee mixed up 'nationality' with 'citizenship': one cannot give up nationality, but when applying for citizenship in the country of residence, an immigrant might have to give up his or her former citizenship).

> [P]eople from the Indian sub-continent ..have all the rights [in Britain],only on the European level, they cannot take part. (Int. 4/B)

The specific problem referred to here is that of those immigrants who have full formal rights in Britain by still holding their original citizenship (i.e. passport) because they come from Commonwealth countries which do not recognize dual nationality/citizenship (such as India). For them, freedom of movement does not even exist in theory because they do not have British citizenship. The fact of being formally recognized as a British citizen (in terms of rights) does, therefore, not necessarily equal formal European citizenship.

*Future prospects* The future likelihood of a beneficial revision of the Treaty of Rome in 1996 - in terms of adding a 'race' dimension to it - is largely viewed as pessimistic, in particular by one interviewee who works for a semi-governmental organization dealing with the workings of the British 'Race Relations Act':

> I do not think that we will win...What I think they are doing is they are going to give Third country nationals permanently resident in Europe basic rights of movement as the buy-off. They will give that and they will not put 'race' in [the Treaty of Rome]. (Int. 4/B)

In the light of coming general elections in various EU-member-states and with the ongoing 'playing of the race and immigration card' - as mentioned by the president of the EU Migrants Forum - this pragmatic view on the future developments seems to be justified. It may, however, not be necessary to put 'race' into the Treaty of Rome. One of the arguments in this thesis is that this issue could be dealt with on the sub-national, i.e. local, level as part of the Committee of the Regions' field of responsibilities.

*Subnational developments* In general, none of the interviewees expressed very clear ideas about the future prospects of the Committee of the Regions established by the Maastricht Treaty and its implications for citizenship. There was no clarity as to what exactly 'regionalism' means. Two interviewees equated it with 'localism'. As suggested previously, this might be related to the fact that this Committee has not existed for very long and that the interviewed organizations have not been involved in one form or other. On a general level, one interviewee (member of the majority) held a positive view:

> I would guess...that it would be a healthy development, both to have a greater sense of supra-nationalism....but also greater localism. I think that would be healthy for everybody, both those trends. (Int. 1/B)

As it stands at present, however, the same interviewee cannot envisage a move "towards a constructive regionalism" as the British government "is either diminishing powers of local authorities or it is actually taking them away to itself". According to this view, 'regionalism' is understood as more 'power' or more involvement of local authorities. A three-dimensional concept of citizenship (local, national and European) seems, therefore, desirable. In highly centralized Britain, however, this concept might not be realizable.

The following interviewee explained his opinion with more specific reference to ethnic minorities :

> I am not sure how many black people are in the ..Committee of the Regions, but *it has just started*...and I doubt that racial equality has reached the agenda or will ever reach the agenda...In that context, it is relevant to the black community...I have got to see...whether giving funds to the regions directly or indirectly benefits the black community. And from what I have seen, whether it is my involvement in the Association of

Local Authorities or as a Councillor or some of my work in the European field, I have not seen that materialized. But, yes, of course, I support the concept to give more influence to the regions. (Int. 3/B; emphasis added)

It is recognized here that the Committee of the Regions is a very new development and it is, therefore, too early to make an assessment of its positive impact on ethnic minorities. Despite the fear that 'racial equality' might never be an issue the Committee will deal with, the general idea of giving more power to the regions is viewed by this interviewee as positive. The recency of the creation of the Committee has also been emphasized by other commentators (Barber & Millns 1993; Taylor 1995) who view that there is potential for 'race' related issues to reach the agenda.

According to the above replies, it can be assumed that the general idea of 'local citizenship' would gain support from the organizations working in the field of 'race relations'. This idea is, however, far removed from present day politics in Britain.

### 9.3.2 The German organizations

*Formal citizenship* The situation for non-European first immigrants in Germany and their descendants has been very different from the situation in Britain in that they were not provided with an equal formal citizenship status upon their arrival. The reason for this has to be partly related to the lack of any 'historical ties' between post-war labour migrants and Germany, as in the British case. All of the interviewees mentioned the fact that large parts of the post-war labour migrants and their children do not have formal citizenship. However, they rendered this issue different degrees of importance.

One interviewee (member of majority) made the lack of any historical ties very clear when stating that:

They [the immigrants] are citizens of another state and they live here with a secure residential status, but they are citizens of another state. If they naturalize, they are citizens of this state. (Int. 2/G)

The same interviewee continued to explain the citizenship situation of those immigrants who have not naturalized:

[Without German citizenship, apart from voting], they cannot become civil servants...Some professions with private practices such as psychologists, lawyers, medical doctors, are linked to citizenship... But they can move freely [within Germany][12]...There are only a few rights which are limited to citizens. The access to social rights - that is not a citizenship right, but a right of the residential population. Most of the rights are either human rights or rights of the residential population in Germany. (Int. 2/G)

These quotes stem from the head of a department which is part of a particular city's governmental structure. This head has been very actively engaged over the years in campaigning and lobbying for the facilitation of naturalization procedures, as well as for ius soli being introduced as a supplement to ius sanguinis. She is not in favour of dual nationality and that is most likely the reason why she insists that the labour migrants are "citizens of another state", which seems to justify in her opinion the non-granting of certain rights, with the only way out of this problem being naturalization.

Furthermore, it is a matter of interpretation to say that there are *only a few* rights withheld from immigrants who otherwise have gained permanent residence status. Some of those rights, the political as well as some of the civil rights, are very important for the 'struggle for equal citizenship' (Turner 1990). Without the general right to assemble or demonstrate, let alone to vote, a strong social movement is hardly feasible. Moreover, the lack of full civil rights has serious implications on the so-called 'secure residential status' of immigrants - an issue mentioned by most of the other interviewees. If immigrants are believed to jeopardize public peace, they can be deported - a matter which recently reached topicality when the government threatened to deport members of the Curdish minority for having taken part in blockades and demonstrations. The notion of being a 'threat to public peace' is very much subject to the discretion of politicians. Without formal citizenship, therefore,

> [f]oreigners are not allowed to be politically active....... [and] they have not got any legal influence.  (Int. 8/G)

> [S]omebody [of the immigrant population] who breaks the law and...who 'jeopardizes German public life' can be deported, even when born in Germany.  (Int. 5/G)

*Social rights (narrow sense)* It is correct that social rights (such as unemployment benefit, pensions, health insurance, child allowances etc.) are in theory not tied to citizenship. However, practical problems might occur when immigrants try to claim them - an aspect neglected by the interviewee 2/G (quoted above), but mentioned by many other interviewees (in particular by members of the Turkish minority).

> [The immigrants have] all social rights [only] to a certain extent, because a person who has been living here for 30 years and who has an unlimited right of abode, but who...has been receiving state benefits for three years comes into conflict with the job centre [Arbeitsamt]. This is not equality. (Int. 5/G)

> Social rights are available. But when an unemployed immigrant goes to the job centre and asks for unemployment benefit, he is certainly

tormented...Day by day immigrants are coming [to see me] who are tormented ...by governmental institutions and although they are legally entitled to and fulfil the preconditions, they do not get their money.... (Int. 6/G)

There seems to be a discrepancy between social rights as legal entitlements of all residents and their perception within the wider public. Discrimination (which is based here on ethnic origin) was said to be involved in the issue of who is a legitimate claimer of state benefits (Int. 6/G) - an aspect which has also been mentioned with reference to the exclusionary effects of national identity. Therefore, it is subliminally indicated here that racial discrimination within civil society and the state structure has a negative impact on the claiming of entitlements. Legal definition as a foreigner is, therefore, reflected in every day treatment by civil society. This also means that the legal right to social rights (in the narrow sense) is accompanied by substantive problems. Thus, the statement that "this is not equality" (Int. 5/G) seems to be justified.

*Civil rights* As mentioned above, some of the civil rights, such as freedom of assembly and of alliance, are tied to citizenship and not residence. This area of rights is

...acutely divided between foreigners and Germans, i.e. between Germans and human beings [in general]....A certain part [of these rights] is limited to Germans. (Int. 3/G)

It was written in the constitution from the very beginning. It is not defined who is citizen [Bundesbürger], but it is defined who is German. (Int. 6/G)

Both interviewees (one member of the majority and one member of the minority) rightly pointed out that the constitution does not describe rights as generally of citizens (by the sole nature of residence and not ethnic background), but that they are either for Germans or they are declaratory (and thus vague) human rights[13]. This reflects the idea of citizenship and nationality being largely treated as one and the same concept.

*Ius sanguinis* Ius sanguinis was regarded by most interviewees (and by all members of the Turkish minority) as a major barrier to the acquisition of formal citizenship rights. One interviewee (member of the majority) thought that

...this principle of descent should be supplemented by the territorial principle, because the basis has to be that all the people who live together in a country and form the residential population must have the same rights and duties. (Int. 2./G)

A Turkish interviewee explicitly referred to sole ius sanguinis as

> [r]acism....People who were born and raised here....are foreigners. This principle of ethnic descent is a unique phenomenon and it is open racism. (Int. 7/G)

This constitutes more evidence of the enmeshing of nationality and citizenship in the German law with clearly racializing effects.

*Dual nationality/citizenship*  Another, even regarded by some interviewees as the main, obstacle to formal citizenship is the "required waiver of the former citizenship" (Int. 7/G), i.e. the non-acceptance of dual citizenship[14]. One interviewee who is the head of a (city)governmental department which exercises policy-making powers explained her opinion on this matter:

> We [the policy-makers] have to accept, in my opinion, dual nationality, ...because identity ...cannot be changed simply by a 'stroke of the pen' and by a different colour passport, but these are processes, and I have to take these processes into account by building a bridge. Bridges are, for example, the dual nationality. It is not a panacea for everything - it is only one aspect towards integration, but it is a vital one, because in a country like Germany, where formalities are so important, it provides for formal equality. Somebody with a dark skin would still not be equal, ...but at least he could claim his rights.  (Int. 4/G)

Important is the metaphor of dual nationality as a 'bridge'. This brings to mind the Swedish approach which regards citizenship as the prerequisite for integration (Hammar 1985a&b). In Germany, by contrast, integration is largely regarded as the prerequisite to citizenship (with the understanding that only persons who are, or feel, fully integrated are prepared to give up their original citizenship), in particular by the governing coalition (see Chapter Eight). This approach totally ignores the fact that immigration is a long-term process which might last for a few generations.

The above quote showed the importance given to formal citizenship - described by another interviewee as "the beginning" of the process of achieving cultural and social equality (Int. 5/G). And yet, it is also indicated above that formal citizenship is not a "panacea for everything" - an aspect which leads to the notion of substantive citizenship.

*Substantive citizenship*  It is acknowledged by many interviewees (members of majority as well as minority) that formal citizenship does not necessarily mean "equality on the social level" (Int. 5/G). It was suggested by one interviewee that the recent arson attacks have reinforced this awareness:

After the terrible arson attacks, many foreigners and Germans who are working in the *Ausländerarbeit* [equivalent to 'race relations' field, N.P.] have said: Of what use is the German passport to foreigners? I think, one of the persons who died had a German passport. Therefore, as their appearance does not alter, they are still recognizable as ethnically non-German. (Int. 1/G)

Non-recognition and non-acceptance as a legitimate part of the socio-national community indicates a dimension which is going beyond legal, civil and social (narrow sense) rights and which has been suggested as being best expressed in terms of substantive citizenship. This non-recognition is related by the above interviewee to immigrants' different ethnicity - an element which has also been mentioned with regard to national identity. The interpretation of nationalistic and racializing processes being involved in this non-recognition by civil society does, therefore, not seem to be too far fetched.

It is also indicated in the above quote that substantive citizenship is not about rights in the same way as formal citizenship, but it is rather a matter of personal freedom and attitude - an aspect also mentioned by the following interviewee:

After all, it is about changing [the majority's] behaviour and attitudes. And this is the big problem...To achieve changes in behaviour is a time-consuming and tedious task. (Int. 2/G)

Legal changes are, therefore, not sufficient. The perception of immigrants as belonging, and thus the minimization of the effects of nationalism and racism, has to be achieved. This could partly be done with the help of anti-discrimination legislation.

*Anti-discrimination legislation* Effective resistance to nationalism and racism might result from anti-discrimination legislation. As for the question why there is no anti-discrimination legislation in Germany such as in Britain,

[t]here are two reasons. There is an objective reason that in Germany ...there are actually possibilities in almost every legal field to fight discrimination...If they were applied, we would not need [extra] legislation...The other reason is ideological. As there are neither minorities nor discrimination or racism, we do not need a law. (Int. 4/G)

The ideological reason for not having any anti-discrimination legislation or for not implementing the legal provisions which already exist is linked to the official (i.e. governmental) denial of racism. Amendments to the *Ausländergesetz* (Foreigners' Law) are the only attempt on the part of the government to improve the position of *Ausländer*.

*The new Foreigners' Law: a source of improvement?* The question whether the new Foreigners' Law of 1991 has actually improved immigrants' citizenship status was largely denied. Only one interviewee thought that "a lot of things have changed" (Int. 2/G). In particular the lowering of fees for naturalization and other facilitations for the first and second generations were regarded by this interviewee as profound changes. This might have to do with the fact that this interviewee is the head of a (city) governmental department which has been very active in achieving formal citizenship status for immigrants by facilitating naturalization procedures (the very first quote at the beginning of this section on the German organizations was by the same person). This positive view on the new law might, therefore, hide the disappointment about the little success of many years of work. It could, however, also show a compromising attitude: the head of this department was described by a colleague as very realistic in terms of her assessment of the progress possible to be achieved under a conservative government and in the present (post-reunification) socio-political climate.

This positive view of the new law is, however, contested by most of the other interviewees:

> As far as the legal position is concerned, the new Foreigners' Law has made a few little improvements, but it has not improved the basic situation of total insecurity with regard to their [the immigrants'] residential status, in particular for young foreigners who can still be deported as soon as they somehow breach the law.... (Int. 3/G)

> [There are] aspects [of the new law] that have deteriorated: before, everybody could obtain a secure residence permit, now only if you have worked here and paid in social security/insurances for five years. (Int. 5/G)

The latter interviewee explains this further with the help of an example from her own family. Her brother was born in Germany and was at the time of the interview only sixteen years old and, therefore, has not yet been in full-time employment for five years as compulsory school education lasts for eight years. Thus, he cannot get a secure residence permit as yet. In his case, however, there is the possibility to naturalize easily as the fees have been drastically reduced and requirements facilitated by the new law for children up to the age of twenty-one. The interviewee calls this policy, therefore, an "insidious assimilation policy" because it is not possible at that age to have worked for five years and thus, to obtain the most secure residential status German law offers, but naturalization is as easy as never before for this particular age group - on the same condition, however, of giving up the original citizenship. Dual nationality/citizenship is officially still not allowed.

There is, however, one aspect which was mentioned as a positive improvement by the new law: the so-called 'return option' (Rückkehroption). This is said to show a change in the official attitude towards the recognition of the 'territorial principle'.

> For adolescents who had to return with their parents as minors, there is the possibility of returning to Germany within five years after having 'come of age' (volljährig). And this is a clear sign that the legislators indeed realize that people who were born and brought up in a country are rooted there. (Int. 1/G)

This interviewee is the public relations officer of interviewee 2/G - the only other person who talked about the new law in mostly positive terms. This underpins what had been said above about the long-term activities of this department aimed at improving naturalization procedures. The 'return option' can certainly be seen as such a 'sign of improvement'. However, it is by no means as thorough as automatically granting immigrants' children full formal citizenship rights upon birth - an aspect felt by all the other interviewees. It is, therefore, a very weak sign of any recognition of a principle based on residence rather than on ethnic ties.

*European citizenship* It is widely acknowledged among the interviewees that most of Germany's non-European immigrants do not benefit from European citizenship as the majority of them does not have German citizenship, which is, however, the prerequisite for entitlements such as the freedom of movement. The main problem, therefore, is - similar to the national level - the formal side of European citizenship.
Interviewee 5/G and 3/G thought that European citizenship means a new and further 'domestic discrimination' (erneute Inlandsdiskriminierung) as it separates EU-nationals from non-EU nationals, whereby the former are given extended rights (such as voting in local and European elections) despite the longer periods of residence of the latter. Even travelling, for example, for school-children on school trips to European neighbour-countries, is not possible without a visa. One interviewee explained this issue further:

> If an [immigrant] lives in Aachen [city in the West of Germany, N.P.] and wants to go on a short visit to Luxembourg, he needs a visa...We always have these problems with our conferences. Just recently, our Vice President who is Moroccan and lives and works in Spain - he did not get a visa for London. He had to go from Barcelona to Madrid in order to get a visa. He had to take off one and half days. Such a hassle!....There is so much of this nonsense which we have to abolish. (Int. 3/G)

*A future 'race' dimension?* The future prospects for the competence of the EU in the field of 'race relations' is viewed as rather pessimistic.

> I do not think so [that there is going to be action]. They [the EU officials] can surely help to increase awareness for this on a national basis...But there is no legal basis for the Community to become active in this field." (Int. 2/G)

> This is not going to work....because each country's regulations are very different. ..I think that would be a bit utopic.  (Int. 5/G)

One problem is the fact that the EC has no legal competence in the field of 'race relations'. The second quote rightly points out that every country has  different regulations which might be the result of different immigration histories.

Despite a generally negative view on common EU integrative policies, it is viewed that 'opinion sharing' on the European level is very positive (Int. 5/G) which is also reflected in the fact that most of the interviewed organizations are involved in 'European networking'. The aspect of 'opinion sharing' had been mentioned in connection with the Committee of the Regions in chapter Six.  It has been suggested that local authorities could get together and exchange experiences and opinions on all sorts of issues, 'race relation' matters included.

*Sub-national developments* In general, there are slightly stronger opinions on regionalism than in the British context which must have to do with Germany's politico-administrative structure giving 'regions' more independence. Regionalism promoted by the EU in form of the Committee of the Regions was, therefore,  mostly seen as positive. One interviewee thought that

> ..what is 'decidable' in smaller entities should be solved and decided by smaller entities. (Int. 3/G)

This indicates the concept of 'subsidiarity', i.e. "that decisions should be taken at the lowest level possible" (The European 1992:34).

More specifically in the context of ethnic minorities, it was felt by another interviewee that

> [e]verything has to be done to create opportunities for disadvantaged groups to participate. (Int. 4/G)

And further regionalism is regarded as promoting such opportunities.  'Participation' could mean 'empowerment' and if coming from a 'sub-national' level, this leads to the idea of local citizenship.

*Local citizenship* When explaining the rather unique responsibilities and workings of her 'institution', one interviewee (4/G) in particular mentioned a number of aspects which could be interpreted as notions of 'local citizenship'. The interviewee is the chief executive of a (city-)governmental department involved in policy-making relating to 'multi-cultural affairs'. The task of this department is not only to deal with ethnic or immigrant minorities' matters, but to incorporate *all* minorities existing within German society (and so far as they exist in that particular city for which this department is responsible). Part of the policy-making process is the consultation with 'grass-root' organizations - which is not at all a unique feature among the interviewed groups, but it is rather the *way* in which this work is described and understood which seems to be special.

In a multi-cultural and multi-ethnic society, as explained by the interviewee, certain mechanisms of solving conflicts (Konfliktlösungs-mechanismen) are necessary. In other words,

> the simple mechanisms for solving conflicts - which could mean fetching the police or not - those are not sufficient anymore. And that is why there have to be other offers which appeal to those groups who are weaker within this society and which give [those groups] the possibility to be understood and to get their rights...

One of those mechanisms necessary in a multi-cultural society - and probably the most important one - is seen by the interviewee as being communication.

> The meaning of communication in a multi-cultural, pluralistic society, which is not closed, which constantly produces new issues, which is full of tensions [is very important to us]. This means, peoplehave to learn how to solve conflicts,..a type of 'management of conflicts' on the part of the responsible persons - we understand [our work as such].

The reason why communication is given such a central position in the problem solving process is further explained:

> To create commitment - what is that supposed to mean? To create commitment means, I have to create loyalty to this city-council, to this state, to this system, to this society. But I cannot achieve this by commanding people. I have to demand duties from a person [by giving him/her] rights.

'Communication' is understood here as a process of 'giving and taking'. In this way, commitment and loyalty can be achieved which is likely to result in collective identification. It is also indicated here that there are different levels of loyalty (i.e. a local and a state level) and that they supplement each other. The last two sentences of the above quote seem to come from a German context where formal citizenship is not enjoyed by most immigrants: Instead of only 'commanding' them (maybe by the Foreigners' Law?) and demanding duties from them (such as tax-paying), citizenship rights should be granted at the same time.

The idea of 'communication' with, and on, the grass-root level and the best solution-finding process for certain conflicts taking place on the local level is expressed in the following quote. It is the response to the question as to what the interviewee thinks of the recent juridical decisions that Turkish girls (as Muslims) do not have to take part in physical education at school because of their religious faith.

> I do not think that is right. I believe one should not decide such matters juridically...What one should have done, is [that] in each individual case which appears one has to negotiate...This means, I have to negotiate [for example] between younger and older generations, between different concepts...Migration is a very hard process for all those involved. It is not solved within one generation...Our institutions...have got the obligation to accompany these processes in a reasonable way and to support all those involved...I cannot only [support one person] - in that case I would do injustice to the other person...To do so, a lot of [experts guiding this communication] are needed.

The interviewee did not only speak here in her professional capacity, but also on the basis of her personal experience as the daughter of a 'mixed' marriage and as the wife of a member of another ethnic minority - and, therefore, her reference to generational and conceptual problems is part of her own experience with migration processes.

One of the issues raised in the above quote is that not all matters should or can adequately be decided juridically. This somehow indicates that apart from formal citizenship - which is clearly about a legal status - problems or conflicts revolving around the substantive side of citizenship should be dealt with in the form of negotiation. It might not be too far fetched (in particular as the above ideas came from an interviewee who works within a federal political structure) to interpret this as negotiation on the local level where these conflicts occur by letting the people involved participate in finding solutions. Taken a bit further, this leads to the conception of 'local citizenship'.

> More concretely, 'local citizenship' means that in a 'situation of conflict' (such as the above example),

> ..we are trying to make all persons involved co-operate....One has to show understanding [for each party] and to lead them [to the solution].

Roughly, this is meant when speaking of more active participation in a solution-finding process. This makes most sense on the local level where peoples' everyday lives are taking place. Here, mutual understanding can be promoted by, for example, sections within the city council being in charge of communicating between *all* residents. This particular institution, of which the interviewee 4/G is the chief executive, is not in favour of specific policies for *immigrant* minorities, but rather for policies promoting inclusion and fair treatment of all possible minorities. Only by taking society as a whole, 'public peace' is seen by the interviewee as maintainable.

It should be added here that the study on racial violence by Björgo & Witte (1993) also mentions the local dimension of these kinds of incidents. In most of these cases, local residents had been the perpetrators of such acts of violence. The authors, therefore, suggest that further involvement of the local community (in terms of showing clear rejection of such acts) could help to stop or reduce violence. More active involvement of the local community could also result in solving other social conflicts.

The general approach by this German city-governmental department, i.e. to take society as a whole, seems to be similar to the approach as set out by the Swann Report (Department of Education and Science 1985), albeit in the context of education only (as quoted by Tomlinson 1990). According to Tomlinson, since the publication of this report, "the focus of multi-cultural education has moved from issues concerned with the education of ethnic minority pupils, to issues concerning the education of *all* pupils in an ethnically diverse society, in which acceptance of all groups as part of the British nation is becoming socially, politically and economically more important." (op. cit.:7; original emphasis).

Education is surely an important part of gaining 'acceptance' for all groups within society, but the emphasis should probably be more on 'education for citizenship in a multi-cultural society' - which is also the title of a book by Lynch (1992) in which he advocates the need for a new concept of citizenship to prepare for a life in multi-cultural and multi-ethnic societies. The main message in his book is that

> the old individualistic, utilitarian neo-classical paradigm is no longer adequate to the needs of a world with galloping economic, social, cultural and economic[15] problems, and that an alternative community-focused paradigm, which can take account of both individual rights and responsibilities and of different levels of 'community-affiliation' is needed, together with a corresponding shift in the paradigm of the education which prepares future members of those communities. (op. cit.: 20)

The future of citizenship might, therefore, lie in a stronger focus on the local level which seems the best way to improve the substantive part of citizenship - in general as well as for immigrant minorities in particular.

### 9.3.3  *The EU Migrants Forum*

*European citizenship - inclusive or exclusive?*  The EU Migrants Forum's president (the interviewee) viewed citizenship as very important in the process to minimize the power of racism. I would suggest to add the power of nationalism, although this was not explicitly done by the interviewee at this point of the interview, but in a few other contexts (such as the 'scapegoating' of ethnic minorities for socio-economic problems). The reason why citizenship is given such a central position could be that it is - in its formal sense - the prerequisite for immigrants to become politically active and fight for their own rights and social justice on the nation-state level as well as for their enjoyment of entitlements provided by European citizenship.

So far, however, the interviewee acknowledged that there are approximately "nine million" people who do not hold citizenship in one of the member-states and are, for that reason, at a disadvantage.

> [T]here are two types of migrant communities living [on EU territory]. One of those ..are Community citizens, others...are legally resident non-Community citizens...Their position is this: they are not recognized.

The term 'non-recognition' refers here to third-country nationals' legal position, as they cannot enjoy the same entitlements provided by the Maastricht Treaty for EU nationals. Thus, formal European citizenship works only inclusively for those immigrants who are citizens in one of the EU-member-states, but exclusively for third country nationals who have not naturalized and whose countries of residence do not allow dual citizenship. Exclusive tendencies, however, exist not only on the formal level.

*Substantive citizenship* For those nine million third country nationals residing within EU-territory, the acquisition of formal European citizenship is the first step towards inclusion and equality. The interviewee realizes, however, that there is a dimension beyond formal equality when stating that

> ...law itself is not enough. Education is important to change the attitude of the mind...To understand other peoples' culture is important.

It is similarly expressed here as by the 'British' and 'German' organizations that formal citizenship alone is not sufficient and that there is a substantive side to it. Educating the 'white' majority is one way suggested by the interviewee to promote a different perception of ethnic minorities, namely "not as a problem, but as an opportunity". The contributions these minorities are making to European societies have to be emphasized, according to the interviewee, to gain recognition and acceptance which might help to minimize racialization and thus, improve ethnic minorities' substantive citizenship.

*European solutions*   To establish citizenship rights for third-country nationals, the EU Migrants Forum proposes a general European Bill of Rights for every citizen. The status of ethnic minorities should also be explicitly enshrined, with a definition of 'minority' which would force Germany to recognize third country nationals as such (i.e. to include labour migrants)[16]. Furthermore,

> we are saying that they should amend the Treaty of Rome...so that Union citizenship could also be given to legally resident non-community citizens.

The idea is that third-country nationals can apply for European Union citizenship without having to go through naturalization procedures in the EU member-state in which they reside. In this way, they could avoid restrictive policies set up by countries such as Germany. They would get the same rights that have been given to European Union nationals. It seems, however, rather utopic that EU officials will and can ignore the various nationally existing regulations. As it stands now, this is impossible as the Maastricht Treaty contains in one of its appendices that nationality as a legal status remains for each member-state to decide upon. In addition, immigration/integration policies remain outside the actual framework of the EC as they are dealt with in the 'second pillar', i.e. in the form of intergovernmental co-operation (see Chapter Three and Six). The only institution of the EC which could be sympathetic to the Migrants Forum's demands is the European Parliament which is still not powerful enough to enforce any changes in the legal structure. More importantly, however, the EP itself recommended the first step towards European citizenship as being changes on the *national* level (European Parliament 1990). Therefore, the idea stated in the above quote does not seem to be realizable - a fact which the interviewee is very well aware of. However, he relates this negative view more to rising nationalism - which also means that any changes on the national level are rather unlikely in the present climate. Nonetheless, the most likely scenario for third-country nationals to acquire European citizenship seems to be the granting of *national* citizenship by which they would automatically become European citizens.

*Sub-national developments*   In addition to further integration of the European Community into the European Union, regionalism is seen by the interviewee as a parallel development.  He understands 'regionalism' as 'federalism' (which follows the German definition).

> [F]ederalism is inevitable. Federalism is regionalism. At the moment we have got a loose federation of the European Union. So what the [European] Council admits [is] "Okay, we should now fund on the regional basis to areas which should have more funds like Portugal, Spain

and Greece, and even Britain is now regarded as one of the poor areas recently...

'Regionalism' is presented here as predominantly a matter of financial support. The reply to the question how beneficial that would be for ethnic minority communities is, therefore, on similar lines:

> That is something we are fighting for. For instance,...at the moment, ...they [the EU-officials] are giving billions and billions of regional development aid, but that development is only  confined to road and transport and that sort of  thing. There is not a  single penny given for housing...We are now putting to Padraig Flynn, the Commissioner for Social Affairs, in his Green Paper, that he should now propagate [that] regional funding [for] housing should be [given]...And that  will benefit the ethnic people.

The predominant concern with funding reflects in a way the main purpose of the European Community, i.e. economic and developmental matters. Nonetheless, financial support for housing would certainly benefit parts of the ethnic minorities. It is, however, difficult to imagine how this could positively affect the situation of immigrant minorities in Germany, which is not exactly regarded as one of the poorer member-states. And if there is any funding, it is most likely spent on the reconstruction of the East.

The interviewee did not express clearer ideas on this matter or, more precisely, on the Committee of the Regions' potential. This could mean that these developments are too recent and the 'output' too low for any further assessment. As for the near future, the interviewee mentioned the particular problem posed by the opposition of countries such as Britain to the idea of federalism (in the German sense) and local empowerment. This might slow down any active involvement of the Committee of the Regions in matters of 'race relations' in the way envisaged by Taylor (1995; see Chapter Six).

### 9.3.4 Commentary

The core issues relating to citizenship raised by the interviewees in Germany, Britain and on EU level clearly reflect the main concerns mentioned in the contexts of national identity and racism.

In Britain, there was a clear preoccupation with the substantive position of ethnic minorities. The interviewees' understanding of racism and nationalism were related mostly to substantive elements of citizenship. The legal side of citizenship was not perceived as a significant problem which must have to do with the fact that post-war labour migrants came from ex-colonial countries and thus, enjoyed a fully equal formal citizenship status. This legal equality was rightly seen as a result of specific historical circumstances (i.e. the Empire). Important to note is, however, that imperial circumstances have not only had positive results. It was rightly pointed out by many interviewees that first immigrants' (and to some extent also their children's) *social* position within British society was, and partly still is, negatively affected by imperial attitudes and prejudiced ways of thinking on the part of the 'white' majority[17]. Thus, the particular historical circumstances were on the one hand responsible for equal formal citizenship, but at the same time they resulted in a less equal substantive status.

In Germany, post-war migration happened in a very different historical context as labour migrants came from countries where there were no historical links as in the British case. This is reflected in the terminology and concept of *Ausländer* which shows that immigrants were and still are treated as 'outsiders', legally as well as socially. Therefore, the interviewees' main concern with regard to citizenship was the lack of formal equality. Those interviewees who acknowledged the existence of racism in one form or other thought of citizenship in legal terms as racist since it is clearly linked to nationality, i.e. ethnic descent or blood-relatedness. This was also reflected in their responses to questions about national identity and nationality as defined by law. Many interviewees had mentioned that the official approach (at least by the present Conservative government) to racism in Germany is to minimize its existence, which is reflected in the non-application of anti-discrimination legislation and the reluctance to amend the citizenship/nationality law to rid it off racializing elements.

In both countries, the interviews indicated (mostly implicitly) the negative effects of nationalism *and* racism on ethnic minorities' citizenship status. The close link of nationalism and racism became clear as some aspects were mentioned in both sections on national identity and racism and reappeared as encroaching immigrants' (formal and/or substantive) citizenship: both, nationalism and racism were seen as rooted in the same historical periods; apart from deeper historical roots, the sources or 'triggers' of both nationalism and racism were seen in the economy (recession, capitalist system), political parties and the media. These are aspects which belong to the category of the substantive side of citizenship and were, thus, rightly seen as the most difficult to improve. It would involve a complex set of measures and changes relating to education and attitudes.

As a result of the above, it can be noticed that the interview replies in Germany, Britain and by the EU Migrants Forum largely underpinned the conceptual division of citizenship into the two dimensions of formal and substantive citizenship. The legal side of citizenship was of 'number one' importance to all 'German' interviewees. For the 'British' organizations, this was more an issue of importance in the European context as many immigrants from the Indian sub-continent do not hold British citizenship and hence, do not have European citizenship. All three sources, however, equally expressed the opinion that legal equality has its limits and is not necessarily reflected in social (broad sense) acceptance. It also became clear that the substantive side of citizenship cannot be regarded as 'rights' in the same way as its legal side and that it is rather about the broader notion of participation and acceptance.

The conceptual division of citizenship into a formal and a substantive dimension also appeared in most of the interviews as an issue in the European context. However, here again the main concerns of the 'German' organizations were related to the lack of formal citizenship on the national level, whereas many 'British' organizations raised issues centring upon substantive problems and the perception of immigrants within the wider European public. The replies of all three sources seemed to suggest that the effects of nationalism and racism on ethnic minorities' European citizenship status conveyed the same problems as on national level. Thus, the European Union was not seen as having made any difference to these effects.

With regard to sub-national developments, the long German tradition of a decentralized governmental structure, i.e. the federal state system, seems to be the reason why these developments occupied a considerable part of the citizenship debate among the 'German' interviewees (also reflected in some explicit replies to national identity, or rather the different layers of collective identity) which stands in contrast to the 'British' replies. The idea of local citizenship was also more concretely deducible from the 'German' interviews than in the British case. This does, however, not mean that the conception of local citizenship could not work in Britain, but rather that this sub-national development lies further away than in Germany.

### 9.4 Citizenship as a mechanism for inclusion - the nature of the interviewed organizations and their demands: concluding remarks

*9.4.1 Demands*

The issues of nationalism/national identity, racism, and citizenship generally appeared in the interviews as the main areas upon which the organizations' activities centre. The mere existence of the interviewed organizations and their activities (campaigning, lobbying, policy-making) in the 'race relations' field already indicate that the power of racism and nationalism are not regarded as irresistible. Although the organizations linked the exclusion from formal and/or substantive citizenship more or less explicitly to racism (or *Ausländerfeindlichkeit*) and nationalism, citizenship was nonetheless understood as a *potential* to minimize the power of nationalism and racism and thus, as a potential mechanism for inclusion. In other words, racism and nationalism were seen as having negative effects on immigrants' citizenship status, and yet, the interviews yielded various ideas how to improve this situation.

On the formal level, improvements were of main concern to the 'German' interviewees. Their replies have shown that racializing and nationalistic elements of formal citizenship - such as the sole provision of ius sanguinis and the ethnic/racial interpretation of the concept of *Volk* - can be eliminated. These were in fact the main demands addressed to policy-makers along with the official acceptance of dual nationality/citizenship. In Britain, the racializing and stigmatizing effects of the 1981 BNA (by introducing an ethnic definition of 'Britishness') were deplored by some interviewees and therefore, suggested for change, albeit with less serious concern than in the German case, as this act affects settled ethnic minorities only indirectly.

With regard to substantive citizenship, however, measures of improvement have to go beyond changing certain laws. The power of racism and nationalism functions in a much more complex way, and according to many interviewees (including the EU Migrants Forum), any resistance cannot work by just amending laws. As it had become clear in particular in the 'British' interviews, there are many instances within civil society which encroach on ethnic minorities' substantive citizenship *despite* formal equality. Their formal citizenship remains challenged and questioned by racist and nationalistic tendencies within the majority population. Therefore, there is acknowledgement in Britain, Germany, and by the EU Migrants Forum that legal equality alone does not function as a mechanism to minimize the effects of racism and nationalism. Changes in attitude on the part of the 'white' majority - which could be caused, e.g., by different emphases in education - were suggested by all three sources as important for the promotion of inclusion. Hence, the 'solution package' for minimizing the power of racism and nationalism on immigrants' citizenship has to consist of complex and long-term strategies.

In one of the German interviews, participation and co-operation in conflict-solving processes on the local level were regarded as crucial 'ingredients' of such a 'solution package' - a suggestion which leads to the idea of local citizenship. Some of the 'British' interviewees and the EU Migrants Forum, too, implicitly expressed the importance of three layers of citizenship - local, national and European. This was reflected in a generally positive (albeit mostly vague) opinion on regionalism and the potential of the Committee of the Regions. The prospects of sub-national developments in Britain were, however, viewed as bleak.

The EU Migrants Forum's demands centred upon a common European 'Race Relations' policy and a common 'Race Relations Act'. To achieve this, the Treaty of Rome needs to be amended in 1996 to allow for the post of a Commissioner for 'Racial Affairs'. The acquisition of European citizenship for all long-term resident third country nationals could be facilitated by granting it directly from the supra-national level, without the necessity to naturalize first.

*Nature of organizations* The equal formal citizenship status of ethnic minorities in Britain seems to have had one important advantage. It has provided them with the opportunity to organize and engage actively in politics. This was very well reflected in the way in which in particular the two members of an ethnic minority (Int. 2/B; 3/B) expressed their views, i.e. the language they used. Their replies were quite often of a rhetorical, challenging and rather uncompromising nature which somehow demonstrates the kind of activities they are involved in: campaigning, 'consciousness-raising', but no policy-making power. Their main concern was that the present 'Race Relations Act' "lacks teeth and bite" (Int. 3/B) and that racial violence should be made an offence as part of the criminal law (Int. 2/B; 3/B). The European Union was also seen by those two interviewees in a very negative and uncompromising way.

The 'activities' the other three 'British' organizations engage in seem to involve a wider range of tasks, such as representing members of ethnic minorities at court or other governmental/administrative institutions or to produce research type of literature. Those interviewees recognized similar problems of racism and nationalism, but tended to be less extreme in the way in which they expressed their thoughts and criticisms (i.e. more compromising). Their demands included: a Bill of Rights (as suggested by two interviewees 1/B; 2/B), the abolition of ius sanguinis and 'racist' elements in the immigration law (5/B) and an education which emphasizes the 'multi-ethnic/racial' reality of Britain (2/B; 3/B).

In Germany, the fact that most ethnic minorities do not have formal citizenship and are only allowed to assemble and to organize if not threatening public peace and order might be the reason for a less extreme language on the part of the Turkish minority members. Dissatisfaction with present policies (such as the new Foreigners Law) was, nonetheless, expressed more by Turkish interviewees than by their indigenous German counterparts. The demands by the latter did not necessarily go as far as allowing dual nationality, replacing the Foreigners Law in favour of an immigration law and introducing (or applying) anti-discrimination legislation. The demands by Turkish and 'German' interviewees, however, clearly centred upon facilitating the acquisition of formal citizenship and involved only secondarily elements linked to substantive citizenship (such as attitudinal changes).

The developments on the European Union level with regard to settled ethnic minorities were viewed by most of the 'British' and 'German' interviewees, as well as by the Migrants Forum, as quite negative. Their replies, however, also reflected that European issues have not been on the agenda for very long and that the national level has priority - this latter point was, however, viewed differently by the EU Migrants Forum with regard to the acquisition of European citizenship as it proposed to 'skip' national citizenship.

The demands expressed by the EU Migrants Forum somehow showed a predominance of 'British' concepts revolving around 'race relations' which might have to do with the fact that the President is a British citizen. The idea of granting European citizenship without having to acquire 'national' citizenship also seems to reflect the more liberal British approach towards dual nationality or the granting of formal citizenship rights to every ex-colonial immigrant, despite not holding British citizenship. This view, however, disregards the complexity of different histories of immigration and the variety of regulations, and thus appears rather utopic.

On the whole, the interviewed organizations are involved in a social movement aimed at improving ethnic minorities' socio-legal position. Like politicians, they lead opinion mainly by drawing attention to problems and articulating goals. As opposed to politicians, however, interest or lobby groups also "stimulate research and encourage the publishing of books, articles and commentary that may educate public opinion." (Margolis & Mauser 1989:310). In this way, their work is more characterized by long-term strategies rather than by short-term tactics (such as the instantaneous winning of votes).

Throughout the interviews, the relationship between racialization, nationalism (i.e. the ethnic understanding of national identity) - both reinforced by socio-economic crises - and this relationship's impact on citizenship for ethnic minorities have become apparent. Ethnic minorities' (formal and/or substantive) citizenship was regarded as being encroached upon by this relationship on national as well as European level. The conditions of (national) citizenship were seen as conveyed on the European level and thus, the EU was not perceived as having had a major impact on ethnic minorities' position.

As it stands at present, therefore, the 'German' interviews have confirmed that the interplay of racism and nationalism results in what Hammar (1990) referred to as 'denizenship' status of immigrants and their children. In Germany and Britain, it was recognized that formal equality does not necessarily lead to social equality. In terms of their social experience, racism and nationalism continue to affect ethnic minorities' perception as equal citizens within civil society.

As for the possibility of citizenship to function more inclusively, it has to be pointed out again that the interviews did not suggest that there are no prospects for improvement, although on the substantive level, the suggested changes are of a more complex and long-term nature. This means that the concept of citizenship could function as a mechanism to minimize the power of racism and nationalism. The notion of citizenship as sub-divided into a European, national and local level was more or less explicitly expressed by many interviewees. The local environment was regarded by some interviewees as the most tangible. This could be interpreted as supporting my argument (see Chapter Six) that the best potential to counteract racism and nationalism exists on the local level as it is there where peoples' daily lives take place and where they could actively participate in the decision-making process in relation to community issues. This should, therefore, be the focus for future policy developments.

## Notes

1      This refers to one of the many arson attacks on refugee or immigrant homes during 1992.

2      See chapter Eight as well as Van Dijk (1993:111).

3      *Kontingent-Flüchtlinge* are refugees who were admitted through humanitarian 'aid' actions or through an official statement by the Ministry of the Interior. This means they are offically recognized refugees whose legal position results from the articles 2-34 of the Geneva Convention (Agreement on the legal position of refugees) of 28.7.85.

4      This document and other leaflets on the activities of the Migrants Forum were provided by the interviewee on the day of the interview as a further source for more detailed information as the interview schedule was very much delayed because of an unexpected matter the interviewee had to attend to. As a result, there was not as much time left for the actual interview as originally planned.

5      This document, which is the idea of various individuals and organizations throughout the EU, is a draft directive in the form a real Community directive might take, agreed upon in 1993. It is aimed at the elimination of racial discrimination. So far, the drafting group has no power, it simply offers this document as a basis for discussion and lobbying. The aim is to obtain a directive eventually, but the first step is to get the Treaty amended in 1996, so as to enable the Community to produce such legislation (The Starting Line 1994; introduction by Dummett).

6      In actual fact, most cases in which anti-discrimination legislation exists and is applied have to do with antisemitic propaganda (Gesetz gegen Volksverhetzung: law against public incitement) or the so called 'denial of Auschwitz' (Auschwitzlüge).

7      Albeit only in the case of antisemitic racism. Racist atrocities committed against gypsies (Sinti and Roma) are even today not officially recognized.

8      See for more details on black stereotypes and racialization in sports in Small (1994:101-106). Also, Bhikhu Parekh has commented on the disrespectful treatment of Linford Christie by the British media and the police in an article for *The Independent* (19 June 1995).

9      According to the interviewee (1/B), this idea draws heavily on the article by Alain Minc in *The Guardian* of 31 January 1994.

10      This connection (between exclusion based on racialization and a 'backward' orientation to ethnic origin) was also made by Modood et al. (1994).

11      Interviewee 5/B who works for a voluntary organization specializing in legal issues revolving around immigration explained: "It depends where you are from and what colour you are how difficult it is going to be [to unify or form a family]. [It is most difficult] for men from countries of the

Indian sub-continent to join their wives already living here. They [policy-makers] picked a difficult something that is known as the 'primary purpose rule'. One bit of the immigration rules about husbands and wives or fiancees coming to join a partner says that the person coming has to satisfy the immigration official that the primary purpose of the marriage is not immigration to the UK...Basically that is intended to be used against people from the Sub-continent. If you are applying from [North] America, you won't be asked these sort of questions." (emphasis added).

12     During the very early stages of the 'guest-worker system' when foreign workers were recruited to do specific jobs, they were not allowed to move freely from one employer to another. Meanwhile, of course, this has changed -and this might be the reason for this remark.

13     Paragraph 1 of Article 1 of the 'Basic Rights' (Grundrechte), for example, states "The dignity of a human being (a person) is inviolable" (Die Würde des Menschen ist unantastbar). Paragraph 1 of Article 3 goes "All human beings are equal before the law" (Alle Menschen sind vor dem Gesetz gleich). In contrast, Article 9, Paragraph 1, goes "All *Germans* have the right to form clubs and societies" (emphasis added) (Alle Deutschen haben das Recht, Vereine und Gesellschaften zu bilden).

14     A survey of 1412 foreign residents in Germany (most of which Turkish nationals, followed by ex-Yugoslavs, Italians and Greeks), undertaken in 1994 by Sen & Karakasoglu, found that 55% of the whole sample would apply for German citizenship if they could keep their original citizenship (62% of the Turkish respondents and 69% of the ex-Yugoslav respondents said so).

15     In the original text, 'economic' is indeed printed twice. One of them could be a printing mistake and should probably be 'ecological' as Lynch mentions ecological problems as global phenomena many times in his book.

16     According to an inquiry by the European Parliament, the German government is said to have officially denied the existence of any ethnic minorities as its definition of a minority is merely regional or national, i.e. only the Danes and Sorbes are recognized as such (Int. 4/G; see Heckmann, 1992: chapter 4, for more details on the typologies for ethnic minorities).

17     This was also an aspect mentioned by Modood et al. in their study on *Changing Ethnic Identities* in which seventy-four individual members of the various ethnic minorities were interviewed (1994).

# 10 Conclusion

In this book, I have attempted to link the concepts of citizenship, nationalism, and racialization. I have argued that there is a symbiotic relationship between nationalism and racism, reflected in the mingling of the concept of citizenship and the notion of nationality. In its formal legal and substantive sense, citizenship defines socio-legal membership and is, thus, the key indicator of inclusion in a socio-national community. The relationship between nationalism and racism, however, has exclusionary tendencies for immigrant or ethnic minorities' ability to acquire and practice citizenship.

My argument linked the theory of racialization with the formation of national identity and what has been conceptualized as 'the Other' (i.e. an immigrant or ethnic minority) drawing boundaries between insiders ('us') and outsiders ('them'). The identification of an 'inferior Other' thereby parallels the definition of the majority as a (superior) 'race' and 'nation', legitimizing the granting or withholding of citizenship.

With regard to legislation, it has been shown that racializing notions of nationality tend to be linked closely to the concept of citizenship with exclusionary effects on immigrants and ethnic minorities. Exclusionary tendencies, however, are not only to be found in law, but also within the policy-making process (i.e. as part of parliamentarians' discourse) and within civil society (in form of general attitudes). Thus, the main concluding argument has been that only a concept of citizenship which is disassociated from nationality can function as a mechanism for inclusion and full participation in post-war (western European) societies constituted of a 'range of fragmented identities' - to use Cohen's expression. Only in this way can citizenship become the source of a post-national, or post-conventional, identity. This does not mean that any sense of ethnicity (or any other cultural identity) has to vanish. The idea and/or practice of treating nationality as the prerequisite for citizenship as laid down in law, however, has to disappear and be replaced by the practice of citizenship as a signifier of 'genuine membership' to minimize conflicts between various ethnic (or cultural) groups. I have argued - based on the interview results - that there are ways in which formal and substantive citizenship can be made less exclusive and that citizenship has the potential to function as a mechanism for inclusion.

As far as future developments are concerned, I envisage a three-layered conception of citizenship ranging from local, to national to European level based on the principle of residence. Of those three layers, I have argued that the local level is probably the most effective to resist the power of racism and nationalism within civil society as it would mean communication and problem solving in the everyday environment of citizens. It would involve active and feasible efforts of ethnic minorities and the indigenous majority. It could also reduce the influence of professional politicians. In this way, citizenship would not merely be 'imagined'.

## 10.1  Citizenship in Germany and Britain: a comparison

In the literature on the historical formation of national identities and its reflection in the concept of nationality/citizenship, German and British developments have been depicted as almost opposing examples. These differences, however, seem to become less significant when approached from the context of post-war immigration. As for formal citizenship, the British notion of the territorial or 'civic' basis of membership and citizenship has reached its limits during its post-imperial era. The distinction between 'patrials' and 'non-patrials' introduced by immigration acts during the 1970s demonstrates an increasing emphasis on the principle of ius sanguinis in the operation of British citizenship/nationality laws, and thus "a retreat from policies which had allowed the entry, settlement and exercise of citizenship rights to substantial numbers of non-white and non-Christian immigrants." (Collinson 1994:114). As for substantive citizenship, the colonial experience of Britain - which is sometimes suggested to have resulted in a greater acceptance of foreign immigration - "almost certainly did more to reinforce the ideas of racial or cultural superiority than to foster tolerance" (op.cit.:115). Thus, although the colonial link has resulted in formal equality, it poses limits on immigrant minorities' substantive citizenship. This was confirmed by the interviewed organizations as well as by the parliamentary discourse and 'mass discourse', all of which placed more emphasis on substantive elements of citizenship. The acquisition of formal citizenship is only an issue for future immigration, in the case of family reunification (or formation), and in the context of European citizenship.

In Germany, by contrast, ius sanguinis has always been the main criterion for membership. In addition, its post-war immigrants originate from countries which do not have any colonial ties. These aspects are mainly responsible for the lack of formal citizenship. Thus, the most urgent demands of the 'German' organizations revolved around the acquisition of formal citizenship (on national as well as European level), with substantive citizenship being of secondary importance. Recent parliamentary debates have also focused on this aspect of citizenship.

As a result, it can be said that specific historical circumstances have resulted in a variation of concepts and terminologies referring to minorities of immigrant origin in Germany and Britain which reflects the bases of immigrant minorities' status in the receiving countries. Apart from historical reasons, these concepts and terms reflect to some extent objective differences in citizenship laws and also indicate the degree to which immigrant minorities are excluded. To distinguish between the indigenous majority and post-war labour migrants, the terminology of 'race' (Neuveu 1989) and 'race relations' is employed in Britain. It has been suggested that this reflects equal *formal* citizenship rights of post-war labour migrants. By contrast, in Germany the terminology of *Ausländer* reflects the foreign workers' status as denizens. With regard to formal citizenship status, therefore, non-European labour migrants in Germany are more directly excluded than their counterparts in Britain.

As for substantive citizenship, immigrant minorities in both countries experience exclusionary tendencies. Two important differences in Germany, however, render the improvement of ethnic minorities' substantive citizenship more difficult than in Britain: One is the absence of anti-discrimination legislation of the British type - which is partly the result of the official denial of discrimination based on racism; the other difference is related to immigrants' insecure residential status and limited civil rights as it negatively affects the success of any political organization or citizens' rights movement for immigrants. The struggle for equality is, thus, a very slow and piecemeal process as reflected in the latest introduction of the 'child citizenship'.

In both countries, formal and substantive citizenship is clearly enmeshed with the notion of nationality (i.e. ethnic descent) and, therefore, characterized by a symbiotic relationship between racism and nationalism. This obstructs the ease with which ethnic minorities can acquire formal citizenship. In Britain, there has been a shift from a general notion of subjecthood to citizenship as defined by nationality which has led to the abolition of the unconditional principle of ius soli. This, however, affects post-war labour migrants and their children mostly indirectly, and naturalization procedures have remained very liberal. Apart from the law, however, there is a tendency in British society, too, towards narrow nationalism and the equating of legitimate membership with 'white Britishness or Englishness' as conveyed by (mainly conservative) political and media discourse in a similar way to that in Germany (Gilroy 1987; van Dijk 1991). One crucial difference in Britain, however, is that there is an advanced understanding of racialization as debates and discourse on issues related to ethnic minorities clearly focus on substantive elements of citizenship.

It can be concluded, therefore, that in terms of legal status, post-war labour migrants have entered Britain on an equal basis as opposed to the situation in Germany. This formally equal citizenship status as enjoyed by immigrant minorities in Britain gives them the possibility of being politically active and to move into representation in public life. In Germany, by contrast, this basis for 'help to self-help' (Hilfe zur Selbsthilfe, Bielefeld 1991:102) is not given. With regard to rising nationalism and the general existence of racialization and racial discrimination, however, ethnic minorities' status in both countries is negatively affected.

This was also reflected in the different concerns and demands of the interviewed groups to render citizenship more inclusive. So far, this was not seen as having been achieved to a satisfactory extent, and the racializing effects of the link to nationality in law was regarded in both countries as still too strong. In addition to legal definitions, the groups have stressed that belonging and active participation are important criteria for citizenship, i.e. membership is not only a matter of legality and laws, but is also a matter of perception and recognition as belonging on the part of civil society.

## 10.2 European identity and citizenship

Based on the findings from the literature, the parliamentarians' discourse, opinion surveys/polls, and the interviews, it can be said that, although a pan-European identity among the majority population seems (more or less tentatively) to emerge, this identity has - in a similar way to national identity - the tendency to be exclusive towards non-European residents. This is perpetuated by the predominant concern by the EU with immigration and border control ('Fortress Europe') and by neglecting policies of integration. As yet, there is no evidence of harmonization or co-operation in granting citizenship to all third-country nationals with long periods of residence in any of the EU member-states. The image of a 'People's Europe' as well as European citizenship does not, therefore, include non-European long-term residents, and thus European identity and citizenship do not offer any mechanisms for overcoming impediments on the national level, but rather perpetuate them.

## 10.3 Future prospects of citizenship

According to Garcia, current debates on European and national identities seem to revolve around two main lines of thought. The first emphasizes the unifying processes taking place in western European industrialized societies. The second stresses the remaining strength of national identities as opposed to a European identity. The two strands do not necessarily conflict, but should be perceived as parallel (1992:9). This view is fully supported here. However, apart from national and an emerging supranational identity, a consciousness for the local level has continued to exist to a lesser or greater extent in western Europe as a third layer of collective identity. This should be reflected in the exercise of citizenship.

With regard to the composition of contemporary societies, citizens' identity does not derive from common ethnic and cultural properties but rather from the praxis of citizenship which has, however, a limited direct impact on national, let alone European, politics. Therefore, the active practice of citizenship at the local level would give the other two levels their legitimation. Local identity as the first and foremost source of collective identity (which seems to be less visible in Britain/England where economic and political centralism has undermined local differentiation and empowerment) can be directed in such a way that attachments need not conflict with national and (the development of a) European consciousness and identity. The three layers of identity and citizenship are to a certain extent expressed in the notion of subsidiarity and the potential of the Committee of the Regions - both of which would, however, need to be clarified to render these levels practicality.

What are possible future solutions for citizenship to function more inclusively for non-European ethnic minorities? For those who do not have formal citizenship, such as the Turks, special agreements between their countries of origin and the EU could allow them the holding of dual nationality and thus, vest them with full formal citizenship rights on national and European level. In the case of Turkey, there have been debates about its likelihood to join the EU (taz, 19.12.94 & 21.12.94 & 12.01.95 & 18.02.95) which would at least result in the same treatment of Turkish immigrants as that of EU-nationals. A further possibility would be to grant third-country nationals citizenship rights after a certain period of residence without the requirement to naturalize, i.e. totally detached from the holding of a passport. This is not at all an unknown practice. Countries such as Sweden and the Netherlands grant foreign residents at least local voting rights (Martin & Miller 1990:11). Also, the European Parliament has recommended the granting of local voting rights after five years of residence for immigrants in all member-states (see Chapter Three).

The addition of a 'race' dimension to the Treaty of Rome - as one aspect of substantive European citizenship - might not be necessary, let alone achieved to a satisfactory extent from the perspective of British ethnic minorities when considering the various different immigration histories of EU member-states and the tendency to agree on the lowest denominator with regard to common EU policies. A better solution might be to approach the field of 'race relations' and integration policies via the Committee of the Regions and the principle of subsidiarity. To deal with these issues on the level of regional/local co-operation may also counteract the rather protectionist atmosphere which is at present prevailing (i.e. retreat to nationalism) - which can partly be explained by the general fear of losing influence on the decision making process of issues which are of local and national interest to European bureaucrats.

As a 'solution package', first of all, citizenship should be given to all (legal)[1] residents within the EU after a certain length of residence[2]. The impetus should come from the national level as suggested by Hoffmann (1992) and by the European Parliament (see Chapter Three) as opposed to the way in which the EU Migrants Forum demands changes (by ignoring the national level and by granting formal (European) citizenship via the EU). According to Hoffmann, it is not a good idea to link the question of citizenship with European integration. He rightly claims that it is not Europe which overcomes the thinking in terms of nation-states, but it is the overcoming of the idea of the nation-state which makes Europe possible.

Therefore, the potential of the Committee of the Regions is an important issue for the future. The Committee has to be given competence to make decisions in matters important for the peaceful co-existence of citizens within a local community.

As for European citizenship, it is impossible to mirror national citizenship on EU level. There are different levels of participation with different degrees of direct influence which exist at the same time. The local level has to be extended in order to promote and legitimize the other two. This is the same with regard to the formation of identity. The reality is, today as much as before, that Europe is only one dimension of collective identity - an aspect which has also become clear in the interviews. The national and local dimensions are equally as important and have to be reflected in political representation. The local level is in actual fact the most flexible in that it represents the variety of people with their various identities in the local community. This has to be recognized, however, in terms of empowerment for local governance and citizenship. All three levels cannot work in exactly the same way and all three levels have to be responsible for different political, economic and social aspects of life.

Overall, an understanding of citizenship detached from nationality should go beyond its formal meaning of the right to carry a passport and should be promoted in its comprehensive sense, emphasizing the relationship between the individual, the local community, the state and the European Union. Only in this way can citizenship minimize the effects of racialization and nationalism. I have argued that this can best be achieved by recognizing the need for the equal importance of the three layers of citizenship. The local level in particular is regarded as being crucial to promote understanding among ethno-culturally different residents. The co-operation of all citizens at the local level will work its way upwards to co-operation and mutual representation on the national and European level, and will thus create a true 'Peoples' Europe'.

To sum up, it is agreed here with Meehan that

a new kind of citizenship is emerging that is neither national nor cosmopolitan but which is multiple in enabling the various identities that we all possess to be expressed, and our rights and duties exercised, through an increasingly complex configuration of common institutions, states, national and transnational interest groups and voluntary associations, local or provincial authorities, regions and alliances of regions....Sometimes interests may coincide with national identity...Sometimes interests and identities will be regional..Social identities and interests sometimes cross national frontiers. (1993b:185)

Most importantly for this new kind of citizenship, made up of different layers - local, national and European - in the context of settled immigrants, is the realization that it has to be separated from nationality to render acquisition of citizenship possible via residential criteria. This is the prerequisite for reducing those impediments to formal and substantive citizenship which result from a symbiotic relationship between racism and nationalism to enable all residents to participate and to develop a form of collective identity in a world of global movement.

## Notes

| | |
|---|---|
| 1 | The issue of 'illegality' has not been dealt with in this thesis. |
| 2 | The European Parliament has recommended a minimum period of five years. |

# Appendix I

**Statistics on foreign residents by nationality**

*a) Foreign residents in the Federal Republic of Germany*

| Nationality | 1983 | 1993 |
|---|---|---|
| Turkey | 1,552,300 | 1,918,400 |
| Former Yugoslavia | 612,800 | 929,600 |
| Italy | 565,000 | 563,000 |
| Greece | 292,300 | 352,000 |
| Spain | 166,000 | 133,200 |
| Portugal | 99,500 | 105,600 |
| Morocco | 44,200 | 82,800 |
| Tunisia | 25,300 | 28,100 |
| Total | 4,534,900 | 6,878,100 |

Source: OECD, 1995

*b) Foreign residents in the United Kingdom*

| Nationality | 1984 | 1993 |
|---|---|---|
| Ireland | 491,000 | 465,000 |
| India | 148,000 | 151,000 |
| Caribbean and Guyana | 131,000 | 106,000 |
| Pakistan | 63,000 | 98,000 |
| Bangladesh | 21,000 | 73,000 |
| Total | 1,601,000 | 2,001,000 |

Source: OECD, 1995

# Appendix II

**EU-drafted documents**

*1 The External Border Convention*
Or, in its full title, Draft Convention of the Member States of the European Communities on the Crossing of External Frontiers. It was expected to be signed in 1991, but the signing has been delayed because of the disagreement between Britain and Spain over the status of the border between Gibraltar and Spain (the British government considers this frontier as internal, whereas Spain considers it as external; Collinson 1994:190, footnote no. 10). This convention is central to the opening up of the internal market, since it sets up external controls and the information system needed to secure the EC's borders, without which the internal borders cannot be removed. Its main purpose is to avoid third country nationals entering the EC by imposing very stringent conditions on entry. A uniform EC visa is intended to be developed, based on common criteria. Third country nationals legally settled in one EC country are not to have the right to free movement and settlement across the EC territory. The only 'improvement' for them is the granting of visa-free travel for three months. This convention, when signed, would be another key element in the creation of 'Fortress Europe'.

*2 The Draft Resolution on Family Reunification'*
This is another draft document which would have much more obvious implications for already settled ethnic minority communities. It was prepared in 1992 with the aim to limit the dependants who can be brought in by non-EC workers who are already living in the EC, and to impose conditions on their admission such as the limitation of family reunion to spouses and children aged up to sixteen or eighteen with the exclusion of other family members (which stands in sharp contrast to family rights of EC nationals working in another EC member-state, who are allowed to bring in spouse, children under 21 or in full-time education, elderly parents and other dependent relatives). This resolution is more stringent than the current British law which allows for the admission of elderly parents and of other relatives under certain circumstances. Britain's infamous 'primary purpose rule' of 1982 is also adopted by this resolution meaning that spouses have to prove that the primary purpose of their marriage was not to obtain admission to the territory before being admitted.

*3 The Draft Resolution on Admission for Employment*
Prepared by the Ad Hoc Group for submission to the immigration ministers in November 1992, looks very much like having a revival of the 'guestworker system' as its aim. It defines the limited and temporary nature

of immigration for employment which the EC will allow to non-EC nationals. It proposes that member-states may admit migrant workers on a temporary basis, for six months, without a special permit; for up to three years as a trainee, and as a contract worker for five years maximum in the first instance. The only category which could lead to settlement is the last, but it envisages five years of tied employment with the same employer before any opportunity for permanent residence arises. There is no guarantee for equal treatment with workers of EC nationality, family union rights are also very limited.

# Appendix III

**The interviewed organizations: their functions and objectives**

*a) In Germany*

*Das Amt für Multikulturelle Angelegenheiten der Stadt Frankfurt am Main (Department for multi-cultural affairs of the city of Frankfurt/Main)* - Function/governance: This department is part of the city council of Frankfurt and therefore, it is solely in charge of multi-cultural matters of Frankfurt which is the city in Germany with the highest percentage of 'foreign' population (immigrant peoples without a German passport; ethnic Germans excluded here), namely 27,55% (Wolf-Almanasreh 1993:10).

This department was set up in 1989 by the 'red-green coalition' (coalition of the Social Democrats and the Green Party in the city council) with the present head of department (Dezernent) being a member of the Green Party. The head of the department (Dezernent) is the political leader and secures access to the city's parliament. The department is given its own financial budget, and the proposing of bills is in its power. As part of the local politico-administrative structure of the city of Frankfurt, this department has been described as having "taken the lead in defending migrant representation" in Germany (Winstone 1993:5).

- Objectives: Its field of activities ranges from advancing public relations, functioning as an ombudsperson, working against discrimination and racism towards more integration (such in the areas of school and education, job training), to promoting inter-cultural communication (support for clubs etc.). The groups these activities are aimed at include *all* citizens of Frankfurt - i.e. any minority group, be it ethnic or social (one example was a homosexual organization which was seeking support from this department to obtain permission to build a monument to commemorate the homosexual victims of the National Socialists which had been previously rejected). Therefore, the point of departure for the department's scope of responsibilities is more global and spreaded out which means that it does not solely focus on lobbying immigrants and ethnic minorities. It holds the view that society has to be seen as a whole in order to minimize social clashes.

- Status of interviewee: The interviewee is the second person in the departmental hierarchy, the chief executive.

*Ausländerbeauftragte der Senatsverwaltung der Stadt Berlin (Commissioner for Foreigners' Affairs of the Senate of Berlin)* - Function/governance: This department is in a similar way as the above part of the public sector, but it is not a department on its own, it is a section of the Department for Social Affairs of the Berlin Senate (city government). Therefore, although it has competence in the specialized field of immigration, it does not have any policy-making powers. The Commissioner of Berlin was the first of its kind in the whole of Germany set up in 1981 (initiated by Richard von Weizäcker who was then Mayor of Berlin). It is responsible for the city of Berlin.

- Objectives: Its range of activities include three main areas: 1. the conception of immigration or 'foreigners' policies' (Ausländerpolitik) for the purpose of lobbying, 2. counselling for individuals in immigration and integration matters, 3. public relations (informing 'foreigners' about their rights and enlightening the majority on matters of the 'foreign' minorities).

- Status of interviewee: The two interviewees from this department are the head, the Commissioner, and the public relations' officer.

*TGB Hamburg e.V. (Bündnis türkischer Einwanderer Hamburg) (Association for Turkish Immigrants Hamburg)* - Function/governance: This organization is an umbrella organization for all sorts of Turkish associations and clubs, political as well as cultural, and individuals in Hamburg. It was initiated in 1985 by its present director (as a registered association - the meaning of the abbreviation "e.V." - since 1986).

- Objectives: The originally main objective for the TGB's establishment was the campaigning for local voting rights and dual citizenship - the former was in fact materialized as a result of the campaigns in the three Nordic *Länder* Schleswig-Holstein, Bremen and Hamburg, but contested by the Conservative Parties CDU and CSU and ruled as unconstitutional by the Federal Constitutional Court. The field of activities ranges now from public relations work, to campaigning and lobbying for certain 'foreigners' policies such as dual citizenship, anti-discrimination legislation and voting rights.

- Status of the interviewee: The interviewee is the president and founder of this organization. He is also member of the city parliament (which is at the same time a *Länder* parliament as Hamburg is a city-state) representing the Social Democrats - a fact which is possible due to him holding dual citizenship.

*BETB e.V. (Bund der Einwanderer/Innen aus der Türkei in Berlin-Brandenburg) (Association for Immigrants from Turkey in Berlin-Brandenburg)* - Function/governance: This organization exists since 1990 and was initiated as an 'action group' (Aktionsgemeinschaft) campaigning against the new Foreigners' Law (Ausländergesetz). All sorts of immigrant groups from all across the political spectrum came together and originally called this action group "Aktionsbündnis türkischer Selbsthilfe und Betroffenen Organisation" (action alliance for Turkish self-help and organization for the persons affected). When the new law was enacted in 1991 despite their campaign, they decided to carry on with their work under a new name - BETB e.V, which is now an umbrella organization including all sorts of immigrant association and individuals. At present, there are twenty-one member organizations.

- Objectives: They make strong efforts for legal, social and political equality of ethnic minorities and for the peaceful co-existence with the indigenous German majority. Thus, the field of public relations and campaigning is one of their main activities, but also individual counselling. They represent all *Berliner* and *Berlinerinnen* (people from Berlin) of Turkish origin vis-à-vis all institutions and departments in Berlin as well as in public in all matters of immigration and 'foreigners' policies. They also organize cultural events, conferences and seminars.

- Status of the interviewee: The interviewee is spokesperson of the executive committee.

*TGB Berlin (Türkische Gemeinde Berlin) (Turkish Community Berlin)* - Function/governance: This organization functions also as an umbrella for smaller Turkish associations and its members come from all sections of social life such as folklore, youth, women, sports and religion. It is non-aligned to any political party. They are non-violent and stand for democracy, liberty and constitutional rights. They welcome everybody - Turks, Germans and others - committed to peaceful co-existence of minorities in Germany.

- Objectives: The Turkish Community engages in social consultant services to German authorities, the churches and individuals. They keep up the dialogue with administrations and policy makers in order to improve the Turkish minority's life in Berlin. They also try to have good relationships with the press and educational organizations to promote mutual understanding and thus, the Turkish Community functions as a bridge between Turkish and German Berliners.

- Status of the interviewee: The interviewee is the head of this organization.

*Forum Buntes Deutschland e.V. - S.O.S. Rassismus (Forum Colourful Germany - S.O.S. Racism)* - Function/governance: This organization was established in 1992 as a federal body for all small and medium initiatives, associations and organizations which are active on the local or *Länder* level in the area of anti-racism work. Until its set up, there had not been a federal anti-racism alliance. The Forum co-ordinates the activities of these local groups and promotes actions from the grass-root level on federal level. It also co-operates with other big federations such as the refugee councils. On European level, it is engaged in the anti-racist network for equality in Europe.

- Objectives: Elimination of racism and the spreading of information of racially motivated discrimination.

- Status of the interviewee: The interviewee is the director of this organization. She used to be a Member of Parliament representing the SPD.

*WIR - Internationales Zentrum, Hamburg (WIR International Centre, Hamburg)* -Function/governance: It was founded in 1981 by Germans and immigrants and functioned in the beginning as an international meeting place (Begegnungsstätte) for immigrants and Germans in Hamburg. It is funded by the Hamburg Senate (city parliament).

- Objectives: It is engaged in individual counselling (social, legal, family matters and advice on return to country of origin). They offer German language courses as well as cultural courses and organize cultural events, campaigns (e.g. for dual citizenship, local voting rights), conferences, seminars, work-shops and projects in schools, community centres etc. and in particular for people working in the field of education (Multiplikatoren) in order to reduce prejudices (anti-racism work). It is a grass-root organization.

- Status of interviewee: The interviewee is one of the three leading organizers.

## b) In Britain

*The Commission for Racial Equality* - Function/governance: It was set up by the 1976 Race Relations Act. It is funded by an annual grant from the Home Office, but works independently of the Government. It is run by Commissioners appointed by the Home Secretary.

- Objectives: Its activities cover work towards the elimination of discrimination, promotion of equality of opportunity and good relations between persons of different racial/ethnic groups. Its main task is to keep under review the working of the Act (monitoring of the way the Act is working) and when required by the Secretary of State or when it otherwise thinks it necessary it can draw up proposals for amending it and submitting it to the Secretary of State. It deals with racial discrimination in the field of employment and education, and it is also engaged on the European level in the set up of the Starting Line (as explained in the Chapter on the EC).

- Status of the interviewee: The interviewee is senior information officer.

*The Joint Council for the Welfare of Immigrants* - Function/governance: It was established in 1967 and has been since then the only national independent voluntary organization which specialized in British immigration and nationality law. It is funded by its members and by donations.

- Objectives: It offers counselling to individuals and gives advice on legal matters concerning immigration and nationality legislation. It represents individuals to the Home Office, Racial Officers, Racial Appeals, and Embassies. It is also engaged in organizing campaigns and lobbying for changes in the law. It produces literature and provides up-to-date information on changes in the law and other briefings for journalists, MPs and its members. It also offers training courses. With regard to European matters, there is an European project worker who is specializing in EC matters.

- Status of the interviewee: The interviewee is the training and information officer.

*The Anti-Racist Alliance* - Function/governance: The Anti-Racist Alliance was established in November 1991. It is a black-led, broad-based coalition, campaigning against racism, anti-Semitism and support for the extreme right. The ARA is supported by major national black and Jewish organizations. The Executive Committee of the ARA is made up of 34 people, who are elected at an Annual General Meeting. The EC is made up of representatives of major black and Jewish organizations, trade unions, black community groups, youth organizations and other organizations. Membership in the ARA is open to organizations and individuals.

- Objectives: They organize and support campaigns and demonstrations locally and nationally against racist murders, attacks and harassment, and they are involved in putting together petitions and in lobbying. One of their main activities is arguing for changes in the racial harassment law. With the help of a monitoring system they catalogue racial attacks and violence. The ARA gives support to victims and families of victims of racial violence by producing leaflets, organizing demonstrations and giving financial help. They also work in liaison with anti-racist organizations in Britain and the rest of Europe and are engaged in the Anti-racist Network for Equality in Europe.

- Status of the interviewee: The interviewee is the head of this organization.

*The Indian Workers' Association* - Function/governance: It was founded in the mid-1950s. The IWA has originally started as a supportive body and has grown up as an anti-racist group with one of its major tasks being to fight against racism in Britain.

They are funded by an annual governmental grant, but recently they have been very restricted with their work because of funding difficulties as the government is not prepared to give them any further funding on the grounds that the IWA has become a political body - an allegation which the IWA denies. It claims to be not affiliated with any political party.

- Objectives: It offers support to the individuals' problems and functions very much as a grass-root organization. They provide service to the people and give support in issues revolving around education, employment, nationality, immigration and citizenship (passport).

- Status of the interviewee: The interviewee is the director of the IWA and also a Labour MP.

*The Runnymede Trust* - Function/governance: It was founded in 1968 by Antony Lester, now Lord Lester, who was also active in the Charter 88 movement. It is funded by its members and by donations.

- Objectives: Its objectives are to help strengthen and shape policies and projects which work towards eliminating all forms of racial discrimination; promote mutual respect, appreciation and learning between different traditions and values; release and develop the resources, talents and skills of all members of society. The Runnymede Trust does not provide any individual counselling, but is engaged in producing literature on race relations' matters and other issues such as nationalism and right-wing extremism as well as in public relations in general.
- Status of the interviewee: The interviewee is the director of this organization.

*c) EU source*

*The European Union Migrants Forum:* - Function/governance: This organization was originally called EC Migrants Forum but since the creation of the European Union by the Maastricht Treaty, it has changed its name to European Union Migrants Forum. The idea of putting together a forum where peoples with immigrant origins could find a political voice and have a dialogue with the European institutions derived from a report of the late MEP Evregenis, presented to the European Parliament in 1985 by the Committee of enquiry on the rise of fascism, racism and xenophobia. The Forum was finally set up in May 1991 by which for the first time political dialogue was institutionalized between the EC and its populations originating outside the EC. It is funded by the Commission of the European Communities with the European Parliament being involved in debating over the Forum's budget. Even though the Forum was initiated and supported by the European Parliament and is funded by the Commission, it is supposed to be a totally independent advisory body to them, and it is politically and religiously non-aligned. It is the only non-governmental organization which is allowed to meet and discuss matters with the rotating presidencies.
The EU Migrants Forum is made up of a 'grass-root structure': there are 110 organizations that are affiliated to the Migrants Forum across the EU memberstates with over 50 various nationals from outside the EU. The Forum has established support groups in each of the 12 member-states and it invites anybody who agrees with their aims and constitutional objectives to join. The members are not only drawn from minority communities, but also from organizations or institutions such as local authorities, the police, trade unions, any European organizations etc.
- Objectives: With a view to the full integration of immigrants in Europe, the Forum sets itself as its objectives and purpose action on attaining equal rights, freedom of movement, the fight against racism, observance of the right of asylum and integration in all respects into a multi-cultural Europe. The Forum lobbies the EP, the Commission, the presidencies and individual memberstates on race relations' and immigration matters. It engages in particular in improving the situation for

Third country nationals who do not hold any EC-memberstates' citizenship, but they are also generally concerned about discrimination and racism against any ethnic minority.

Two of the Forum's main initiatives are the European Manifesto against Racism and Suggestions for the White Paper on a Social Europe of 1994.

- Status of the interviewee: The interviewee is the president.

# Appendix IV

**The interview questions**

*In Britain:*

*A*

1. First of all, I would like to talk about national identity: Do you think British people have a sense of national identity?

2. Is the idea of national identity important to British people right now in 1994? I wonder what you think about it.

3. That is generally, now I would like to know what exactly is the content of national identity for British (English?) people? What does it mean to them?

4. Do you have any idea where the sense of national identity is fostered? Is there any source which promotes this idea in particular?

5. I wonder, how far the idea of national identity is exclusive? Do you think, it excludes any groups in Britain which are not of 'white' British origin? If yes, which groups?

6. Do you think the cultural particularities and/or cultural contributions of ethnic minority groups are adequately recognized by British society? Why (not)?

7. Are they in this respect visible or invisible parts of the nation?

8. Britain has traditionally been the prime example of a country where the principle of ius soli has applied. Since the British Nationality Act of 1981 this has been modified (in that any child born in the UK is British citizen only if it has a parent who is British citizen or 'settled'). What implications does this Act have? Does that mean the number of persons born in the UK without British citizenship has considerably risen? What is your opinion about this Act?

9. I would like to repeat: Whenever Britain is presented as a nation, do you think ethnic minority groups are considered as a part of it?

10. Do you think a stronger consciousness for the region would be beneficial to immigrants with regard to their ability to feel accepted as an

equal member? (I am asking this question with regard to Germany which has a federal state structure and with regard to the changes in Britain during the last 10,15 years towards further centralization; also with regard to the EC which does not only promote the idea of supra-nationality, but also of regionalism)

11. How do you see the future of national identity in view of a more integrated Europe? Is the emphasis more going to be on regional and/or supranational, i.e. European, identity?

12. Is European identity going to replace national identity in the sense that it will work in the same exclusive way as the identity of 'white' Europeans or do you see any chance for all the various ethnic groups to be included?

13. Do you think the generally promoted idea of national identity in Britain contains any elements which you would call racist? If yes, what are they and what are their purposes?

*B*

14. Generally speaking, do you think racism in any form exists in British society?

15. How is this racism recognisable?

16. If you look back to British history, has racism changed in any way? For instance, are the targets/victims different? Is the articulation different?

17. In the literature on racism, it is said that racism can be explained/defined culturally in that cultural differences are pictured as innate and unchangeable. Do you think cultural racism can be applied to the British situation?

18. I would like to ask you where racist ideas come from? Where are they fostered? Maybe you could comment on the following 'list':
1. by the media?
2. by the government?
3. by politicians? If yes, of which party alliance are they?
4. by racist groups?
5. by anybody else?

19. Does your work include the fight against racism and inequality of immigrants? If yes, what is the most difficult aspect in your anti-racism work?

20. What concerns your fight against racism and inequality of immigrants, what is your strongest concern for the future? What would you like to see changed?

21. Do you think there will be joint action against racism by the EC? How do you view the future prospectus of an EC-wide anti-discrimination legislation? Is it likely to be on the level of the British legal provisions?

*C*

I would like to move on to the issue of citizenship.

22. Do you think there is any difference between the term 'nationality' and 'citizenship' in Britain?

23. In what sense, do you think, are members of ethnic minority groups British citizens? Is there any difference to the citizenship status of indigenous white British people?

24. Does your work here include citizenship issues? What is your most important concern? Is there anything that you would like to see in the near future?

25. Do you see any future prospects for a European citizenship? Is it going to include minority groups?

Some summarizing/concluding questions:

26. Coming back to the activities your organization is involved in, which of the three issues we have discussed (citizenship, national identity, racism) is the most important? What are your priority concerns?

27. Which issue should the national government turn to first and foremost?

28. Which issue should the EC turn to first and foremost?

Terminological question:
term 'black': what is your approach or opinion? Is 'black' a useful term which should be preserved? If not, any alternative?

Section A:
        The first three questions were asked to find out whether 'national identity' exists and whether it is still important (in view of European integration) or even more important (rising nationalism) and what elements are claimed to be 'British'. Question four was meant to indicate where ideas about national identity come from (political parties etc.), question five and

six should show whether ethnic minorities are included or excluded in these ideas and whether their presence is recognized (question seven). Possible changes which the BNA of 1981 had brought about were explored in question 8, and question 10 should test the interviewees' opinion on regionalism (the potential of the EU's Committee of the Regions). Question 11 and 12 were asked to find out whether the EC as supranational entity has had any impact on national identity and where ethnic minorities are placed within it. Question 13 was meant to bridge the first issue (national identity) with the following issue (racism)[1].

Section B:
        Question 14 and 15 were meant to find out what elements in British society were viewed as racist. Question 16 should test the theory that there are different racisms (or racialization processes) and that there are 'racisms without race'. Question 17 refers to the 'cultural racism' theory (as opposed to biological racism). With question 18, the source of racist ideas was explored. Question 19 and 20 referred to the organizations' activities and concerns in this area. The likelihood of the European Community to become active in this field was tested.

Section C:
        Question 22 was meant to find out whether there is a sense for people being of different nationality but having the same citizenship rights (so that it would be possible to be a recognized citizen as an immigrant of different nationality). This question was also originally meant (before 'discovering' that both concepts might be coterminous in the British context as well) to explore whether there is any difference to Germany where both concepts tend to be regarded as the same in the sense that a person has to be of German nationality to be a German citizen. Question 23 was asked to test in which way ethnic minority members' citizenship is equal to the majority's citizenship. Question 24 referred to the organizations' activities in this field, and question 25 explored the European dimension.

*In Germany:*

A

1. Zuallererst möchte ich über nationale Identität sprechen: Denken Sie, dass die Deutschen einen Sinn für nationale Identität haben?

2. Ist der Begriff/die Vorstellung der nationalen Identität heute, also im Jahre 1994, wichtig für Deutsche?

3. Das war allgemein. Ich hätte jetzt gerne gewusst, was genau beinhaltet dieser Begriff (der nationalen Identität) für Deutsche?

4. Wo werden diese Vorstellungen am meisten betont/herausgehoben? Woher kommen diese Vorstellungen der nationalen Identität?

5. Haben diese Vorstellungen sich seit der Wiedervereinigung irgendwie verändert? Wenn ja, wie?

6. Ich möchte gerne wissen, inwieweit diese Vorstellungen eine ausschliessende Wirkung haben? Glauben Sie, dass nationale Identität irgendwelche Immigranten- oder andere Gruppen in Deutschland ausschliesst? Wenn ja, welche Gruppen?

7. Denken Sie, dass die kulturellen Besonderheiten der Immigranten und ihre kulturellen Beiträge von der deutschen Gesellschaft angemessen anerkannt werden? Warum (nicht)?

8. Sind die Immigranten in dieser Hinsicht 'sichtbarer' oder 'unsichtbarer' Teil der Nation?

9. Das rechtliche Prinzip der deutschen Staatsangehörigkeit/Nationalität wird oft als 'blut-bezogen' bezeichnet, weil das ius sanguinis bestimmt, wer die deutsche Nationalität bekommen kann; haben Sie eine Vorstellung, woher dieses Prinzip kommt?

10. Denken Sie, dass dieses Konzept beibehalten/aufrechterhalten werden sollte?

11. In der Debatte über die Interpretation des "Volk"-Konzeptes scheint die überwiegende juristische Meinung zu sein (wie es ja in der Entscheidung des Bundesverfassungsgerichts reflektiert ist), dass mit Volk nur die Deutschen gemeint sind; ich hätte gerne ihre Meinung dazu gewusst!

12. Wie sehen Sie die Zukunft der nationalen Identität im Hinblick auf ein stärker integriertes Europa? Wird die Betonung auf eine regionale und supra-nationale, sprich europäische, Identität sein?

13. Wird eine europäische Identität nur einfach die nationale Identität ersetzen in dem Sinne, dass sie in derselben ausschliessenden Art und Weise funktionieren wird als Identität von einheimischen Europäern oder sehen Sie eine Chance für alle verschiedenen ethnischen Gruppen darin miteinbegriffen zu sein?

14. Denken Sie, dass eine regionale Identität sich vorteilhaft auf die Fähigkeit der Immigranten, sich mit ihrer neuen Heimat zu identifizieren und sich akzeptiert zu fühlen, auswirken würde?

15. Glauben Sie, dass der Begriff der nationalen Identität Elemente enthält, die Sie als rassistisch bezeichnen würden? Wenn ja, was genau sind sie?

*B*

16. Besonders seitdem seit kurzem Attacken aller Art auf Immigranten und Asylbewerber angestiegen sind, berichten die Medien viel über "Ausländer-feindlichkeit" und Xenophobia; ich hätte gerne gewusst, warum wir in diesem Zusammenhang zögern, den Begriff 'Rassismus' anzuwenden wie er z.B. in Grossbritannien benutzt wird?

17. Wir wissen von unserer Geschichte, dass Rassismus auf biologische Differenzierung basiert, dennoch kann Rassismus auch kulturell definiert werden, indem kulturelle Verschiedenheiten als angeboren und unveränderlich dargestellt werden; was, glauben Sie, ist heutzutage ausschlaggebender in Deutschland: Der auf das Biologische basierende oder der auf das Kulturelle basierende Rassismus?

18. Denken Sie, dass der Rassismus/Anti-Semitismus der Nazi-Ära irgend-einen Einfluss auf das Denken der Deutschen über heutigen Rassismus hat? Würden Sie irgendeinen klaren Unterschied sehen zur Nazi-Zeit (andere Artikulation von Rassismus, andere Zielgruppen?) oder auch eine gewisse Kontinuität?

19. Ich möchte gerne wissen, ob Sie eine Vorstellung haben, woher rassistische Ideen kommen? Wo werden Sie besonders genährt? Vielleicht könnten Sie die folgende "Liste" kommentieren:
1. von den Medien?
2. von der Regierung?
3. von Politikern? Wenn ja, welcher Partei gehören sie an?
4. von rechtsextremistischen Gruppierungen?
5. von anderen?

20. Denken Sie, dass es Elemente in der deutschen Gesellschaft gibt, die man als rassistisch bezeichnen könnte? Welche?

21. Zurück zu ihrer Arbeit: Beinhaltet Ihre Arbeit den Kampf gegen Rassismus und gegen Ungleichheit der Immigranten? Wenn ja, was ist der schwierigste Aspekt in Ihrem Kampf?

22. Weshalb, glauben Sie, hat Deutschland kein Anti-Diskriminierungsgesetz wie z.B. Grossbritannien?

23. Glauben Sie, dass es eine 'gemeinsame Aktion' von seiten der EG gegen Rassismus geben wird? Wie sehen Sie die Zukunftsaussichten einer EG-weiten Anti-Diskriminierungsgesetzgebung?

C
Ich möchte jetzt gerne zum dritten Thema kommen: Staatsbürgerschaft

24. Es gibt ja im Deutschen zwei Begriffe: Nationalität und Staatsbürgerschaft; könnten Sie mir sagen, ob es irgendeinen Unterschied gibt im Deutschen in der Interpretation dieser Begriffe?

25. In welchem Sinne, glauben Sie, sind Immigranten Staatsbürger hier in Deutschland? Der oft benutzte Begriff "Ausländer" deutet ja an, dass die Immigranten nicht als gleiche und vollberechtigte Bürger angesehen werden, aber was sind die genauen Elemente, die die Ausländer von den Inländern unterscheiden?

26. Können Sie sich eine Erklärung vorstellen, warum die deutsche Regierung den inzwischen fest etablierten Immigranten immer noch keinen vollen staatsbürgerlichen Status gewährt?

27. Wenn Sie zurückblicken auf die Anfangsphase des Gastarbeitersystems, gab es seitdem irgendwelche Veränderungen bezüglich des staatsbürger-lichen Status der Immigranten?

28. Befassen Sie sich hier mit staatsbürgerlichen Angelegenheiten im Hinblick auf Immigranten?

29. Glauben Sie an Zukunftsaussichten für eine Europäische Staatsbürgerschaft? Wird diese auch Immigrantengruppen einbeziehen? Wenn nein, warum nicht?

Zusammenfassende Fragen:
30. Wenn Sie an Ihre Arbeit hier denken, welches der drei Themen, die wir besprochen haben, ist am wichtigsten? Wo liegen Ihre Prioritäten?

31. Welchem Thema sollten sich Ihrer Meinung nach die Bundesregierung zuerst zuwenden?

32. Im Zusammenhang mit der europäischen Integration, welches dieser drei Themen ist für Sie von grösstem Belang?

Terminologische Frage:
Was ist Ihre Meinung zu dem Begriff "Ausländer"?

In Section A, the additional questions referred to any changes in the perception of national identity since unification (rise of nationalism?), to the *ius sanguinis* principle of German nationality law and the specific *Volk*-concept. In Section B, the first question (No. 16) was meant to find out why the term 'hostility towards foreigners' is so often used and hardly ever 'racism' as in the British case. Question 18 was asked to discover whether contemporary German approach to 'racism' is still influenced by the experiences during the Nazi-period. Question 22 referred to the fact that Germany has not got any anti-discrimination legislation and it was asked to find out why this legislation does not exist. In Section C, question 25 and 26 refers to the different approach towards immigrants' citizenship rights in Germany and was meant to find out why they are still not given full equal (formal) rights. Question 27 has to be seen in the same context: the objective was to explore whether there have been any (positive) changes since the days of the '*Gastarbeiter*' system and it refers to the various amendments in the "Foreigners' Law".

In the case of the interview with the EU Migrants Forum, the 'British questions' were adjusted to the European context. Therefore, instead of asking, for instance, "Do British people have a sense of national identity", it was asked whether national identity plays as important role in each single member-state. Moreover, country-specific questions (as on the 1981 BNA or the German *Volk*- concept) were omitted.

## Notes

1    This question looks like a 'leading question', but it was meant to function as a 'bridge' between the two sections. In the actual interview situation, this question was not once asked in this way as the interviewees referred to this aspect in one way or another as part of their replies to the previous questions in section A. This was the same in the 'German' context (see question no. 15, section A).

# Bibliography

Akçam, D. (1993). *Deutsches Heim - Glück allein. Alaman Ocagi. Wie Türken Deutsche sehen.* Göttingen: Lamuv.

Albrow, M. & King, E. (Eds.) (1990). *Globalization, Knowledge, and Society.* London: Sage.

Allen, S. & Macey, M. (1992). *Race And Ethnicity In The European Context* - paper for the conference on 'Social Order in Post-Classical Sociology', University of Bristol.

Allen, S. & Macey, M. (1994). 'Some issues of race, ethnicity and nationalism in the "New" Europe: rethinking sociological paradigms'. In Brown, P. & Cromption, R. (Eds.), *A New Europe? Economic Restructuring and Social Exclusion* (pp. 108-135). London: UCL Press Limited.

Anderson, B. (1983). *Imagined Communities - Reflections on the Origin and Spread of Nationalism.* London: Verso.

Anthias, F. (1995). 'Cultural racism or racist culture? Rethinking racist exclusions'. *Economy and Society,* 24(2), 279-301.

Anthias, F. & Yuval-Davis, N. (1992). *Racialized boundaries - Race, nation, gender, colour and class and the anti-racist struggle.* London: Routledge.

Antrata, O. & Kaschuba, G. & Leiprecht, R. & Wolf, C. (Eds.) (1989). *Theorien über Rassismus.* Hamburg: Argument-Verlag.

Arendt, H. (1951). *The Origins of Totalitarianism* (Second edition of 1958 ed.). London: Allen & Unwin Ltd.

Arendt, H. (1958). *The Human Condition.* Chicago: University of Chicago Press.

Arendt, H. (1986). *Elemente und Ursprünge Totaler Herrschaft.* München: Serie Piper.

Ausländerbeauftragte des Senats von Berlin (1990a). *Deutsche und türkische Jugendliche in wichtigen Fragen einig - Gegenseitige tolerante Einstellungen überwiegen.* Berlin: AuslB.

Ausländerbeauftragte des Senats von Berlin (1990b). *Zusammenleben mit Ausländern in Ost- und West-Berlin: Ja zu kultureller Vielfalt - Bedenken gegen weitere Zuwanderung.* Berlin: AuslB.

Bade, K. J. (Ed.) (1992). *Deutsche im Ausland - Fremde in Deutschland. Migration in Geschichte und Gegenwart.* München: C.H. Beck.

Bahringhorst, S. (1991). *Fremde in der Stadt - Multikulturelle Minderheitenpolitik, dargestellt am Beispiel der nordenglischen Stadt Bradford.* Baden-Baden: Nomos.

Bahringhorst, S. (1993). Multikulturalismus und Anti-Diskriminierungspolitik in Grossbritannien. In Robertson-Wensauer, C.Y. (Ed.), *Multikulturalität - Interkulturalität? Probleme und Perspektiven der multikulturellen Gesellschaft* (pp. 193-211). Baden-Baden: Nomos.

Baimbridge, M. & Burkitt, B. & Macey, M. (1994). The Maastricht Treaty: exacerbating racism in Europe? *Ethnic and Racial Studies,* 17(3), 420-441.

Baimbridge, M. & Burkitt, B. & Macey, M. (1995). 'The European Parliamentary Election of 1994 and racism in Europe'. *Ethnic and Racial Studies*, 18, 128-130.

Balibar, E. (1991). 'Es gibt keinen Staat in Europa: Racism and Politics in Europe Today'. *New Left Review*(186), 5-19.

Balibar, E. & Wallerstein, I. (1990). *Rasse Klasse Nation - Ambivalente Identitäten*. Hamburg: Argumente-Verlag.

Balibar, E. & Wallerstein, I. (1991). *Race, Nation, Class - Ambiguous Identities*. London: Verso.

Banton, M. (1977). *The Idea of Race*. London: Tavistock.

Banton, M. (1991). 'The race relations problematic'. *British Journal of Sociology,* 42(1), 115-130.

Barbalet, J. M. (1988). *Citizenship: Rights, Struggle and Class Inequality.* Milton Keynes: Open University Press.

Barber, S. & Millns, T. (1993). *Building the new Europe - The role of local authorities in the UK*. London: Association of County Councils.

Baring, A. (Ed.) (1994). *Germany's New Position in Europe*. Oxford: Berg.

Barker, M. (1981). *The New Racism*. London: Junction Books.

Bauman, Z. (1989). *Modernity and the Holocaust*. Cambridge: Polity Press.

Bauman, Z. (1992). 'Soil, blood and identity'. *The Sociological Review*, 40(4), 675-701.

Beauftragte der Bundesrepublik für die Belange der Ausländer (1993a). *Bericht der Beauftragten der Bundesregierung für die Belange der Ausländer über die Lage der Ausländer in der Bundesrepublik Deutschland*. Bonn: Beauftragte der Bundesrepublik für die Belange der Ausländer.

Beauftragte der Bundesrepublik für die Belange der Ausländer (1993b). *"Ausländerkriminalität" oder "kriminelle Ausländer" - Anmerkungen zu einem sensiblen Thema*. Bonn: Die Beauftragte der Bundesregierung für die Belange der Ausländer.

Bergmann, W. & Erb, R. (1991). *Antisemitismus in der Bundesrepublik Deutschland - Ergebnisse der empirischen Forschung von 1946-1989*. Opladen: Leske & Budrich.

Bhavnani, K.-K. (1993). 'Towards a Multicultural Europe?: 'Race', Nation and Identity in 1992 and Beyond'. *Feminist Review*(45), 30-45.

Bielefeld, U. (1991). *Das Eigene und das Fremde - Neuer Rassismus in der Alten Welt*? Hamburg: Junius.

Björgo, T. (1993). 'Role of the Media in Racist Violence'. In Björgo, T. & Witte, R. (Eds.), *Racist Violence in Europe* London: Macmillan.

Björgo, T. & Witte, R. (Eds.) (1993). *Racist Violence in Europe*. London: Macmillan.

Bös, M. (1993). 'Ethnisierung des Rechts? Staatsbürgerschaft in Deutschland, Frankreich, Grossbritannien und den USA'. *Kölner Zeitschrift für Soziologie und Sozialpsychologie,* 45(4), 619-643.

Bowling, B. & Saulsbury, W. (1993). 'A Local Response to Racial Violence'. In Björgo, T. &. Witte, R. (Eds.), *Racist Violence in Europe* London: Macmillan.

Brah, A. (1992). 'Difference, Diversity and Differentiation'. In Donald, J. & Rattansi, A. (Eds.), *'Race', Culture & Difference* (pp. 126-145). London: Sage.

Brah, A. (1993). 'Re-Framing Europe: En-gendered Racisms, Ethnicities and Nationalisms in Contemporary Western Europe'. *Feminist Review*(45), 9-28.

Brah, A. (1994). 'Time, Place and Others: Discourses of Race, Nation, and Ethnicity' (Review Essay). *Sociology,* 28(3), 805-813.

Brown, C. (1984). *Black and White Britain - The Third PSI Survey.* Aldershot: Gower.

Brown, R. (1995). 'Racism and immigration in Britain'. *International Socialism,* 68(autumn), 3-35.

Brubaker, W. R. (1992). *Citizenship And Nationhood In France and Germany.* London: Harvard University Press.

Brubaker, W. R. (Ed.) (1989). *Immigration and The Politics of Citizenship in Europe & North America.* London: University Press of America.

Bundesrepublik Deutschland (1994). *Grundgesetz für die Bundesrepublik Deutschland.* Bonn: Bundeszentrale für politische Bildung.

Bundesverfassungsgericht (1989). 'Wahlrecht für Ausländer bei Kommunalwahlen'. *Neue Juristische Wochenzeitschrift,* 42(2), 3147-3148.

Bunyan, T. (1993). *Statewatching the new Europe - a handbook on the European state.* Nottingham: Russell Press.

Burgleih, M. & Wippermann, W. (1991). *The Racial State - Germany 1933-1945.* Cambridge: Cambridge University Press.

Buruma, I. (1994). *Wages of Guilt - Memories of War in Germany and Japan.* London: Jonathan Cape.

Butterwege, C. & Jäger, S. (Eds.) (1992). *Rassismus in Europa.* Köln: Bund-Verlag.

Callovi, G. (1992). 'Regulation of Immigration in 1993: Pieces of the European Community Jig-Saw Puzzle'. *International Migration Review,* 26, 353-372.

CARF (1994). 'Deadly Europe'. *Campaign Against Racism & Fascism* (CARF)(18 (Jan./Feb.), 4-8.

Castles, S. (1984). *Here for Good - Western Europe's New Ethnic Minorities.* London: Pluto Press.

Castles, S. (1993). 'Migrations and Minorities in Europe. Perspectives for the 1990s: Eleven Hypotheses'. In Wrench, J. & Solomos, J. (Eds.), *Racism and Migration in Western Europe,* Oxford: Berg.

Castles, S. (1995). 'How nation-states respond to immigration and ethnic diversity'. *New Community,* 21(3), 293-308.

Castles, S. & Kosack, G. (1973). *Immigrant Workers and Class Structure in Western Europe.* London: Oxford University Press.

Çelik, H. (1995). *Die Migrationspolitik bundesdeutscher Parteien und Gewerkschaften.* Bonn: Protext-Verlag.

Centre for Contemporary Cultural Studies (1982). *The Empire Strikes Back.* London: Routledge.

Churches' Commission for Migrants in Europe (Ed.) (1994). *Combatting Racism in Europe.* Bruxelles: Churches' Commission for Migrants in Europe.

Çinar, D. (1993). 'Von "Gastarbeitern" zu "ethnics"?' *Migration - A European Journal of International Migration and Ethnic Relations,* 17(1), 63-85.

Clemens, J. (1983). *Polls, Politics and Populism.* Aldershot: Gower.

Closa, C. (1992). 'The Concept of Citizenship in the Treaty on European Union'. *Common Market Law Review,* 29(6), 1137-1169.

Cohen, S. (1991). *Imagine there's no countries.* Manchester: Greater Manchester Immigration Aid Unit.

Cohen, R. (1994). *Frontiers of Identity - The British and the Others.* London: Longman.

Cohn-Bendit, D. & Schmid, T. (1992). *Heimat Babylon - Das Wagnis der multikulturellen Demokratie.* Hamburg: Hoffmann und Campe.

Colley, L. (1992). *Britons - Forging the Nation 1707-1837.* New Haven: Yale University Press.

Collinson, S. (1994). *Europe and International Migration* (Second ed.). London: Royal Institute of International Affairs.

Commichau, I. (1990). 'Ausländer in der DDR - die ungeliebte Minderheit'. *Deutschland Archiv,* 9, 1432-1439.

Commission of the European Communities (1990). *Member States' National Legislation Applicable To Non-Community Citizens.* Brussels: Commission of the European Communities.

Commission of the European Communities (1991a). 'Meeting of Ministers responsible for immigration'. *Bulletin of the European Communities*(6), 134-135.

Commission of the European Communities (1991b). *Eurobarometer, No. 35.* Brussels: Commission of the European Communities.

Commission of the European Communities (1992). *Legal Instruments to Combat Racism and Xenophobia.* Brussels: Directorate General Employment, Industrial Relations and Social Affairs.

Commission of the European Communities (1993a). *Green Paper - European Social Policy, Option for the Union.* Luxembourg: Office for Official Publications of the European Communities.

Commission of the European Communities (1993b). *Eurobarometer, No. 39.* Brussels: Commission of the European Communities.

Council of Europe (1987). *Colloquy: "Migrants and the Media - from 'guest workers' to linguistic and cultural minorities"*. Strasbourg: Council of Europe.

Council of Europe (1991a). 'Immigration. Europe in search of new arrangements'. *Forum*(November), 40-43.

Council of Europe (1991b). 'Is "freedom of movement" a threat for Europe?' *Forum*(February), 38-41.

Council of the European Communities (1990a). Council Directive of 28 June 1990 on the right of residence. *Official Journal of the European Communities, L 180/26*(90/364/EEC).

Council of the European Communities (1990b). Council Directive of 28 June 1990 on the rights of residence for employees and self-employed persons who have ceased their occupational activity. *Official Journal of the European Communities, L180/28*(90/365/EEC).

Council of the European Communities (1990c). Council Directive of 28 June 1990 on the right of residence for students. *Official Journal of the European Communities, L 180/30*(90/366/EEC).

Council of the European Communities & Commission of the European Communities (1992). *Treaty on European Union*. Luxembourg: Office for Official Publication of the ECs.

DISS (1992). *SchlagZeilen - Rostock: Rassismus in den Medien*. Duisburg: Duisburger Institut für Sprach- und Sozialforschung.

Dominelli, L. (1992). 'An uncaring profession? An examination of racism in social work'. In Braham, P. & Rattansi, A. & Skellington, R. (Eds.), *Racism and Antiracism - Inequalities, Opportunities and Policies*, London: Sage.

Donald, J. & Rattansi, A. (Eds.) (1992). *"Race", Culture & Difference*. London: Sage.

Dummett, A. & Nicol, A. (1990). *Subjects, Citizens, Aliens and Others - Nationality and Immigration Law*. London: Weidenfeld and Nicolson.

Dummett, A. & Niessen, J. (1993). *Immigration and Citizenship in the European Union*. Bruxelles & London: Churches Commission for Migrants in Europe & Commission for Racial Equality.

Economist (1991). 'Immigration: The other fortress Europe.' *The Economist, 01.06.91*(No. 7709), 47-48.

Economist (1992). E'urope's Immigrants'. *The Economist, 15.2.92*(No. 7746), 17-20.

Elias, N. (1992a). *Über den Prozess der Zivilisation: Soziogenetische und psychogenetische Untersuchungen (first volume)* (17th ed.). Frankfurt am Main: Suhrkamp.

Elias, N. (1992b). *Über den Prozess der Zivilisation: Soziogenetische und psychogenetische Untersuchungen (second volume)* (17th ed.). Frankfurt am Main: Suhrkamp.

Elias, N. (1992c). *Studien über die Deutschen - Machtkämpfe und Habitusentwicklung im 19. und 20. Jahrhundert* (first ed.). Frankfurt am Main: Suhrkamp.

Engelmann, B. (1991). *Du deutsch? - Geschichte der Ausländer in Deutschland.* Göttingen: Steidl Verlag.

Essed, P. (1991). *Understanding Everyday Racism.* London: Sage.

Estel, B. (1991). 'Grundaspekte der Nation - Eine begrifflich-systematische Untersuchung'. *Soziale Welt, 42,* 208-231.

European Commission (1993). *Eurobarometer, No. 40.* Brussels: European Commission.

European Commission (1994). *Eurobarometer, No. 41.* Brussels: European Commission.

European Commission (1995). *Eurobarometer No. 42.* Brussels: European Commission.

European Commission (1996). *Standard Eurobarometer No. 44.* Brussels: European Commission.

European documentation. 'Europe on the move' (1992). *From Single Market to European Union.* Luxembourg: Office for Official Publications of the European Communities.

European documentation. 'Europe on the move' (1993). *A Citizen's Europe.* Luxembourg: Office for Official Publications of the European Communities.

European documentation. 'Europe on the move' (1994). *European Union.* Luxembourg: Office for Official Publications of the European Communities.

European Parliament (1990). *Report of the Committee of Inquiry Into Racism And Xenophobia.* Strasbourg: European Parliament.

European Parliament (1992). *Maastricht - The Treaty on European Union.* Luxembourg: European Communities.

European Parliament (1993). 'Resolution on the resurgence of racism and xenophobia in Europe and the danger of right-wing extremist violence'. *Official Journal of the European Communities, Information and Notices, C150,* 127-132.

European Union (1993). *Selected instruments taken from the Treaties.* Luxembourg: Office for Official Publications of the European Communities.

European Union Migrants Forum (1993). *European Manifesto against Racism.* Bruxelles: European Union Migrants Forum.

Eurostat (1992). *Basic Statistics of the Community.* Luxembourg: Office for Official Publications of the European Communities.

Eurostat (1993). *Basic Statistics of the Community.* Luxembourg: Office for Official Publications of the European Communities.

Faist, T. (1994a). 'Immigration, integration and the ethnicization of politics'. *European Journal of Political Research, 25*(4), 439-459.

Faist, T. (1994b). 'How to Define a Foreigner? The Symbolic Politics of Immigration in German Partisan Discourse', 1978-1992. *West European Politics, 17*(2), 50-71.

Faist, T. (1995). 'Ethnicization and racialization of welfare-state politics in Germany and the USA.' *Ethnic and Racial Studies, 18*(2), 219-250.

Federalist (1993). 'European Citizenship and Post-National Identity'. *Federalist, 35*(1), 3-8.

Feldhoff, J. (1990). 'Vom Nationalstaat zur multikulturellen Gesellschaft - zur Auseinandersetzung mit dem neuen Ausländergesetz.' *Neue Praxis, 3*, 197-206.

Fernandes, M. (1992). 'The Free Movement of Persons: The Ever Changing Face of Europe'. *European Business Law Review, 3*(12), 327-30.

Ferstl, L. & Hetzel, H. (1990). *"Wir sind immer die Fremden" - Aussiedler in Deutschland*. Bonn: J.H.W. Dietz.

Ford, G. (1992). *Fascist Europe - The Rise of Racism and Xenophobia*. London: Pluto Press.

Forsythe, D. (1989). 'German Identity and the Problem of History'. In Tonkin, E. & McDonald, M. & Chapman, M. (Eds.), *History and Ethnicity* (pp. 137-156). London: Routledge.

Forudastan, F. (1990). 'Ein Gesetz, das grundlegende Rechte beschneidet'. *taz* (25.04.90)

Frankfurter Rundschau (1994). 'Diffamierung der Ausländer'. *Frankfurter Rundschau* (14.11.94).

Friedrich, W. & Schubarth, W. (1991). 'Ausländerfeindliche und rechtsextreme Orientierungen bei ostdeutschen Jugendlichen - Eine empirische Studie'. *Deutschland Archiv, 10,* 1052-1065.

Fryer, P. (1984). *Staying Power - The History of Black People in Britain*. London: Pluto Press.

Funcke, L. (1991). 'Wie lange ist ein Zuwanderer "Ausländer"?' In Iranbomy, S.S. (Ed.), *Einwanderbares Deutschland oder Vertreibung aus dem Wohlstandsparadies?* (pp. 35-43). Frankfurt/Main: Horizonte Verlag GmbH.

Gallup political & economic index (1992). *Report No. 384 (August)*. London: The Gallup Organization.

Gallup political & economic index (1995). *Report No. 421 (September)*. London: The Gallup Organization.

Gallup political & economic index (1996). *Report No. 428 (April)*. London: The Gallup Organization.

Garcia, S. (1992). *Europe's Fragmented Identities and the Frontiers of Citizenship*. London: The Royal Institute of International Affairs.

Garcia, S. (1994). *European Citizenship: Issues of Culture, Convergence and Legitimacy* - paper for the International Seminar on "Citizenship, Work & Income in Europe", Sheffield University, 22 October 1994.

Gebhardt, J. (1993). 'Verfassungspatriotismus als Identitätskonzept der Nation'. *Aus Politik und Zeitgeschichte*(B14/93), 29-37.

Geissler, H. (1991). 'Deutschland - ein Einwanderungsland?' In Iranbomy, S.S. (Ed.), *Einwanderbares Deutschland oder Vertreibung aus dem Wohlstandsparadies?* (pp. 9-23). Frankfurt/Main: Horizonte Verlag GmbH.

Geissler, R. & Marissen, N. (1990). 'Kriminalität und Kriminalisierung junger Ausländer - Die tickende soziale Zeitbombe - ein Artefact der Kriminalstatistik'. *Kölner Zeitschrift für Soziologie und Sozialpsychologie, 42*(4), 663-687.

Gellner, E. (1983). *Nations and Nationalism.* Oxford: Blackwell.

George, S. (1990). *An Akward Partner - Britain in the European Community.* Oxford: Oxford University Press.

George, S. (1991). Politics and Policy in the European Community. Oxford: Oxford University Press.

Giddens, A. (1985). *The Nation-State And Violence.* Cambridge: Polity Press.

Gill, D. & Mayor, B. & Blair, M. (Eds.) (1992). *Racism and Education - Structure and Strategies.* London: Sage.

Gilroy, P. (1987). *There Ain't No Black In The Union Jack.* London: Hutchinson.

Goldberg, D. T. (1993). *Racist Culture - Philosophy and the Politics of Meaning.* Oxford: Blackwell.

Gordon, P. (1985). *Policing Immigration - Britain's Internal Controls.* London: Pluto Press.

Gordon, P. (1989). *"Fortress Europe? The meaning of 1992".* London: Runnymede Trust.

Gordon, P. (1990). *Racial violence and harassment.* London: Runnymede Trust.

Gordon, P. (1992). 'Black people and the criminal law - Rhetoric and Reality'. In Braham, P. & Rattansi, A. & Skellington, R. (Eds.), *Racism and Antiracism* London: Sage.

Gordon, P. (1993). 'The Police and Racist Violence in Britain'. In Björgo, T. & Witte, R. (Eds.), *Racist Violence in Europe* London: Macmillan.

Gordon, P. & Rosenberg, D. (1989). *Daily Racism - The press and black people in Britain.* London: Runnymede Trust.

Gottschlich, J. (1990). 'Politisch ignorant und ideologisch borniert.' *taz* (01.11.90).

Goulbourne, H. (1991). *Ethnicity and nationalism in post-imperial Britain.* Cambridge: Cambridge University Press.

Grant, R. (1993). 'New Right. In Outhwaite,' W. & Bottomore, T. (Eds.), *The Blackwell Dictionary of Twentieth-Century Social Thought.* Oxford: Blackwell.

Greenfeld, L. (1992). *Five Roads to Modernity.* London: Harvard University Press.

Guardian (1995). 'Challenge to EU border scheme'. *The Guardian,* (25.03.95).

Guendelsberger, J. W. (1992). 'Access to Citizenship for Children Born Within the State to Foreign Parents. *American Journal of Comparative Law, 40*(2), 379-429.

Habermas, J. (1989). *The New Conservatism.* Cambridge: Polity Press.

Habermas, J. (1992). 'Staatsbürgerschaft und nationale Identität '(1990). In Habermas, J., *Faktizität und Geltung* (pp. 632-660). Frankfurt am Main: Suhrkamp.

Habermas, J. (1994). 'Citizenship and National Identity'. In van Steenbergen, B. (Ed.),_The Condition of Citizenship_ (pp. 20-35). London: Sage.

Hall, J. A. (1993). 'Nationalisms: Classified and Explained'. *Daedalus - Journal of the American Academy of Arts and Sciences, 122(3)*, 1-28.

Hall, S. (1978). 'Racism and Reaction'. In Commission for Racial Equality (Ed.), *Five Views Of Multi-Racial Britain.* London: Commission for Racial Equality.

Hall, S. (1988). 'New Ethnicities'. In ICA Document 7 (Ed.), *Black Film/British Cinema* (pp. 27-31). London: ICA.

Hall, S. (1992). 'The West and the Rest: discourse and power'. In Hall, S. & Gieben, B. (Eds.), *Formations of Modernity.* Cambridge: Polity Press.

Hall, S. & Held, D. (1989). 'Citizens and Citizenship'. In Hall, S. & Jacques, M. (Eds.), *NEW TIMES - The Changing Face of Politics in the 1990s* (pp. 173-188). London: Lawrence & Wishart.

Hammar, T. (1985a). 'Dual Citizenship and Political Integration'. *International Migration Review, 19(3)*, 438-450.

Hammar, T. (Ed.) (1985b). *European immigration policy - A comparative study.* Cambridge: Cambridge University Press.

Hammar, T. (1986). 'Citizenship: Membership of a Nation and of a State'. *International Migration, 24(4)*, 735-747.

Hammar, T. (1990). *Democracy and the Nation State: Aliens, Denizens and Citizens in a World of International Migration.* Aldershot: Gower.

Hammersley, M. (1992). *What's wrong with Ethnography?* London: Routledge.

Hammersley, M. & Atkinson, P. (1983). *Ethnography - Principles in Practice.* London: Tavistock Publications.

Hannoversche Allgemeine Zeitung (1994). *'Die Bonner Pläne vertiefen den Riss innerhalb vieler Ausländerfamilien'.* HAZ (18.11.94).

Heater, D. (1990). *Citizenship - The Civic Ideal In World History, Politics And Education.* London: Longman.

Hechter, M. (1975). *Internal Colonialism - The Celtic Fringe in British National Development, 1536-1966.* London: Routledge & Kegan Paul.

Heckmann, F. (1992). *Ethnische Minderheiten, Volk und Nation. Soziologie inter-ethnischer Beziehungen.* Stuttgart: Ferdinand Enke Verlag.

Held, D. (1991). 'Between State and Civil Society: Citizenship'. In Andrews, G. (Ed.), *Citizenship.* London: Lawrence & Wishart.

Herbert, U. (1986). *Geschichte der Ausländerbeschäftigung in Deutschland 1880 bis 1980 - Saisonarbeiter, Zwangsarbeiter, Gastarbeiter.* Bonn: J.H.W. Dietz Nachf.

Hoffmann, L. (1991). 'Das 'Volk' - Zur ideologischen Struktur eines unvermeidbaren Begriffs'. *Zeitschrift für Soziologie, 20*(3), 191-208.

Hoffmann, L. (1992 (second edition). *Die unvollendete Republik - Zwischen Einwanderungsland und deutschem Nationalstaat.* Köln: PapyRossa Verlag.

Hoffmann, L. & Even, H. (1984). *Soziologie der Ausländerfeindlichkeit - Zwischen nationaler Identität und multikultureller Gesellschaft.* Weinheim: Beltz Verlag.

Holdaway, S. (1996). *The Racialisation of British Policing.* Basingstoke: Macmillan.

Holmes, C. (1979). *Anti-semitism in British society.* London: Edward Arnold.

Holmes, C. (1991). *A tolerant country? - Immigrants, Refugees and Minorities in Britain.* London: Faber and Faber Ltd.

Husbands, C. T. (1992). 'The kindness of strangers? Citizenship, immigration and political asylum in the new Europe'. *conference paper.*

Husbands, C. T. (1994). 'Crises of national identity as the 'new moral panics': Political agenda-setting about definitions of nationhood'. *New Community, 20*(2), 191-206.

Institut für Migrations-und Rassismusforschung e. V. (1992). *Rassismus und Migration in Europa.* Hamburg: Argumente-Verlag.

IPOS (1990). *Einstellungen zu aktuellen Fragen der Innenpolitik 1990 in der Bundesrepublik Deutschland und in der DDR.* Mannheim: Institut für praxisorientierte Sozialforschung.

IPOS (1992). *Einstellungen zu aktuellen Fragen der Innenpolitik 1992 in Deutschland.* Mannheim: Institut für praxisorientierte Sozialforschung.

IPOS (1993). *Einstellungen zu aktuellen Fragen der Innenpolitik 1993 in Deutschland.* Mannheim: Institut für praxisorientierte Sozialforschung.

IPOS (1995). *Einstellungen zu aktuellen Fragen der Innenpolitik 1995 in Deutschland.* Mannheim: Institut für praxisorientierte Sozialforschung.

Jackson, P. & Penrose, J. (Eds.) (1993). *Constructions of race, place and nation.* London: UCL Press.

Jäger, S. (1992). 'Elitediskurs und Alltagsbewusstsein - zu den Ursachen der Eskalation rassistisch motivierter Gewalttaten in Deutschland'. *Forum Wissenschaft, 3,* 6-11.

Jäger, S. (1993). *BrandSätze - Rassismus im Alltag.* Duisburg: DISS.

Jäger, S. & Januschek, F. (Eds.) (1992). *Osnabrücker Beiträge zur Sprachtheorie - Der Diskurs des Rassismus.* Osnabrück: Verein zur Förderung der Sprachwissenschaft in Forschung und Ausbildung e.V.

Jäggi, C. J. (1992). *Rassismus - Ein globales Problem.* Zürisch: Orell Füssli.

John, B. (1990). 'Wer ist ein Deutscher? - Von der Abstammungsideologie zum Territorialrecht'. *Die Neue Gesellschaft Frankfurter Hefte, 37*(7), 888-922.

Jones, T. (1996). *Britain's Ethnic Minorities* (Student Edition). London: Policy Studies Institute.

Jowell, R. & Airey, C. (Eds.) (1984). *British Social Attitudes - the 1984 report*. Aldershot: Gower.

Jowell, R. et al. (Eds.) (1986). *British Social Attitudes - the 1986 report*. Aldershot: Gower.

Jowell, R. et al. (Eds.) (1989). *British Social Attitudes - special international report (6th report)*. Aldershot: Gower.

Jowell, R. et al. (Eds.) (1992). *British Social Attitudes - the 9th report*. Aldershort: Dartmouth Publishing Company Ltd.

Jowell, R. et al. (Eds.) (1995). *British Social Attitudes - the 12th report*. Aldershot: Dartmouth Publishing Company Ltd.

Kalpaka, A. & Räthzel, N. (Eds.) (1990). *Die Schwierigkeit, nicht rassistisch zu sein*. Leer: Mundo Verlag.

Kennedy, P. & Nicholls, A. (Eds.) (1981). *Nationalist and Racialist Movements in Britain and Germany before 1914*. London: Macmillan Press Ltd.

King, J. (1993). *Ethnic Minority Communitites and The Politics of Europe*. paper for the conference on "Racism, Ethnicity and Politics in Contemporary Europe", Loughborough University, 24-26 September 1993.

Klusmeyer, D. B. (1993). 'Aliens, Immigrants, and Citizens: The Politics of Inclusion in the Federal Republic of Germany'. *Daedalus - Journal of the American Academy of Arts and Sciences, 122*(3), 81-114.

Kluxen-Pyta, D. (1990). 'Verfassungspatriotismus und Nationale Identität'. *Zeitschrift für Politik, 37*(2), 117-133.

Koch-Arzberger, C. (1993). 'Die Ausländer in den Augen der Deutschen'. In Koch-Arzberger, C. (Ed.), *Einwanderungsland Hessen? Daten, Fakten, Analysen* (pp. 17-29). Opladen: Westdeutscher Verlag.

Korell, J. (1994). 'Schläger in Uniform?' *taz* (30.09.94).

Kulluk, F.E. (1996). 'The political discourse on quota immigration in Germany'. *New Community, 22*(2), 301-320.

Layton-Henry, Z. (1991). 'Citizenship and Migrant Workers in Western Europe'. In Vogel, U. & Moran, M. (Eds.), *The Frontiers of Citizenship*, London: Macmillan.

Layton-Henry, Z. (Ed.). (1990). *The political rights of migrant workers in Western Europe*. London: Sage.

Layton-Henry, Z. (1992). *The Politics of Immigration*. Oxford: Blackwell.

Leggewie, C. & Senoçak, Z. (1993). *Deutsche Türken - Türk Almanlar*. Hamburg: Rowohlt.

Lester, Lord of Herne Hill (1994). 'Discrimination: What Can Lawyers Learn from History?' *Public Law*, 224-237.

Liegmann, G. (1990). *Kommunales Wahlrecht für Ausländer in den Bundesländern und Europa: Dokumentation und Stellungnahme*. Stuttgart: Richard Boorberg Verlag.

Lillich, R. B. (1984). *The human rights of aliens in contemporary international law*. Manchester: Manchester University Press.

Llobera, J. R. (1994). *The God of Modernity - the development of nationalism in western europe.* Oxford: Berg.

Lynch, J. (1992). *Education For Citizenship In A Multi-cultural Society.* London: Cassell Education.

Macdonald, S. (Ed.) (1993). *Inside European Identities.* Oxford: Berg.

Maier, C. S. (1988). *The Unmasterable Past - History, Holocaust, and German National Identity.* London: Harvard University Press.

Mann, M. (1992). 'The emergence of modern European nationalism'. In Hall, J.A. & Jarvie, I.C. (Eds.), *Transition to Modernity* (pp. 137-165). Cambridge: Cambridge University Press.

Mann, M. (1993a). 'Nation-States in Europe and Other Continents: Diversifying, Developing, Not Dying'. *Daedalus - Journal of the American Academy of Arts and Sciences, 122*(3), 115-140.

Mann, M. (1993b). *The Sources of Social Power: The rise of classes and nation-states, 1760-1914.* Cambridge: Cambridge University Press.

Mansel, J. & Hurrelmann, K. (1993). 'Psychosoziale Befindlichkeit junger Ausländer in der Bundesrepublik Deutschland'. *Soziale Probleme,* 4(2): 167-192.

Margolis, M. & Mauser, G. A. (eds.) (1989). *Manipulating Public Opinion - Essays on Public Opinion as a Dependent Variable.* Pacific Grove, California: Brooks/Cole Publishing Company.

Marshall, T. H. (1950). *Citizenship And Social Class - and other essays.* Cambridge: Cambridge University Press.

Marshall, T. H. & Bottomore, T. (1992). *Citizenship and Social Class.* London: Pluto Press.

Martin, P. L. & Miller, M. J. (1990). 'Guests or Immigrants?' *Migration Worlds, 18*(1), 8-13.

Mason, D. (1992). *Some Problems With The Concepts Of Race And Racism.* Leicester: University of Leicester.

Mason, D. (1994a). 'Employment and the labour market.' *New Community, 20*(2), 301-308.

Mason, D. (1994b). 'Employment and the labour market.' *New Community, 20*(4), 673-677.

Mason, D. (1995). *Race & Ethnicity in Modern Britain.* Oxford: Oxford University Press.

Meehan, E. (1991). 'European Citizenship and Social Policies'. In Vogel,U. & Moran, M. (Eds.), *The Frontiers of Citizenship.* London: Macmillan.

Meehan, E. (1993a). *Citizenship and the European Community.* London: Sage.

Meehan, E. (1993b). 'Citizenship and the European Community'. *The Political Quarterly, 64*(2), 172-186.

Melber, H. (1992). 'Kontinuitäten totaler Herrschaft: Völkermord und Apartheid in "Deutsch-Südwestafrika". Zur kolonialen Herrschaftspraxis im Deutschen Kaiserreich"'. *Jahrbuch für Antisemitismusforschung, 1*(1), 91-116.

Menski, W. (1994). *The impact of immigration: the German and British experience.* London: Anglo-German Foundation for the Study of Industrial Society.

Mergner, G. (1992). '"Unser Nationales Erbe" vom deutschen Kolonialismus. Rassistische Bilder - Mitleid mit den Opfern - die Unschuld der Erben"'. In Foitzik, A. & Leiprecht, R. & Marvakis, A. & Seid, U. (Eds.), *"Ein Herrenvolk von Untertanen"* (pp. 143-162). Duisburg: DISS.

Messina, A. M. (1990). 'Political impediments to the resumption of labour migration to Western Europe'. *Western European Politics, 13*(1), 31-46.

Migration News (1996a). Vol. 3(6). migrant@primal.ucdavis.edu.

Migration News (1996b). Vol. 3(7). migrant@primal.ucdavis.edu.

Miles, R. (1982a). *Racism and migrant labour.* London: Routledge & Kegan Paul.

Miles, R. (1982b). 'Racism and nationalism in Britain'. In Husband, C. (Ed.), *'Race in Britain - Continuity and change* London: Hutchinson.

Miles, R. (1987). 'Recent Marxist theories of nationalism and the issue of racism'. *British Journal of Sociology, 38,* p. 24-43.

Miles, R. (1989). *Racism.* London: Routledge.

Miles, R. (1993). *Racism after 'race relations'.* London: Routledge.

Miles, R. (1994). 'Explaining Racism in Contemporary Europe'. In Rattansi, A. & Westwood, S. (Eds.), *Racism, Modernity and Identity - On the Western Front.* Cambridge: Polity Press.

Miller, M. J. (1981). *Foreign Workers in Western Europe: An Emerging Political Force.* New York: Praeger.

Mitchell, M. & Russell, D. (1994). 'Race, citizenship and "Fortress Europe".' In Brown, P. & Crompton, R. (Eds.), *A New Europe? Economic Restructuring and Social Exclusion* (pp. 136-156). London: UCL Press Limited.

Modood, T. (1992a). *If Races Do Not Exist, Then What Does? Racial Categorisation and Ethnic Relations.* Paper for the conference on "Social Order in Post-Classical Sociology". University of Bristol.

Modood, T. (1992b). *Not Easy Being British - colour, culture and citizenship.* London: Runnymede Trust and Trentham Books.

Modood, T. et al. (1994). *Changing Ethnic Identities.* London: Policy Studies Institute.

Mouffe, C. (Ed.) (1992). *Dimension of Radical Democracy - Pluralism, Citizenship, Community.* London: Verso.

Nairn, T. (1981). *The Break-Up of Britain - Crisis and Neo-Nationalism.* London: Verso.

Nederveen Pieterse, J. (1991). 'Fictions of Europe'. *Race & Class, 32*(3), 3-10.

Nederveen Pieterse, J. (1994). 'Unpacking the West: How European is Europe?' In Rattansi, A. & Westwood, S. (Eds.), *Racism, Modernity and Identity - On the Western Front.* Cambridge: Polity Press.

Neveu, C. (1989). *Ethnic Minorities, Citizenship and Nationality: A case study for a comparative approach between France and Britain.* Warwick: Centre for Research in Ethnic Relations, University of Warwick.

Nicklas, H. (1993). 'Die Nation im Kopf: Die Pathologie der Nationalität.' *Arkaden - Interkulturelle Zeitschrift,* 2(3), 9-13.

Niessen, J. (1992). 'European Community Legislation and Intergovernmental Cooperation on Migration'. *International Migration Review,* 26, 676-684.

Niessen, J. (1994). *The Making of European Immigration Policies.* Bruxelles: Churches Commission for Migrants in Europe.

Noelle-Neumann, E. (Ed.) (1981). *The Germans - Public Opinion Polls, 1967-1980.* London: Greenwood Press.

O'Brien, P. (1992). 'German-Polish Migration: The Elusive Search for a German Nation-State'. *International Migration Review,* 26, 373-387.

O'Leary, S. (1992). 'Nationality Law and Community Citizenship: A Tale of Two Uneasy Bedfellows'. *Yearbook of European Law,* 12, 353-384.

Oberndörfer, D. (1993). *Der Wahn des Nationalen.* Freiburg: Herder Spektrum.

OECD (1991). *Continuous reporting system on migration.* Paris: OECD.

OECD (1995). *Continuous reporting system on migration.* Paris: OECD.

Office for Official Publications of the European Communities (1987). *Treaties Establishing the European Communities* (Abrigded Edition ed.). Luxembourg: Office for Official Publication of the ECs.

Owen, D. (1993a). *Ethnic Minorities in Britain: Economic Characteristics.* University of Warwick: Centre for Research in Ethnic Relations, National Ethnic Minority Data Archive, 1991 Census Statistical Paper No. 3.

Owen, D. (1993b). *Ethnic Minorities in Britain: Housing and Family Characteristics.* University of Warwick: Centre for Research in Ethnic Relations, National Ethnic Minority Data Archive, 1991 Census Statistical Paper No. 4.

Owen, D. & Green, A. (1992). 'Labour market experience and occupational change amongst ethnic groups in Great Britain'. *New Community, 19*(1), 7-29.

Philip, A. B. (1994). E'uropean Union Immigration Policy: Phantom, Fantasy or Fact?' *West European Politics, 17*(2), 168-191.

Pinn, I. & Nebelung, M. (1992). *Vom "klassichen" zum aktuellen Rassismus in Deutschland - Das Menschenbild der Bevölkerungstheorie und Bevölkerungspolitik.* Duisburg: DISS (Duisburger Institut für Sprach- und Sozialforschung).

Piper-Verlag (Ed.) (1987). *"Historikerstreit" - Die Dokumentation der Kontroverse um die Einzigartigkeit der nationalsozialistischen Judenvernichtung.* München: R. Piper GmbH.

Plender, R. (1990). 'Competence, European Community Law and Nationals of Non-Member States'. *International and Comparative Law Quarterly, 39*(July), 599-610.

Poole, R. (1992). 'On National Identity - A Response to Jonathan Ree'. *Radical Philosophy, 62*(Autumn), 14-19.

Ram, Monder (1992). 'Coping with Racism: Asian Employers in the Inner-City'. *Work, Employment & Society, 6*(4): 601-618.

Räthzel, N. (1995). '*Aussiedler* and *Ausländer*: Transforming German National Identity'. *Social Identities, 1*(2), 263-282.

Rattansi, A. (1994). "'Western' Racisms, Ethnicities and Identities in a 'Postmodern' Frame'. In Rattansi, A. & Westwood, S. (Eds.), *Racism, Modernity and Identity - On the Western Front* (pp. 15-86). Cambridge: Polity Press.

Rattansi, A. & Westwood, S. (Eds.) (1994). *Racism, Modernity and Identity - On the Western Front.* Cambridge: Polity Press.

Reinharz, S. (1992). *Feminist Methods in Social Research.* Oxford: Oxford University Press.

Rex, J. (1983). *Race Relations In Sociological Theory* (second edition). London: Routledge & Kegan Paul.

Rex, J. & Tomlinson, S. (1979). *Colonial Immigrants in a British City - A Class Analysis.* London: Routledge.

Rhodes, P. J. (1994). 'Race-Of-Interviewer Effects: A Brief Comment'. *Sociology, 28*(2), 547-558.

Rich, P. (1991). 'Patriotism and the Idea of Citizenship in Postwar British Politics'. In Vogel, U. & Moran, M. (Eds.), *The Frontiers of Citizenship.* London: Macmillan.

Rich, P. B. (1986). *Race and Empire in British Politics.* Cambridge: Cambridge University Press.

Roche, M. (1987). 'Citizenship, social theory, and social change'. *Theory and Society*(16), 363-399.

Roche, M. (1992). *Rethinking citizenship.* Cambridge: Polity Press.

Roche, M. (1994a). *European Social Citizenship: Notes on post-national citizenship and social exclusion.* Paper for the International Seminar on "Citizenship, Work & Income in Europe". October 22nd 1994. Sheffield University.

Roche, M. (1994b). 'Citizenship and Nationhood in France and Germany', Rogers Brubaker (book review). *Theory and Society(23), 889-902.*

Roche, M. (1995). 'Citizenship and modernity'. *The British Journal of Sociology, 46*(4), 715-733.

Robertson, R. (1992). *Globalization - Social Theory and Global Culture.* London: Sage.

Rose, E. J. B. (1969). *Colour and Citizenship - A Report on British Race Relations.* London: Oxford University Press.

Rudolph, Hedwig (1996). 'The new*gastarbeiter* system in Germany'. *New Community, 22*(2), 287-300.

Rutherford, J. (Ed.) (1990). *Identity - Community, Culture, Difference.* London: Lawrence & Wishart.

Saggar, S. (1993). 'Black participation and the transformation of the 'race issue' in British politics'. *New Community, 20*(1), 27-41.

Said, E. W. (1995). *Orientalism - Western Conceptions of the Orient.* London: Penguin.

Samuel, R. (Ed.) (1989). *Patriotism: The Making and Unmaking of British National Identity - Minorities and Outsiders.* London: Routledge.

Schiffauer, W. (1991). *Die Migranten aus Subay - Türken in Deutschland: Eine Ethnographie.* Stuttgart: Klett-Cotta.

Schnapper, D. (1994). 'The Debate on Immigration and the Crisis of National Identity'. *West European Politics, 17*(2), 127-139.

Schönwälder, K. (1991). 'Zu viele Ausländer in Deutschland? Zur Entwicklung ausländerfeindlicher Einstellungen in der Bundesrepublik'. *Vorgänge, 4*, 1-11.

Schönwälder, K. (1995). 'No constitutionally guaranteed respect for minorities in Germany'. *New Community, 21*(3), 421-424.

Scott, A. & Peterson, J. & Millar, D. (1994). 'Subsidiarity: A 'Europe of the Regions' v. the British Constitution?' *Journal of Common Market Studies, 32*(1), 47-67.

Sen, F. & Karakasoglu, Y. *(1994). Einstellungen zum kommunalen Wahlrecht, zu Parteien und zu der doppelten Staatsangehörigkeit bei Ausländern in der Bundesrepublik Deutschland.* Essen: Zentrum für Türkeistudien.

Senoçak, Z. (1992). *Atlas des tropischen Deutschland.* Berlin: Babel Verlag.

Senoçak, Z. (1994). *War Hitler Araber? Essays.* Berlin: Babel Verlag Hund & van Uffelen.

Seton-Watson, H. (1977). *Nations and States - An Enquiry into the Origins of Nations and the Politics of Nationalism.* London: Methuen & Co.

Skellington, R. & Morris, P. (1992). *'Race' in Britain Today.* London: Sage.

Small, S. (1994). *Racialised Barriers - The Black Experience in the United States and England in the 1980s.* London: Routledge.

Smith, A. D. (1971). *Theories of Nationalism.* London: Duckworth.

Smith, A. D. (1988). 'The myth of the "Modern Nation" and the myths of nations'. *Ethnic and Racial Studies, 11*(1), 1-26.

Smith, D. J. & Tomlinson, S. (1989). *The School Effect - A Study of Multi-Racial Comprehensives.* London: Policy Studies Institute.

Smith, J. (1994). *Citizens' Europe? The European Elections and the Role of the European Parliament.* London: The Royal Institute of International Affairs.

Smith, S. J. (1989). *The Politics of 'Race' and Residence - Citizenship, Segregation and White Supremacy in Britain.* Oxford: Polity Press.

Solomos, J. & Back, L. (1994). 'Conceptualising Racisms: Social Theory, Politics and Research'. *Sociology - the Journal of the British Sociological Association, 28*(1), 143-161.

Solomos, J. & Wrench, J. (1993). 'Race and Racism in Contemporary Europe'. In Wrench, J. & Solomos, J. (Eds.), *Racism and Migration in Western Europe* Oxford: Berg.

Soysal, Y. N. (1994). *Limits of Citizenship - Migrants and Postnational Membership in Europe.* London: University of Chicago.

Stanley, L. & Wise, S. (1993). *Breaking Out Again.* London: Routledge.

Starting Line (1994). 'The Starting Line: A proposal for a draft Council Directive concerning the elimination of racial discrimination'. *New Community, 20*(3), 530-538.

Sternberger, D. (1990). *Verfassungspatriotismus.* Frankfurt am Main: Insel Verlag.

Taylor, K. (1995). 'European Union: The Challenge for Local and Regional Government.' *The Political Quarterly, 66*(1), 74-83.

taz (1994). 'Doppelte Staatsbürgerschaft - Referendumsinitiative mahnt zur Reform des Staatsbürgerschaftsgesetzes'. *taz* (26.04.94)

taz (1994). TOP 1: 'Polizeskandal'. *taz* (19.09.94)

taz (1994). 'Ein Schuss, der nach hinten losging'. *taz* (28.09.94)

taz (1994). S'echs Haftbefehle nach Kurden-Demonstration'. *taz* (30.09.94)

taz (1994a). 'Ausländer bleibt Ausländer'. *taz* (15.11.94)

taz (1994b). 'Eine Troika von wahren Freunden'. *taz* (15.11.94)

taz (1994). 'Wer darf schnuppern?' *taz* (21.11.94)

taz (1994). 'Abschiebungen: Kanther bleibt hart'. *taz* (08.12.94)

taz (1994). 'Rückt Europa ab von der Türkei?' *taz* (19.12.94)

taz (1994). 'Die Menschenrechtsfrage in der Aussenpolitik: Die Türkei muss in die EU!' *taz* (21.12.94)

taz (1995). 'Stichtag 20. Januar'. *taz* (05.01.95)

taz (1995). 'Isolation wäre das Schlimmste!' *taz* (12.01.95)

taz (1995). 'Bayern international am Pranger.' *taz* (31.01.95)

taz (1995). 'Zuspruch und Kritik für die Türkei (Zollunion mit der EU gefordert)'. *taz* (18.02.95)

Teasdale, A. L. (1993). 'Subsidiarity in Post-Maastricht Europe'. *The Political Quarterly, 64*(2), 187-197.

Teich, N. & Porter, R. (Eds.) (1993). *The National Question in Europe in Historical Context.* Cambridge: Cambridge University Press.

TGB (Bündnis Türkischer Einwanderer e.V.) (1988). *Dokumentation zum kommunalen Wahlrecht für Ausländer in Hamburg* (third ed.). Hamburg: TGB.

Tomlinson, S. (1990). *Multicultural Education in White Schools.* London: B.T. Batsford Ltd.

Turner, B. S. (1986). *Citizenship and Capitalism - The Debate Over Reformism.* London: Allen & Unwin.

Turner, B. S. (1990). 'Outline of a Theory of Citizenship'. *Sociology, 24*(2), 189-217.

Turner, B. S. (Ed.) (1993). *Citizenship and Social Theory.* London: Sage.

Twine, F. (1994). *Citizenship and Social Rights - The Interdependence of Self and Society.* London: Sage.

van Dijk, T. A. (1991). *Racism andthe Press.* London: Routledge.

van Dijk, T. A. (1993b). *Elite Discourse and Racism.* London: Sage.

van Steenbergen, B. (Ed.). (1994). *The Conditions of Citizenship.* London: Sage.

Vogel, U. & Moran, M. (1991). *The Frontiers of Citizenship.* London: Macmillan.

Wallerstein, I. (1974). *The modern world-system I - Capitalist agriculture and the origins of the European world-economy in the sixteenth century.* London: Academic Press.

Wallerstein, I. (1987). 'The Construction of Peoplehood: Racism, Nationalism, Ethnicity'. *Sociological Forum, 2*(2), 373-388.

Wallraff, G. (1985). *Ganz unten.* Köln: Kiepenheuer & Witsch.

Weber, E. (1976). *Peasants into Frenchmen - The modernization of rural France 1870-1914.* London: Chatto & Windus.

Weidenfeld, W. & Korte, K.-R. (1991). *Die Deutschen - Profil einer Nation.* Stuttgart: Klett-Cotta.

Welsh, J. M. (1993). 'A People's Europe? European Citizenship and European Identity'. *Politics, 13*(2), 25-31.

Wieviorka, M. (1994). R'acism in Europe: Unity and Diversity.' In Rattansi, A. & Westwood, S. (Eds.), *Racism, Modernity and Identity - On the Western Front.* Cambridge: Polity Press.

Wilpert, C. (1991). 'Migration and ethnicity in a non-immigration country: Foreigners in a united Germany'. *New Community, 18*(1), 49-62.

Wilpert, C. (1993). 'The Ideological and Institutional Foundations of Racism in the Federal Republic of Germany.' In Wrench, J. & Solomos, J. (Eds.), *Racism and Migration in Western Europe.* Oxford: Berg.

Winstone, P. (1993). 'Stemming the Tide? - Local Authorities develop Race Relations in Europe'. *European Information Service*(140), 3-6.

Wolf-Almanasreh, R. (1992). 'Zuwanderungs- und Flüchtlingspolitik in einem sich öffnenden Europa'. *VDJ Forum - Zeitschrift demokratischer Juristinnen und Juristen*(1), 8-11.

Wolf-Almanasreh, R. (1993). *Zweieinhalb Jahre Amt für Multikulturelle Angelegenheiten.* Frankfurt am Main: Amt für Multikulturelle Angelegenheiten.

Wrench, J. & Solomos, J. (1993). 'The Politics and Processes of Racial Discrimination in Britain'. In Wrench, J. & Solomos, J. (Eds.), *Racism and Migration in Western Europe* Oxford: Berg.

Wrench, J. & Solomos, J. (1994). *Racism and Migration in Western Europe.* Oxford: Berg Publishers.

Young, N. (1967). 'Prometheans or Troglodytes? The English Working Class and the Dialectics of Incorporation'. *Berkeley Journal of Sociology, 12,* 1-43.

Yuval-Davis, N. & Anthias, F. (1989). *Woman - Nation - State*. London: Macmillan.

Zentrum für Türkeistudien (Ed.) (1995). *Das Bild der Ausländer in der Öffentlichkeit*. Opladen: Leske & Budrich.

Zubaida, S. (1978). 'Theories of Nationalism'. In Littlejohn, G. & Smart, B. & Wakeford, J. & Yuval-Davis, N. (Eds.), *Power andThe State* (pp. 52-71). London: Croom Helm.